DRUG TRANSIT AND DISTRIBUTION, INTERCEPTION AND CONTROL

U.S. DRUG SUPPLY, INVESTIGATIONAL DRUGS AND E-PRESCRIPTIONS

Drug Transit and Distribution, Interception and Control

Additional books and e-books in this series can be found on Nova's website under the Series tab.

American Political, Economic, and Security Issues

Additional books and e-books in this series can be found on Nova's website under the Series tab.

DRUG TRANSIT AND DISTRIBUTION, INTERCEPTION AND CONTROL

U.S. DRUG SUPPLY, INVESTIGATIONAL DRUGS AND E-PRESCRIPTIONS

EMIL R. BERG
EDITOR

snova
New York

Library of Congress Cataloging-in-Publication Data

ISBN: 978-1-53617-442-7

Published by Nova Science Publishers, Inc. † New York

CONTENTS

PREFACE

Chapter 1 reports on the U.S. drug supply and the complex way it is interwoven with multiple stakeholders involved in each step of the process.

When investigational drugs show promise for treating serious or life-threatening diseases, patients are often interested in obtaining access to them. Congress included a provision in the FDA Reauthorization Act of 2017 for GAO to review actions taken to facilitate access to these drugs. Chapter 2 describes (1) actions FDA and drug manufacturers have taken to broaden eligibility criteria for clinical trials, (2) actions FDA has taken to facilitate access to investigational drugs outside of clinical trials, and (3) information drug manufacturers have communicated to patients and physicians about access to investigational drugs outside of clinical trials.

Chapter 3 reports on requiring e-prescriptions for coverage under part D of the Medicare program for prescription drugs that are controlled substances.

Chapter 1 - This is an edited, reformatted and augmented version of Hearing before the Subcommittee on Health of the Committee on Energy and Commerce, House of Representatives, One Hundred Fifteenth Congress, First Session, Serial No. 115–88, dated December 13, 2017.

Chapter 2 - When investigational drugs show promise for treating serious or life-threatening diseases, patients are often interested in obtaining access to them. Congress included a provision in the FDA Reauthorization Act of 2017 for GAO to review actions taken to facilitate access to these drugs. This chapter describes (1) actions FDA and drug manufacturers have taken to broaden eligibility criteria for clinical trials, (2) actions FDA has taken to facilitate access to investigational drugs outside of clinical trials, and (3) information drug manufacturers have communicated to patients and physicians about access to investigational drugs outside of clinical trials. GAO reviewed laws, regulations, FDA documents, and manufacturer policies and interviewed FDA officials and a non-generalizable selection of 10 manufacturers and 14 other stakeholders (including patient advocacy and physician organizations). The manufacturers were developing drugs to treat serious or life-threatening diseases, and were selected for variation in company size. GAO also reviewed information that a non- generalizable selection of 29 manufacturers communicated through their websites about access to investigational drugs outside of clinical trials. GAO selected manufacturers for variation in the type of serious diseases their investigational drugs were intended to treat, company size, and other factors. HHS provided technical comments on a draft of this chapter, which GAO incorporated as appropriate.

Chapter 3 - This is an edited, reformatted and augmented version of Committee of the Whole House on the State of the Union, House of Representatives, 115th Congress, 2d Session, Serial No. 115–748, dated June 12, 2018.

In: U.S. Drug Supply, Investigational Drugs …
Editor: Emil R. Berg
ISBN: 978-1-53617-442-7

Chapter 1

EXAMINING THE DRUG SUPPLY CHAIN*

Subcommittee on Health

The subcommittee met, pursuant to call, at 10:00 a.m., in room 2123 Rayburn House Office Building, Hon. Michael Burgess (chairman of the subcommittee) presiding.

Members present: Representatives Burgess, Guthrie, Barton, Shimkus, Blackburn, Latta, Lance, Griffith, Bilirakis, Long, Bucshon, Brooks, Mullin, Hudson, Collins, Carter, Walden (ex officio), Green, Schakowsky, Matsui, Castor, Sarbanes, Lujan, Schrader, Cardenas, Eshoo, DeGette, Welch, and Pallone (ex officio).

Staff present: Ray Baum, Staff Director; Mike Bloomquist, Deputy Staff Director; Adam Buckalew, Professional Staff Member, Health; Kelly Collins, Staff Assistant; Zack Dareshori, Legislative Clerk, Health; Jordan Davis, Director of Policy and External Affairs; Paul Edattel, Chief Counsel, Health; Adam Fromm, Director of Outreach and Coalitions; Ali Fulling, Legislative Clerk, Oversight & Investigations, Digital Commerce and Consumer Protection; Jay Gulshen, Legislative Associate, Health; James Paluskiewicz, Professional Staff, Health; Jennifer Sherman, Press Secretary; Danielle Steele, Counsel, Health; Hamlin Wade, Special Advisor, External Affairs; Jeff Carroll, Minority Staff Director; Tiffany Guarascio, Minority Deputy Staff Director and Chief Health Advisor; Una Lee, Minority Senior Health Counsel; Rachel Pryor, Minority Senior Health Policy Advisor; Samantha Satchell, Minority Policy Analyst; Andrew Souvall, Minority Director of Communications, Outreach and Member Services; Kimberlee Trzeciak, Minority Senior Health Policy Advisor; and C.J. Young, Minority Press Secretary.

* This is an edited, reformatted and augmented version of Hearing before the Subcommittee on Health of the Committee on Energy and Commerce, House of Representatives, One Hundred Fifteenth Congress, First Session, Serial No. 115–88, dated December 13, 2017.

Opening Statement of Hon. Michael C. Burgess, a Representative in Congress from the State of Texas

Mr. BURGESS. The subcommittee will come to order. I will recognize myself for 5 minutes for an opening statement.

I want to thank everyone for being here today. We are going to talk about the U.S. drug supply and the complex way it is interwoven with multiple stakeholders involved in each step of the process. Improving access to lifesaving treatments for consumers and patients should be a nonpartisan priority for every person in the room. Two weeks ago, the Health Subcommittee held a hearing on the implementation of the 21st Century Cures Act. We heard testimonies from officials at the helm of the National Institute of Health and the Food and Drug Administration about the law's transformative impact on maintaining our nation's global leadership in biomedical innovation. Built into that very concept is the expectation that innovative and breakthrough treatments will get developed, approved, and introduced into the therapeutic market to cure diseases or effectively manage chronic conditions so people lead healthier, fuller lives.

Today's hearing will serve as an important educational opportunity to better understand the intricacies of our nation's drug supply chain. To help us work toward that goal, we will hear from a diverse group of representatives—ten to be exact—that represent many facets of the supply chain process, and I do want to welcome each of you to the subcommittee this morning. It is my hope that our discussion today is substantive and will be focused on the patients who are prescribed these medications because, at the end of the day, it is the patients who matter most in our conversation.

Practicing medicine, I cared most about prescribing for my patients a drug that was efficacious and safe, and really not wanting to think too much whether or not they would be able to fill their prescription at the pharmacy. But now, the conversation has shifted to a complicated back and forth between doctors, patients, insurance companies, pharmacies about drug co-pays, prior authorizations, drug formularies, step therapies, amongst other things. Over the last few years, we have also learned about acquisitions and mergers within the various drug supply chain as companies seek out increased integration of their operations with an eye towards more efficiencies.

Prescription drugs continue to play a vital role in the United States health care system. From significantly improving patients' lives to producing health care savings through fewer hospitalizations and medical procedures. A patient's access to prescription drugs is a key health care issue for Americans and within that context now the debate is over affordability.

I will be frank with you. I expect disagreement this morning. But while there are legitimate differences of opinion, I recognize that every participant here this morning does aspire to the common goal of saving lives and alleviating human suffering. And so out of these areas of disagreement, I hope to begin to identify areas of consensus so that we can begin delivering solutions to the problems that we do identify this morning.

These stakeholders here include pharmaceutical manufacturers that primarily research, develop, and produce brand name and generic drugs, biologic, and biosimilars. These medicines treat a spectrum of diseases and conditions from allergies, infections, hypertension to cancer, diabetes, and rheumatoid arthritis.

Next, the pharmaceutical wholesalers purchase these drugs and store them in regional distribution centers for delivery points that include our pharmacies, our supermarket retailers, hospitals, physician groups, and other health care providers. Wholesalers also provide other ancillary services such as repackaging, consulting, inventory management, and patient discount programs.

Overall, pharmacy benefit managers manage prescription drug benefits on behalf of employer-sponsored health plans, health maintenance organizations, state and federal health programs including Medicare Part D, and Medicaid-managed care plans. These managers impact the lives of 226 million insured Americans with most of them enrolled in private health plans. So they have a special role in the drug supply chain that includes determining payments and pricing for drugs, processing pharmacy drug claims, negotiating rebates and discounts from drug manufacturers, designing drug plan formularies, and operating mail order businesses.

Retail pharmacies have a large neighborhood presence representing large drug store chains, pharmacy departments in local supermarkets and big box retailers, and independent community pharmacies that occupy a unique and essential role within the drug supply chain. Many drug stores contract with payers and pharmacy benefit managers to join health plan pharmacy networks. Some larger pharmacy chains have also entered into joint ventures with PBMs and insurers.

Finally, private health insurance plans are likely recognized by most Americans to have a direct impact on their ability to access prescription drugs, largely due to the dictates of federal laws such as the Affordable Care Act on benefit requirements and out-of-pocket spending limits. They employ utilization controls to manage cost such as multi-tier drug formularies, step therapies, prior authorizations for certain high-cost brand name medicines.

Again, I want to welcome all of our witnesses here today. As you see, we have the entire panoply of the supply chain here before us.

I look forward to your testimony and we will recognize Mr. Green of Texas, the ranking member of the subcommittee, 5 minutes for an opening statement.

[The prepared statement of Mr. Burgess follows:]

Chairman Michael C. Burgess, MD, Opening Statement, Energy and Commerce Subcommittee on Health Hearing "Examining the Drug Supply Chain," December 13, 2017

The Subcommittee will come to order.

The Chair will recognize himself for an opening statement.

The multifaceted nature of the current U.S. drug supply chain system is complex and interwoven with multiple stakeholders involved in each step of the process. Improving access to life-saving treatments for consumers should be a non-partisan priority for all of us. Two weeks ago, the Health Subcommittee held a hearing on the implementation of the 21st Century Cures Act and heard testimonies from officials at the helm of the National Institutes of Health and the Food and Drug Administration about the law's transformative impact on maintaining our nation's global leadership in biomedical innovation. Built into that very concept is the expectation that innovative and breakthrough treatments will get developed, approved, and introduced into the therapeutic market to cure diseases or effectively manage chronic conditions, so people can lead healthier, fuller lives.

Today's hearing will serve as an important educational opportunity to better understand the intricacies of our nation's drug supply chain. To help us work toward that goal, we will hear from a diverse group of representatives – ten to be exact – that represent the many facets of the supply chain process. I want to welcome each of you to the subcommittee this morning. It is my hope our discussion today is substantive and largely focused on the patients who are prescribed these medications because, at the end of the day, they are who matter most in this conversation.

Practicing medicine, I cared most about prescribing my patients a drug that was efficacious and safe without thinking too much about whether they would be able to fill their prescription at the pharmacy. Now, the conversation has shifted to a complicated back-and-forth between doctors, patients, insurance companies, and pharmacies about drug copays, prior authorizations, and drug formularies, among other things. Over the last few years, we have also learned about acquisitions and mergers within and amongst the various drug supply chain as companies seek out increased integration of their operations with an eye towards more efficiencies over the larger continuum of the system.

Prescription drugs continue to play a vital role in the United States health care system, from significantly improving patients' lives to producing health care savings through fewer hospitalizations and medical procedures. A patient's access to prescription drugs is a key healthcare issue for Americans, and within that context is the debate over affordability.

Now, I also expect disagreement. But, while there are legitimate differences of opinion, I recognize that every participant here this morning does aspire to the common goal of saving lives and alleviating human suffering. And so out of these areas of disagreement – I hope to begin to identify areas of consensus so that we can begin delivering solutions to the problems identified this morning.

These stakeholders include pharmaceutical manufacturers that primarily research, develop, and produce brand-name and generic drugs, biologics, and biosimilars. These medicines treat a spectrum of diseases and conditions, such as allergies, infections, and hypertension to cancer, diabetes, and rheumatoid arthritis.

Next, pharmaceutical wholesalers purchase these drugs and store them in regional distribution centers for delivery points that include pharmacies, supermarket retailers, hospitals, physician groups, and other healthcare providers. Wholesalers also provide other ancillary services such as repackaging, consulting, inventory management, and patient discount programs.

Overall, pharmacy benefit managers (PBMs) manage prescription drug benefits on behalf of employer-sponsored health plans, health maintenance organizations, state and federal health programs, including Medicare Part D and Medicaid managed care plans. PBMs impact the lives of 266 million insured Americans, with most them enrolled in private health plans. They have a special role in the drug supply chain that include determining payments and pricing for drugs, processing pharmacy drug claims, negotiating rebate and discounts from drug manufacturers, designing drug plan formularies, and operating mail-order and specialty pharmacies.

Retail pharmacies have a large neighborhood presence, representing large drug store chains, pharmacy departments in local supermarkets and big-box retailers, and independent (community) pharmacies that occupy a unique and essential role within the drug supply chain. Many drug stores contract with payers and PBMs to join health plan pharmacy networks; some larger pharmacy chains have also entered into joint ventures with PBMs and insurers.

Finally, private health insurance plans are likely recognized by most Americans to have a direct impact on their ability to access prescription drugs, largely due to the dictates of federal laws, such as the Affordable Care Act, on benefit requirements and out-of-pocket spending limits. They employ utilization controls to manage costs, such as multi-tiered drug formularies, step therapies, and prior authorizations for certain high-cost brand-name medicines.

I again want to welcome our witnesses and thank you for being here. I look forward to your testimony.

Opening Statement of Hon. Gene Green, a Representative in Congress from the State of Texas

Mr. GREEN. Thank you, Mr. Chairman, and thank you to our witnesses for being here this morning.

Too many Americans face real barriers in accessing the medications they need. Annual drug spending in the U.S. is expected to reach more than $500 billion by 2018.

In 2015, the rise in prescription drug spending outpaced all other health care services, surpassing hospital care as well as physician and clinical services.

While new life changing and lifesaving therapies continue to enter the market each year, patients must be able to afford these treatments in order to benefit from these breakthroughs.

The issue of high drug costs is not a simple challenge with a simple solution. Instances of bad actors buying up off-patent generic drugs with only one manufacturer astronomically jacking up the price has posed one type of challenge while breakthrough treatments capable of curing previously incurable disease but will have staggering price tags poses a different one.

These challenges are magnified by the proliferation of the high deductible plans which expose more and more consumers to the full list of their medications.

We have a responsibility to explore the full spectrum of the supply chain to protect patients which are distinct for generic and brand name drugs and frustratingly complex.

The United States leads the world in biomedical development, but having 21st Century Cures means much less if people cannot access because of the high prices.

It's important to also recognize that pharmaceutical companies sponsor the research that leads to these advances. We must find a workable solution that incentivizes competition in the pharmaceutical marketplace, reward value, and encourage the development of these affordable and high quality drugs.

We must also monitor steep prescription drug price increases when they rise, particularly when no additional research or development has occurred.

There are a number of policy proposals that are represented to address the issue of high prescription drug costs. Transparency and value-based approaches are some of the keys to market-based reforms that will lead to better prices, continued investment in research and development, and ensure that taxpayers receive a real return on their investment.

I want to note that in pursuit of the lower drug prices, Congress must be careful to avoid the policies that will diminish patient safety.

Filling out an application to the FDA is one step in what can be a decades-long process to get from the lab table to the bedside.

Proposals that would lower FDA safety and effective standards effectively outsource FDA oversight to other countries, push the stage of three trials into the post-approval space are unlikely to translate into meaningful savings for customers and are likely to put patients at risk.

Making the FDA approval process as sophisticated and efficient as it can be is one thing, but rolling back patient protections in the name of lower drug prices is not an acceptable path.

We should be looking on how we pay for drugs and reward real value in the order of safety and meaningful, address the rising costs of prescription drugs.

Following our bipartisan work on the 21st Century Cures Act, our recent work to reauthorize the FDA user fee programs, it is my hope that we can advance bipartisan policies to address rising drug costs.

This problem demands a bipartisan and thoughtful process that includes a full spectrum of stakeholders. The American people expect us to work together to find answers and I believe we can do so.

I want to thank you for being here today and look forward to the day's discussion. And Mr. Chairman, I have one more minute. I'd like—anybody would like to have a minute? No? OK.

I'd like to ask unanimous consent to place into the record, Mr. Chairman, a letter from AARP.

Mr. BURGESS. Without objection, so ordered.

[The information appears at the conclusion of the hearing.]

Mr. BURGESS. I believe the chair actually already used your minute.

Does the gentleman yield back?

Mr. GREEN. I yield back.

Mr. BURGESS. The chair thanks the gentleman.

Mr. GREEN. You owe me a minute sometime.

Mr. BURGESS. Oh, next week.

The chair now recognizes the gentleman from Oregon, the chairman of the full committee, Mr. Walden, 5 minutes, please.

[The prepared statement of Mr. Green follows:]

Opening Statement, Health Subcommittee Hearing: "Examining the Drug Supply Chain" Rep. Gene Green, December 13, 2017

Thank you Mr. Chairman, and thank you to our witnesses for being here this morning.

Too many Americans face real barriers to accessing the medications they need.

Annual drug spending in the U.S. is expected to reach more than $500 billion by 2018.

In 2015, the rise prescription drug spending outpaced all other health care services, surpassing hospital care as well as physician and clinical services.

While new life-changing and life-saving therapies continue to enter the market each year, patients must be able to afford these treatments in order to benefit from these breakthroughs.

The issue of high drug costs is not a simple challenge with a simple solution.

Instances of bad actors buying up off-patent generic drugs only made by one manufacturer and astronomically jacking up the price poses one type of challenge, while breakthrough treatments capable of curing previously un-curable disease but have a staggering price tag poses a different one.

These challenges are magnified by the proliferation of high-deductible plans, which expose more and more consumers to the full list price of their medications.

We have a responsibility to explore the full spectrum of the supply chain to protect patients, which are distinct for generic and brand-name drugs, and frustratingly complex.

The United States leads the world in biomedical development, but having 21st century cures means much less if people cannot access them because of high prices.

It is important to also recognize that pharmaceutical companies sponsor the research that leads to these advances.

We must find workable solutions that incentivize competition in the pharmaceutical marketplace, reward value, and encourage the development of affordable and high quality drugs.

We must also monitor steep prescription drug price increases when they arise, particularly when no additional research and development has occurred.

There are a number of policy proposals that have been presented to address the issue of high prescription drug costs.

Transparency and value-based approaches are some of the keys to market-based reforms that will lead to better prices, continued investment in research and development, and ensure that taxpayers receive a real return on their investment.

I want to note that in the pursuit of lower drug prices, Congress must be careful to avoid policies that will diminish patient safety.

Filing an application with the FDA is the last step in what can be a decade's long process to get from the lab table to the bedside.

Proposals that would lower FDA safety and effective standards, effectively outsource FDA oversight to other countries, or push stage three trials into the post-approval space are unlikely to translate into meaning savings for consumers and are likely put patients at risk.

Making the FDA approval process as sophisticated and efficient as it can be is one thing, but rolling back patient protections in the name of lower drug prices is not an acceptable path.

We should be looking at how we pay for drugs, and reward real value in order to safely and meaningfully address the rising costs of prescription drugs.

Following our bipartisan work on the 21st Century Cures Act and our recent work to reauthorize the FDA user fee programs, it is my hope that we can advance bipartisan policies to address rising drug costs.

This problem demands a bipartisan, thoughtful process that includes the full spectrum of stakeholders.

The American people expect us to work together to find answers and I believe we can do so.

Thank you all for being here today, and I look forward to today's discussion.

OPENING STATEMENT OF HON. GREG WALDEN, A REPRESENTATIVE IN CONGRESS FROM THE STATE OF OREGON

Mr. WALDEN. Dr. Burgess, thank you for holding this important discussion. I appreciate your comments and those of Mr. Green's about the full set of issues before us and the overwhelming desire by our constituents that we dive deep into the whole drug chain and figure out how we can put consumers first not only in developing new medicines and new innovation and better pricing as well.

As Mr. Green mentioned, this community unanimously reauthorized and the president signed into law the FDA Modernization Act. This committee last Congress championed the 21st Century Cures Act with Congresswoman DeGette and Congressman Upton at the helm of that, celebrating its one-year anniversary.

But, clearly, there is more to be done, and as chairman of the committee, I felt it was really important that we hear from the entire sector from the development of new drugs to the final end place where we buy them, we consume them, we use them.

For more than 4 years, members of this committee have listened to patients. We have listened to providers. We have listened to payors. The Federal Government is one of the biggest payors in this effort and we are all about accelerating the discovery, development, and delivery of innovative drugs and medical devices. That was a lot of what was behind passage and implementation of 21st Century Cures.

We have heard from Dr. Gottlieb and we have heard from the head of NIH about the progress they are making already with the legislation we have enacted.

Today, though, we want to get a more full appreciation for the drug supply chain, and I think you all would have to acknowledge its complexity, and we want to ask questions instead of jumping to conclusions.

I encourage members on both sides of the aisle to dismiss, to a certain extent, any of your preconceived notions and let's focus on how each stage of the drug supply chain impacts access, delivery, and delivery of drugs and, of course, costs.

We need to listen to the complex journey from molecular discoveries to patient deliveries that one dose of medicine takes along the way and we all need to learn about the impact each participant in the supply chain has in the ultimate cost to patients.

And we have no shortage of witnesses today to help us gain a better understanding, and we appreciate you all being here. We have representatives from the manufacturers, the distributors, the payers, the pharmacists, the providers, and the patients.

And I promise today's hearing will be an informative discussion and, I dare say, not the last as we move forward to better educate ourselves and then look at the public policy changes that need to be made to move America forward in these areas.

So I thank you all for your participation. I think you'll find the committee is very interested in every step of this process and with that, Mr. Chairman, I would yield the balance of my time to the chairwoman of the Telecommunications Subcommittee, the gentlelady from Tennessee, Mrs. Blackburn.

[The prepared statement of Mr. Walden follows:]

Opening Statement of Chairman Walden, Subcommittee on Health, "Examining the Drug Supply Chain," December 13, 2017

Thank you, Dr. Burgess, for holding this important discussion.

As we all know, no one is immune to sickness and disease. This is, in part, why our committee – under the bipartisan leadership of former Chairman Fred Upton and Congresswoman Diana DeGette – championed the 21st Century Cures initiative.

For more than four years, members of this committee listened to patients, providers, and payors. Accelerating the discovery, development, and delivery of innovative drugs became a nationwide mantra for the passage of Cures. And I'm proud to say that *today* – thanks to the tireless advocacy of patients across the country and the endurance of members of this committee – we celebrate the one-year anniversary of this landmark bill being signed into law.

But our work isn't done. As Dr. Burgess has said, "As we continue to build on the success of the transformative 21st Century Cures act, our committee must fully comprehend how each step of the drug supply chain process impacts consumers."

He's right. And it is why we are here today – to learn from patient and industry experts and improve our understanding of the drug supply chain.

In order to fully appreciate the drug supply chain you have to acknowledge its complexity and ask questions instead of jumping to conclusions. I encourage members on both sides of the aisle to dismiss any preconceived notions and focus on how each stage of the drug supply chain impacts access and delivery of drugs. Listen to the complex journey – from molecular discoveries to patient deliveries – that one dose of medicine takes.

Now, I'll be up front: For me, this isn't a drug pricing hearing. There's enough rhetoric about the cost of drugs. But having said that I know that I have more to learn about the impact each participant in the supply chain has in the ultimate cost to patients. And we have no shortage of witnesses to question! As you can see, we have invited witnesses from each step of the process: manufacturers, distributers, payors, pharmacists, providers, and patients. I promise today's hearing will be an informative discussion.

On that note, I'd like to welcome to each of our expert panelists. I appreciate your generosity and willingness to participate today. And I yield to Mrs. Blackburn of Tennessee, who would like to offer a few opening remarks.

Mrs. BLACKBURN. Thank you, Mr. Chairman, and I thank Chairman Burgess for the hearing and to each of you. We know it is the busy time of year. We are appreciative that you are here before us and, as Chairman Burgess said, we have the entire panoply of the system.

And most of my constituents will tell you they understand how their doctor, their insurance plan, and the pharmacy play into the prescriptions they receive. They do not have the understanding, as Chairman Walden said, of the complex system that goes from research to the time they pick up that prescription, and we are so interested in looking at this access, delivery, and cost issue within this entire spectrum.

It does affect health care delivery, and being from middle Tennessee, we have a lot of health care in my congressional district and this entire supply chain is an issue that we discuss often.

And we are excited about some of the new innovations that are coming your way with technology. So that will enter into our discussion today. Thank you for your presence and, Mr. Chairman, I will yield back to you the balance of the time and if there is another member who would like to claim that time.

Yield back.

Mr. BURGESS. Seeing none, the gentlelady yields back. The chair thanks the gentlelady.

The chair recognizes the gentleman from New Jersey, the ranking member of the full committee, Mr. Pallone, 5 minutes for an opening statement, please.

OPENING STATEMENT OF HON. FRANK PALLONE, JR., A REPRESENTATIVE IN CONGRESS FROM THE STATE OF NEW JERSEY

Mr. PALLONE. Thank you, Mr. Chairman.

This committee has spent considerable time examining the drug supply chain both through the Drug Quality Security Act and, more recently, through the 21st Century Cures, and today is actually the 1-year anniversary of when President Obama signed 21st Century Cures. Both of these legislative efforts were the result of considerable oversight and discussion as to how the drug supply chain worked, how it could be better secured and how we could encourage efficiencies to improve drug development. And these bipartisan efforts have helped to address the post-market security of products and the regulatory review process. But neither effort focused on how prescription drugs move through the supply chain through the financial lens.

Prescription drug prices are higher than ever, and while the dramatic rise in prescription spending has come down a little, we know addressing drug costs continues to be a top priority for many American families. The costs of prescriptions have forced so many American families to make tough choices. For some, it is a choice of filling their prescriptions or filling their tank of gas to get to work. For others, they are leaving prescriptions unfulfilled, skipping doses, or cutting pill in half so they don't have to purchase their prescriptions that often, and none of these choices is acceptable.

Today, prescription drug spending represents about 14 percent of overall health care spending. It is no wonder that six in 10 Americans have said that lowering prescription drug costs should be a top priority for Congress and this administration and I am pleased that there has been such bipartisan interest in this topic both during consideration of the FDA Reauthorization Act and at recent member briefings, and I do believe that making prescription drugs more affordable for the average consumer is an issue that we all care about and can support.

And that is why today's hearing is so important. This morning, we have the opportunity to better understand the drug supply chain and the often-complicated ways that drugs move through the supply chain to the patient. As my colleagues have pointed out, we will hear from each of our witnesses about the role they play regarding drug delivery, the impact they have on the cost of drugs, and the value they bring to patients and consumers, and I hope and expect that today's hearing will serve as a foundation for future hearings on policy solutions that may help reduce prescription drug costs in our health care system.

While understanding how the supply chain works is critically important to this committee, I also would urge Chairman Walden to schedule a legislative hearing in the early part of next year to examine specific proposals to address the high prices of prescription drugs.

Our constituents want and expect us to take concrete action to address this growing problem. And the problems we are seeing in the supply chain cannot be addressed through one policy solution and all of our witnesses have a role to play in these solutions.

It is long past time for Congress to take a serious look at all solutions that will help American families to afford the medications they depend on and I look forward to further bipartisan discussion on what that broad range of policy solutions may look like.

And I want to thank each of our witnesses for being here and look forward to learning more about your role in the drug supply chain and how we can improve access to drugs for patients in the future, and I would like to yield the remainder of my time to Congressman Luja´ n from New Mexico.

[The prepared statement of Mr. Pallone follows:]

PALLONE OPENING REMARKS AT DRUG SUPPLY CHAIN HEARING

"Making prescription drugs more affordable for the average consumer is an issue that we all care about and can support."

Washington, D.C. – Energy and Commerce Ranking Member Frank Pallone, Jr. (D-NJ) delivered the following opening remarks today at a Subcommittee on Health hearing titled "Examining the Drug Supply Chain:"

This Committee has spent considerable time examining the drug supply chain both through the Drug Quality Security Act, and more recently through 21st Century Cures. Both of these legislative efforts were the result of considerable oversight and discussion as to how the drug supply chain worked, how it could be better secured, and how we could encourage efficiencies to improve drug development. These bipartisan efforts have helped address the post market security of products and the regulatory review process, but neither effort focused on how prescription drugs move through the supply chain through the financial lens.

Prescription drug prices are higher than ever, and while the dramatic rise in prescription spending has come down some, we know addressing drug costs continues to be a top priority for many American families. The costs of prescriptions have forced so many American families to make tough choices. For some, it's a choice of filling their prescription or filling their tank of gas to get to work. For others, they are leaving prescriptions unfilled, skipping doses, or cutting pills in half so that they don't have to purchase their prescriptions as often. None of these choices are acceptable.

Today prescription drug spending represents about 14 percent of overall healthcare spending. It's no wonder that six in ten Americans have said that lowering prescription drug costs should be a top priority for Congress and this Administration. I am pleased that there has been such bipartisan interest in this topic – both during consideration of the

Food and Drug Administration Reauthorization Act and at recent Member briefings. I do believe that making prescription drugs more affordable for the average consumer is an issue that we all care about and can support.

That is why today's hearing is so important. This morning we have the opportunity to better understand the drug supply chain and the often complicated ways that drugs move through the supply chain to the patient. As my colleagues have pointed out, we will hear from each of our witnesses about the role they play regarding drug delivery, the impact they have on the cost of a drug, and the value that they bring to patients and consumers.

I hope and expect that today's hearing will serve as a foundation for future hearings on policy solutions that may help reduce prescription drug costs in our healthcare system. While understanding how the supply chain works is critically important to this Committee, I urge Chairman Walden to schedule a legislative hearing in the early part of next year to examine specific proposals to address the high prices of prescription drugs. Our constituents want and expect us to take concrete action to address this growing problem.

The problems we are seeing in the supply chain cannot be addressed through one policy solution and all of our witnesses have a role to play in these solutions. It is long past time for Congress to take a serious look at all solutions that will help American families to afford the medications they depend on. I look forward to further bipartisan discussion on what that broad range of policy solutions may look like.

I want to thank each of our witnesses for being here. I look forward to learning more about your role in the drug supply chain and how we can improve access to drugs for patients in the future.

Thank you.

Mr. LUJAN. Thank you, Mr. Pallone, and Mr. Chairman, thank you for this important hearing.

There is so much going on in the health care arena right now—CHIP, community health centers, National Health Services Corps, special diabetes program, Medicare extenders, Puerto Rico's Medicaid program—items that all need attention and need it now.

With all these priorities competing for attention, it would be easy to lose sight of which should be our guiding star—finding ways to balance innovation and affordability.

We depend on different approaches to give us more time with the ones we love, whether it is a brother who lives with diabetes or a mother with a new cancer diagnosis. Our lives have been improved by many tools including pharmaceutical therapies. To realize the promise of these innovations, we must ensure patients can access the cures that manufacturers spend so much energy and effort developing. It doesn't help to hold out hope for a cure if there is no hope that regular people can afford it.

It is unrealistic to think the answer to making prescription drugs affordable for everyone is ending the 340B program or allowing for off-label communication.

We must all look holistically at what affordable accessible health care means. I am also real interested, Mr. Chairman—on a bit of a sidebar here—because we have everyone in the room to work with you and make sure that we are pushing pain management treatments that are nonaddictive.

This is critically important. We have a huge problem facing our country and we need to work together to get that done. We also need serious treatments from everyone here to make sure that we are addressing the cravings that come from opioids and alcohol.

Simply having medications that make someone sick if they use is not going to stop the craving and not going to stop use.

I am hopeful this is the first of many hearings examining how we ensure affordable accessible prescription drugs and I look forward to working with everyone here on real solutions.

Thank you, Mr. Chairman.

Mr. BURGESS. Chair thanks the gentleman. Gentleman yields back.

This will conclude member opening statements and the chair would remind members that pursuant to committee rules, all members' opening statements will be made part of the record.

And once again, we do want to thank our witnesses for being here today, taking time to testify before the subcommittee. Each witness is going to have an opportunity to give a three-minute opening statement and that will be followed by questions from members.

So today, in order, we are going to hear from Lori Reilly, the Executive Vice President for Policy, Research, and Membership at the Pharmaceutical Research and Manufacturers Association of America; Tom DiLenge, President, Advocacy, Law, and Public Policy, Biotechnology Innovation Organization; Chip Davis, President and CEO for the Association for Accessible Medicines; Elizabeth Gallenagh, Senior Vice President, Government Affairs and General Counsel, Health Care Distribution Alliance; Mark Merritt, President and CEO for the Pharmaceutical Care Management Association; Matt Eyles, the Senior Executive Vice President and Chief Operating Officer for Policy and Regulatory Affairs at America's Health Insurance Plans; Tom Nickels, the Executive Vice President for Government Relations and Public Policy for the American Hospital Association; Gerald Harmon, M.D., Chairman of the Board of Trustees of the American Medical Association; Douglas Hoey, the CEO of the National Community Pharmacists Association; and David Mitchell, the Founder and President of Patients for Affordable Drugs.

We do appreciate you all being here this morning. Ms. Reilly, you are now recognized for 3 minutes to give a summary of your opening statement.

Statements of Lori Reilly, Executive Vice President for Policy, Research, and Membership, Pharmaceutical Research and Manufacturers of America; Tom Dilenge, President, Advocacy, Law, and Public Policy, Biotechnology Innovation Organization; Chip Davis, President and Ceo, Association for Accessible Medicines; Elizabeth

Gallenagh, Senior Vice President, Governmental Affairs and General Counsel, Healthcare Distribution Alliance; Mark Merritt, President and Ceo, Pharmaceutical Care Management Association; Matt Eyles, Senior Executive Vice President and Chief Operating Officer for Policy and Regulatory Affairs, America's Health Insurance Plans; Tom Nickels, Executive Vice President for Government Relations and Public Policy, American Hospital Association; Gerald Harmon, M.D., Chair, Board of Trustees, American Medical Association; B. Douglas Hoey, Ceo, National Community Pharmacists Association; David Mitchell, Founder and President, Patients for Affordable Drugs

STATEMENT OF LORI REILLY

Ms. REILLY. Thank you, Chairman Burgess, Chairman Walden, and Ranking Members Green and Pallone.

My name is Lori Reilly and I am the Executive Vice President for Policy and Research at PhRMA and it is my pleasure to be here today.

Over the past 20 years, more than 500 new medicines have been approved to come to market to treat some our nation's most challenging and costly conditions. In the midst of this progress, prescription drug medicine growth is growing slowly. Just last week, CMS released new data to show that prescription drug spending in 2016 grew at 1.3 percent. That was lower than any other category of spending. To put that into context, hospital spending growth grew at three and a half times that amount. In the last 7 out of 10 years, prescription drug spending growth has been below national spending growth.

Today, medicines consume about 14 percent of the health care dollar, and many assume, when they see that number, that all, or substantially all, of that flows back to the brand name manufacturers. However, less than half of that, or 47 percent, is attributable to brand name drug spending. The remainder, 23 percent, goes to generic firms and 31 percent goes to the supply chain.

Going forward over the next decade, medicines are projected to remain 14 percent of the health care dollar, and many question how is that possible knowing all of the new innovations that are coming to market in the coming years. And there are a few reasons for that, the first being that over $100 billion worth of medicines will be going off-patent over the next five years and that will put cost pressure as new generics and biosimilars enter the marketplace. The second is the fact that there is significant cost constraint in the prescription drug market as three large pharmacy benefit managers buy on behalf of over 70 percent of all prescriptions in this country.

These PBMs exert significant cost pressure to keep prices and spending in check. One of the ways they do that is by extracting significant discounts and rebates from pharmaceutical manufacturers. In fact, discounters and rebates increased 40 percent over the last 4 years and now total over $100 billion a year. Unfortunately, oftentimes those discounts and rebates are captured by intermediaries and don't make their way back to patients. This problem has become more acute over time as we've seen a dramatic increase in the number of patients that today have a deductible for their medicine.

So take, for example, a patient who takes an insulin product with a list price of $400 and that medicine carries a discount of about 65 percent. A patient with a deductible today goes to the pharmacy counter and will be asked to pay $400 for that medicine despite the fact that the insurance company is paying nothing while earning $239 on every sale. Given the rapid rise in deductibles, this must change. Insurance companies and PBMs must be pushing these discounts and rebates back to patients to lower their out-of-pocket spending.

With that, my time is up and I look forward to questions today. Thank you.

[The prepared statement of Ms. Reilly follows:]

TESTIMONY OF LORI M. REILLY, EXECUTIVE VICE PRESIDENT, POLICY, RESEARCH, AND MEMBERSHIP PHARMACEUTICAL RESEARCH AND MANUFACTURERS OF AMERICA, BEFORE THE U.S. HOUSE COMMITTEE ON ENERGY AND COMMERCE, SUBCOMMITTEE ON HEALTH, DECEMBER 13, 2017

Full Committee Chairman Walden and Ranking Member Pallone, Health Subcommittee Chairman Burgess and Ranking Member Green, and Members of the Subcommittee, thank you for inviting me to participate in today's hearing. Understanding the role the drug delivery system plays in determining what patients pay for medicines is a critical part of the discussion about what can be done to improve patient access and affordability and I appreciate the opportunity to explore this topic with you in depth.

PhRMA represents the country's leading innovative biopharmaceutical research companies, which are devoted to discovering and developing medicines that enable patients to live longer, healthier, and more productive lives. The biopharmaceutical sector is one of the most research-intensive industries in the U.S.: since 2000, PhRMA member companies have invested more than half a trillion dollars in the search for new treatments and cures, including $65.5 billion in 2016 alone.

Medicines Have Transformed the Treatment of Many Diseases, Helping Patients Live Longer and Healthier Lives

We are in a new era of medicine in which breakthrough science is transforming patient care and enabling us to more effectively treat chronic disease, the biggest cost driver in our health care system. Innovative medicines represent significant scientific advancements that revolutionize the treatment and thus the downstream healthcare costs of complex and costly diseases, such as cancer, hepatitis C, HIV/AIDS, and cardiovascular disease. In this new era of medicine, many diseases previously regarded as deadly are now manageable and even curable. Today, more than 7,000 medicines are in development worldwide, of which 80% have the potential to be first in class and 42% are personalized medicines.[1] Prescription medicines produce unparalleled value and savings for the health care system, preventing or slowing the progression of disease, and reducing the need for more intensive medical care. Continued advances in biopharmaceutical innovation represent the best opportunities to improve health outcomes and control future health care costs.

New medicines help contain overall health care spending by preventing costly complications and hospitalizations, and replacing other medical interventions. A 2013 study by IMS Institute for Healthcare Informatics estimated that the U.S. health care system could save $213 billion annually by improving the use of medicines.[2] Similarly, research published in *Health Affairs* found that just an extra $1 spent on medicines for adherent patients with congestive heart failure, high blood pressure, diabetes and high cholesterol can generate $3 to $10 in savings on emergency room visits and inpatient hospitalizations.[3]

Based on the growing body of evidence about medicines' benefits, the Congressional Budget Office (CBO) recognizes reductions in other medical expenditures associated with increased use of prescription medicines in Medicare Part D.[4] Research indicates that the savings may be three to six times greater than estimated by the CBO for seniors with common chronic conditions like diabetes and hypertension,[5] and less prevalent conditions such as Parkinson's disease.[6] More recent research has shown that increased use of

---

[1] Long G. The Biopharmaceutical Pipeline: Innovative Therapies in Clinical Development. Analysis Group. 2017; Tufts Center for the Study of Drug Development (CSDD). Personalized Medicine Gains Traction But Still Faces Multiple Challenges. *Tufts CSDD Impact Report*. 2015;17(3).

[2] *IMS Institute for Healthcare Informatics. Avoidable Costs in U.S. Healthcare: The $200 Billion Opportunity from Using Medicines More Responsibly*. June 2013.

[3] Roebuck MC, Lieberman JN, Gemmill-Toyama M, et al. Medication Adherence Leads to Lower Care Use And Costs Despite Increased Drug Spending. *Health Affairs*. 2011;30(1):99.

[4] Congressional Budget Office. *Offsetting Effects of Prescription Drug Use on Medicare's Spending for Medical Services*. November 29, 2012.

[5] Roebuck MC. Medical Cost Offsets from Prescription Drug Utilization Among Medicare Beneficiaries. *Journal of Managed Care Pharmacy*. 2014;20(10):994-995.

[6] Wei YJ, Palumbo FB, Simoni-Wastila L, et al. Antiparkinson Drug Adherence and its Association With Health Care Utilization and Economic Outcomes in a Medicare Part D Population. *Value in Health*. 2014;17(2):196-204.

medicines among patients is associated with reductions in expenditures from avoided use of inpatient and outpatient services in Medicaid as well. For example, among patients with schizophrenia, improved adherence to antipsychotic medicines yielded annual net savings of up to $3.3 billion, or $1,580 per patient per year, driven by lower hospitalizations, outpatient care, and criminal system involvement.[7] Another study found that if 60% of the children enrolled in Medicaid achieved high adherence to asthma treatment in just 14 states, Medicaid could achieve $57.5 million in savings annually.[8]

The Competitive Market for Prescription Medicines Balances Innovation, Patient Access, and Cost Containment

The competitive market is the engine that drives the innovative biopharmaceutical research and development ecosystem. The dynamics of the private, market-based system in the U.S. promote incentives for continued innovation and patient access to needed medicines while leveraging competition to achieve cost containment. Since 2000, biopharmaceutical companies have brought more than 500 new medicines to the U.S. market, resulting in significant progress against some of the most costly and challenging diseases.[9] Through innovation, the death rate for HIV/AIDs death has dropped 86% and more recently, decades of work are paying off in cancer as new therapies launched over the past few years are recognized as game changers that are transforming the treatment of many cancers. Today, because of scientific advances, many other conditions are now manageable and sometimes even curable. Yet, due to robust negotiation and competition in the marketplace, spending on medicines is growing at the slowest rate in years.[10]

Government, market analyst, and pharmacy benefit manager data all point to the same conclusion: that after peaking in 2014—an anomaly year in which millions of uninsured patients gained coverage and a record number of new medicines were approved—prescription drug spending growth has fallen substantially. National health expenditure data just released show that retail prescription medicine spending grew more slowly than overall health care cost growth in seven of the last ten years, and grew just

---

[7] Predmore ZS, Mattke S, Horvitz-Lennon M. Improving Antipsychotic Adherence among Patients With Schizophrenia: Savings for States. *Psychiatric Services*. 2015; 66:343–345.

[8] Rust G, Zhang S, McRoy L. Potential Savings From Increasing Adherence to Inhaled Corticosteroid Therapy in Medicaid-Enrolled Children. *American Journal of Managed Care*. 2015;21(3):173-180.

[9] US Food and Drug Administration. Summary of NDA Approvals & Receipts, 1938 to the Present. http://www.fda.gov/aboutfda/whatwedo/history/productregulation/summaryofndaapprovalsreceipts1938tothepresent/default.htm; US Food and Drug Administration. New Drugs at FDA: CDER's New Molecular Entities and New Therapeutic Biological Products. 2012 – 2015. https://www.fda.gov/drugs/developmentapprovalprocess/druginnovation/default.htm.

[10] Quintiles IMS Institute. *Medicine Use and Spending in the US: A Review of 2016 and Outlook to 2021*. April 2017.

1.3% in 2016, less than one-third of the rate of overall health care spending growth.[11] Accounting for discounts and rebates, multiple other sources report historically low growth rates.[12] As a result of negotiation and competition in the marketplace, spending on retail and physician-administered medicines continues to represent only 14% of overall health care spending, even though scores of new medicines are approved every year. And at the state level, Medicaid programs spent just 4.9% of their budgets on prescription drugs, including new medicines, in 2016, relative to 26% for hospital care and 18.2% for provider services.[13]

The U.S. biopharmaceutical marketplace promotes innovation and affordability through cost containment that is built into the prescription drug lifecycle. While the price of a medicine may increase or decrease over its lifetime, prices fall dramatically as competition occurs among brand-name medicines, and typically fall even further (up to 80%) with the introduction of generics.[14] For instance, the price of one common statin (atorvastatin, known in the branded form as Lipitor) used to lower cholesterol and prevent cardiovascular disease, dropped by about 92% from 2005 to 2013 when generic alternatives came to market.[15] Meanwhile, the average charge for percutaneous transluminal coronary angioplasty (PTCA) – a surgical procedure to treat cardiovascular disease – increased by almost 66% during that same time period.[16]

The U.S. market is structured to take maximum advantage of savings from brand competition and from generics. Three large, sophisticated pharmacy benefit managers (PBMs) manage about 70% of all prescriptions filled.[17] They use brand competition to obtain discounts from manufacturers and take full advantage of the presence of generics to drive savings. This drives the rapid shift of market share to generics (and, looking forward, to biosimilars), a system with few analogues in other health care sectors. As one example of the growing influence of PBMs, industry leader Express Scripts has publicly stated their success in leveraging substantial rebates for hepatitis C medicines led to those

---

[11] Hartman M, Martin AB, Espinosa N, Catlin A, et al. National Health Spending in 2016: Spending and Enrollment Growth Slow After Initial Coverage Expansions. *Health Affairs*. 2018;37(1) Available online ahead of print at https://www.healthaffairs.org/doi/abs/10.1377/hlthaff.2017.1299.

[12] Quintiles IMS Institute. *Medicine Use and Spending in the US: A Review of 2016 and Outlook to 2021.* April 2017; CVS Health. *CVS Health PBM Clients Achieved Lowest Prescription Drug Trend in Four Years, Despite Rising Drug Prices.* March 15, 2017. http://www.prnewswire.com/news-releases/cvs-health-pbm-clients-achieved-lowest-prescription-drug-trend-in-four-years-despite-rising-drug-prices-300423726.html; Express Scripts. 2016 Drug Trend Report. February 2017. https://lab.express-scripts.com/lab/drug-trend-report; Which PBM Best Managed Drug Spending in 2016: How Did OptumRx Compare? Drug Channels. April 25, 2017. http://www.drugchannels.net/2017/04/which-pbm-best-managed-drug-spending-in.html#more.

[13] Prescription drug pre-rebate expenditures tabulated by The Menges Group using FY2016 CMS State Drug Utilization data files and CMS brand/generic indicators for each National Drug Code. Rebate information obtained from FY2016 CMS-64 reports. Post-rebate expenditures derived through The Menges Group tabulations using above information.

[14] IMS Institute for Healthcare Informatics. *Price Declines After Branded Medicines Lose Exclusivity in the US January 2016.*

[15] Atorvastatin, known in the branded form as Lipitor 10mg: IMS National Sales Perspective (NSP) Invoice Price in 2005 (Branded Lipitor) and in 2013 (Generic Atorvastatin).

[16] Data adapted from: HCUP Hospital Charge Database 2005 to 2013, Average Hospital Charges.

[17] Fein AJ; Drug Channels Institute. *The 2017 economic report on U.S. pharmacies and pharmacy benefit managers.* Exhibit 72. February 2017.

treatments being less expensive in the U.S. than in many other western countries.[18] And the competitive market will continue to generate savings in the years ahead, as more than $140 billion of U.S. brand sales are projected to face generic competition between now and 2021.[19] Competition from biosimiliars is estimated to account for $38 billion of the loss in brand spending.

List Prices for Medicines Do Not Reflect Substantial Rebates and Discounts and Provide an Increasingly Inaccurate Picture of Prescription Drug Costs

Much of the public debate about the cost of medicines has focused on list prices, which do not account for the rebates and discounts that PBMs and health plans commonly negotiate with biopharmaceutical companies in exchange for preferred formulary placement on lower cost-sharing tiers. For certain medicines used to treat chronic conditions like asthma, high cholesterol, hepatitis C, and diabetes, these discounts and rebates can reduce list prices by as much as 30% to 70%.[20] Biopharmaceutical companies are also required to provide sizable statutory rebates, discounts, and fees to government programs, which have increased in recent years due to an increase in the Medicaid rebate, closing of the Medicare Part D "donut hole" and expansion of the 340B program. These mandatory payments grew by more than 40% between 2013 and 2015, increasing from $29.6 billion to $41.8 billion.[21]

Excluding rebates and discounts from discussions about the cost of prescription medicines provides an increasingly inaccurate picture of marketplace trends. According to PBMs and industry analysts, list prices for brand medicines have grown by an estimated 9% to 12% annually since 2015, while net prices (which take discounts and rebates into account) have grown by just 2.5% to 3.5%.[22] A recent study from the QuintilesIMS Institute demonstrates that net prices for medicines that have been on the

---

[18] LaMattina J. For Hepatitis C Drugs, U.S, Prices Are Cheaper Than in Europe. *Forbes*. December 4, 2015. http://www.forbes.com/sites/johnlamattina/2015/12/04/for-hepatitis-c-drugs-u-s-prices-are-cheaper-than-in-europe/#7ced43f564bb.

[19] Quintiles IMS Institute. *Medicine Use and Spending in the US: A Review of 2016 and Outlook to 2021*. April 2017.

[20] Quintiles IMS Institute. *Estimate of Medicare Part D Costs After Accounting for Manufacturer Rebates*. October 2016; Gronholt-Pedersen J, Skydsgaard N, Neely J. Novo Nordisk Defends U.S. Diabetes Drug Pricing. *Reuters*. November 4, 2016. http://www.reuters.com/article/us-novo-nordisk-prices-idUSKBN12Z184; Silverman E. What the 'Shocking' Gilead Discounts on its Hepatitis C Drugs Will Mean. *Wall Street Journal*. February 4, 2015. https://blogs.wsj.com/pharmalot/2015/02/04/what-the-shocking-gilead-discounts-on-its-hepatitis-c-drugs-will-mean/ Barrett P, Langreth R. The Crazy Math Behind Drug Prices: Intermediaries that Negotiate to Lower Prices May Cause Them To Increase Too. *Bloomberg Businessweek*, June 29, 2017. https://www.bloomberg.com/news/articles/2017-06-29/the-crazy-math-behind-drug-prices.

[21] Berkeley Research Group. *The Pharmaceutical Supply Chain: Gross Drug Expenditures Realized by Stakeholder*. January 2017.

[22] Quintiles IMS Institute. *Medicine Use and Spending in the US: A Review of 2016 and Outlook to 2021*. April 2017; Express Scripts. 2016 Drug Trend Report. February 2017. https://lab.express-scripts.com/lab/drug-trend-report; SSR Health. *US Brand Pharmaceutical Net Prices Fell 0.3% in 3Q16*. January 18, 2017. http://www.ssrllc.com/publication/us-brand-pharmaceutical-net-prices-fell-0-3-in-3q16/.

market for at least two years *declined* by an average of 2.5% annually from 2010 to 2016, driven by patent expirations and increased competition from generics.[23] The QuintilesIMS report also notes that over the next five years, net prices for existing medicines will continue to decline between 1% and 4% annually, highlighting the important role rebates and discounts will continue to play in containing prescription medicine spending growth in the future.

Claims from PBMs, payers, and others about the skyrocketing prices of medicines almost always focus solely on list prices, which are not reflective of actual spending trends. When new hepatitis C medicines offering cure rates exceeding 90% entered the market, PBMs claimed that these life-saving treatments and cures would bankrupt the health system and their costs were simply unsustainable. Instead, competition among brand manufacturers quickly drove deep discounts averaging 40% to 65% off the list price.[24] Express Scripts now states that their aggressive negotiations have saved Americans $4 billion, cured more patients with hepatitis C than any time in history, and that the discounted price makes it affordable to treat all patients with the infection.[25]

Prior to the launch of PCSK9 inhibitors, a new type of cholesterol lowering medicine that represents a significant advance in treatment of heart disease, PBMs made alarming claims about their cost, projecting up to $150 billion to $200 billion per year in spending for these medicines.[26] The Centers for Medicare and Medicaid (CMS) Office of the Actuary, however, projected a much more modest impact, based on expected competition leading to discounts and continued widespread use of generic statins.[27] The Actuary's refusal to accept these inflated claims proved to be the right approach. In fact, PBMs quickly made deals to cover both of the brand competitors on the market and emphasized that the drugs' cost is "far lower than industry forecasts."[28] New research shows that PBMs have also effectively used strict prior authorization and high cost-sharing requirements to suppress utilization of these medicines, resulting in less than one-third of patients prescribed a PCSK9 inhibitor being able to access therapy.[29]

---

[23] Quintiles IMS Institute. *Understanding the Drives of Drug Expenditure in the US*. September 2017.

[24] What Gilead's Big Hepatitis C Discounts Mean for Biosimilar Pricing. *Drug Channels*. February 5, 2015. http://www.drugchannels.net/2015/02/what-gileads-big-hepatitis-c-discounts.html.

[25] Express Scripts. *The $4 Billion Return on a Promise Kept*. January 27, 2015. http://lab.express-scripts.com/lab/insights/specialty-medications/the-4-billion-return-on-a-promise-kept.

[26] Shrank W, Lotvin A, Singh S, Brennan T. In the Debate About Cost and Efficacy, PCSK9 Inhibitors May Be The Biggest Challenge Yet. *Health Affairs Blog*. February 17, 2015. http://healthaffairs.org/blog/2015/02/17/in-the-debate-about-cost-and-efficacy-pcsk9-inhibitors-may-be-the-biggest-challenge-yet/.

[27] Kelly C. U.S. Drug Spending Will Increase 7.6% in 2015, Including PCSK9 Costs – CMS. *The Pink Sheet*, July 2015.

[28] *Express Scripts*. "Express Scripts Includes Innovative Cholesterol-Lowering Drugs on National Preferred Formulary." October 6, 2015. http://www.prnewswire.com/news-releases/express-scripts-includes-innovative-cholesterol-lowering-drugs-on-national-preferred-formulary-300155222.html.

[29] Navar AM, Taylor B, Mulder H, et al. Association of Prior Authorization and Out-of-Pocket Costs With Patient Access to PCSK9 Inhibitor Therapy. *JAMA Cardiology*. Published online September 27, 2017. doi:10.1001/jamacardio.2017.3451.

A Complex Distribution and Payment System Shapes the Prices Patients, Health Plans, and the Government Pay for Medicines

The process by which prescription medicines move from biopharmaceutical manufacturers to patients involves multiple stakeholders and numerous financial transactions. This process has evolved significantly in recent years, as supply chain entities have grown to play a larger role in drug distribution and payment. Wholesalers, pharmacies, plan sponsors, and patients all pay different prices for medicines, and the amount that is ultimately paid is determined by confidential negotiations between stakeholders. Many discounts provided by manufacturers do not flow directly through to the patients taking the medicine, and in some cases the full discounts may also not flow through to employers or plan sponsors.[30]

Some manufacturer rebates and discounts are required by law, while others are negotiated between biopharmaceutical companies and powerful commercial payers, many of which cover tens of millions of patients. In recent years, as payers have consolidated and competition between brand medicines has increased, negotiated rebates and discounts have also grown. Multiple data sources indicate that growth in manufacturer rebates and discounts has been substantial and that an increasing share of these discounts and rebates are retained by middlemen involved in distributing and paying for prescription medicines.[31] According to a recent study by the Berkeley Research Group, on average, more than a third of the initial list price of a medicine is rebated back to insurance companies, PBMs and the government, or retained by other stakeholders along the biopharmaceutical supply chain.[32] And the gap between list prices and net prices is growing every year as more of medicine costs are being retained by middlemen in the system.

As shown in Figure 1, accounting for the discounts, rebates and fees paid to PBMs, payers, and the government, brand biopharmaceutical companies realize less than half of total net spending on prescription medicines.[33] Of the $469 billion spent on prescription drugs in the U.S. in 2015, brand manufacturers realized $219 billion; the remainder went to generic manufacturers or was retained as earnings by entities along the supply chain

---

[30] Midwestern Business Group on Health. *Drawing a Line in the Sand: Employers Must Rethink Pharmacy Benefit Strategies*. September 2017. https://higherlogicdownload.s3.amazonaws.com/MBGH/4f7f512a-e946-4060-9575-b27c65545cb8/UploadedImages/Specialty%20Pharmacy/DMJ_MBGH_Line_in_the_Sand_RV12_9617.pdf.

[31] Quintiles IMS Institute. *Medicine Use and Spending in the US: A Review of 2016 and Outlook to 2021*. April 2017; Berkeley Research Group. The Pharmaceutical Supply Chain: Gross Drug Expenditures Realized by Stakeholder. January 2017; Dross D. Will Point-of-Sale Rebates Disrupt the PBM Business? *Mercer*. July 31, 2017. https://www.mercer.us/our-thinking/healthcare/will-point-of-sale-rebates-disrupt-the-pbm-business.html.

[32] Berkeley Research Group. *The Pharmaceutical Supply Chain: Gross Drug Expenditures Realized by Stakeholder*. January 2017.

[33] *Ibid.*

and other stakeholders.[34] The $219 billion realized by the brand biopharmaceutical industry accounts for just 6.8% of the $3.2 trillion spent on health care overall in the U.S. in 2015.[35]

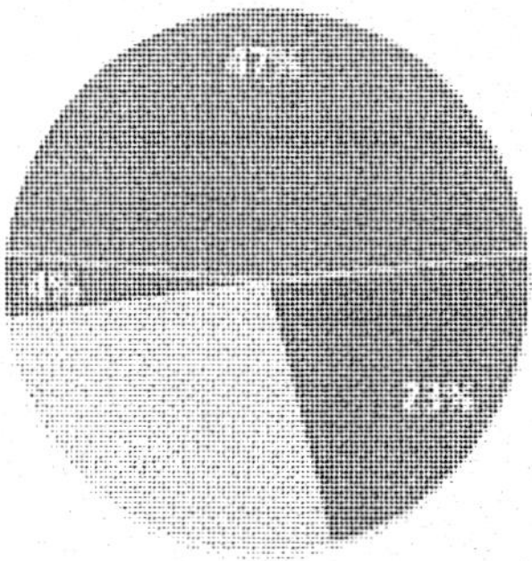

Figure 1. Share of 2015 Net Prescription Medicine Spending Realized by Manufacturer and Non-Manufacturer Stakeholders.

Patients Do Not Directly Benefit from Significant Price Negotiations Happening in the Market Today

Savings generated from price negotiations between biopharmaceutical companies and payers do not always make their way directly to patients facing high cost-sharing for their medicines. Unlike care received at an in-network hospital or physician's office, health plans base cost-sharing for prescriptions filled in the deductible or with coinsurance on undiscounted list prices, rather than on prices that reflect negotiated rebates and discounts. Enrollment in high deductible health plans and use of coinsurance for prescription medicines has grown sharply in recent years, increasingly exposing patients to high out-of-pocket costs based on undiscounted prices, creating scenarios in which medicines appear to be more costly than other health care services. High cost-sharing is a cause for concern, as a substantial body of research clearly demonstrates that increases in out-of-pocket costs are associated with both lower medication adherence and increased abandonment rates, putting patients' ability to stay on needed therapies at risk.[36]

---

[34] *Ibid.*

[35] Martin AB, Hartman M, Washington B, et al. National Health Spending: Faster Growth in 2015 As Coverage Expands and Utilization Increases. *Health Affairs*. 2017;36(1):166-176.

[36] IMS Institute for Healthcare Informatics. *Emergency and Impact of Pharmacy Deductibles: Implications for Patients in Commercial Health Plans.* September 2015; Doshi JA, Li P, Huo H, et al. High Cost Sharing and Specialty Drug Initiation Under Medicare Part D: A Case Study in Patients with Newly Diagnosed Chronic Myeloid Leukemia. *American Journal of Managed Care*. 2016;22(4 Suppl):S78-S86; Brot-Goldberg ZC, Chandra A, Handel BR, et al. What Does A Deductible Do? The Impact of Cost-Sharing on Health Care Prices, Quantities, and Spending Dynamics. *NBER Working Paper* 21632, October 2015; Eaddy MT, Cook

Over the past 10 years, patient cost-sharing has risen substantially faster than health plan costs. For workers with employer-sponsored health insurance, out-of-pocket spending for deductible and coinsurance payments increased by 230% and 89%, respectively, compared to a 56% increase in payments by health plans.[37] Whereas cost-sharing for prescription medicines once consisted almost entirely of copays, use of deductibles and coinsurance has increased rapidly particularly for new medicines that represent the most innovative therapies and treat the sickest patients. The share of patient out-of-pocket drug spending represented by coinsurance more than doubled over the past ten years in the commercial market, while the share accounted for by deductibles tripled.[38]

The growing use of deductibles and coinsurance for prescription medicines creates affordability challenges for many patients. Patients enrolled in high deductible health plans may be asked to pay thousands of dollars out-of-pocket before any of their prescriptions are covered, while patients with coinsurance are responsible for as much as 30% to 40% of the total cost of their medicines.

Due to the growing gap between list and net prices, patients' cost sharing for medicines is increasingly based on prices that do not reflect plan sponsors' actual costs. For example, market analysts report that negotiated discounts and rebates can lower the net price of insulin by up to 50% to 70%, yet health plans require patients with deductibles to pay the full undiscounted price. As a result, a patient in a high-deductible health plan who pays the list price each month for insulin maybe paying hundreds—or even thousands—more annually than their insurer.

As a hypothetical example, imagine a patient enrolled in a high-deductible health plan who takes an insulin with a list price of $400. The patient's insurer has negotiated a 65% rebate, which substantially reduces the cost to the plan. However, because the patient has not yet met his deductible, his insurer does not provide any coverage for his prescription, and the patient's bill reflects the insulin's full cost of $400. Despite paying nothing for this patient's insulin, the insurer still collects the rebate, earning over $200.[39]

Unfortunately, as the number of patients with deductibles and coinsurance rises, this situation is becoming more common. Analysis by Amundsen Consulting shows that more

---

CL, O'Day K, et al. How Patient Cost-Sharing Trends Affect Adherence and Outcomes. *Pharmacy & Therapeutics*. 2012;37(1):45-55.

[37] Claxton G, Levitt L, Long M, et al. Increases in Cost-Sharing Payments Have Far Outpaced Wage Growth. *Peterson-Kaiser Health System Tracker*. October 4, 2017. https://www.healthsystemtracker.org/brief/increases-in-cost-sharing-payments-have-far-outpaced-wage-growth/#item-start.

[38] Claxton G, Levitt L, Long M. Payments for Cost Sharing Increasing Rapidly Over Time. *Peterson-Kaiser Health System Tracker*. April 2016. http://www.healthsystemtracker.org/insight/examining-high-prescription-drug-spending-for-people-with-employer-sponsored-health-insurance/.

[39] Pharmaceutical Research and Manufacturers of America. *Follow the Dollar*. November 2017. http://phrma-docs.phrma.org/files/dmfile/Follow-the-Dollar-Report.pdf.

than half of patients' out-of-pocket spending for brand medicines is based on the list price of the medicine, even though their health insurer may be receiving a steep discount.[40]

Health plans typically use some portion of negotiated rebates to reduce premiums for all enrollees, rather than to directly lower costs for patients facing high cost-sharing due to deductibles and coinsurance. According to one actuarial firm, this results in a system of "reverse insurance," whereby payers require patients with high drug expenditures to pay more out-of-pocket, while rebate savings are spread out among all health plan enrollees in the form of lower premiums.[41] Asking sicker patients with high drug costs to subsidize premiums for healthier enrollees is the exact opposite of how health insurance is supposed to work.

Some patients also end up paying more at the pharmacy counter when they use their insurance, not knowing that their prescriptions would be cheaper if they were paying in cash. Many PBM contracts require pharmacies to charge patients the exact amount negotiated between the PBM and the pharmacy, even if that amount exceeds what the pharmacy would charge to a patient without insurance. Gag-clauses in PBM contracts prohibit pharmacists from informing insured patients about the lower cash price, at the risk of the pharmacy being excluded from the PBM's network. In these instances, pharmacies must instead overcharge patients, requiring them to pay the full amount of their copayment, over and above the actual cost of the medication. These overpayments are then "clawed back" from the pharmacy by the PBM.[42]

PBMs Negotiate Lower Medicine Prices for Health Plans and Employers, but Don't Always Pass Along All of the Savings

PBMs commonly retain a portion of the rebates they negotiate on behalf of their health plan and employer clients. While the remainder of the rebates are generally passed on to plan sponsors, smaller employers and health plans may not benefit from all of the price concessions the PBM has negotiated with manufacturers, particularly if the PBM decides not to define certain fees or other concessions as "rebates." For example, one benefits consultant has observed that PBMs are increasingly changing the contractual definition of rebates to exclude certain administrative fees, allowing the PBM to retain these payments rather than passing them back to the plan sponsor.

---

[40] Amundsen Consulting. *Commercially-Insured Patients Pay Undiscounted List Prices for One In Five Brand Prescriptions, Accounting for Half of Out-of-Pocket Spending on Brand Medicines*. March 2017. http://www.phrma.org/report/commercially-insured-patients-pay-undiscounted-list-prices-for-one-in-five-brand-prescriptions-accounting-for-half-of-out-of-pocket-spending-brand-medicines.

[41] Girod CS, Hart SK, Weltz S. 2017 *Milliman Medical Index*. May 2017. http://www.milliman.com/uploadedFiles/insight/Periodicals/mmi/2017-milliman-medical-index.pdf.

[42] Hopkins JS. You're Overpaying for Drugs and Your Pharmacist Can't Tell You. *Bloomberg*. February 24, 2017. https://www.bloomberg.com/news/articles/2017-02-24/sworn-to-secrecy-drugstores-stay-silent-as-customers-overpay.

These administrative fees can be as high as 25% to 30% of the total rebate negotiated with the manufacturer and are often not reported to the plan sponsor by the PBM.[43]

In addition to the rebates they negotiate with biopharmaceutical companies, PBMs are increasingly requiring that if a medicine's list price increases by more than a certain percentage, the manufacturer must provide an additional price protection rebate reimbursing the PBM for all price increases above the threshold. Lack of transparency in contracts between employers and PBMs has led many plan sponsors to question the share of rebate savings being passed through, how much the PBM is retaining for administrative fees, and whether the PBM is disclosing and passing on other price concessions, such as savings from price protection rebates.[44]

Both the portion of the rebate retained by the PBM and the administrative fees they charge their clients are typically based on a percentage of a medicine's list price. Accordingly, some PBMs may prefer that their formularies include medicines with high list prices and large rebates, rather than medicines with a lower list price. Thus, if a manufacturer were to lower the list price of a medicine in lieu of a higher rebate, the PBM's revenue would decline. Because PBMs hold the key to market access through their decisions about formulary coverage and placement, such a manufacturer decision could result in reduced formulary access.

In its most recent report to Congress, the Medicare Payment Advisory Commission discussed incentives that may drive Part D plan sponsors to give formulary preference to medicines with large rebates, rather than lower cost alternatives.[45] These incentives arise because sizable portions of the Part D benefit are not paid for by plan sponsors (e.g., beneficiaries and manufacturers pay for the majority of costs in the coverage gap). Similarly, CMS has noted that coverage of medicines with high list prices and large rebates "ease[s] the financial burden borne by Part D plans essentially by shifting costs to the catastrophic phase of the benefit, where plan liability is limited"[46] and that plans have "weak incentives, and in some cases even, no incentive, to lower prices at the point of sale or to choose lower net cost alternatives to high cost-highly rebated drugs when available."[47] Recently, CMS addressed this concern in a Request for Information issued as part of a proposed regulation for Medicare Part D. In an effort to better align plan incentives with the interests of beneficiaries and the Medicare program, CMS is soliciting

---

[43] Dross D. Will Point-of-Sale Rebates Disrupt the PBM Business? *Mercer.* July 31, 2017. https://www.mercer.us/our-thinking/healthcare/will-point-of-sale-rebates-disrupt-the-pbm-business.html.

[44] Midwestern Business Group on Health. *Drawing a Line in the Sand: Employers Must Rethink Pharmacy Benefit Strategies.* September 2017. https://higherlogicdownload.s3.amazonaws.com/MBGH/4f7f512a-e946-4060-9575-b27c65545cb8/UploadedImages/Specialty%20Pharmacy/DMJ_MBGH_Line_in_the_Sand_RV12_9617.pdf.

[45] Medicare Payment Advisory Commission. *Status Report on the Medicare Prescription Drug Program (Part D).* March 2017. http://medpac.gov/docs/default-source/reports/mar17_entirereport.pdf.

[46] Centers for Medicare & Medicaid. *Medicare Part D—Direct and Indirect Remuneration (DIR).* January 19, 2017. https://www.cms.gov/Newsroom/MediaReleaseDatabase/Fact-sheets/2017-Fact-Sheet-items/2017-01-19-2.html.

[47] 82 FR 56419 (November 28, 2017).

feedback on a potential future proposal to require Part D plans to share negotiated rebate savings directly with beneficiaries at the point of sale.

Hospital Markups on Medicines Increase Cost-Sharing for Commercially-Insured Patients

The pharmaceutical distribution and payment process differs for medicines administered in a physician office or health care facility vs. those purchased at a pharmacy. Providers typically purchase medicines directly, often through a Group Purchasing Organization (GPO). After the physician administers the medicine to the patient, the patient's insurance reimburses the provider for the cost of the medicine as part of the patient's coverage for medical care.

The amount that providers charge for medicines and how much insurers pay varies widely based on where the medicine is administered to the patient. For example, commercial insurers often pay hospital outpatient departments twice as much as physician offices for administering the exact same medicines, including for diseases such as cancer or autoimmune disorders.[48] This is because large hospitals can demand much higher prices from commercial insurers than small physician practices. The Senior Vice President of Oncology and Genetics at UnitedHealthcare described the effect for chemotherapy treatment at high profile cancer centers, "Put simply, the hospitals are saying, 'If you want our beds, you have to take our prices for oncology treatment.'"[49]

The results of hospital markups are astounding. Recent research shows that for twenty medicines administered in hospital outpatient departments, hospitals charge prices that are on average nearly five times higher than their acquisition costs and are reimbursed up to three and a half times their acquisition cost by commercial insurers.[50] For a vast majority of the medicines included in the analysis, this means that the manufacturer—who made the substantial time and R&D investments including clinical trials necessary to develop the treatment—was paid less for the medicine than the hospital.

Hospital markups on prescription medicines have a substantial effect not just on overall healthcare costs, but also on patient affordability. For patients with commercial insurance, coinsurance is the most common form of cost-sharing for provider-administered medicines, which means that the amount the patient must pay is equal to a percentage of the total price the insurer reimburses the provider for the medication. So, when a hospital is paid two or three times the acquisition cost for a medicine, patients are

[48] Magellan RX Management. Medical Pharmacy Trend Report: 2016 Seventh Edition. March 2017.

[49] Newcomer LN. Those Who Pay Have A Say: A View On Oncology Drug Pricing and Reimbursement. *The Oncologist*. 2016;21(7):779-81.

[50] The Moran Company. *Hospital Charges and Reimbursement for Drugs: Analysis of Markups Relative to Acquisition Cost.* October 2017.

also paying higher coinsurance. As the same United insurance executive quoted above noted "it is immoral to force vulnerable patients to pay triple-digit mark-ups because they have cancer."[51]

Market Distortions Created by the 340B Program Lead to Higher Health Care Costs

The 340B program, a program originally intended to provide discounts on medicines for safety-net providers, is contributing to higher health care costs and economists suspect that it is also leading to higher list prices for medicines. This program started in 1992, and its basic structure has not been updated since then, despite dramatic changes in the health care system over the past 25 years. The current structure of the program is causing higher health care costs for three main reasons.

First, the 340B discount, which is structured as a percentage discount, creates incentives for hospitals to earn a larger spread from the 340B discounts by prescribing more medicines and higher cost medicines. Economists have noted this may lead prescribing to "shift toward more expensive drugs because profit margins will in general be larger."[52] A 2015 Government Accountability Office study found evidence that 340B was leading to the prescribing of more drugs and more expensive drugs for Medicare patients.[53]

Second, evidence suggests the 340B program shifts care to more expensive and less convenient settings. Government reports suggest that hospitals are taking advantage of guidance that has not been revisited since 1994 which allows hospitals to obtain more 340B discounts by buying community-based physician practices, so that prescriptions written by those physicians then qualify for 340B discounts.[54] As a result, patients are left with fewer community-based provider options and are pushed into higher cost hospital-based settings. Analysis by the IMS Institute for Healthcare Informatics found that average costs for administering cancer drugs are typically twice as high at hospital outpatient departments compared to community-based oncologists, which can lead to "higher patient cost responsibility."[55] Researchers from Memorial Sloan Kettering have noted 340B is helping to drive consolidation of physician practices into hospitals, and

---

[51] Newcomer LN. Those Who Pay Have A Say: A View On Oncology Drug Pricing and Reimbursement. *The Oncologist*. 2016;21(7):779-81.

[52] Conti R, Bach P. Cost Consequences of the 340B Drug Discount Program. *Journal of the American Medical Association*. 2013;309(19):1995-1996.

[53] Government Accountability Office. *Medicare Part B Drugs: Action Needed to Reduce Financial Incentives to Prescribe 340B Drugs at Participating Hospitals*. GAO-15-442, June 2015.

[54] 59 Federal Register 47884.

[55] IMS Institute for Healthcare Informatics. *Global Oncology Trend Report: A Review of 2015 and Outlook to 2020*. June 2016.

that in the absence of reforms "the trend toward consolidation will continue to drive up the cost of commercial insurance..."[56]

Third, the scale of the program as well as its rapid growth may be affecting market prices for prescription drugs. In 2015, roughly 45 percent of all hospitals participated in 340B.[57] In an analysis of prescription drug pricing published in the *New England Journal of Medicine,* economists at Harvard University and the University of Chicago concluded that "lawmakers could lower the price of prescription drugs by reforming the federal 340B Drug Pricing Program. [...]The scope of the 340B program is currently so vast for drugs that are commonly infused or injected into patients by physicians that their prices are probably driven up for all consumers."[58] Another study in *JAMA* noted that list prices for drugs are likely higher than they otherwise would be "to offset revenue losses incurred as a larger number of drug sales become eligible for 340B discounts (and thus fewer drugs are sold at full price)."[59] Certain drug classes are disproportionately impacted by the 340B program. Thus, the price distorting impact may be concentrated in certain therapeutic areas, such as medicines for cancer. For example, sales to 340B hospitals account for 33% of *all* Medicare Part B reimbursement for certain types of cancer drugs.[60]

Market-Based Approaches Are the Best Solution for Addressing Health Care Affordability and Controlling Costs

The competitive U.S. health care market provides a sound framework for balancing and supporting patient access, cost containment, and continued progress for patients. Meaningful efforts to address the cost of prescription medicines must include all stakeholders in the supply chain, including biopharmaceutical companies, PBMs, health plans, wholesalers, hospitals, and pharmacies. Policies targeted solely at brand manufacturers—which account for just half of total net spending on prescription medicines and just 6.8% of total U.S. health care spending—are insufficient for addressing broader health care sustainability challenges and risk diminishing the incentives for future innovation.

---

56 Bach P and Jain RH. Physician's Office and Hospital Outpatient Setting in Oncology: It's About Prices, Not Use. *Journal of Oncology Practice* 2017; 13(1), 4-5.

57 Medicare Payment Advisory Commission. *Report to the Congress: Overview of the 340B Drug Pricing Program.* May 2015.

58 Conti R and Rosenthal M. Pharmaceutical Policy Reform—Balancing Affordability with Incentives for Innovation. *New England Journal of Medicine*. 2016; 374:703-706.

59 Conti R, Bach P. Cost Consequences of the 340B Drug Discount Program, *Journal of the American Medical Association.* 2013;309(19):1995-1996.

60 Drugs sold to 340B hospitals account for 33% of *all* Part B reimbursement for breast cancer and multiple myeloma drugs. Vandervelde A and Blalock E. *Measuring the Relative Size of the 340B Program: 2012-2017.* Berkeley Research Group, July 2017.

Strategies for strengthening and enhancing the competitive market include encouraging payers to share negotiated savings with patients at the pharmacy; reforming outdated regulations hindering the adoption of value-based payment arrangements; reforming the 340B drug discount program, which is distorting the market, so that it better serves the purpose for which it was created; and continuing to modernize the Food and Drug Administration (FDA) and assure that there is robust generic and biosimilar competition once a brand medicine loses its exclusivity.

Sharing Negotiated Savings with Patients

Changes in insurance coverage for prescription medicines, and the growing use of deductibles and coinsurance in particular, have created affordability challenges for many patients. Health plans should be encouraged to directly pass on more of the savings from negotiated rebates in the form of lower patient out-of-pocket costs, just like they do for other types of health care services. This should be executed in a way that maintains the confidentiality of proprietary pricing information that the Federal Trade Commission has identified as important to the effective functioning of competitive markets. Payers have begun to recognize that using the undiscounted price of a medicine to set cost-sharing is problematic for patients: recent statements from the two largest PBMs note that high deductibles for medicines put patients in a "very difficult position" and indicate that sharing rebate savings directly with patients should be considered as a "best practice."[61] Actuarial research indicates that sharing negotiated savings could save certain commercially insured patients enrolled in plans with high deductibles and coinsurance between $145 and $800 annually, while increasing premiums by 1% or less.[62]

To help patients afford their medicines, biopharmaceutical companies have entered into partnerships with third parties, such as Blink Health and GoodRx, to offer discounted prices directly to patients, outside of their insurance benefit.[63] Encouraging health plans to allow the cost of prescriptions purchased through these third-party programs to count towards patients' deductibles and maximum out-of-pocket spending limits would further reduce patient affordability barriers.

Copay assistance programs offered by biopharmaceutical companies provide another valuable source of assistance for many commercially insured patients who are struggling to afford their out-of-pocket costs, as do manufacturer-sponsored patient assistance

---

[61] Seeking Alpha. Express Scripts Holding (ESRX) *Q4 2016 Results – Earnings Call Transcript.* February 15, 2017. http://seekingalpha.com/article/4046365-express-scripts-holding-esrx-q4-2016-results-earnings-call-transcript; Seeking Alpha. CVS Health (CVS) *Q4 2016 Results – Earnings Call Transcript.* February 9, 2017. http://seekingalpha.com/article/4044425-cvs-health-cvs-q4-2016-results-earnings-call-transcript?part=single.

[62] Bunger A, Gomberg J, Petroske J. *Sharing Rebates May Lower Patient Costs and Likely Has Minimal Impact on Premiums.* October 12, 2017. http://www.phrma.org/report/point-of-sale-rebate-analysis-in-the-commercial-market.

[63] Thomas K. New Online Tools Offer Path to Lower Drug Prices. *New York Times.* February 9, 2016. https://www.nytimes.com/2016/02/10/business/taming-drug-prices-by-pulling-back-the-curtain-online.html.

programs that help underinsured and uninsured patients obtain the medicines they need for free or nearly free.

Recent efforts by health plans to restrict use of copay assistance programs, including no longer counting the full amount patients are asked to pay out-of-pocket towards their deductibles or out-of-pocket maximums, unfairly penalize patients and threaten their ability to stay on needed medicines.

Reforming Outdated Regulations Hindering the Adoption of Value-Based Payment Arrangements

Changes in the science and pressures for cost containment in the competitive market are driving rapid evolution of payment and care delivery systems, and biopharmaceutical companies are playing a role in this transformation. As therapies become more personalized, and as the health care market moves away from fee-for-service care and toward more integrated care systems, biopharmaceutical companies are increasingly partnering with payers to develop new payment arrangements that reward improvements in care and better health outcomes for patients. These arrangements can improve patient access to medicines and lead to savings for the health care system.

Yet while the science and market are moving rapidly, efforts to develop new ways to pay for medicines have been slowed by regulations designed for an earlier era. Such regulations can have the unintended consequence of making it more difficult for payers to prioritize results that matter to patients, and for biopharmaceutical companies to increase the amount of risk they share with payers. For example:

- Ambiguity in FDA rules governing manufacturer communications about their medicines can prevent biopharmaceutical companies from entering into contracts on metrics that matter to payers, such as the ability of their medicine to reduce hospitalizations or other medical services. This is because of concerns that such contracts might be perceived as promoting the medicine for an unapproved indication.
- Lack of clarity in the anti-kickback statute (AKS) can inhibit value-based contracts due to lack of certainty as to whether contracts fit within existing safe harbors and exceptions. By revising the AKS regulations to add a value-based arrangements safe harbor, policymakers can facilitate an expansion of these arrangements between insurers and manufacturers.
- Price reporting rules such as Medicaid Best Price can limit the amount of risk biopharmaceutical companies share with payers within a value based arrangement, because any increased discount beyond the statutory minimum must be offered not only to that payer, but also to all of Medicaid. These rules should be modernized to create flexibility for new innovative contracting arrangements.

CMS' Center for Medicare and Medicaid Innovation (CMMI) recently released a New Direction RFI which expressed interest in testing value based payment arrangements, among other models. Unfortunately, CMMI is not the right venue to make the changes needed to allow for new contracting approaches between insurers and manufacturers. It does not have waiver authority to address challenges posed by Food and Drug Administration (FDA) communication rules or Medicaid Best Price. While CMMI can waive the Anti-Kickback Statute, such a waiver could discourage beneficial arrangements outside of CMMI, which would not have the benefit of the waiver. Instead of a demonstration, we are seeking permanent regulatory reforms to encourage value-based arrangements.

Modernizing the FDA

As the pace of scientific discovery accelerates, it is critical to assure that our regulatory infrastructure keeps up with the science and that FDA regulations are up-to-date, practical, clear and not overly burdensome to foster efficiency, predictability, and the ability of biopharmaceutical companies to innovate and bring new medicines to patients. The Committee's recent action to reauthorize the Prescription Drug User Fee Act creates a solid foundation not only to accelerate approval of new life-saving treatments, but also assure that there is robust generic and biosimilar competition. We thank the Committee for its rapid and bipartisan action.

Accelerating the introduction of new medicines allows the forces of private market competition to keep costs in check and increases the number lifesaving drugs becoming available to patients. Importantly, key provisions of the prescription drug, biosimilar, and generic drug user fee acts will help to eliminate the generic drug application backlog, increase resources to prevent future backlogs, and to streamline the review process and enhance FDA's expertise related to drug-device combination products, an area in which regulatory uncertainties and delays have previously deterred brand and generic manufacturers from investments. Additional opportunities to improve competition include finalizing FDA guidance related to biosimilars and enhancing incentives for generic manufacturers to enter the marketplace where there are no intellectual property or regulatory incentives preventing generic entry but, due to small patient population sizes, there are no brand or generic competitors. Increased competition from generics could be spurred by waiving user fees for eligible products, providing a transferable generic drug priority review voucher, and expediting review of such products and the inspection of their facilities.

Finally, the FDA can further spur efficiency in the market and free up scarce resources through elimination of certain outdated regulations. For example, regulations requiring biopharmaceutical companies to submit post-marketing reports in a format unique to the U.S. are inefficient and burdensome and provide no appreciable benefit compared to the format used globally. A more logical approach for submission of post-marketing reports would be to streamline the formats. Similarly, requiring biopharmaceutical companies to submit all promotional materials to the FDA at the time of dissemination—even if only minor, non-substantive changes have been made to previously submitted pieces—results in submission of thousands of pieces per company per year with no benefit to public health.

Reforming the 340B Drug Discount Program

To protect the health care safety net, it is critical to ensure that the underlying market works. The 340B program needs both Congressional and administrative updates to help prevent it from continuing to raise costs for consumers and the overall health care system. Stronger rules for hospitals participating in the program will help ensure the program targets the patients and true safety-net facilities it was intended to help. Specific reforms for hospitals participating in the program should include stricter 340B eligibility criteria, limits on contract pharmacy arrangements, requirements that patients see a benefit from the program, a tighter definition of patient eligibility, and limits on which hospital-owned physician practices can participate in 340B.

Assuring Robust Competition and Continuing to Modernize the FDA

Economists have reinforced the critical role of boosting competition to address drug cost and access issues. To increase competition:

- Key provisions of the prescription drug, biosimilar, and generic drug user fee acts will spur competition, including policies to eliminate the generic drug application backlog and increased resources to prevent future backlogs, expand FDA's expertise related to drug-device combination products, and reduce the regulatory uncertainty and streamline review of drug-device combination products. Biopharmaceutical companies have stated that current regulatory uncertainties and delays have deterred both generic and brand manufacturers from investments in these areas.
- Reducing the length and increasing the efficiency of drug development will increase competition on both price and clinical effects. Given that the cost of innovator drug development has doubled over the past decade, in part due to increasing FDA requirements, the Prescription Drug User Fee Act includes a range of provisions aimed at reducing uncertainty and creating efficiencies in the both the development and regulatory review of new medicines. Accelerating the introduction of new medicines would allow the forces of private market competition to keep costs in check and increase the number of lifesaving drugs becoming available to patients.
- Enhancing incentives for generic manufacturers to enter the marketplace in areas where there are no intellectual property or regulatory incentives preventing

generic entry but due to small population sizes there are no brand or generic competitors. Increased competition from generics could be spurred by waiving user fees for eligible products, providing a transferable generic drug priority review voucher, and expediting review of such products and the inspection of their facilities.

- Finalizing the various FDA guidances related to biosimilars is necessary to reduce regulatory uncertainties for biosimliar manufacturers and to accelerate the market entry of biosimilars. Biosimilar medicines are an important way to spur competition that will lead to more choices for patients and lower prices for patients and the health care system.

Sustaining Incentives for Innovation Is Critical to Solving Future Health Care Challenges

Looking ahead, it is clear that medicines offer some of the clearest opportunities to address the challenge of growing health care costs as our population ages. For example, the number of Alzheimer's cases is projected to increase rapidly over the next decade as Baby Boomers begin to reach retirement age, resulting in an enormous human and economic cost. If we can achieve treatment advances that delay Alzheimer's by just five years beginning a decade from now, 2.5 million fewer Americans will be afflicted by the disease and we would avoid $367 billion annually by 2050 in costs for long-term care and similar services for persons with Alzheimer's.[64] Alzheimer's remains a major focus of biopharmaceutical research companies despite high risks; since 1998 there have been 123 unsuccessful attempts to develop a medicine for Alzheimer's, and just four approved medicines.[65] In just the last two years, several promising new therapies failed in mid- and late-stage trials, resulting in the loss of billions of dollars of human, political, and monetary capital.[66]

As with Alzheimer's disease, there is a significant unmet medical need for patients with rare diseases which collectively affect 30 million Americans. But only 5% of these diseases have available treatment options.[67] Given the many diseases where there is significant unmet need, maintaining incentives for the continued development of new

---

[64] Alzheimer's Association. "Changing the Trajectory of Alzheimer's Disease: How a Treatment by 2025 Saves Lives and Dollars." https://www.alz.org/documents_custom/trajectory.pdf.

[65] PhRMA. *Researching Alzheimer's Medicines: Setbacks and Stepping Stones.* Summer 2015. Available at: http://phrma.org/sites/default/files/pdf/alzheimers-setbacks-and-stepping-stones.pdf.

[66] Ogg JC. The List of Failed Alzheimer's Drug Treatments Keeps Growing. *24/7 Wall Street.* September 26, 2017. http://247wallst.com/healthcare-business/2017/09/26/the-list-of-failed-alzheimers-drug-treatments-keeps-growing/.

[67] Pharmaceutical Research and Manufacturers of America (PhRMA). *Spurring Innovation in Rare Diseases: 2017 update.* http://phrma-docs.phrma.org/files/dmfile/Rare-Disease-Udpate_FINAL.pdf.

medicines will be crucial in addressing the most costly and challenging diseases of our time.

Yet there is evidence that rising costs in drug development, combined with an increasingly competitive market, have resulted in more uncertainty and lower average returns in recent years. Analysis by a Massachusetts Institute of Technology economist and the IMS Institute finds that increasing market competition has eroded much of the economic profitability of newly launched brand medicines, such that on average financial returns for medicines launched between 2005 and 2009 were insufficient to recoup average R&D and operating costs.[68]

Even drugs that succeed at launch may quickly be supplanted as other new brand competitors enter the market, as occurred with first generation of hepatitis C medicines. For example, despite initial success, two protease inhibitors launched in 2011—seen at the time as substantial advances in treatment of hepatitis C —found that they were supplanted by more effective treatments following the introduction of the next generation of medicines in 2013. Thus, despite substantial investment and many years of research and development, competition from newer brands led these medicines to be withdrawn from the market within two years.[69] This underscores the extraordinary risk biopharmaceutical companies confront to bring new treatments to market.

Mr. BURGESS. Chair thanks the gentlelady.

The chair recognizes Mr. DiLenge for 3 minutes for your opening statement, please.

STATEMENT OF TOM DILENGE

Mr. DILENGE. Thank you, Mr. Chairman, Ranking Member Green, Mr. Walden, Ranking Member Pallone. Thank you for the opportunity to testify today about how to sustain the biomedical innovation that is bringing home and cures to the patients who need them the most.

I am Tom DiLenge. I am Vice President for Advocacy, Law, and Public Policy. While BIO represents the entire biomedical eco-system—universities, startups, investors, large drug companies— the vast majority of our members—about 80 percent—are small companies with no marketed products and no profits. They rely heavily on outside investors and partners to fund the cutting-edge research that they do, and it is these small companies that are leading 70 percent of the nearly 6,000 clinical trials that are underway today.

[68] Berndt ER, Nass D, Kleinrock M, Aitken M. Decline in Economic Returns from New Drugs Raises Questions About Sustaining Innovations. *Health Affairs*. 2015;34(2):245-252.

[69] Loftus P. Merck Will No Longer Sell its Victrelis Hepatitis C Drug in the US. *Wall Street Journal*, Jan 21, 2015, http://blogs.wsj.com/pharmalot/2015/01/21/merck-will-no-longer-sell-its-victrelis-hepatitis-c-drug-in-the-u-s/.

Another key fact—almost 60 percent of all new medicines are innovated right here in America, more than the rest of the world combined. We lead because America has a public policy environment that incentivizes the investment and innovation and this committee, on a bipartisan basis, has led the way on that for decades. This is critical because, while NIH funds really important research, it is the private sector that spends $150 billion every year in applied R&D to bring products from research to the marketplace.

This investment provides more than 1.7 million American jobs and we are growing jobs at twice the rate of the national average. More importantly, we are having an awe-inspiring record of public health accomplishment, transforming HIV/AIDS from a death sentence to a manageable condition, increasing cancer survival in children to 83 percent today, and hundreds of other new medicines for once-debilitating diseases.

We are saving millions of lives. We are saving trillions of dollars in the process. We are making discoveries that were once unimaginable—immuno-oncology, in which we activate the body's own immune system to attack cancer—gene therapy, which we can repair defective genes or use the patient's own cells to make a medicine tailored for that patient.

Precision and personalized medicine is here. Thus, to understand the pricing dynamics of our market, it is important to consider a couple of facts. Ninety percent of clinical programs fail. Ninety-two percent of our companies are unprofitable. Ten to 15 years and $2.6 billion, the average time and cost to bring a medicine through approval, that number has doubled since 2003, and nearly 90 percent of prescriptions today in America are for cheap generic copies of once-branded drugs. Thus, it is the revenues from the 10 percent of successful clinical programs that have to be sufficient to incentivize this entire wonderful innovation ecosystem.

We have repeatedly seen biotech investment jeopardized by the spectre of government price setting. The small companies are the proverbial canaries in the coal mine when it comes to that.

We also recognize that patients, even those with insurance, cannot afford many of these lifesaving miracles. We share this commitment to solving the problem. BIO has joined the coalition with a lot of people at the table and others—insurers, PBMs, patient groups—to come up with market-based ways to lower drug costs. We'd love to work with this committee on doing that.

Reward volume, reward value, not volume, inject more competition, empower patients. So with Congress' continued support, we are going to put more Americans to work, we are going to lower health care costs, and we are going to heal the world in the process.

Thank you, and I am happy to answer any questions you have. [The prepared statement of Mr. DiLenge follows:]

Testimony of Tom DiLenge, President, Advocacy, Law and Public Policy, Biotechnology Innovation Organization, before the U.S. House of Representatives, Energy and Commerce Committee Subcommittee on Health, Hearing on "Examining the Drug Supply Chain," December 13, 2017

Mr. Chairman, Ranking Member Green, and Members of the Subcommittee: BIO appreciates the opportunity to speak with you today about the innovative biopharmaceutical development and delivery system and its enormous contributions to patient health and the U.S. economy.

My name is Tom DiLenge and I am the President for Advocacy, Law and Public Policy at the Biotechnology Innovation Organization, or BIO. BIO is the world's largest trade association representing biotechnology companies, academic institutions, state biotechnology centers, and related organizations across the United States and in more than 30 other nations. BIO is a unique association because it represents an entire technology, rather than a particular industry or sector. Our members operate at the intersection of biology and technology to discover innovative ways to not only heal the world, but also to help feed and fuel our planet in more sustainable and environmentally friendly ways.

BIO also represents the entire biotech innovative ecosystem – from universities and research institutes, to start-up biotechnology companies, to the private investors that risk massive amounts of capital to fund these companies, to the larger, established companies that play a critical role in bringing these amazing innovations through the development and approval process and into the marketplace.

Of our approximately 1,000 members, the vast majority of them are small companies engaged in some of the most challenging, cutting-edge research in the world. They typically have no marketed products and no profits, and thus are heavily reliant on private capital to fund their work. They take enormous risks every day to develop the next generation of biomedical breakthroughs for the millions of patients suffering from diseases for which there currently are no effective cures or treatments.

BIO is enormously proud of their entrepreneurial and innovative spirit, and the dedication of all of our members to alleviating human suffering. I am honored to testify before you on their behalf today to explain what it takes to sustain this dynamic ecosystem and to bring new cures through the incredibly risky development and regulatory approval processes to the patients who need them.

AMERICA'S ROLE IN BIOMEDICAL INNOVATION

Let me emphasize at the outset a fundamental fact about biomedical innovation: American biopharmaceutical innovation delivers more new drugs than the rest of the world combined.

Almost 60 percent of all new medicines that treat patients across the world are innovated right here in the United States.[70]

This dominant American leadership is made possible by a number of factors:

- Outstanding scientists;
- Savvy entrepreneurs;
- World-class research universities;
- A culture of learning from setbacks;
- And investors willing to take risky bets on life-saving cures.

Yet other countries have similar capabilities, but don't drive innovation to the degree that America does. Why does America stand out and lead the world? Because we have a public policy environment that incentivizes investment in innovation. These policies include:

- Strong support for continued advancement and funding of scientific understanding;
- Strong and predictable intellectual property (IP) rights and a reliable system for IP transfer, licensing and collaboration;
- An efficient and predictable regulatory environment that strives to keep up with advances in biomedical science; and
- Payment systems that reward innovation and encourage free-market competition.

Yes, the American public has always had a love-hate relationship with drug companies, dating back to the late 1800s. But fortunately, even in the face of public pressure, Congress has steadfastly remained focused on curing disease and has opted against rash policy actions, including a refusal to impose artificial limits on the rewards for successful innovation.

Congress' strong, bipartisan support for the National Institutes of Health (NIH) biomedical research enterprise, which BIO has consistently endorsed, has been a critical component of our nation's success. Yet while NIH funds the basic academic research that often leads to breakthrough discoveries about our biology and genetics, it is the private

---

[70] DeVol, R., Bedroussian, A, Yeo, B, "The Global Biomedical Industry: Preserving U.S. Leadership," *Milken Institute*, 2011, at p. 5.

sector that drives the applied R&D and approval of actual new medicines based on those new scientific understandings.

In fact, the biopharmaceutical industry's collective annual research budget is more than $150 billion – roughly five times the entire NIH budget – and our investments are growing much more rapidly than NIH funding.[71] About half of this private sector research – $75 billion a year – is invested right here in the United States, far more than any other industry in America.[72] In any given year, biopharmaceutical companies spend five times more on R&D than the aerospace industry – and more than double that of the software industry.[73] Indeed, our industry plows more of our revenues back into research and development than any other American industry – period – roughly one out of every five dollars of revenue we generate.[74]

These investments are paying off in big ways not only for patients living with terrible diseases and conditions, but also for American workers and our economy. Today, more than 1.7 million Americans are employed in the biosciences across the United States, and we are growing jobs at a rate double the national average.[75] These are good-paying, highly skilled jobs, and support another seven million American jobs throughout the economy.[76]

Biotechnology: A Young Industry with Enormous Public Health Contributions

Modern biotechnology is a young industry. But in just a few decades, the entrepreneurs, scientists, researchers and investors working in this field have firmly established themselves at the forefront of medical innovation. Indeed, biotechnology's strong track record can be traced directly to the men and women working in the field. For them, biotechnology is not just an occupation. It is a mission and a calling to solve the greatest challenges of our time: to unlock the essence of life itself and to use what they learn to treat and cure disease. These individuals are entrepreneurial. They are risk takers. They are driven by science and are stubborn in their refusal to accept human suffering or the status quo. So, let's pause to examine the miracles our young industry already has made possible.

---

[71] See https://report.nih.gov/fundingfacts/fundingfacts.aspx; *World Preview 2017, Outlook to 2022, Evaluate Pharma*, 2017, at p. 19; Factset, *BIO Industry Analysis*.

[72] Factset, *BIO Industry Analysis*.

[73] Pitts, P. J., Why people don't trust drug makers. *New York Post* (September 24, 2015). Retrieved from https://nypost.com/2015/09/24/why-people-dont-trust-drug-makers/.

[74] Factset, BIO Industry Analysis.

[75] TEConomy/BIO, *The Value of Bioscience Innovation in Growing Jobs and Improving Quality of Life*, 2016. Retrieved from https://www.bio.org/value-bioscience-innovation-growing-jobs-and-improving-quality-life-2016.

[76] Ibid.

Thirty years ago, the HIV/AIDS epidemic pushed our country and our healthcare system to the brink. Facing more than one million people infected – and nearly 100,000 deaths – American biopharmaceutical companies went to work, supported by an active patient community who demanded more flexibility from federal regulators.

By 1996, with the development and FDA approval of the first wave of antiretroviral drugs, the HIV epidemic abated. Death rates have plummeted by nearly 85% since 1995.[77] Since then, nearly a million premature HIV/AIDS deaths have been prevented, saving our economy $1.4 trillion dollars.[78]

What was once thought to be untreatable is now beatable. Today, a 20-year-old diagnosed with HIV can expect to live into their early 70s – a life expectancy comparable to that of a person without the disease.[79]

The biotech story doesn't end there.

Medical breakthroughs are delivering meaningful, measurable results for millions of patients facing a wide variety of serious diseases. For example:

- There has been a 22% decrease in the cancer death rate since 1991, resulting in millions of lives saved and an estimated $2 trillion in economic savings;[80]
- Today, 83% of children with cancer survive, compared to just 58% in the mid-1970s;[81]
- Today, 80% of people with Chronic Myeloid Leukemia experience 10-year survival rates, compared to only 20% a decade ago;[82]
- Heart disease death rates decreased by nearly 30% between 2001 and 2010 alone;[83]
- In a single year in America, statins that lower cholesterol save 40,000 lives, prevent 60,000 heart attacks, and avert 22,000 strokes;[84] and
- New therapies are delivering more than a 90% cure rate for Hepatitis C, saving our health care system billions in reduced hospital costs, liver cancer treatments, and liver transplants.[85]

[77] U.S Department of Health and Services, Centers for Disease Control, "Health, United States, 2013, With Special Feature on Prescription Drugs," 2014.

[78] Philipson T, Jena AB. "Who Benefits from New Medical Technologies? Estimates of Consumer and Producer Surpluses for HIV/AIDS Drugs. Forum for Health Economics and Policy." 2006;9 (2) *Biomedical Research and the Economy*, Article 3.

[79] 1 Samji H, Cescon A, Hogg RS, Modur SP, Althoff KN, et al., Closing the Gap: Increases in Life Expectancy among Treated HIV-Positive Individuals in the United States and Canada. *PLoS ONE* 8(12): e81355 (2013).

[80] Lakdawala DN, et al. An economic evaluation of the war on cancer. *Journal of Health Economics*. May 2010. 29(3):333-346.

[81] See https://www.bio.org/sites/default/files/BIO_Cancer%20Medicine.pdf.

[82] *Journal of Managed Care*, Nov. 2012.

[83] American Heart Association, *Annual Statistical Update Report,* December 2014. Retrieved from http://newsroom.heart.org/news/new-statistical-update-looks-at-worldwide-heart-stroke-health.

[84] Health Affairs, at content.healthaffairs.org/content/31/10/2276.abstract.

[85] Kabiri M, Jazwinski AB, Roberts MS, Schaefer AJ, Chatwal J. "The changing burden of hepatitis C virus infection in the United States: Model-based predictions." *Annals of Internal Medicine*. 2014;161 (3):170-180.

Innovation truly saves – not just lives, but real dollars as well. In fact, if biopharmaceutical researchers are able to develop a new medicine that delays the onset of Alzheimer's disease by just five years, America would save $367 billion in healthcare services by 2050.[86] To meaningfully bend the troubling healthcare cost curve, increased investment in new medicines is essential.

The Next Wave of Biomedical Advances Are Here

This is an extraordinary time for biotechnology. The therapies in development and coming to the market are unlike any we've seen in the history of medicine. Our companies are making discoveries that were unimaginable a decade ago. We truly are in a new era of medicine, and the science and its promise for alleviating human suffering is galloping forward.

The days of traditional chemical drugs that treat broad classes of patients in blunt ways are giving way to the development of entirely new ways to treat and ultimately cure disease for targeted patient populations using living organisms, including a patient's own cells.

These include advances such as immuno-oncology – in which we attack cancer by activating the body's own immune system against it, while leaving healthy cells alone. And cellular and gene therapy – in which we use a patient's own cells to develop a medicine tailored for that patient, or use other genetic techniques to repair or replace defectives genes causing disease. We've already seen the first wave of these advances reach the marketplace, with many more already in the FDA regulatory process, including novel medicines that utilize these techniques to treat childhood leukemia and blindness.

Overall, our industry has nearly 6,000 new medicines in development for a wide range of life-threatening or debilitating diseases, with 74% of these clinical projects targeting new mechanisms of action – so called "first in class" medicines that work in entirely new ways to treat and cure disease.[87]

This is innovation at its best. The only thing that can stop our march forward is bad public policy.

---

[86] Alzheimer's Association, *Changing the Trajectory of Alzheimer's Disease: How a Treatment by 2025 Saves Lives and Dollars*. Retrieved from https://alz.org/documents_custom/ALZ_Trajectory_InfoSheet_01.26.15_Final.pdf.

[87] Emerging Therapeutic Company Investment and Deal Trends 2007-2016, BIO Industry Analysis, 2017, at bio.org/iareports; Long, G. The Biopharmaceutical Pipeline: Innovative Therapies in Clinical Development, Analysis Group, 2017; The Analysis Group, *The Biopharmaceutical Pipeline: Innovative Therapies in Clinical Development*. July 2017. Retrieved from: http://phrma-docs.phrma.org/files/dmfile/Biopharmaceutical-Pipeline-Full-Report.pdf.

The Biopharmaceutical Ecosystem by the Numbers

As *The Economist* magazine has noted, "Creating new drugs through biotechnology is at the risky end of a business in which superhuman stamina and bottomless pockets are minimum requirements."[88] Thus, to understand the biopharmaceutical innovation ecosystem and its pricing dynamics, you have to understand the numbers. Here are the key ones:

- 70%: that's the percentage of innovative clinical programs that are being led by small companies, which rely heavily on venture capitalists, angel investors, or partnerships with larger pharmaceutical companies to provide the enormous amounts of private capital required to fund these challenging and incredibly risky endeavors.[89]
- 90%: that's the percentage of clinical programs that ultimately fail to lead to an FDA approval; in fact, the success rate of clinical trials can be even less than that, particularly in areas like Alzheimer's and cancer.[90]
- 92%: that's the percentage of biopharmaceutical companies that are unprofitable at any given time.[91]
- 10-15 Years: that's the time it takes on average to secure FDA approval of a new medicine, from initial discovery of a potential new molecule or approach, through pre-clinical and clinical programs, and through the FDA regulatory and approval processes.[92]
- $2.6 Billion: that's the average cost to develop and secure approval of a new medicine, taking into account all the trial and error and research failures along the way, and the cost of capital; this figure has skyrocketed in recent years, doubling since just 2003.[93]
- 36th: that is where the biopharmaceutical industry ranks among domestic industries in terms of return on investment, despite the popular media narrative of excessive drug industry profits.[94]

---

[88] Biotechnology: Fever Rising. *The Economist* (Feb. 14, 2014). Retrieved from: https://www.economist.com/news/business/21596557-there-are-reasons-hope-latest-biotech-boom-will-not-be-followed-another.

[89] Emerging Therapeutic Company Investment and Deal Trends 2007-2016, *BIO Industry Analysis*, 2017, at bio.org/iareports.

[90] Clinical Development Success Rates 2006-2015, BIO Industry Analysis, 2016, at bio.org/iareports; for example, since 1998, 123 medicines in development for Alzheimer's have not made it through clinical trials, while only 4 have been approved – resulting in a 97% failure rate. See PhRMA, *Researching Alzheimer's Medicines: Setbacks and Stepping Stones*, Summer 2015. Retrieved from http://phrma-docs.phrma.org/sites/default/files/pdf/alzheimersetbacksreportfinal912.pdf.

[91] Factset, BIO Industry Analysis.

[92] DiMasi J., Grabowski, H., Hansen, R. Innovation in the Pharmaceutical Industry: New estimates of R&D Costs. *Journal of Health Economics*, 2016, at pp. 20-33.

[93] Ibid.

[94] Factset, *BIO Industry Analysis*.

- 89%: that's the percentage of all prescriptions in America that are for lower-cost generic copies of once-branded pharmaceuticals.[95]

The hundreds of billions of dollars needed to support this private biopharmaceutical ecosystem each year come from two basic sources: private and public investors, and sales revenues from existing marketed medicines. Thus, it is the revenues from the 10% of successful clinical programs, and the 11% of prescriptions for branded medicines, that have to reward investors and support the continuing R&D innovation cycle. And they must do that before generics can copy them and enter the market, because once generics enter the market, prices and innovator market share fall dramatically. Notably, no other component of healthcare (e.g., hospital or physician fees) experiences such reductions in price over time – a fact that is often ignored during debates regarding drug pricing.

As noted above, the costs of drug innovation have increased dramatically over the past 15 years. This is partly due to increased regulatory and payer demands for more and better data on drug safety and effectiveness. But it also has much to do with the new era of genomic and personalized medicine. We are tackling the most challenging of problems, and the more we learn about our biology and the basis of disease, the more complex our R&D processes become. Furthermore, while these costs go up and up, the patient populations to be served are becoming more and more targeted, reducing the ability to spread these costs across wide patient populations.

Thus, this critically important innovation ecosystem can continue to flourish only if it has the confidence and financial backing of investors. Biotech investors – like all investors – expect a reasonable return on their investments, free from artificial, government-imposed restrictions or erroneous assumptions about investment returns.

So, let me be absolutely clear here: investment in the biotech sector is directly influenced by the public policy debate in Congress and the states, and by the policy positions taken by our leading public officials. We have seen that impact over and over again over the decades, with the latest example occurring just last year amid all the negative focus on drug prices during the 2016 presidential campaign. While the stock index for market-stage drug companies declined slightly during 2016 (only 3%), the index representing small, research-stage biotech companies plummeted 38% over that same time.[96] Here are some more troubling data points from 2016:

- The number of new biotech IPOs dropped in half;
- The dollars spent of acquisitions of small biotech companies dropped by 43%;

[95] Association for Accessible Medicines. *Generic Drug Access & Savings in the U.S.* (2016). Retrieved from https://accessiblemeds.org/sites/default/files/2017-07/2017-AAM-Access-Savings-Report-2017-web2.pdf.

[96] Based on index performance in 2016 for the LifeSci Biotechnology Clinical Trials Index and the LifeSci Biotechnology Products Index. See Life Sci Index Partners, at http://www.bioshares.com; Factset, *BIO Industry Analysis.*

- The dollars invested by venture capital in late-stage financing rounds dropped by 33%; and
- The number of biotech licensing deals dropped by 17% and the value of upfront payments to small biotech companies as a result of such deals was cut in half.[97]

Indeed, these smaller companies – the ones that account for 70% of the cutting-edge clinical programs underway today – are the proverbial canaries in the coal mine. When the public and policy debates turn against innovation, these small companies are the first to feel the negative results – making it harder for them to raise the capital needed to advance their R&D programs. And for patients waiting for the next modern biotech miracle, that is really bad news.

Yes, in the biotech sector, risk is an everyday reality. Indeed, biotech is synonymous with risk. But political and policy risk is something different. It can cripple innovation.

The Right Way to Enhance Patient Access and Affordability of New Drugs

BIO and our members recognize that too many patients, even those with insurance, cannot afford access to the life-saving cures and treatments that biotech companies are developing. We stand with the Members of this Committee, the Congress, and the Trump Administration in our shared commitment to addressing this serious problem.

But to accomplish this, we have to harness – not abandon – the free market that has delivered amazing innovations for patients and made America first in the world in biomedical innovation. BIO supports enhancing drug affordability through competition. If we act smartly to promote market-based reforms that spur greater competition and efficiencies in our healthcare sector, we can improve patient access to the innovations of today, while preserving incentives to discover the next generation of innovations for the patients of tomorrow.

That's why BIO has joined with stakeholders across the healthcare spectrum – including insurers, PBMs, employers, and patient groups – in a coalition that developed and supports consensus, market-based reforms to lower drug costs without harming innovation. Through the Council for Affordable Health Coverage,[98] BIO and our allies are working to:

---

[97] Emerging Therapeutic Company Investment and Deal Trends 2007-2016, *BIO Industry Analysis*, 2017, at bio.org/iareports.

[98] https://www.cahc.net/prescription-drugs/.

- Increase marketplace competition by speeding regulatory approval of more innovative drugs, and promoting greater and faster generic and biosimilar entry once patents and exclusivities for innovator drugs have expired;
- Move towards a drug payment system that is based on value and patient outcomes rather than volume, by removing regulatory and legal barriers that hamper value-based arrangements and communications between innovators and payers;
- Empower patients and providers with more data on drug costs and value to help them make more informed choices; and
- Oppose innovation-killing ideas like price controls, drug importation, or direct government "negotiation" of drug prices in Medicare.

The Council estimates that, if fully adopted and implemented, these reforms could lower national health expenditures by $71 billion a year.[99] This approach also is consistent with the landmark 21st Century Cures Act shepherded through Congress last year by this Committee on a strongly bipartisan basis, as well as this Committee's more recently enacted Food & Drug Administration Reauthorization Act (FDARA). BIO was a strong supporter of both of these bills, which we believe will help expedite the delivery of new innovations to patients in need, while also speeding competition among branded medicines and from more generics and biosimilars. We all want to see FDA approve generic drugs as efficiently as possible and for the backlog of generic drug applications to be reduced quickly. More choice and competition is good for patients and the healthcare system overall.

That said, it should be noted that, generally speaking, the United States has a robustly competitive market for drugs, where innovators compete vigorously with one another to produce safer and more effective medicines within the same class, and then compete on price as part of negotiations with powerful, sophisticated, and aggressive commercial middlemen such as insurance companies and pharmacy benefit managers who control patient access to these innovative products. While there are pockets of exceptions to this competitive environment, the reality is that the average innovator drug has a short period of time on the market without competition from other similar products (roughly two years[100]), and nearly nine out of every 10 prescriptions filled in America are for cheaper generic copies of once-branded drugs.[101]

---

[99] Ibid.

[100] See "Nearly All Later Entrants to Drug Classes Were in Clinical Testing or Regulatory Review Before First-in-Class Approval," Tufts Center for the Study of Drug Development, November 3, 2015, at http://csdd.tufts.edu/news/complete_story/pr_ir_november_december_2015.

[101] Association for Accessible Medicines. *Generic Drug Access & Savings in the U.S.* (2016). Retrieved from https://accessiblemeds.org/sites/default/files/2017-07/2017-AAM-Access-Savings-Report-2017-web2.pdf.

Conclusion

America is one of the only countries left in the world that doesn't treat a vibrant, risk-taking biotech industry like a regulated public utility – because we know that doing so will cause investors to flee this critical sector and put their money elsewhere. And this much we also know: If we adopt price restrictions favored in countries with socialized medicine, we can expect to get the level of innovation found in countries with socialized medicine.[102]

BIO recognizes that it's sometimes easy to think of biotech companies as simply manufacturers of expensive pills and biologics. But nothing could be further from the truth. Whether we are suffering from disease or caring for a loved one who is, the biomedical innovation ecosystem gives every one of us the most precious gifts of all – hope that tomorrow will be better than today, and more time to share with those who mean the most to us.

We're life savers.

We're the "cure" to the growing societal cost of disease.

And we're job creators, investors, and drivers of American economic growth and global technological leadership.

With Congress' continued support, we will put more people to work, lower health care costs, and heal the world.

Thank you for the opportunity to present our views today. For more information on drug costs and value, I would encourage you to visit www.drugcostfacts.org, a comprehensive website that answers many of the questions patients and policymakers frequently ask about the drug supply system by reference to expert studies and other independent data sources.

And I stand ready to answer any questions you may have during my testimony as well.

Mr. BURGESS. The chair thanks the gentleman.

Mr. Davis, you're recognized for 3 minutes for an opening statement, please. And your microphone.

STATEMENT OF CHIP DAVIS

Mr. DAVIS. Sorry about that. Good morning, Chairman Burgess, Ranking Member Green, Chairman Walden, and Ranking Member Pallone, members of the subcommittee. Thank you for the invitation and opportunity to testify today.

---

[102] Joseph H. Golec and John A. Vernon, "Financial Effects of Pharmaceutical Price Regulation on R&D Spending by EU versus US Firms," *Pharmacoeconomics* 28, no. 8, (2010): 615–628.

As stated, my name is Chip Davis. I am the President and CEO of the Association for Accessible Medicines. We are the leading trade association for manufacturers of FDA-approved generic and biosimilar medicines. Our members manufacture more than 61 billion doses of medication at over 150 facilities here in the United States on an annual basis.

As you know, Americans across the political spectrum are calling for action to lower the cost of prescription drugs, making it a fore-most health priority, which is why we are all here today. Despite a lot of well-intentioned rhetoric, over the last year the problem of high drug prices by and large continues unabated.

Last month, the nominee for secretary of health and human services, Alex Azar, said that drug prices are too high and must be lowered. FDA Commissioner Scott Gottlieb recently characterized drug costs as a public health concern.

Congress now has the opportunity to take meaningful action to lower the cost of prescription drugs. Over 30 years ago, through Hatch-Waxman, Congress sought to strike a careful balance between encouraging innovation in drug development, which we all support, and accelerating access to lower cost generic alternatives for patients.

Unfortunately, the patient access side of Hatch-Waxman is absolutely unequivocally in jeopardy as we speak. This is due to a combination of factors, including a failure of policy to keep pace with a changing pharmaceutical market, a growing market and balance between generic buyers and sellers, and an increase in anti-competitive business practices deployed by certain brand companies who have been increasing these activities so much in recent years that recently Commissioner Gottlieb counseled the industry last month, and I am quoting, ''to end the shenanigans,'' during his formal remarks at an FTC hearing.

The generic industry operates in a rapidly changing often-commoditized marketplace with significant and unique pressures that distinguish it from the monopolized brands sector. As a result, generics continue to experience accelerated price deflation. In fact, it is ironic in many ways that at a time when the overall costs of prescription drugs is such a high profile issue that generic medicines are currently experiencing an unprecedented degree of price deflation, which impacts the national health estimate figures that were mentioned previously. In fact, according to IQVIA, which is formerly Quintiles IMS, for 16 consecutive months generic drugs prices have declined.

Our members operate in a consolidated market where three large buying consortiums of wholesalers and retail pharmacies now control 90 percent of the retail generic market. Portfolio decisions related to what medicines they will continue to manufacture, announcing pending closures of manufacturing facilities, and significant anticipated job layoffs in the generic sector are all things that we are currently experiencing.

Should the market not evolve itself and should Congress fail to take action, these trends will continue, threatening uninterrupted patient access to the needed generic medicines. When generics and biosimilars are available, competition increases and patients benefit from access to safe and affordable treatment options.

We have provided this committee with recommendations that Congress could take today to increase competition and increase patient access.

I thank you again for the opportunity to testify and look forward to your questions today.

Thank you.

[The prepared statement of Mr. Davis follows:]

Statement of Chester "Chip" Davis, Jr., U.S. House of Representatives, Energy and Commerce Health Subcommittee, Examining the Drug Supply Chain, December 13, 2017

Introduction

Chairman Burgess, Ranking Member Green and members of the committee, thank you for the invitation to testify today. I am Chip Davis, President and CEO of the Association for Accessible Medicines (AAM). AAM is the nation's leading trade association for manufacturers and distributors of FDA-approved generic and biosimilar prescription medicines. Our members provide more than 36,700 jobs at nearly 150 facilities, and manufacture more than 61 billion doses in the United States every year. AAM's core mission is to improve the lives of patients by advancing timely access to affordable generic and biosimilar medications.

I commend you for convening today's hearing to examine the critical challenge of high and rising drug prices.

Generic medicines represent greater than 89 percent of all prescriptions dispensed in the U.S., but only 26 percent of expenditures on prescription drugs, saving patients and payers nearly $5 billion every week.[103] Our industry is proud to be able to deliver these savings to the healthcare system.

It is sobering to consider what America's patients would face if there were no FDA-approved generic or biosimilar medicines to provide reliable access to affordable treatments. Generics don't just deliver the most medicine at the lowest cost and greatest savings; generics cushion the significant impact dealt to patients and the healthcare system by high brand name drug prices every day.

[103] $253 billion total savings in 2016, equivalent to approximately $5 billion every week. *AAM 2017 Generic Drug Access & Savings in the U.S.*, http://accessiblemeds.org/sites/default/files/2017-07/2017-AAM-Access-Savings-Report-2017-web2.pdf.

Put another way, the availability of low-cost generics offsets the impact of high brand drug prices. Whereas prices for FDA-approved generic medicines are currently declining by over 7 percent year-over-year, prices for brand drugs, especially biologics and specialty medicines, are increasing at an unsustainable rate. From 2007 to 2016, brand specialty medicines grew to occupy almost 43 percent of spending. These products treat less than 3 percent of the population, and can often cost patients thousands of dollars per treatment.

To illustrate this fact, consider that generic drug revenue has declined for 16 consecutive months and that 80 percent of the top 20 generic companies had negative dollar growth over the past year.[104] Contrast this with the expectation published last week by Moody's Investors Service that net prices on brand drugs would continue to rise.[105]

Consider the costs that patients would face in the absence of these levels of generic competition. Last year, use of generic medicines saved $253 billion. It has produced $1.67 trillion in savings over the last ten years. This has produced meaningful and sustained patient access. Without generic medicines, spending on cholesterol drugs would be more than three-and-a-half times higher, diabetes drugs almost three times higher, and spending on breast cancer drugs eight times higher.[106]

However, the sustainability of a competitive generic market and the availability of generic medicines for patients, uninterrupted by shortages, is in jeopardy. In 1984, Congress enacted the Hatch-Waxman Act which represents a model of successful, bipartisan public policy. Over its more than 30-year history, the Act has produced a thriving and constantly-changing marketplace by balancing innovation in drug development and accelerating the availability of lower cost generic alternatives. This has important effects on public health, allowing patients to live longer, healthier lives.

This balance is now threatened by three factors:

- changing and increasingly challenging market and reimbursement frameworks;
- the abuse of laws and regulations by bad actors; and,
- a failure of policy to account for the unique challenges facing generic and biosimilar medicines.

In fact, while brand drug innovation has benefited from a series of subsequent laws establishing incentives and development tools, the generic and biosimilar marketplace and patient access has not received an equivalent level of attention. That neglect, combined with current market and anticompetitive realities, reinforces why the continued

---

[104] IVQIA, analysis of National Sales Perspectives and National Prescription Audit data through October 2017.

[105] *Moody's: Outlook for global healthcare industry in 2018 is stable*. Business Standard. (2017, Dec. 8). Retrieved from http://www.business-standard.com/article/news-cm/moody-s-outlook-for-global-healthcare-industry-in-2018-is-stable-117120800572_1.html.

[106] *AAM 2017 Generic Drug Access & Savings in the U.S.*, http://accessiblemeds.org/sites/default/files/2017-07/2017-AAM-Access-Savings-Report-2017-web2.pdf.

attention to this issue – including the FDA's public hearing and the FTC's recent public workshop – are so important.

Congress must act to support generic and biosimilar competition and supply to ensure continued access for patients. It can do so by:

1) Repealing the misguided Medicaid penalty on generic drugs;
2) Preventing brand abuses designed to block generic and biosimilar competition by passing the bipartisan CREATES Act and FAST Generics Act; and,
3) Ensuring that biosimilar medicines have a level and competitive playing field in Medicare.

Generic Drug Markets Are Fundamentally Different Than Brands

First, it is important to provide context about the generic marketplace. Not only is the FDA approval process different for generics and brand-name drugs, but their respective markets and the path by which they reach patients diverge significantly, with important policy implications.

The 1984 Drug Price Competition and Patent Term Restoration Act, commonly referred to as the Hatch-Waxman Act, created an abbreviated pathway for generic drugs. This allows manufacturers to rely upon the existing clinical data of the brand product and demonstrate to FDA that their product is the same as the reference product.

Hatch-Waxman also provided numerous lucrative incentives for brand-name drug companies, including extensions of patent terms, regulatory exclusivities that guarantee market monopolies regardless of the intellectual property status, and a clear litigation pathway for asserting intellectual property claims against generic manufacturers.

Supply Chain Differences Drive Model Differences

The balance established by Hatch-Waxman also created a new and different market for generic drugs – separate from brand drugs – that has supported growth in generic utilization and its attendant savings for patients. Although brand manufacturers often criticize pharmacy benefit managers (PBMs) and health plan formulary and rebate practices, the supply chain and pricing models they criticize do not represent the vast majority of prescription drugs distributed in this country. The 89 percent of prescriptions filled by generic medicines are subject to a different set of economic incentives and arrangements – the result of multiple manufacturers marketing identical products and competing exclusively on price, in a commodity-style market.

When brand manufacturers leverage the pricing power granted by their patents and regulatory exclusivities, PBMs, distributors, and payers rely on formulary management and rebating agreements to control costs.

However, upon generic entry, payers typically shift away from rebate models of reimbursement and rely on distribution channels to effectively lower the price of the medicine. Rather than providing rebates to lower the cost, generic manufacturers must compete for sales to wholesalers. Because the products are virtually identical, the primary leverage manufacturers have is their ability to lower the price and provide the necessary volume. With more than 200 generic manufacturers recognized by the FDA, competition is fierce and prices decline rapidly. The wholesalers, often in collaborative purchasing agreements with pharmacies across the country, then distribute generic medicines to various retail pharmacies. Generic manufacturers may have to compete even further by negotiating separate payments to pharmacies to stock their product.

The different business model leads to a different type of business planning by generic and biosimilar manufacturers. As part of this, the decisions by which generic and biosimilar manufacturers select which products to develop can take into account multiple variables. Considerations include the complexity in reverse engineering the original product, the state of the intellectual property claimed by the brand manufacturer over the product, the size of the patient population served, the number of likely competitors for that product, the product development and manufacturing capabilities and costs.

Generic drug reimbursement is also different. Rather than relying on per-transaction rebates, PBMs and insurers typically establish a "Maximum Allowable Cost" (MAC) list that sets a specific reimbursement rate for the product, regardless of the generic product cost to the pharmacy. These MAC lists create additional incentives for pharmacies to maximize their dispensing margins by finding the lowest-cost source for generic products.

The result is a business model that differs significantly from the brand business model. While brand companies typically market a small number of high-margin products, many generic manufacturers market hundreds of products with varying levels of profitability or loss.

Generics Face Increasing Supply Chain Pressures

These differences in the generic and brand marketplaces create vastly different incentives for the various manufacturers, wholesalers, distributors, PBMs, insurers, and retail pharmacies that make up the supply chain. To put it simply, virtually all other actors in the supply chain enjoy significant financial benefits from the manufacture of generic medicines.

This phenomenon was most recently examined by a group of researchers at the USC Leonard D. Schaeffer Center for Health Policy & Economics. That analysis, "The Flow of Money Through the Pharmaceutical Distribution System," identified two items relevant to today's hearing:

- First, for every sale of a brand name drug to a patient, the brand manufacturer captures approximately 76 percent of that revenue. Comparatively, generic manufacturers keep only half of that percentage. Moreover, generic manufacturers cannot rely on capturing the total volume within the market as the brands do, and therefore individual generic manufacturers are forced to rely on much smaller revenue streams. To put it simply, brand drugs capture a higher percentage of the spend of a higher-value market.
- Second, the supply chain captures significantly more of the revenue spent on generic medicines than on brand-name drugs. For every $100 spent on dispensing generic medicines in this country, approximately $65 goes to the distribution and reimbursement of those products by the members of the supply chain. PBMs make nearly three times as much on generics as they do on brands. Wholesalers make about eight times more. Pharmacies make more than 10 times more for every $100 on generics than brands.[107]

While the analysis demonstrates a series of strong incentives to drive patients to generic medicines, supply chain consolidation may jeopardize that success.

Compared to the fragmented generic drug market, consolidation in the wholesale market and contractual arrangements between pharmacy chains and the wholesalers have left generic manufacturers with only a small number of purchasers. The result is a market where three purchasers account for more than 90 percent of all wholesale revenue.[108]

As these purchasers move more and more toward single-source contracts for generic drugs, it often creates a dynamic where it is possible that no more than three generic manufacturers may be able to successfully market any given product. This risks future competitive success in the generic market as generic drug manufacturers may be forced to maximize economies of scale and consolidate themselves.

Patients Face Growing Cost Pressures

Patients thrive because of generic medicines, both in terms of health outcomes and financial savings. For insured patients, more than 90 percent of generic prescriptions are filled for $20 or less out-of-pocket. That is in comparison to just 39 percent for brands at that price.[109]

Data shows patients are far less likely to fill a prescription for a high-priced brand drug. In fact, brand-name drugs make up 20 percent of approved claims but account for 40 percent of all abandoned claims for new patients. Moreover, new patient abandonment

---

[107] Sood, et al., "The Flow of Money Through the Pharmaceutical Distribution System." June 2017. http://healthpolicy.usc.edu/documents/USC%20Schaeffer_Flow%20of%20Money_2017.pdf.

[108] Fein, Adam J. Fein. *The 2016-2017 Economic Report on Pharmaceutical Wholesalers and Specialty Distributors*, September 2016.

[109] *AAM 2017 Generic Drug Access & Savings in the U.S.*, http://accessiblemeds.org/sites/default/files/2017-07/2017-AAM-Access-Savings-Report-2017-web2.pdf.

rates for generics are three times lower than for branded products.[110] Patient abandonment has a serious effect on patient health – leading to hospitalizations, deaths and extensive health system costs.

This is not to say that the market functions perfectly in providing patients with the lowest cost possible. Many generic medicines are subject to significant markups after they leave the generic manufacturer. As an example, amoxicillin/potassium clavulanate, commonly referred by its branded name Augmentin and used for the treatment of infections, is sold by the generic manufacturer for pennies per pill. However, by the time a patient picks it up at the pharmacy counter, it may have a cash price as high as $60 for 20 pills, or $20 for a fill for patients with commercial insurance.[111]

It is clear the significant benefits for patients of reliable access to affordable generic medicines are at risk. Notwithstanding the economic principle that more suppliers of a good or service creates lower prices for consumers, it is unclear that the new imbalance between 200 generic competitors and a handful of purchasers is sustainable. Some industry analysts have already begun to forecast consolidation among generic manufacturers.

An unfortunate yet foreseeable consequence of fewer generic manufacturers is a significantly increased risk of drug shortages. Evidence suggests that generic drugs are particularly susceptible to drug shortages, potentially related to existing market incentives as well as low reimbursement.[112] Such shortages have a serious effect on patient care. Responding to a series of drug shortages in 2011, Dr. Scott Gottlieb testified before Congress that many such shortages were a direct result of low reimbursement for older, low-margin products and that "many hospitals are being forced to ration key medicines and patients to sit on waiting lists for vital drugs."[113]

Policymakers Should Recognize Market Differences

It is critical that policymakers take steps to ensure the continued supply of affordable FDA-approved generic medicines. Failure to do so threatens a stable supply of generic medicines.

Congress recently created a new inflation-based penalty in the Medicaid program for generics as part of the Bipartisan Budget Act of 2015.The legislation inappropriately applied a tool crafted for the brand drug market to generic markets, essentially conflating what transpires in a monopolized market with what occurs in a commoditized market with multiple competitors. Under the legislation, generic manufacturers are now subject

---

[110] *Id.*

[111] Data on manufacturer sales from CMS Average Manufacturer Price (AMP) data. Typical pharmacy prices from GoodRx.com.

[112] Stromberg, C. (May 2014). *Drug Shortages, Pricing, and Regulatory Activity*. National Bureau of Economics Working Paper. http://www.nber.org/chapters/c13102.pdf.

[113] Gottlieb, Scott. "Drug Shortages: Why they happen and what they mean" Testimony before the Senate Finance Committee. December 2011. https://www.finance.senate.gov/imo/media/doc/Gottlieb%20Testimony1.pdf.

to additional rebates for products *even in the absence of changes in the actual price* of the product. This is a direct result of a flawed application of a brand drug scheme that fails to recognize the significant volatility in generic prices.

As a result, manufacturers of affordable generic medicines are now paying millions of dollars in "penalties" on products that have not been subject to a price increase. In many instances, changes in customer mix from one quarter to another have triggered penalties solely due to purchasers getting lower discounts on smaller volume orders – a normal occurrence in a competitive market. These changes do not necessarily reflect any new price being set by the manufacturer, but may merely reflect new purchasing patterns.

These unpredictable, onerous penalties on often low-margin medicines creates significant risk for manufacturers that would consider entering these markets, and makes it more challenging for manufacturers to continue participating in those markets. A recent analysis concluded that the penalty would "increase uncertainty, reduce revenues, encourage manufacturers to exit the market, and discourage the entry of new manufacturers. The predictable effect of discouraging entry into competitive markets is that product availability will be hampered: shortages will be more likely, and the market forces that lead prices to fall will be dampened."[114] Ironically, the analysis also concluded that the penalty "will not only have little effect on generic prices, but it will also have the unanticipated and unintended consequence of increasing the likelihood of shortages for potentially life-saving generic medicines."[115] Accordingly, we urge Congress to repeal this penalty.

AAM and its members strongly support innovation. The generic and biosimilar marketplaces rely on the existence of a vibrant brand medicine industry. Fortunately, innovation continues to flourish. FDA has already approved more new molecular entities this year than it did in all of 2016. This is good news for all of us. But the balance between innovation and access requires a clear opportunity for FDA-approved generic or biosimilar entry. Without that competition, there can be no savings for patients or taxpayers. Unfortunately, many brand drug companies have responded to the threat of competition by deploying new and controversial ways to extend their high monopoly prices.

Shenanigans Extend to Intellectual Property

Recently, one company went so far as to pay a Native American tribe to rent its tribal sovereign immunity by taking ownership of certain brand name drug patents facing a challenge. Allergan, Plc (Allergan), a Dublin, Ireland-based drug company, transferred the patent rights to its blockbuster drug Restasis® to the St. Regis Mohawk Tribe in a

---

[114] Manning and Selck, "Penalizing Generic Drugs with the CPI Rebate will Reduce Competition and Increase the Likelihood of Drug Shortages," September 2017. https://www.accessiblemeds.org/sites/default/files/2017-09/Bates-White-White-Paper-Report-CPI-Penalty-09-12-2017.pdf.

[115] *Id.*

blatant effort to shield those patents from an administrative review process established by Congress in 2011 and block generic competition.

The deal stands to be a profitable one for Allergan. Restasis generated $1.4 billion in 2016 sales.[116] For less than 0.1 percent of the drug's annual sales, Allergan's deal could delay patient access to affordable generic drugs for six more years. This is a supply chain failure that Congress should prevent.

According to press reports, Allergan provided an initial payment of $13.75 million to the St. Regis Mohawk Tribe and $15 million in annual licensing fees. Every day Allergan delays competition, the company takes in more than $4 million in revenue due to the lack of generic competition. Allergan will recoup this licensing fee in around four days.

Allergan's transfer of its patents to the St. Regis Mohawk Tribe is an end-run around the legal process established by Congress to challenge questionable patents. If Congress wants to ensure that Americans have access to affordable prescription drugs, it must address schemes like Allergan's to delay generic competition by renting sovereign immunity. The action by Allergan to ensure that patients and payors do not benefit from timely generic competition to Restasis is an alarming example of the steps that brand name drug companies will take to put profits above the public interest. But it is by no means the only such example. Congress should outlaw these practices and strengthen the *Inter Partes Review* (IPR) system.

Barriers to Generic and Biosimilar Development Threaten Access & Savings

As this committee is aware, many generic and biosimilar manufacturers face significant challenges obtaining the samples needed for generic or biosimilar development. This is a result of the misuse of systems designed to ensure the safety of medicines by certain brand drug companies focused on delaying or prevent competition. Such delays created by misuse, abuse or regulatory failure deserve Congressional attention. In short, if generic and biosimilar development is frustrated, they will never enter the supply chain.

FDA Commissioner Gottlieb has repeatedly highlighted the abuse of FDA-mandated restricted distribution systems and restricted distribution systems that brand companies create on their own, without any mandate from FDA, to delay or completely prevent generic competition.

This occurs when brand companies, using a Risk Evaluation and Mitigation System (REMS) or their own voluntary "safety" program as an excuse, refuse to sell samples of their products to generic and biosimilar companies so that they can conduct the requisite bioequivalence and other testing. AAM members that have sought to purchase brand products from wholesalers in the supply chain are often informed that the wholesalers'

---

[116] Alllergan plc, *Annual Report (Form 10-K)*, at 59 (February 2017) (link).

contracts prohibit the sale of the brand product for generic studies. To date, FDA has received more than 150 complaints of specific challenges to obtaining samples.

These abusive practices are directly counter to Congressional intent reflected in both Hatch-Waxman, which seeks to create generic competition as soon as brand monopoly protection has expired, and the Food and Drug Administration Amendments Act, which specifically prohibited the use of REMS to delay generic competition.

The FDA has taken steps to limit these kinds of abuses. In 2014, the FDA released a draft guidance that attempted to assist prospective generic and biosimilar applicants in their efforts to acquire the samples necessary to conduct bioequivalence testing. Under the guidance, the FDA reviews bioequivalence protocols. Following its review and identification of any required changes, the FDA sends a letter to the brand sponsor indicating that the proposed testing contains safety protections that provide the same level of patient-protection as those in the applicable brand's safety protocol and that the FDA will not consider it a violation of the law for the brand sponsor to provide samples to the designated potential generic or biosimilar applicant. Although well-intentioned, the draft guidance has failed to solve the problem and patients wait in vain for FDA-approved generic and biosimilar versions of these medicines.

Generic applicants are also challenged by brand companies' refusal to negotiate in good faith the creation and implementation of a single-shared REMS system (SSRS). Under current law, if a brand drug is subject to a REMS that contains Elements To Assure Safe Use (ETASU), generic versions cannot be approved unless they are subject to a SSRS to implement the ETASU elements. Moreover, the Federal Food Drug and Cosmetic Act provides that a generic drug must utilize a shared system along with the brand drug unless FDA waives this requirement for one of the reasons set forth in the statute. In other words, the brand and generic must agree on how to implement the existing safety protocol jointly, unless the FDA says otherwise.

The creation of a shared system should be relatively straightforward and simple—generic applicants merely join the existing safety system. Fundamentally, this is the business of generic manufacturers: taking a sole-source product and making it a multi-source product. However, brand companies regularly use a variety of tactics to systematically delay and extend the brand/generic negotiations.

This refusal to engage in good faith negotiations can delay the approval of the generic product and force consumers to pay more to fill their prescriptions.

This abuse injures competition. Commissioner Gottlieb recently testified that:

> brand companies often have an incentive to refuse to agree to a single, shared system REMS. By prolonging the negotiations over a single, shared system REMS, they further

delay generic drug approval and competition. We see prolonged negotiations and inability to agree on the terms of a single, shared system REMS regularly.[117]

AAM applauds Commissioner Gottlieb's leadership to develop a "Drug Competition Action Plan" to address regulatory issues that are impeding competition, including abuse of restricted distribution and REMS systems. However, AAM is concerned that FDA's enforcement authorities as provided in FDAAA will not be adequate to fully stem the brand abuses that have become so widespread in recent years. For instance, the civil monetary penalties available under FDA's enforcement authority pale in comparison to the revenue available by impeding generic entry. Center for Drug Evaluation and Research (CDER) Director Dr. Janet Woodcock noted that "fines and everything might simply be considered a cost of doing business because there's so much at stake in delaying generic competition."[118] Also, the FDA's authority to address the brand abuses using voluntarily imposed restricted distribution system are highly limited.

Brand manufacturers who have recognized the incentives created by REMS-related delays have developed novel distribution schemes that mimic these programs even when the FDA has not recognized any inherent safety risk with the handling or use of the medicine. According to a recent study,[119] 74 drugs are subject to restricted access programs (i.e., drugs that are either subject to REMS or self-imposed restricted distribution programs) with total sales of $22.7 billion in 2016. Of these, 41 drugs are restricted by REMS programs, with $11.5 billion in sales in 2016. The remaining 33 drugs are restricted by the brands in a voluntarily imposed non-REMS program, with $11.2 billion in sales in 2016. And a 2014 study concluded that REMS abuse costs the U.S. healthcare system $5.4 billion annually.[120] Consumers pay $960 million of that cost while Medicare and Medicaid incur $1.8 billion; private insurers bear the remaining $2.4 billion.[121] This estimate is conservative "and should not be construed as the entirety of the lost savings from REMS misuse, either currently or going forward."[122]

AAM and its members are committed to ensuring that all Americans have access to safe, effective and affordable medicines and believe that the FDA's REMS programs can and do serve a compelling public good – namely, the safe distribution and use of certain pharmaceuticals that have a higher risk profile. We do not support any policies that would jeopardize patient safety. Any suggestion to the contrary is simply an effort to

[117] Gottlieb, Scott. "Antitrust Concerns and The FDA Approval Process," Testimony before the House Committee on the Judiciary, Subcommittee on Regulatory Reform, Commercial and Antitrust Law, July 2017. https://www.fda.gov/NewsEvents/Testimony/ucm568869.htm.

[118] Testimony of Dr. Janet Woodcock at "Generic Drug User Fee Amendments: Accelerating Patient Access to Generic Drugs." Senate Committee on Health, Education, Labor and Pensions, January 2016.

[119] Alex Brill, REMS and Restricted Distribution Programs: An Estimate of the Market (June 2017), *available at* http://www.gphaonline.org/media/cms/Alex_Brill_REMS_Study_June_2017.pdf.

[120] Alex Brill, *Lost Prescription Drug Savings from Use of REMS Programs to Delay Generic Market Entry*, at 5 (2014), *available at* http://www.gphaonline.org/media/cms/REMS_Studyfinal_July2014.pdf.

[121] *Id.*

[122] *Id.*

distract us from the real issue we need to focus on: addressing the use of REMS or non-FDA mandated restrictions on drug supply that are designed to block lower cost generics and biosimilars from coming to market. By refusing to sell their product for research purposes, or restricting its sale to a named patient, brand manufacturers can distort the supply chain to limit competition.

To address this problem once and for all, Congress must pass the CREATES Act, bipartisan and bicameral legislation introduced by Representatives Marino and Cicilline, to prevent the misuse of REMS and restricted distribution schemes to delay generic drug competition. AAM also supports Rep. David McKinley and Rep. Peter Welch's FAST Generics Act.

The cost of failure is significant, and will only encourage anti-competitive practices to grow. In the absence of Congressional action, AAM members today must consider the difficulty involved in obtaining branded drugs when determining which generic development programs to pursue. Where access to brand drugs is subject to restricted access programs, some AAM members have determined that generic development was not feasible and decided against initiating these development programs. This means that patients and taxpayers lose out on opportunities for affordable access to life-saving medicines and our nation's health care system leaves savings on the table.

Biosimilar Medicines are Critical to Future Savings

Nowhere is the need for lower-priced alternatives, and the challenges facing them, more real than among high-priced biologic medicines. Biologics, many of which are specialty medicines, are the most rapidly growing segment of increasing brand-name prescription drug costs in the United States, with more than $100 billion in annual spending. And the role of biologic drugs in the health care system is expanding — while only 2 percent of America's patients use biologics, they account for about 40 percent of prescription drug spending in the United States.[123] These products are often life-saving therapies for serious illnesses, but they come at steep expense to patients, taxpayers and insurers. Many biologics cost tens of thousands of dollars per year per patient — some more than $200,000.

To help bring down prices for patients, Congress designed and approved the Biologics Price Competition and Innovation Act (BPCIA) in 2010 – creating an abbreviated approval pathway for biological products that are demonstrated to be "highly similar" (biosimilar) to or "interchangeable" with an FDA-approved biological product. The BPCIA also gave brand biologic drug manufacturers a 12-year market exclusivity period for their products to ensure a return on investment for new medicines. This period

[123] *Medicine Use and Spending in the U.S.: A Review of 2016 and Outlook to 2021*, April 2017.

is longer than anywhere else in the world that has a similar abbreviated pathway for biosimilars.

Biosimilar medicines represent a key step forward in reducing high drug prices. They are safe, effective and affordable versions of costly brand biologics. By the year 2025, over 70% of drug approvals are expected to be biological products.[124] Experts estimate that FDA-approved biosimilars could save between $44 billion and $250 billion over the next 10 years.[125] In doing so, they will mean greater access to lifesaving cures for 1.2 million U.S. patients, according to a new analysis. Women, lower income, and elderly patients would particularly benefit from access to biosimilar medicines.

Today, there are 38 biosimilars approved for use in the European Union, but only eight in the United States and only three are currently marketed. However, more than 66 biosimilar programs are under FDA review for development of 20 different biologic products. The ability of biosimilars to fulfill their potential is threatened by market abuses and policy challenges.

Anticompetitive Threats Even Greater to Biosimilars Availability

As discussed above, while the abuse of restricted distribution programs continues to impede generic development, the problem of access to samples is likely to be even more acute for biosimilar development. Biosimilars are more complex and difficult to develop than traditional generic drugs. Their development requires multiple lots of the brand product produced over time. If access to the variability that is inherent in brand lot development of biologics is denied, the development of the biosimilar will be greatly delayed and patients will be held hostage to higher prices and fewer options. Plus, unlike with small molecule generic drugs, the development of biosimilars is more likely to involve clinical trials requiring even more samples of the reference product. Restricted access to samples at any point during the clinical trial could cause a study to fail. This further highlights the importance of Congressional action on the CREATES Act and the FAST Generics Act.

And it now appears that brand manufacturers of biologic drugs are misusing their negotiating leverage to insist on contract terms that effectively block use of biosimilar alternatives by physicians. In a recent lawsuit, one branded company has alleged that another company that manufactures Remicade has misused its negotiating power to force PBMs and purchasers to block access to a biosimilar product. Such actions could threaten the ability of biosimilars to deliver on the promise of savings for patients.

Finally, it is critical to reiterate that biosimilars are just as safe and effective as their reference product. While we understand that physicians must remain directly involved in their patients' treatment, it is also important to recognize that some have sought to create uncertainty around the efficacy and pharmacovigilance standards of biosimilars in

[124] U.S. Pharmacist, "Biosimilars: Current Approvals and Pipeline Agents," October 2016 (link).
[125] AAM, "Generic Drug Access & Savings in the U.S.," June 2017 (link).

comparison to their reference products. These messages are in direct contradiction to the standards established in the BPCIA, and enforced by the FDA. Differentiation between biosimilars and their reference products risks undermining the important provider education that is already being done by FDA. It is also directly in contradiction to the medical evidence found in Europe and other advanced countries that have more experience with biosimilars, and have seen no measurable clinical differences between biosimilars and their reference products.

Policy Barriers Impede Biosimilar Adoption

Biosimilars present a significant opportunity for patient and program savings in the Medicare Part D program. However current law creates barriers to biosimilar access for patients in Part D, who may be forced onto higher-priced biologics.

Because of the structure of Medicare Part D, the 50 percent discount required of brand biologics is counted towards a patient's out of pocket costs – but competing biosimilars are barred from providing such a discount. This creates a perverse incentive for health plans and patients to use a higher-priced brand biologic – moving patients through the coverage gap and into catastrophic coverage faster and with lower out-of-pocket costs compared to a lower-cost biosimilar.

This approach creates substantial barriers for biosimilar manufacturers, as it may be effectively impossible to ever offer sufficient discounts to be included on Part D formularies. The resulting imbalance severely undermines the market potential for biosimilar competition. Ultimately, patients, payers, and Medicare all pay more for brand biologics than they would if the Coverage Gap Discount program were amended to include biosimilars.

Congress should amend the Part D coverage gap discount program to classify biosimilars as "applicable drugs." This change would allow biosimilar manufacturers to pay the 50 percent discounts paid by their brand competitors, and participate on a level playing field to compete for placement on the Part D plan's formulary. It would reduce both patient out-of-pocket costs and save at least $1 billion over the next ten years for the Medicare Part D program.

Conclusion

AAM and its members commend the committee for holding today's hearing addressing the challenge of high drug prices through the lens of the pharmaceutical supply chain. Generic and biosimilar medicines are a critical part of the solution for patients and America's health care system. But they are under threat from market imbalances, policies that fail to distinguish their business model from brand drugs, and anti-competitive behavior by other supply chain actors. AAM stands ready to work with you to ensure uninterrupted access to affordable therapies for patients and taxpayers.

Mr. BURGESS. The chair thanks the gentleman.

Ms. Gallenagh, you're recognized for 3 minutes, please, to summarize your opening statement.

STATEMENT OF ELIZABETH GALLENAGH

Ms. GALLENAGH. Good morning, Chairman Burgess, Ranking Member Green, Chairman Walden, and Ranking Member Pallone and members of the subcommittee.

Thank you for the chance to participate in today's hearing. Health Care Distribution Alliance represents 35 primary pharmaceutical distributors, the vital link between the nation's pharma-ceutical manufacturers and more than 200,000 pharmacies, hospitals, and other providers nationwide. Their expertise streamlines the supply chain to ensure safety and efficiency while achieving cost savings for our nation's health care system.

Without HDA members, pharmacies and providers would have to carry weeks of inventory and undertake the time consuming process of placing daily individual orders with every manufacturer. By working with full line distributors, pharmacies can maintain just-in-time inventories, saving them the expense and staff necessary to carry extensive inventories or manage large storage facilities.

While our members are logistics experts, pharmaceutical distribution has evolved over the last decade. This is no longer an industry focused solely on moving products from point A to point B. In exchange for a variety of distribution and logistics services that primary distributors provide to manufacturers, they charge bona fide service fees. These fees, which are not passed on to the customer, represent a fair market value for itemized services actually performed on behalf of the manufacturer that the manufacturer would have to perform otherwise for themselves.

Our industry is a very high volume yet low profit margin industry with the industry margin just over 1 percent on average in 2016. Moreover, in a recent 2017 study, the Berkeley Research Group concluded the pharmaceutical wholesale distributor profit on overall branded drug costs was just under 1 percent.

Traditional pharmaceutical wholesale distributors purchase pharmaceuticals from manufacturers based on the wholesale acquisition cost, or WAC—a publicly available figure reported for each product by the manufacturer. WAC represents the manufacturer's list price and does not include rebates, prompt payment, or other adjustments in price resulting from downstream or proprietary negotiation. Manufacturers set the WAC prices for their products and distributors are not privy to how that pricing decisions are made.

Primary distributors typically sell branded drugs to downstream customers based on those WACs established solely by those manufacturers. Distributors might also sell generic drugs to downstream customers based on WACs or they may be based in part on response to the market, which includes competing generic drugs. In other words, wholesale distributors do not control the price of pharmaceuticals, but rather the price of pharmaceuticals is dictated by list prices determined by their manufacturers and other market forces including the WACs of generic drugs that compete with given generic drug products.

HDA distributor members add value within the supply chain and have minimal impact on the overall cost of drugs. Ultimately, the services provided by our members result in benefits to patients and consumers and have made the U.S. pharmaceutical supply chain one of the safest and most efficient in the world.

Thank you. I would be happy to answer any question. [The prepared statement of Ms. Gallenagh follows:]

TESTIMONY OF ELIZABETH GALLENAGH, SENIOR VICE PRESIDENT, GOVERNMENT AFFAIRS AND GENERAL COUNSEL FOR THE HEALTHCARE DISTRIBUTION ALLIANCE (HDA), HOUSE ENERGY AND COMMERCE SUBCOMMITTEE ON HEALTH, DECEMBER 13, 2017

Good morning, Chairman Burgess, Ranking Member Green and members of the Committee. Thank you for the opportunity to participate in today's hearing. I am Liz Gallenagh, Senior Vice President, Government Affairs and General Counsel for the Healthcare Distribution Alliance (HDA). HDA is the national trade organization representing primary pharmaceutical distributors — the vital link between the nation's pharmaceutical manufacturers and more than 200,000 pharmacies, hospitals, long-term care facilities, clinics and others nationwide.

Since 1876, HDA has helped members navigate regulations and innovations to get the right medicines to the right patients at the right time, safely and efficiently. HDA's members include 35 national, regional and specialty primary distribution companies who are not just distributors, but are technology innovators, information management experts, security specialists and efficiency professionals. Their expertise streamlines the supply chain to ensure safety and efficiency, while also achieving cost savings for our nation's healthcare system.

Role in the Supply Chain

The U.S. healthcare supply chain is complex, and the nation's primary pharmaceutical distributors play a vital role within it. Each day hundreds of thousands of healthcare provider locations must receive needed medicines and other healthcare products from thousands of manufacturers. These manufacturers and providers are served predominantly by HDA's primary distributors, who operate out of about 176 warehouses and purchase directly from authorized manufacturers — a relatively small, but highly efficient and effective network. In fact, most pharmaceutical sales in the U.S. flow through primary distributors (95.7%).[126]

Every day HDA members work around the clock to safely and efficiently ship 15 million healthcare products (medicines, medical supplies, durable medical equipment, et al.) to pharmacies, hospitals and other healthcare providers to keep their shelves stocked with the medications and products they need to treat and serve their patients.

Distributors are unlike any other supply chain participants — their core business is not manufacturing, and they do not prescribe medicines or dispense to patients. Their key role is to serve as a conduit for medicines to travel from manufacturer to patient while making sure the supply chain is fully secure and as efficient as possible.

HDA distributor members focus significant resources on the safety and security of the supply chain, and their secure supply chain efforts may in fact be the most important service distributors provide to the overall pharmaceutical delivery system. With this committee's support several years ago, HDA strongly advocated for the enactment of the Drug Supply Chain Security Act (DSCSA), Title II of the Drug Quality Security Act, which sets a framework for unit level traceability of medicines by 2023. Today, HDA members are in the midst of Phase I implementation efforts and work to collaborate with FDA, state regulatory authorities and trading partners to build the systems and processes necessary to achieve unit-level traceability of prescription drugs by 2023, as outlined in the law.

Relationship with Provider Customers

On a daily basis, pharmacies, hospitals and other healthcare providers place orders with HDA distributor members for the medicines, supplies and equipment they need to serve their patients. Without pharmaceutical distributors, pharmacies and providers would have to carry weeks of inventory and undertake the time-consuming process of placing individual orders with each and every manufacturer for products needed by the healthcare provider on a daily basis. By working with full-line distributors, providers can maintain just-in-time inventories, saving pharmacies and hospitals the expense and staff necessary to carry extensive inventories or have large storage facilities, both of which would add significantly to their cost of operations.

[126] HDA Research Foundation, *88" Edition HDA Factbook: The Facts, Figures and Trends in Healthcare (2017-2018},* 2017.

While distributors provide many services to the pharmacy provider community, the core services are supply chain related — providing on-time and complete shipment of ordered drugs in a safe and efficient manner. In addition, they often provide financial credit, pharmacy management systems and in-store retail support, among many other services.

Traditional distributors serve a broad array of provider types — mostly retail and hospital settings, including chain pharmacy warehouses, mass merchandisers and food chains, and chain pharmacies (42%); hospitals, HMOs, clinics and nursing homes (22.7%); independent pharmacies (15.7%); mail order (16.4%). Specialty distributors (and specialty subsidiaries) serve other provider settings such as physician offices, home care, specialty pharmacy and some retail pharmacy.[127]

Relationship with Manufacturer Suppliers

The work of primary distributors also enables manufacturers to concentrate on developing and producing needed medicines without the added expense and logistical challenges of determining how to get those medicines to the providers and patients across the U.S. However, pharmaceutical distribution has evolved over the last decade from simply managing warehouses and shipping goods. While HDA members are primarily supply chain logistics and operations experts, this is no longer an industry focused solely on moving products from point A to point B. Rather, pharmaceutical distributors provide a wide array of supporting services that enable the pharmaceutical supply chain to function efficiently and safely, delivering significant value to manufacturers and healthcare providers — and ultimately to patients. Some examples of these core services include: receiving orders and shipping pharmaceutical products in a safe, efficient manner; inventory handling and inventory management, providing manufacturers with data about where (and in which settings) their products are utilized; verifying downstream customer eligibility to purchase products at pricing established under various programs or contracts between such customers and given manufacturers; and processing relevant chargebacks to manufacturers.

In exchange for the variety of distribution and logistics services that primary distributors provide to manufacturers, they charge manufacturers what are referred to as "bona fide service fees" for the provision of these services. These fees, which are not passed on to the customer, represent a fair market value for a bona fide, itemized service actually performed on behalf of the manufacturer that the manufacturer would otherwise perform (or contract for) in the absence of the service arrangement. This model reduces demand volatility — aligning order patterns more closely to actual patient demand and,

---

[127] HDA Research Foundation, *BB" Edition HDA Foctbook: The Facts, Figures and Trends in Healthcare (2017-2018)*, 2017.

eliminating artificial demand spikes, allowing for a supply chain that operates more smoothly and predictably.

It should also be noted that without HDA members, each manufacturer would have to ensure that more than 200,000 pharmacy and provider settings receive the medications they need when they need them, employing substantial financial, logistical and staff resources to provide medicines and supplies to hundreds of thousands of dispensing sites. Because distributors provide these logistical, inventory and other service support which manufacturers and pharmacies would otherwise have to perform themselves, the pharmaceutical supply chain is more efficient, reliable and secure, and patients are able to get the medicines they need in a timely fashion, saving our healthcare system approximately $42 billion each year.[128]

Primary Wholesale Distributors' Role in Drug Pricing[129]

The primary pharmaceutical distribution industry is a very high-volume, yet very lowprofit margin industry, with the industry margin just over one percent on average in 2016. In fact, overall profitability for the primary distribution sector shows little notable change over the past several years, even during recent market volatility.[130] Moreover, in a recent 2017 study, the Berkeley Research Group concluded that the pharmaceutical wholesale distributor profit on overall branded drug costs was just under one percent.[131]

Traditional pharmaceutical wholesale distributors purchase pharmaceuticals from manufacturers based on the Wholesale Acquisition Cost ("WAC"), a publicly available figure reported for each pharmaceutical product by the manufacturer to various compendia such as Medi-Span and RedBook, which publish such prices. WAC represents the manufacturer's list price, and does not include rebates, prompt payment, or other adjustments in price resulting from proprietary negotiations between the manufacturer and wholesaler, downstream payer groups or other customers. Manufacturers (pharmaceutical, biologic, generic, etc.) set the WAC price for their products. Wholesale distributors are not privy to how such WAC pricing decisions are made. Wholesale distributors typically purchase pharmaceuticals from manufacturers based on WAC and

---

[128] The Center for Healthcare Supply Chain Research, *The Role of Distributors in the U.S. Healthcare Industry*, 2011.

[129] HDA's antitrust policy strictly prohibits any discussions which constitute or imply an agreement or understanding between or among its members concerning: 1) prices, discounts, or terms or conditions of sale; 2) profits, profit margins or cost data; 3) market shares, sales territories or markets,; 4) allocation of customers or territories; 5) selection, rejection or termination of customers or suppliers; 6) restricting the territory or markets in which a company may resell products; 7) restricting the customers to whom a company may sell; or 8) any matter which is inconsistent with the proposition that each members company of HDA must exercise its independent business judgment in pricing its services or products, dealing with its customers and suppliers and choosing the markets in which it will compete.

[130] Data obtained from Annual *HDMA/HDA Factbook*, compiled and compared across multiple years.

[131] *The Pharmaceutical Supply Chain: Gross Drug Expenditures Realized by Stakeholders*; 2017; Table 2 http://www.thinkbrg.com/media/publication/863_Vandervelde_PhRMA-January-2017_WEB-FINAL.pdf.

they also charge manufacturers distribution fees related to their services, as previously discussed.

Wholesale distributors typically sell branded drugs to downstream customers based on WACs established solely by pharmaceutical manufacturers. Wholesale distributors might also sell generic drugs to downstream customers based on WACs established solely by pharmaceutical manufacturers and published in the various pricing compendia or they may price generic drugs sold to downstream customers in response to the market, which includes supply of competing generic drug and considers the WACs for such generic drug products and competitors to such drug products. As such, wholesale distributors do not control the price of pharmaceuticals rather the price of pharmaceuticals is dictated by published WAC or other list prices determined solely by manufacturers of such products and other market forces, including the WACs of generic drugs that compete with a given generic drug product.

Conclusion

As I noted earlier, primary pharmaceutical distributors have evolved from providing basic inventory management and distribution to now offering a suite of services supporting many different operations of both manufacturers and healthcare providers. Ultimately, these services result in benefits to patients and consumers and have made the U.S. pharmaceutical supply chain one of the safest and most efficient in the world.

Traditional pharmaceutical wholesale distributors' goal in the pharmaceutical supply chain is a simple one: add efficiency, security and timely delivery of products so providers can concentrate on patient care and ensure their patients have regular access to the medications they need. Historically, HDA distributor members have effectively achieved this goal and have had a positive effect on the supply chain and patients while taking costs out of the pharmaceutical supply chain and having minimal impact on the overall cost of drugs.

Thank you. I am happy to answer any questions you may have.

Mr. BURGESS. The chair thanks the gentlelady.

The chair recognizes Mr. Merritt for 3 minutes. Summarize your opening statement, please.

STATEMENT OF MARK MERRITT

Mr. MERRITT. Thank you, Mr. Chairman, and members of the committee.

Pharmacy benefit managers are the industry that employers and others hire to negotiate discounts and reduce prescription drug costs.

We see too many reasons why drug pricing has become a focal point in recent years. First, as drug makers shift from making blockbuster drugs like Lipitor, which cost maybe $3 a day, to making much more expensive products like Sovaldi—a great product, but it costs $1,000 a day. Second, in the face of rising medical costs, more health plans are raising deductibles in order to keep premiums as low as possible. This means for the first time some patients who had grown accustomed to paying $2,500 for a $500 drug are now seeing how expensive some of these drugs really are.

It's important to note that while the subject of today's hearing— the drug supply chain—is important and worthy to be discussed, it has nothing to do with why drug companies raise prices. As always, pricing power and pricing decisions in any industry are driven by supply and demand and competition, not supply chains.

Prices are set exclusively by drug companies with zero input from anybody else in the supply chain including PBMs. Further, supply chains are a routine part of how consumers access products in the marketplace today. Every industry uses them. They are not unique to health care or prescription drugs.

In the simplest terms, the prescription drug marketplace is like any other—a market of sellers and buyers. Drug makers are the sellers and, like all sellers, set prices according to whatever they think the market will bear. Likewise, buyers, who we represent, want to pay as little as possible. These are the employers, unions, health plans, and government programs that hire PBMs to negotiate rebates, discounts, and other price concessions from drug makers and drug stores. These savings are used to reduce premiums, cost sharing, and other expenses. And some drug makers have tried to blame their own pricing decisions on the supply chain but this makes little sense. For example, Mylan used this excuse when they raised EpiPen prices 400 percent at a time when supply chain costs were relatively flat. Sovaldi had a launch price of $84,000 even though it involved no rebates at all.

Some of the highest prices are in Medicare Part B, as in boy, where payments are set by the Federal Government without negotiations from PBMs or rebates. In any case, almost half of the RFPs large employers use when hiring PBMs now require PBMs to pass through 100 percent of the rebates and about 90 percent of rebates are passed through overall in the marketplace.

While PBMs are proud that, according to CMS, drug trend only grew 1 percent last year despite rising list prices, we welcome manufacturers to offer alternatives to rebates as a way to get discounts. Payers—our clients—just want the lowest net cost wherever they can get them.

Thank you for having me here today and I look forward to answering any questions you may have.

[The prepared statement of Mr. Merritt follows:]

Testimony of Mark Merritt, Pharmaceutical Care Management Association, before the United States House of Representatives, Energy and Commerce Committee, Subcommittee on Health, "Examining the Drug Supply Chain," December 13, 2017

Introduction

Good morning. My name is Mark Merritt, President and CEO of the Pharmaceutical Care Management Association (PCMA). I appreciate this opportunity to appear before the Subcommittee at this hearing, "Examining the Drug Supply Chain." PCMA is the national association representing America's pharmacy benefit managers (PBMs), which administer prescription drug plans for more than 266 million[132] Americans with health coverage provided through self-insured employers, health insurers, labor unions, Medicare, Medicaid, SCHIP, and the Federal Employees Health Benefits Program (FEHBP).

At the outset, I want to thank the Energy and Commerce Committee for your work with the Senate HELP Committee to improve generic competition and lower the cost of prescription drugs. FDA's faster approvals for generics and the listing of single-source, off-patent brand drugs, as contained in the FDA Reauthorization Act of 2017 (FDARA), should help foster a more competitive marketplace to improve the affordability and accessibility of prescription drugs for patients and guard against sudden, astronomical price hikes of decades-old prescription drugs. I also want to acknowledge the Committee's important work on Medicare Part D and Medicaid to ensure affordable prescription drug benefits for millions of vulnerable Americans.

My testimony will describe the role PBMs play in helping patients and payers get the most for their benefit dollars. I will also outline how the Part D program vividly illustrates the value that PBMs bring and that making major changes could destabilize that successful program. Finally, I offer a number of common-sense, market-based policy proposals to reduce the cost of prescription drugs and to help curb the nation's opioid crisis.

What Is a Supply Chain?

Manufacturers in all industries use supply chains to help bring their goods to market. Generally speaking, manufacturers sell in bulk to wholesalers, who then resell to retailers

[132] PR Newswire, "PBMs Provide Policy Solutions to Increase Competition, Reduce Rx Costs," Feb 04, 2016.

who in turn resell to consumers. Often manufacturers offer rebates, discounts, and other incentives to encourage greater sales of their products versus competing products. Since every supply chain involves some costs, manufacturers only use them to the degree they offer the most cost-effective means of distributing their product.

Supply chains are not generally associated with why manufacturers raise prices. As always, pricing decisions and pricing power are primarily determined by supply, demand, and the level of competition a product faces in the marketplace—not distribution costs.

All this is true in the drug supply chain, too, except that third party payers (employers, unions, insurers, government programs)—not consumers—pay most of the costs of prescription drug coverage. Typically, payers cover two-thirds and patients pay the other one-third in the form of premiums and out-of-pocket costs. Payers hire PBMs (which are not part of the supply chain per se) to reduce costs by promoting generics and negotiating rebates and discounts from drugmakers and drugstores that want to be included in the benefit.

Operating in a competitive environment, PBMs typically reduce drug costs by 30%[133]. Thousands of America's largest, most sophisticated payers choose to hire PBMs, even though none are required to. The Centers for Medicare & Medicaid Services' (CMS) latest National Health Expenditure data also shows that even in the midst of rising drug prices PBMs are continuing to keep overall spending and out-of-pocket costs down.

The Role of Rebates

Central to manufacturer-PBM negotiations, brand drug manufacturers compete for formulary placement by offering rebates for moving market share, which are typically calculated and paid weeks or months after a drug is dispensed. As a result of these negotiations, PBMs can recommend benefit designs that stretch payers' finite dollars and reduce premiums and cost-sharing. These designs include cost-sharing incentives for patients to use the most affordable drugs, which often are generics. The highest cost-sharing is typically reserved for drugs with the least competitive discounts, or in the case of many high-priced, single-source drugs, no discount at all. PCMA supports benefit designs that ensure patients do not pay more in cost-sharing than the actual cost of the drug and innovations like electronic prior authorization that reduce physicians' administrative burden.

Payers typically use rebate savings to reduce premiums and out-of-pocket costs for patients. Each payer determines what percentage of rebates is passed back to it, and how much (if any) it wants the PBM to retain as payment for services. While on average

[133] Visante: *Pharmacy Benefit Managers (PBMs): Generating Savings for Plan Sponsors and Consumers*, February 2016.

payers elect to receive 90% of rebates negotiated by PBMs,[134] an increasing number require PBMs to pass through all of them. About 46% of commercial PBM contracts are negotiated with full pass-through of rebates to payers,[135] and 100% of rebates in the Medicare Part D program are required to be reported to CMS. PBMs are committed to providing rebate transparency and audit rights to their clients.

There Is No Connection between the Prices Drugmakers Set and the Rebates They Negotiate with PBMs

A recent study of the top 200 self-administered, patent-protected, brand-name drugs shows no correlation between the launch prices or price increases manufacturers set and the rebates they pay to PBMs.[136] Some high-priced drugs have low rebates and some low-priced drugs have high rebates. Some high-priced drugs have no rebate at all. Like manufacturers in other industries, drugmakers set prices according to supply, demand, and the level of competitive alternatives available.

Competition drives manufacturer price concessions. Evidence shows a strong correlation between lower net prices for, and more competition between, substitutable drugs.[137] An analysis by Credit Suisse finds "a strong correlation" between the size of drug rebates and the extent that drugs are substitutable.[138] Thus, drug manufacturers with "more unique" products can negotiate lower rebates than companies with more substitutable products.[139] This analysis confirms that PBMs negotiate lower drug costs when they can bring competition to bear.

Exploring Trade Offs to Point-of-Sale (POS) Rebates

POS rebates refer to contract arrangements where negotiated price concessions are estimated before the transaction and then applied immediately when a drug is dispensed. In the commercial market, though PBMs could implement it, few payers have chosen to apply rebates at the pharmacy counter. Frustration over high drug prices has led some public policymakers to explore ways to reduce costs for consumers, including requiring health plans in government programs to use rebates to reduce POS costs rather than

---

134 Written Testimony of Joanna Shepherd, Ph.D., Emory University for the ERISA Advisory Council Hearing on PBM Compensation and Fee Disclosure, June 19, 2014, Citing J. P. Morgan, "Pharmacy Benefit Management, Takeaways from Our Proprietary PBM Survey," May 21, 2014.

135 See, Pharmacy Benefit Management Institute, "PBMI Research Report: Trends in Drug Benefit Design," 2016.

136 Visante, Inc. *Increasing Prices Set by Drugmakers; Not Correlated With Rebates*, June 2017. Analysis prepared for PCMA.

137 Credit Suisse, "Global Pharma and Biotech: Exploring Future U.S. Pricing Pressure," April 18, 2017.

138 Credit Suisse, "Global Pharma and Biotech: Exploring Future U.S. Pricing Pressure," April 18, 2017.

139 Credit Suisse, "Global Pharma and Biotech: Exploring Future U.S. Pricing Pressure," April 18, 2017.

premiums. However, such policies do not reduce costs; they only shift costs from one group of patients to another.

POS Rebates Do Not Work in Medicare Part D

POS rebates have proven unworkable in Medicare Part D and pose risks that could destabilize the program. Already permitted in Part D, POS rebates have been tried—unsuccessfully—in the past. They lead to significant adverse selection and would increase premiums for all Medicare beneficiaries while reducing costs for a small minority. Requiring POS rebates in Part D would significantly increase costs to the program and taxpayers. According to CMS estimates, requiring 100% of rebates to be passed through at POS would, over the next 10 years: increase government costs up to \$82.1 billion; increase beneficiary premiums up to \$28.3 billion; and provide a windfall to drug manufacturers of up to \$29.4 billion.[140]

Additionally, requiring direct and indirect remuneration (DIR) pharmacy payments to be paid at POS would be a step backward from policymakers' goals to transform the Medicare program from a wasteful fee-for-service payment model to one based on quality and value. PDPs and PBMs use performance-based payments to reward pharmacies that improve quality through, for example, increasing generic dispensing, improving medication adherence, and reducing inappropriate drug use. Alternatively, pharmacies that underperform and do not meet the performance metrics may not earn contractually agreed-upon bonus payments. Because such value-based arrangements use quarterly or annually measured incentives, a typical pharmacy's performance cannot be determined at POS. These arrangements are agreed upon and acknowledged in advance by pharmacies in their network contracts.

Finally, mandating POS rebates and pharmacy DIR would expose plans to other risks, such as accusations of False Claims Act violations if they incorrectly estimated the size of rebates, which would be a virtual certainty. These points are especially important in light of CMS's current open docket request for information on the prospect of implementing POS rebates and POS pharmacy DIR in Part D.

Negotiations with Pharmacies Reduce Costs for Consumers and Payers

PBMs also use value-based contracting to build a network of high-performing pharmacies. As noted above, based on negotiated, agreed-upon performance metrics,

---

140 CMS, "Medicare Program: Contract Year 2019 Policy and Technical Changes to the Medicare Advantage, Medicare Cost Plan, Medicare Fee-for-Service, the Medicare Prescription Drug Benefit Programs, and the PACE Program," *Federal Register*, November 28, 2017.

PBMs hold pharmacies accountable for performance on certain activities such as generic dispensing, cost-effective dispensing, improving medication adherence, and reducing inappropriate drug use. In turn, pharmacies performing well on such metrics earn bonus payments and preferred status. The ability of health plans and PBMs to construct networks that include some, but not all, providers—has long been used to increase quality of care and lower costs for patients. Nonetheless, for decades, pharmacies have lobbied to force PBMs to open up their networks to "any willing provider" meeting the same terms and conditions as other network members. If pharmacies know they will automatically be included in networks, they have a reduced incentive to offer PBMs the most competitive terms. Thus, any willing pharmacy (AWP) laws significantly reduce providers' incentive to engage in price competition and be held accountable for the quality of their care. An "any-willing pharmacy" bill introduced in Congress last year would undermine the availability of lower cost, preferred pharmacies and increase Medicare spending by $21 billion over the next 10 years, according to an analysis. PBM pharmacy networks include independent pharmacies that usually hire pharmacy services administrative organizations (PSAOs) to negotiate and contract with PBMs and other third-party payers on their behalf. A typical PSAO represents thousands of pharmacies. More than 80% of independent pharmacies (18,103 of the 21,511 pharmacies identified by National Council for Prescription Drug Programs data) use PSAOs. PSAOs provide access to pooled purchasing power, negotiating leverage, and contracting strategies similar to those of large, multi-location chain pharmacies.

The Success of Part D Showcases the Value of PBMs

In the decade plus since the creation of the Medicare Part D Prescription Drug Benefit, policymakers and other observers have taken heightened interest in the work of PBMs. Widely recognized as one of the more successful government programs in recent history, Part D has provided unprecedented access to needed drugs for millions of Medicare beneficiaries, while consistently spending far below estimated levels. This success has been due to the structure of Part D, which allows PBMs to use the negotiating and management tools at their disposal to manage drug benefits. To make major changes to this successful system would be a mistake.

Medicare Part D: A Case Study for How PBMs Use Direct and Indirect Remuneration (DIR) to Keep Part D Costs Down and Beneficiary Premiums Low

PBMs have been able to replicate the successful drug benefit management techniques they have long used in the private sector to benefit Medicare Part D. The program works through DIR, which is a technical term created by CMS specific to Part D that includes both manufacturer rebates and certain incentive payments to pharmacies. The vast majority of DIR payments in Part D comprise PBM-manufacturer negotiated rebates. A much smaller share is made up of incentive payment terms that pharmacies (or their PSAOs on their behalf) contractually negotiate with PBMs.

According to a recent study, the price concessions PBMs negotiate with drug manufacturers and drugstores and report to CMS as DIR are generating significant savings for the federal government and are projected to save enrollees in stand-alone Part D plans $48.7 billion on their premiums over the next 10 years.[141]

CMS has also found that DIR contributes significantly to keeping Part D premiums low. Earlier this year, CMS released a report that found negotiated DIR price concessions have grown in recent years to moderate beneficiary premiums and reduce costs for the government.[142] The CMS report highlights how negotiated price concessions reduce premiums for Medicare Part D beneficiaries, which also lead to lower costs for the federal government—negotiated price concessions lowered per-beneficiary costs in Part D 28% on average.[143] Stable and affordable premiums have contributed to a 90% satisfaction rate among Part D enrollees.[144]

Policy Recommendations to Improve Competition and Reduce Costs

PCMA supports policies to lower drug costs through increased competition. The vast majority of the policy proposals outlined below to help increase competition in the marketplace and in federal programs would come under Energy and Commerce Committee jurisdiction. Our industry would be pleased to work with you and other stakeholders on the following proposals.

- Eliminate use of Risk Evaluation and Mitigation Strategies (REMS) to delay competition. Some manufacturers have used REMS to prevent generic or biosimilar developers from getting sufficient quantities of a drug or biologic to develop a competitor to the innovator product. REMS were never intended for this purpose; this practice should be prohibited. The Fair Access for Safe and Timely Generics "FAST" Act, introduced by Representatives McKinley and

---

[141] Milliman, "Value of Direct and Indirect Remuneration (DIR): Impact on Medicare Part D Prescription Drug Plan (PDP) Program Stakeholders," Commissioned by Pharmaceutical Care Management Association, July 2017. https://www.pcmanet.org/wp-content/uploads/2017/07/Value-of-PDP-DIR_20170706.pdf.

[142] CMS, "Medicare Part D – Direct and Indirect Remuneration (DIR)" January 19, 2017. https://www.cms.gov/Newsroom/MediaReleaseDatabase/Fact-sheets/2017-Fact-Sheet-items/2017-01-19-2.html.

[143] CMS, Op. Cit.

[144] Morning Consult for Medicare Today, "Ten Years After Implementation, Nearly Nine in 10 Seniors are Satisfied with Part D," July 2016. http://medicaretoday.org/resources/senior-satisfaction-survey/.

Welch and cosponsored by Representatives Schrader, DeGette, and Schakowsky would address these abuses.

- Stop anticompetitive product adjustments, i.e., "evergreening." Drug manufacturers sometimes use tactics such as "product hopping" or "evergreening," submitting applications to the FDA for approval of a "new" product that is essentially the same as the original product. These product lifecycle management tactics artificially extend drug exclusivity periods and delay the take-up of lower-cost generics.
- Allow for FDA accelerated approval of brand drugs based on increasing competition. Accelerated review is granted to new drug applications that address "unmet need." The economic need for competition to lower prices should be a criterion of unmet need.
- Revisit and improve biosimilar labeling and naming. Substitutable biosimilars should bear identical names and labels to their innovator analogs. Use of different names will confuse patients and providers and inhibit prescribing of biosimilars.
- Reduce innovator biologic exclusivity to seven years. Seven years of data exclusivity would still provide a sufficient return to manufacturers, while also speeding more affordable biosimilars to market.

PCMA also supports enhancing tools in Medicare Part D, Medicaid, and commercial markets to increase competition and affordability. PBMs and health plans can best drive competition among drug manufacturers when they can give plan enrollees a strong incentive to use a competing, higher-value drug. This reduces costs and helps improve adherence among patients. Below are some strategies to strengthen these efforts.

- Create a safe harbor for value-based drug price negotiations from Medicaid Best Price. Today any drug manufacturer must offer state Medicaid programs the lowest price it offers any other payer. This provision is seen as a price floor and is inhibiting creative value-based pricing arrangements.
- Expand drug coverage options for Health Savings Account (HSA)-eligible high-deductible health plans (HDHPs). HDHPs associated with HSAs should have the option of covering prescription drugs with low or no cost-sharing prior to reaching the deductible, especially drugs that qualify for a preventive drug list. This policy can be achieved by expanding the current preventive drug list used by HDHPs.
- Remove Medicare Part D's protected classes. Designating "classes of clinical concern" where all or substantially all drugs in a class must be covered allows drug manufacturers to name their price. CMS already applies careful plan formulary coverage checks to assure proper coverage.

- Make biosimilars subject to the 50% Part D coverage gap discount. The ACA did not apply to biosimilars the 50% Part D coverage gap discount. This could have the unintended consequence of encouraging prescribing of more expensive innovator biologics when lower cost biosimilars are available.
- Encourage greater use of generics for Medicare Part D Low Income Subsidy (LIS) enrollees. MedPAC recommended allowing the Secretary of HHS to lower cost-sharing on generics and raise it for brands that have generic competition. Increasing the differential between brands and generics and allowing plans to lower generic cost-sharing would save money for enrollees and Medicare.
- Eliminate the tax deduction for direct-to-consumer (DTC) drug ads that mention a specific product. While DTC drug ads may encourage some people to see a doctor, they drive up unnecessary utilization and the cost of health care.

In addition to proposals to find savings and efficiencies in the market and public programs, we also commend the Subcommittee for its work in helping to curb the nation's opioid crisis. Below are three policy proposals that we believe would help that effort.

- Require E-prescribing (e-Rx) for Controlled Substances. Requiring e-prescribing for controlled substance prescriptions would circumscribe pharmacy shopping, enable better prescription tracking, and reduce fraud. I want to thank Representative Mullin and the other cosponsors on the Energy and Commerce Committee, Representatives Kennedy, Tonko, and Long, for your work on H.R. 3528, the Every Prescription Conveyed Securely Act.
- Seven Day Opioid Prescription Limits for Acute Pain. To prevent patients from getting addicted to pain medication, prescriptions for acute pain should be limited to a seven days' supply. The limit would not apply to treatment of cancer or chronic pain, or the use of opioids in treating addiction or for patients in hospice care. This aligns with a recent recommendation of the Centers for Disease Control and Prevention.
- Achieve Timely and Flexible Implementation of the Comprehensive Addiction and Recovery Act (CARA) Lock-In. CMS included in its recent proposed Part D rule suggested regulations for implementing the CARA pharmacy and prescriber lock-in. Inexplicably, CMS has proposed that once beneficiaries are identified as being at-risk, they should have a six-month delay before being locked-in for controlled substances to a pharmacy. PCMA believes that at-risk beneficiaries should be locked in as quickly as possible to avoid further harm to themselves and also to prevent fraud if they are diverting drugs. This program was established by Representative Bilirakis' *Medication Safety and Drug Abuse Prevention Act*, which passed last Congress and was cosponsored by

Representatives Lujan and Long. Thank you for your leadership and we hope you will express concerns to CMS about their proposal.

Conclusion

PBMs evolved into their current role because they increase the value of prescription drug benefits. PCMA's member companies harness market forces and competition to corral drugs costs and deliver high-quality benefits and services to their payer clients and enrollees. In its search for solutions to address high drug costs, PCMA encourages the Subcommittee to pursue policies that foster and encourage competition to keep prescription drug costs and pharmacy benefits more affordable for employers, enrollees, taxpayers, and government programs.

Thank you for the opportunity to testify. I am happy to answer any questions.

Mr. BURGESS. The chair thanks the gentleman.

Mr. Eyles, you are recognized for 3 minutes to summarize your opening statement, please.

STATEMENT OF MATT EYLES

Mr. EYLES. Good morning, Mr. Chairman, members of the subcommittee. I am Matt Eyles, Chief Operating Officer of America's Health Insurance Plans, the national association whose members provide coverage for health care.

I appreciate the opportunity to testify on behalf of our members this morning and my testimony focuses really on three topics. First, the consequences of out of control drug prices, both excessive launch prices and supersized price increases, and the impact they have on consumers and the factors pointing to a broken pharmaceutical market. Second, any discussion of drug prices and the supply chain must begin with the list price, set solely by drugs companies, and which act as the starting point for plans and PBMs to negotiate lower prices for consumers. Third, AHIP's policy solutions to promote more affordable drug prices.

Out of control prices are the result of drug companies taking advantage of a market skewed in their favor. Too often, this skewed market has granted economic power to drug companies through price-dictating monopolies. For example, with no generic competitors, the list price of popular insulin increased almost 300 percent since 2007, while the CPI rose only about 15 percent.

If you remember one message this morning, it is that the entire pricing process is driven off the list price of a branded drug, solely determined by the drug company, not anyone else, and the end result is everyone pays more.

AHIP's members negotiate with providers and drug manufacturers to cover high-quality treatments and services at the most affordable prices. Looking at the drug supply chain, we must keep two points in mind. First, health insurers offer comprehensive coverage under the pharmacy benefit for prescriptions delivered through retail pharmacies. This represents about 70 percent of drug spending. Second, plans provide coverage under the medical benefit for physician-administered drugs delivered in outpatient and inpatient settings. This covers about 30 percent of spending.

Our discussion today focuses largely on that first bucket covered under the pharmacy benefit but plans provide coverage for both types and therefore have a unique perspective into the broader drug market. A 2017 AHIP analysis found that 22 cents of every dollar spent on insurance premiums goes toward prescription drugs. This is a conservative estimate by excluding hospital spending on drugs.

But here's the bottom line.: The 22 percent outpaces spending on physicians, inpatient hospital, and outpatient hospital services. So when drug prices go up, insurance premiums go up, and that's an economic reality.

For the committee's consideration, we included recommendations in our written statement with three categories of policy solutions— first, delivering real competition through generics and biosimilars; second, ensuring open and honest pricing with greater transparency into how drug prices are set and when prices increase excessively; and third, delivering value to patients by expanding efforts to link drug prices to clinical value and outcomes.

Thank you for the opportunity this morning. We look forward to working with the committee to find solutions to affordable medications.

[The prepared statement of Mr. Eyles follows:]

THE PHARMACEUTICAL SUPPLY CHAIN AND PRESCRIPTION DRUG COSTS: "THE PROBLEM IS THE PRICE," BY MATT EYLES, SENIOR EXECUTIVE VICE PRESIDENT AND CHIEF OPERATING OFFICER, AMERICA'S HEALTH INSURANCE PLANS FOR THE HOUSE ENERGY AND COMMERCE COMMITTEE, SUBCOMMITTEE ON HEALTH, DECEMBER 13, 2017

Introduction

Chairman Burgess, Ranking Member Green and members of the subcommittee, I am Matt Eyles, Senior Executive Vice President and Chief Operating Officer of America's Health Insurance Plans (AHIP). AHIP is the national association whose members provide coverage for health care and related services to millions of Americans every day. Through these offerings, we improve and protect the health and financial security of families, businesses, communities and the nation. We are committed to market-based solutions and public-private partnerships that improve affordability, value, access and well-being for the American people.

We appreciate this opportunity to testify on issues surrounding the pharmaceutical supply chain and solutions that are needed to help millions of Americans who are burdened by out-of-control prescription drug prices. AHIP's members negotiate with health care providers and pharmaceutical manufacturers on behalf of consumers and other health care purchasers (e.g., employers, government) to provide coverage for high-quality treatments and services at the most competitive prices possible. Health insurance providers offer comprehensive coverage under the pharmacy benefit for prescription drugs delivered through retail, mail order, and specialty pharmacies. Health plans also provide coverage under the medical benefit for physician-administered drugs, biologics, and devices in outpatient and inpatient settings. This gives health plans a unique perspective into the pharmaceutical supply chain and a 360-degree view of the broader U.S. health care system – working with pharmacy benefit managers and negotiating with drug and device manufacturers, pharmacies, physicians, and hospitals to ensure that enrollees have coverage for the treatments and services they need.

As the committee explores the role of various participants in the supply chain, we urge you to recognize that the entire pricing process is driven entirely by the original list price of a branded drug – which is determined solely by the drug company, not by the market or any other participant in the pharmaceutical supply chain. Congress needs to address this reality – that the problem is the price – as part of any strategy for reducing pharmaceutical costs for the American people.

Out-of-control prescription drug prices are a direct consequence of pharmaceutical companies taking advantage of a broken market for their own financial gain at the expense of patients. The lack of competition, transparency, and accountability in the prescription drug market has created extended, price-dictating monopolies with economic power that exist nowhere else in the U.S. economy. The end result is that everyone pays more – from patients, businesses and taxpayers to hospitals, doctors, and pharmacists.

Bold steps are needed, at both the legislative and regulatory levels, to ensure that people have access to affordable medications. With the right solutions that increase competition, choice, and patient control, we can deliver affordable prescription drugs – while at the same time protecting and supporting innovations to deliver new treatments and cures for patients.

Our statement focuses on the following topics:

- The consequences that out-of-control prescription drug prices have on consumers;

- How health plans work hard on behalf of all consumers to negotiate lower prescription drug costs, while prescription drug manufacturers set sky-high list prices that serve as the starting point for rebate negotiations and the overall pricing process; and
- Our recommendations for reducing prescription drug prices through market-based solutions that deliver real competition, create more consumer choice, and ensure that open and honest drug pricing is tied to the value delivered to patients.

The Impact of Out-of-Control Prescription Drug Prices

Rising prescription drug prices and costs impose a heavy burden on all Americans. From patients who cannot afford life-saving medications, to consumers who pay higher and higher premiums because of higher and higher drug prices, to employers who must divert dollars that could be used for salaries to pay for more expensive health services, to hardworking taxpayers who fund public programs like Medicaid and Medicare, the consequences are profound.

It is important to understand the unambiguous root causes of this problem: lack of real market competition due to the extension and distortion of government-granted exclusivity and patent protections, opaque pharmaceutical pricing practices, questionable sales and marketing practices, and limited correlation between drug prices and the value they deliver to patients.

Even for products that have been on the market for decades, sharp price increases are not uncommon. For example, one study shows that the price of insulin has increased more than 240 percent over the past decade – from $88.20 per vial in 2007 to $307.20 per vial today – despite the fact that insulin has been widely available for the last 90 years. With no generic competition in the U.S., diabetes patients are limited to brand-name versions costing hundreds of dollars per vial.[145,146]

EpiPens offer another good example. The unjustified price increases for EpiPens generated well deserved scrutiny last year. From 2008 to 2016, the list price of an EpiPen 2-Pak rose an astonishing 500 percent – with zero improvements to the quality of the medication. Because of this out-of-control price spike, the cost of co-insurance to cover the medication increased by 477 percent ($127)[147]. The consequence for hardworking

---

[145] Jeremy A. Green, M.D., Ph.D. and Kevin R. Riggs M.D., M.P.H. "Why Is There No Generic Insulin? Historical Origins of a Modern Problem." *New England Journal of Medicine;* March 19, 2015.

[146] Several Probes Target Insulin Drug Pricing, *Kaiser Health News*, October 28, 2017 https://www.nbcnews.com/health/health-news/several-probes-target-insulin-drug-pricing-n815141.

[147] Calculated by using EpiPen list prices from 2008 and 2016, assuming a 30% co-insurance rate off of PBM payment rate, and using CBO's reported "typical" PBM payment rate of 85% of list price plus a $2.00 dispensing fee (https://www.cbo.gov/sites/default/files/110th-congress-2007-2008/reports/01-03-prescription drug.pdf).

families is that they have less money in their pockets to buy gas, groceries, or save for college or retirement.

Spending on prescription drugs continues to grow at a rapid and unsustainable rate, driven in large part by both high launch prices for new therapies and treatments as well as price increases for existing brand-name drugs. In 2015, U.S. spending on prescription drugs totaled $457 billion and represented 16.7 percent of total personal health care spending (includes retail prescription drugs and drugs provided in a hospital setting).[148] According to the Centers for Medicare & Medicaid Services (CMS), total prescription drug spending is projected to reach $597.1 billion by 2025.[149]

According to the Milliman Medical Index, a widely used benchmark for estimating health care costs for a family of four with employer-sponsored health insurance coverage, prescription drug spending will increase by 8 percent in 2017, which is more than double the 3.6 percent increase in overall medical trend.[150] The report notes that "because prescription drug expenses have grown more quickly than other healthcare expenditures, drugs have increased from approximately 13% of the total MMI in 2001 to 17.1% in 2017."[151] Similarly, Segal Consulting, a prominent benefits consulting firm, estimates that prescription drug spending for employer-sponsored plans will increase by 10.3 percent in 2018 – with a 17.7 percent cost increase in specialty drugs and biologics.[152] Prescription drug spending trends are primarily driven by price inflation (8.8%) as opposed to increases in utilization (2.1%), according to the Segal Consulting study.[153]

The pharmaceutical cost crisis is clearly demonstrated by numerous research findings:

- Out-of-Control Drug Prices and Costs Are a Major Component of Premiums: A March 2017 AHIP analysis concluded that 22 cents of every dollar spent on health insurance premiums goes to pay for prescription drugs – outpacing the amount spent on physician services, inpatient hospital services, and outpatient hospital services.[154] These costs impose a heavy burden on consumers, employers, government programs, taxpayers, and the entire health care system.

---

[148] HHS-ASPE *Report—Observations on Trends in Prescription Drug Spending.* March 8, 2016. https://aspe.hhs.gov/pdf-report/observations-trends-prescription-drug-spending.

[149] National Health Expenditure Projections, 2016-2025: Price Increases, Aging Push Sector to 20 Percent of Economy. Sean P. Keehan, et al. *Health Affairs;* March 2017. https://www.healthaffairs.org/doi/pdf/10.1377/hlthaff.2016.1627.

[150] *2017 Milliman Medical Index.* Chris Girod, Sue Hart, and Scott Weltz. May 2017. http://www.milliman.com/uploadedFiles/insight/Periodicals/mmi/2017-milliman-medical-index.pdf 7 2017 Milliman Medical Index. Chris Girod, Sue Hart, and Scott Weltz. May 2017. http://www. milliman.com/uploadedFiles/insight/Periodicals/mmi/2017-milliman-medical-index.pdf.

[151] Ibid.

[152] Segal Consulting--*High Rx Cost Trends Projected to Be Lower for 2018.* Fall 2017.

[153] Ibid.

[154] "Prescription Drugs Are Largest Single Expense of Consumer Premium Dollars," *AHIP,* March 2, 2017. https://www.ahip.org/health-care-dollar/. This AHIP estimate understates the actual impact of prescription drugs on insurance premiums, as drugs administered in hospital inpatient settings were excluded.

When prescription drug prices go up, the cost of health insurance goes up. That is a fundamental economic reality: rising health care costs, including drug costs, are driving increases in the cost of health coverage.

- Financial Burden on Hospitals and Providers: An October 2016 study commissioned by the American Hospital Association and the Federation of American Hospitals cautioned that hospitals "bear a heavy financial burden when the cost of drugs increases and must make tough choices about how to allocate scarce resources." This study highlighted an example of one hospital for which the price increases of four common drugs (which ranged between 479 and 1,261 percent) cost the same amount in 2015 as the salaries of 55 full-time nurses.[155]
- Unfair Burden of High Drug Prices for American Consumers, Businesses and Taxpayers: In a March 2017 *Health Affairs* blog, researchers at the Memorial Sloan Kettering Center for Health Policy and Outcomes analyzed the 15 companies selling the top 20 drugs (by sales) in the United States. Researchers reported that: (1) list prices in other developed countries averaged just 41 percent of U.S. net drug prices; and (2) the additional income generated by higher U.S. net drug prices totaled $116 billion in 2015.[156] The authors further stated: "We found that the premiums pharmaceutical companies earn from charging substantially higher prices for their medications in the US compared to other Western countries generates substantially more than the companies spend globally on their research and development. This finding counters the claim that the higher prices paid by US patients and taxpayers are necessary to fund research and development. Rather, there are billions of dollars left over even after worldwide research budgets are covered."
- Higher Prices Often Do Not Mean Better Outcomes: While some recent high-priced, breakthrough medications have improved patient outcomes, this is not always the case. For example, an April 2015 study by researchers from the National Institutes of Health (NIH) in *JAMA Oncology* examined 51 oncology drugs approved by the Food and Drug Administration (FDA) from 2009 through 2013. Researchers concluded that current pricing models were irrational and had no connection to better patient outcomes. Remarkably, the NIH researchers found that prices had no significant correlation to improvements in progression-free survival or overall survival.[157] With new cancer drugs now often costing well over $100,000 annually, manufacturers appear to be setting the price of new

---

155 "Trends in Hospital Inpatient Drug Costs: Issues and Challenges," *NORC*, October 11, 2016. http://www.aha.org/content/16/aha-fah-rx-report.pdf.

156 "R&D Costs For Pharmaceutical Companies Do Not Explain Elevated US Drug Prices," Nancy Yu, Zachary Helms, and Peter Bach, March 7, 2017. http://healthaffairs.org/blog/2017/03/07/rd-costs-for-pharmaceutical-companies-do-not-explain-elevated-us-drug-prices/.

157 "Five Years of Cancer Drug Approvals: Innovation, Efficacy, and Costs," Sham Mailankody, MB BS; Vinay Prasad, MD, MPH, *JAMA Oncology*, July 2015. http://oncology.jamanetwork.com/article.aspx?articleid=2212206.

therapies based on the highest-priced oncology treatment approved most recently by the FDA rather than the value or the improved outcomes they deliver to patients.

- "Unreasonable" Drug Prices Forcing Tradeoffs between Taking Medicines and Other Necessities: A September 2016 tracking poll from the Kaiser Family Foundation found that 77 percent of Americans believe that prescription drug costs are "unreasonable."[158] The difficulty in affording unreasonably priced prescription drugs can lead to treatment non-adherence, which can harm patient health creating adverse outcomes and leading to expensive complications. According to a survey by *Consumer Reports*, many respondents took "potentially dangerous" steps to limit the impact of high drug costs: not filling a prescription (17 percent), skipping a scheduled dose (14 percent), or taking an expired medication (14 percent). This survey also found that 19 percent of respondents spent less on groceries, and 15 percent postponed paying other bills so they could afford their prescription drugs.[159]

These facts paint a clear picture of the crisis we face: drug companies exploit a broken market to set seemingly unbounded prices for seemingly unlimited periods while consumers, businesses, and taxpayers bear the staggering costs.

Understanding the Role of Health Plans in the Supply Chain: Negotiating Lower Costs for All Consumers

Consumers are taking a more active role in their health decisions, including how to manage the rising prices and cost of prescription drugs, and health plans are providing better cost and quality comparison tools for individuals and families to make informed choices about their care. According to an AHIP study published in the *American Journal of Managed Care (AJMC)*, 90 percent of plans with price estimator tools educated consumers on their potential out-of-pocket costs, such as co-pays, coinsurance, and deductibles that they might incur for specific procedures or services.[160] Research shows that the advance availability of price information can help consumers make health care decisions tailored to their specific care needs. Additionally, many of these resources are easily-accessible consumer tools available through mobile apps, including coverage

---

[158] Kaiser Health Tracking Poll: September 2016. http://www.kff.org/health-costs/report/kaiser-health-tracking-poll-september-2016/.

[159] "Some Americans take risks with needed drugs due to high costs," *Consumer Reports*, September 2014. http://www.consumerreports.org/cro/2014/09/some-americans-take-risks-with-needed-drugs-due-to-high-costs/index.htm.

[160] "Characterizing Health Plan Price Estimator Tools: Findings From a National Survey," Higgins A, Brainard N, Veselovskiy G., *AJMC*, February 2016.

information, provider directories listing the network of participating and/or preferred pharmacies. This information gives consumers more control over their care and more choices for their coverage.

Overall, when compared to the total spending for retail prescription drugs, consumer out-of-pocket spending – cash payments, deductibles, coinsurance, and copayments – have significantly decreased since the 1990s. Consumer out-of-pocket spending has declined from 57 percent of U.S. retail drug spending in 1990 to 14 percent in 2015, and spending by commercial and government payers rose from 43 percent to 86 percent of U.S. retail drug expenditures during this same period.[161] A 2016 Kaiser analysis found that after insurance coverage for individuals in employer-sponsored coverage, the average out-of-pocket cost for a person who purchases prescription drugs is $12 a month.[162]

Importantly, since 2014, nearly all consumers with minimum essential coverage have been protected by annual limits on maximum out-of-pocket (MOOP) costs. With the exception of certain grandfathered plans in effect before March 2010, all health plans in the individual and group markets (including large group and self-insured plans) have maximum out-of-pocket limits. This includes protecting patients against catastrophic exposure and financial ruin because of rising drug costs. These MOOP limits are reset and updated annually, providing the financial protection that patients deserve. While the federal limit for individual coverage is $7,150 and $14,300 for family coverage in 2017, many health plans have set their out-of-pocket limits far lower. The vast majority of individuals with employer-sponsored coverage (and those covered under Medicare Advantage prescription drug plans and Medicaid) have substantially lower limits.[163]

Prices for specialty-drug medications often significantly exceed a health plan's maximum out-of-pocket limits – protecting consumers from one of the highest and fasting growing prescription drug segments. An AHIP analysis of 150 drugs on specialty-drug formularies found that over half cost more than $100,000 year – in other words, the *monthly cost* of many specialty drugs exceeds the annual MOOP.[164] While these drugs often provide tremendous clinical benefits when medically necessary, their high prices and growing use for treatment of chronic conditions in larger populations threatens the

---

[161] Centers for Medicare & Medicaid Services (CMS), "National Health Expenditures Projections 2016-2025," and National Health Expenditure (NHE), "Historical and Projections 1960-2025," at https://www.cms.gov/Research-Statistics-Data-and-Systems/Statistics-Trends-and-Reports/NationalHealthExpendData/NationalHealthAccountsProjected.html The NHE accounts detail how much consumers pay each year to fill retail prescriptions including cash purchases, insurance deductibles, co-payments, and coinsurance. Annual insurance premiums are not included in out-of-pocket spending.

[162] The Henry J. Kaiser Family Foundation. "New Analysis Finds Out-of-Pocket Prescription Drug Spending Decreasing on Average, But More People Spending in Excess of $1,000 a Year." October 2016.

[163] "Employer Health Benefits 2016 Annual Survey" (exhibit 7.36), Kaiser Family Foundation and Health Research and Educational Trust, 2016. http://files.kff.org/attachment/Report-Employer-Health-Benefits-2016-Annual-Survey 20 "High Priced Drugs: Estimates for Annual Per-Patient Expenditures for 150 Specialty Medications," *AHIP*, April 2016.

[164] "High Priced Drugs: Estimates for Annual Per-Patient Expenditures for 50 Specialty Medications," *AHIP*, April 2016.

availability of affordable coverage options for *all consumers*. With an expected 225 new specialty drugs coming to market over the next five years, health plans, employers, and other stakeholders are searching for innovative, market-based strategies to restrain cost growth while simultaneously maintaining access to safe and effective drugs for patients.

Reducing Prescription Drug Costs through Rebate Negotiations

While prescription drug pricing in the private sector is complex, in many cases, health plans are able to negotiate with manufacturers to provide savings for all consumers. Health plans negotiate with drug manufacturers for lower prices – and then pass those savings on in the form of lower premiums and lower out-of-pocket costs for all consumers. The focus on how some of these savings, which sometimes take the form of "rebates," are distributed to consumers – whether to a small group of patients or across the broader covered population – is a deliberate tactic to obscure the more serious issues surrounding the lack of competition, transparency, and accountability in the pricing of prescription drugs.

In discussing rebates, it is important to understand the role they play within the broader system for setting the cost of drugs that consumers pay at the pharmacy. It is also important to understand that for some branded drugs and biologics without therapeutic alternatives, manufacturers' willingness to negotiate on price is small or nonexistent. Further, rebates are not commonly found for physician-administered drugs, which account for 30 percent of prescription drug spending.[165]

The bottom line is that the original list price of a drug is solely determined and controlled by the drug company – not the market – and it drives the entire pricing process. And if the original list price is high, the final cost that a consumer pays will be high. It is that simple: the problem is the price.

Unfortunately, manufacturers of branded drugs and biologics are working to divert attention from high prescription drug prices and instead point to problems in the drug supply chain and the role of wholesalers and pharmacy benefit managers (PBMs). However, we should focus on how the supply chain actually works. Manufacturers sometimes sell their products directly to the pharmacy (e.g., large chain retail pharmacies), but more often sell their products through a wholesaler. The price that pharmacies and wholesalers pay is highly correlated to the original list price set by the manufacturer. Wholesalers and some pharmacies may acquire the drug at a modest reduction off the list price as a result of volume and/or prompt pay discounts. These discounts are not significant because wholesalers do not influence the "market share" of specific prescription drugs. Wholesalers then take possession of the drug and distribute

[165] "Trends in Specialty Drug Benefits," *Pharmacy Benefit Management Institute*, 2017.

and resell the drug to pharmacies (e.g., smaller community pharmacies) after a small markup above the discounted price.[166] This total cost represents the pharmacy's acquisition cost.

At this point, the consumer enters the process. For individuals who lack health insurance but are prescribed a medication, they often pay the highest prices, especially for branded drugs. Typically, they pay the full list price set by the drug company (or the pharmacy acquisition cost) plus a markup.

By contrast, for individuals with insurance who are dispensed a prescription drug from a pharmacy in the health plan's network, the pharmacy typically communicates electronically with a PBM, which administers drug benefits under a contract with the health plan. From the PBM, the pharmacy receives confirmation of coverage; whether the drug is subject to any utilization management tools, such as prior authorization; whether there are any potential safety issues, such as quantity limits or drug-drug interactions; the reimbursement amount to be paid by the plan; and the co-payment or co-insurance owed by the consumer. The total payment to the pharmacy is typically based on a negotiated contract rate between the pharmacy and the health plan (or the PBM acting on behalf of the health plan). This contract reimburses the pharmacy for its acquisition cost and provides a dispensing fee.

The amount that the consumer or patient pays depends on several factors: (1) the negotiated rate between the plan and pharmacy; (2) the type of drug (i.e., branded or generic); (3) the plan's benefit design (e.g., co-pay or co-insurance); and (4) where the enrollee is within that benefit design at the time of purchase (e.g., in the deductible period, copayment period, MOOP limit or catastrophic phase for those in Medicare Part D). The pharmacy collects the appropriate cost sharing amount from the consumer and receives the remainder from the health plan or PBM at later settlement time based on the payment terms under the contract. (The process described above assumes that there are no manufacturer-sponsored drug coupons and/or co-payment cards, where the manufacturer directly pays a large portion of the consumer's cost sharing. These payment schemes are not operationally transparent to payers, distort an already dysfunctional pricing market, and further complicate a confusing process for consumers.)

Given that the amounts charged by pharmacies for branded drugs reflects the pharmacies' acquisition costs, *these charges are closely correlated to the list price set exclusively by the pharmaceutical manufacturer*. That is why out-of-control drug prices show up at pharmacy counters. It is also why health plans aggressively negotiate with manufacturers for ways to reduce the impact of these prices, so they can pass savings onto consumers. For example, if a health plan's pharmacy and therapeutics committee determines that two or more drugs are therapeutically equivalent and eligible for formulary inclusion, health plans (or PBMs) negotiate with manufacturers for rebates in

---

[166] "Prescription Drug Pricing in the Private Sector," Congressional Budget Office, 2007. https://www.cbo.gov/sites/default/files/110th-congress-2007-2008/reports/01-03-prescriptiondrug.pdf.

exchange for plans placing the drugs on a preferred formulary tier and/or waving utilization management tools, such as step therapy protocols. Since drug costs comprise a significant portion of a health plan's total costs, these discounts, which typically take the form of rebates, reduce the net price of the drug.

Rebate amounts typically are calculated and paid by a manufacturer to a health plan on an aggregate basis, long after an individual prescription is filled by a consumer. Because rebates are extended based on actual aggregated utilization by a specific population, they are paid several months after the drug has been prescribed and dispensed and all the data can be reconciled. In designing their plan benefits and developing premium rates in advance of the upcoming coverage year, health plans calculate an estimate of the aggregate rebates they expect to receive. Since drug costs comprise a significant portion of a health plan's total costs, plans may use these estimated discounts to reduce the premiums they charge for the overall benefit. Alternatively, plans may incorporate the estimates into lower point-of-sale pricing for individual drugs that generate the rebates.

By reducing the net price and cost of drugs, all consumers benefit. The savings from discounts and rebates are passed on through improvements to benefit packages, reductions in premiums, and/or lower out-of-pocket costs. This represents a broad and direct benefit for millions of consumers whether they get their coverage through Medicare, on their own, or through their employer.

An example of successful private sector negotiations between health plan sponsors and manufacturers can be found in Medicare Part D. Medicare prescription drug costs have increased by 8 percent annually, from about $67 billion in 2011 to almost $100 billion in 2016. During that same time, the average premium paid by beneficiaries only increased by $2 or about 1 percent annually.[167]

Preserving these health plan practices is essential to supporting market-based solutions, which we discuss in the next section, for providing consumers relief from high prescription drug costs.

AHIP's Recommendations for Reducing Prescription Drug Prices

The problem with prescription drug pricing does not lie with health plans, wholesalers, pharmacies, providers, or patients. The cost crisis is a direct result of actions by the pharmaceutical industry to take advantage of a broken market. As the committee explores strategies for reducing prescription drug prices, we urge you to consider our recommendations for effective, market-based solutions in three areas: (1) delivering real competition; (2) ensuring open and honest drug pricing; and (3) delivering value to

[167] Medicare Trustees 2017 report. https://www.cms.gov/Research-Statistics-Data-and-Systems/Statistics-Trends-and-Reports/ReportsTrustFunds/Downloads/TR2017.pdf.

patients. Many of these recommendations were raised in a report recently released by the National Academies of Sciences, Engineering, and Medicine entitled, "Making Medicines Affordable: A National Imperative."[168]

Delivering Real Competition

- Create a Robust Biosimilars Market: Biosimilars offer great promise in generating cost savings for consumers. Some of the costliest and most widely-used biologics have been on the market for decades without biosimilar competition. To achieve this promise, it is important to ensure that the FDA promulgates regulations that promote a robust market and ensure providers and patients have unbiased information available to them about the benefits of biosimilars. For example, FDA policies for the labeling, naming, and interchangeability of biosimilars should provide clarity, ensure safety, and avoid unnecessary regulatory hurdles. We also need to address anti-competitive strategies by pharma companies, such as the development of "patent estates," and tactics aimed at delaying the availability of biosimilars.
- Reduce Rules, Regulation and Red Tape to Generic Entry: The FDA should be provided the necessary resources to clear the backlog of generic drug applications, particularly for classes of drugs with no or limited generic competition. To address patent abuses, anti-competitive tactics such as "pay for delay" settlements and "product hopping" should be prohibited, and the Inter Partes Review (IPR) process through the U.S. Patent and Trademark Office should be preserved. Additional legislation is needed to require brand manufacturers to share information and scientific samples to promote the development of generic drugs.
- Revisit and Revise Orphan Drug Incentives: The Orphan Drug Act is being exploited. We urge Congress to ensure that the Orphan Drug Act's incentives are used by those developing medicines to treat rare diseases – not as a gateway to premium pricing and blockbuster sales beyond orphan indications. In cases of rare diseases for which no effective therapy yet exists, we need to ensure that newly approved drugs are priced in accordance with their efficacy.

Ensuring Open and Honest Price Setting

- Publish True R&D Costs and Explain Price Setting and Price Increases: As part of the FDA approval process, manufacturers should be required to disclose

---

[168] National Academies of Sciences, Engineering, and Medicine. 2017. Making Medicines Affordable: A National Imperative. Washington, DC: The National Academies Press. https://doi.org/10.17226/24946.

information regarding the intended launch price, the use of the drug, and direct and indirect research and development costs. After approval, manufacturers should provide appropriate transparency into list price increases.

- Limit Third-Party Schemes that Raise Costs: Policymakers should examine and address the impact of drug coupons and co-pay card programs – and related charitable foundations – on overall pharmaceutical cost trends. These programs often work to steer consumers towards higher priced drugs, and hide the true impact of rising prescription drug costs. It is important to ensure that existing protections aimed at prohibiting their use in certain federal programs are sufficient. In the commercial market, payers need more transparency into when co-pay cards and coupons are being used.
- Evaluate DTC Advertising Impact: According to an article in the *Washington Post*, nine out of the ten biggest pharmaceutical companies spend nearly twice as much on sales, marketing, and advertising than they spend on research and development.[169] We urge the committee to assess the impacts of the growth in direct-to-consumer (DTC) advertising, particularly broadcast advertising, and evaluate the best approaches for conveying information to consumers. As part of this assessment, it is important to examine the impact of DTC advertising on physician prescribing behavior and/or its effect on generic drug availability and utilization.

Delivering Value to Patients

- Inform Patients and Physicians on Effectiveness and Value: Increased funding is needed for private and public efforts to provide information to physicians and their patients on the comparative and cost-effectiveness of different treatments. These tools can help facilitate appropriate assessments about the value and effectiveness of different treatment approaches, particularly those with very high costs. The *New York Times* has highlighted a prime example from one of AHIP's members that has developed a "counter-detailing" program where the health plan uses representatives who previously worked in the pharmaceutical industry to educate physicians on lower cost but equally effective generic alternatives to high-priced branded drugs.[170]
- Expand Value-Based Formulary Programs: It is important to promote value-based payments in public programs like Medicare for drugs and medical technologies, based on agreed-upon standards for quality and outcomes.

[169] "Big pharmaceutical companies are spending far more on marketing than research," *Washington Post*, February 11, 2015.

[170] "Selling Doctors on Cutting Drug Costs," *New York Times*, June 6, 2017.

- Reduce Regulatory Barriers to Value-Based Pricing: We encourage Congress and the Administration to address existing statutory and regulatory requirements (e.g., Medicaid best price rules) that may inhibit the development of pay-for-indication and other value-based strategies in public programs. Specifically, it is important to examine whether Medicaid's best price requirements are negatively impacting private sector negotiations between plans/PBMs and manufacturers by essentially creating a price floor for prescription drugs.[171]

Thank you for considering our perspectives on these important issues. We are strongly committed to solving the cost crisis. With the right solutions that deliver real competition and create more consumer choices, we can bring down the cost of prescription drugs. We look forward to working with the committee to advance market-based solutions to ensure that consumers have access to affordable medications.

Mr. BURGESS. Thank you, Mr. Eyles.

Mr. Nickels, you're recognized for 3 minutes, please, to summarize your opening statement.

STATEMENT OF TOM NICKELS

Mr. NICKELS. Mr. Chairman, my name is Tom Nickels. I am Executive Vice President of the American Hospitals Association. I appreciate the opportunity to be here today on behalf of the——

Mr. WALDEN. Your mic's not on.

Mr. NICKELS. Thank you very much—our 5,000 hospital and health system members. I would like to briefly address three issues: the drug supply chain, drug pricing, and the 340B program.

America's hospitals rely on innovative drug therapies to save lives every day. Modern pharmaceuticals play a critical role in getting patients healthy and helping them maintain that health.

The drug supply chain is, as Chairman Walden said, complex, with the number of steps between the development and delivery of a drug. Hospitals primarily intersect with the drug supply chain in their role as purchasers and dispensers of pharmaceuticals. At the beginning of the chain, our academic medical center members play a leading role in both the development and testing of new drug therapies. Studies show that these efforts discover drugs that have a disproportionately important clinical effect in therapies that

[171] "Health Policy Brief: Medicaid Best Price," *Health Affairs*, August 10, 2017. https://www.healthaffairs.org/do/10.1377/hpb20171008.000173/full/.

can be used for widespread public health concerns. Further down the supply chain all hospitals are major purchasers of drugs used in clinical settings.

Hospitals work with manufacturers and group purchasing organizations to negotiate the best prices for the drugs they use and reduce administrative expenses. Most hospitals do retain some direct contracting with drug manufacturers primarily for branded therapies for which there is no competition. Once a hospital acquires a drug, it manages its supply in hospital-based pharmacies who work with prescribing clinicians to develop and manage the formulary, following standards that take into account evidence-based clinical, ethical, legal, and other factors.

Pharmacists also manage the dispensing of medications to the appropriate clinical staff who then deliver the drug to the patient. In terms of pricing, spending on pharmaceuticals, as has been noted, has increased dramatically over the last several years and the primary driver is higher prices. We see both higher launch prices for new drugs and increases in prices for existing drugs. Limited competition and drug shortages have also facilitated this growth.

Whether GPO or a hospital is negotiating, the starting price, as has been pointed out, is the price set by the manufacturer. The ability of the GPO or hospital to obtain a discount off the price largely has to do with volume and whether and how much competition exists. In instances where no competition exists such as for many of the new high-cost specialty drugs, large discounts are not available.

The burden of these high prices falls on all purchasers including patients and the providers who treat them. For example, hospitals frequently see patients show up in the emergency department or return for follow-up care sicker than when they left because they were unable to afford their drugs.

Hospitals as drug purchasers also face significant resource constraints as spending on drugs increase. Hospitals must make trade-offs between investments in staff, technology, and facilities upgrade and paying more for drugs.

Lastly, I want to mention the 340B program which permits safety net hospitals to care for communities with a high number of low-income and uninsured to stretch scarce federal resources as far as possible, reaching more eligible patients and providing more comprehensive services.

The 340B program enables these hospitals to serve their communities by reinvesting savings from reduced drug prices into programs that benefit vulnerable patients at no additional cost.

Thank you very much for the opportunity to testify. [The prepared statement of Mr. Nickels follows:]

Statement of the American Hospital Association, before the Health Subcommittee of the Committee on Energy and Commerce of the U.S. House of Representatives, "Examining the Drug Supply Chain," December 13, 2017

On behalf of our nearly 5,000 member hospitals, health systems and other health care organizations, and our clinician partners – including more than 270,000 affiliated physicians, 2 million nurses and other caregivers – and the 43,000 health care leaders who belong to our professional membership groups, the American Hospital Association (AHA) appreciates the opportunity to submit for the record our comments on the drug supply chain and the cost of medications.

America's hospitals rely on innovative drug therapies to save lives every day. Without them, more lives would be lost to diseases like cancer and AIDS, and others who now can live comfortably while managing their chronic conditions would see their quality of life deteriorate. In short, modern pharmaceuticals play a critical role in getting patients healthy and helping them maintain health. Hospitals primarily interact with the drug supply chain in their role as purchasers and dispensers of pharmaceuticals. They also play a crucial role in the development of new drug therapies.

Spending on pharmaceuticals has increased dramatically over the past several years. The burden of this increase falls on all purchasers, including patients and the providers who treat them. For example, hospitals frequently see patients show up in the emergency department or return for follow up care sicker than when they left because they were unable to afford their medications. Just as many patients face difficult choices when considering purchasing medications, hospitals, as drug purchasers, face significant resource constraints and trade-offs as spending on drugs increases.

The primary driver behind increased drug spending is higher prices, not increases in utilization. Within the health care field, "pharmaceuticals" was "the fastest growing category" in terms of pricing for every month of 2016 and for most months of 2017.[172] We see both higher launch prices for new drugs and increases in prices for existing drugs. Limited competition and drug shortages have facilitated this price growth.

Hospitals work with manufacturers and group purchasing organizations (GPOs) to negotiate the best prices for the drugs they use. However, for many drugs, the starting point for the negotiation is high, with some new drugs hitting the market at $55,000,[173]

---

[172] Altarum Institute, "Price Briefs," October 2017, September 2017, August 2017, July 2017, June 2017.

[173] Toich, L., "Will Hepatitis C Virus Medication Costs Drop in the Years Ahead?" *Pharmacy Times*, February 8, 2017. http://www.pharmacytimes.com/resource-centers/hepatitisc/will-hepatitis-c-virus-medicaton-costs-drop-in-the-years-ahead.

$475,000,[174] and even $750,000[175] for a course of treatment. This price does not include the cost of managing and delivering the drug, or any of the ancillary services required to support the patient undergoing treatment.

We explore these challenges in more detail below.

How Hospitals and Health Systems Interface with the Drug Supply Chain

The drug supply chain is complicated, with a number of steps between the development and the delivery of a drug. America's hospitals and health systems did not design the supply chain, but they do interface with it. At the very beginning of the chain, academic medical centers are responsible for a significant amount of the research used to develop and test new drugs. Closer to the end of the chain, all hospitals are major purchasers of drugs used in clinical settings. Below we provide more information on our members' roles in the drug supply chain.

Research and Development

Academic medical centers play a leading role in both the development of the underlying science supporting new drug therapies (basic science research), as well as the development and testing of new therapies (applied or translational research). A combination of public and private funding supports this work, including grants from the National Institutes of Health, philanthropy and biopharmaceutical companies.

A report from Tufts University underlined that "a close and synergistic relationship between [the biopharmaceutical and academic medical center] sectors is critical to ensuring a robust national capacity."[176] The report noted that more than 50 percent of researchers at academic medical centers contribute to drug and device medical trials, and partnerships between biopharmaceutical companies and academic hospitals have increased in recent years.

A *New England Journal of Medicine* report underscored the benefits provided by public-sector research institutions (PSRI), which include academic medical centers and their affiliated universities. Specifically, the study's authors found that PSRI were responsible for 153 drugs, vaccines or new indicators for existing drugs approved by the Food and Drug Administration (FDA) between 1970 and 2009. They also found that hospitals and PSRIs were predisposed to discover drugs that have a disproportionately

---

[174] Sagonowsky, E. "At $475,000, is Novartis' Kymriah a bargain—or another example of skyrocketing prices?" *FiercePharma*, August 31, 2017, https://www.fiercepharma.com/pharma/at-475-000-per-treatment-novartis-kymriah-a-bargain-or-just-another-example-skyrocketing.

[175] Picci, A., "The cost of Biogen's new drug: $750,000 per patient," *CBS News*, December 16, 2016. https://www.cbsnews.com/news/the-cost-of-biogens-new-drug-spinraza-750000-per-patient/.

[176] Milne, Christopher-Paul, et al. *Academic-Industry Partnerships for Biopharmaceutical Research & Development: Advancing Medical Science in the U.S. Tufts Center for the Study of Drug Development.* April 2012. http://csdd.tufts.edu/files/uploads/tuftscsdd_academic-industry.pdf.

important clinical effect[177] and those that could be used for widespread public health concerns, including the treatment of cancer and infectious diseases, as well as vaccination development.[178]

Role as Purchasers and Providers

Hospitals purchase drugs that clinicians use to treat patients in their facilities. Hospitals use several different approaches to acquire drugs. Nearly all hospitals work with GPOs to negotiate prices with manufacturers and to contract with wholesalers for delivery. GPOs enable hospitals to reduce administrative expenses by precluding the need to maintain the staff it would take to negotiate contracts for thousands of drugs. Instead, by relying on GPOs, this contracting function, which is not insignificant, is shared across hundreds or thousands of hospitals. This also often enables hospitals to achieve the best price, as they benefit from the negotiating power the GPO has as a result of aggregating purchasing volume. GPOs can save hospitals 10 to 18 percent on the cost of drugs.[179] Hospitals pay GPOs in different ways, which may include a combination of upfront administrative fees, transaction fees and/or a percentage of discount obtained. One report found that GPOs save the health care system between $25 billion and $55 billion per year.[180]

Most hospitals do retain some direct contracting with drug manufacturers. This is primarily true for branded therapies for which there is no competition. In these instances, manufacturers are not compelled to negotiate with GPOs. In those instances, hospitals may directly negotiate with the manufacturer and contract with the wholesaler for delivery. Only a handful of hospitals directly contract for all of their drug supply. These are larger organizations that have both the patient volume and the staff capacity to make one-on-one negotiations worthwhile. A significant challenge arises for small hospitals that have neither the staff capacity nor the volume to enter into direct negotiations with manufacturers. In some instances, small, rural hospitals have been unable to obtain access to certain therapies.

Whether hospitals are contracting directly or relying on GPOs, the pharmaceutical manufacturers set the starting price in negotiations. The ability of the GPO or hospital to obtain a discount off this initial price largely has to do with volume and whether, and how much, competition for such a therapy exists. In instances where no competition exists, such as for many of the new, high-cost specialty drugs, large discounts are not available.

---

177 Forty-six percent of drugs developed by PSRIs received priority reviews from the FDA – an indication that the drugs offered a substantial improvement over existing treatments. Only 20 percent of new drugs from the private sector received a priority review designation.

178 Stevens, Ashley J., et al. The Role of Public-Sector Research in the Discovery of Drugs and Vaccines. *New England Journal of Medicine* 364: 535-541. February 2011.

179 DeBenedette, V., "The Evolution of Group Purchasing Organizations," *Modern Medicine*, October 10, 2016. http://drugtopics.modernmedicine.com/drug-topics/news/evolution-group-purchasing-organizations?page=0,3.

180 Ibid.

Once a hospital acquires a drug, it manages the supply in hospital-based pharmacies. Hospital pharmacists work with prescribing clinicians to develop and manage the formulary and follow standards for formulary development, which takes into account "evidence-based clinical, ethical, legal, social, philosophical, quality-of-life, safety and economic factors that result in optimal patient care."[181] Pharmacists also manage the dispensing of medications to the appropriate clinical staff, who then deliver the drug to the patient.

Hospital Experience with Drug Spending

Purchasers of prescription drugs have faced significant increases in spending over the past several years. Last week, the Centers for Medicare & Medicaid Services (CMS) released updated National Health Expenditures (NHE) data that showed that retail drug spending increased by 1.3 percent in 2016. While this level of growth may appear low, it follows two consecutive years of expansive growth in retail drug spending: 12.4 percent in 2014 and 8.9 percent in 2015. In other words, the lower growth comes on top of a much higher spending base for drugs. In addition, these figures capture *retail* drug spending only; they do *not* include spending on drugs purchased by providers, such as hospitals.

Detailed non-retail drug spending data is not publicly available, as it is not easily collected. Nearly all payments to hospitals for inpatient care are made on a per discharge (Diagnostic Related Group or DRG) or per diem basis, which means that all input costs are rolled into a single payment. Hospitals are responsible for managing input costs within that fixed payment amount and not all input costs are systematically reported publicly.

In order to explore the experience of non-retail drug purchasers, the AHA and the Federation of American Hospitals worked with the NORC at the University of Chicago last year to collect and evaluate data on inpatient drug spending (see Appendix A). The NORC found that increases in drug spending for inpatient care outpaced what the NHE reported for retail drug spending. Specifically, the NORC found that while retail spending on prescription drugs increased by 10.6 percent between 2013 and 2015, hospital spending on drugs in the inpatient space rose percent per admission during the same period.[182,183]

---

[181] American Society for Health-System Pharmacists, "ASHP Guidelines on the Pharmacy and Therapeutics Committee and the Formulary System," Accessed Dec. 9, 2017 at: https://www.ashp.org/-/media/assets/policy-guidelines/docs/guidelines/gdl-pharmacy-therapeutics-committee-formulary-system.ashx?la=en&hash=EF1E4214CC91C65097AEEECE91BF6EC985AE3E56.

[182] National Health Expenditure Data for 2013 – 2015.

[183] "Trends in Hospital Inpatient Drug Costs: Issues and Challenges," American Hospital Association and the Federation of American Hospitals, October 11, 2016. http://www.aha.org/content/16/aha-fah-rx-report.pdf.

Price, not volume, is the primary driver of this increased spending. After examining data from two GPOs that collectively purchase drugs for more than 1,400 hospitals, the NORC was able to track changes in price, utilization and total spending for a select group of drugs. Consistently, changes in pricing drove increases in spending. These price increases, from the hospitals' perspective, appeared to be random, inconsistent and unpredictable: large unit price increases occurred for both low- and high-volume drugs and for both branded and generic drugs.

Our members were not surprised to learn that their purchasing experience differs from what the NHE reports for retail drugs. In testimony to the Committee on Oversight and Government Reform of the U.S. House of Representatives, one drug manufacturer acknowledged targeting hospital-administered drugs for price increases. Howard Schiller, then-interim CEO and director of Valeant Pharmaceuticals, stated: "Because these drugs are hospital-administered, and not purchased by patients directly, increasing the cost of the drugs to hospitals would affect the hospital's profits on these procedures, but it should not reduce patient access."[184]

While the NORC study supports Mr. Schiller's admission that manufacturers target hospitals for price increases, we challenge his assessment that such practices do not reduce patient access. Researchers at the Cleveland Clinic found that patient access to Valeant drugs nitroprusside and isoproterenol declined after the company increased the prices for both substantially. From 2012 to 2015, 53 percent fewer patients were treated with nitroprusside and 35 percent less were treated with isoproterenol.[185] This is because hospitals bear a heavy burden when the cost of drugs increases, in large part due to how hospital reimbursement it structured, and this has direct implications for the availability of certain drug therapies. Medicare, which is one of the largest payers for most hospitals and on which many commercial insurers base their rates, cannot keep up with new and frequently changing drug prices. The program relies on drug pricing data collected and reported by the Bureau of Labor Statistics, which does a full "refresh" of drug pricing information only every five to seven years. This data lag means that hospital reimbursement does not necessarily increase proportionally to drug price increases. As a result, hospitals must divert other resources to cover higher drug costs, forcing difficult choices between providing adequate compensation to employees, many of whom are highly skilled in professions facing shortages; upgrading and modernizing facilities; purchasing new technologies to improve care; or paying for drugs.

A number of factors contribute to the increase in drug spending, and those factors have evolved over time. In the past several years, hospital have faced widespread price

---

[184] Statement of Howard B. Schiller, Interim Chief Executive Officer and Director, Valeant Pharmaceuticals International, Inc. before the Committee on Oversight and Government Reform of the U.S. House of Representatives, February 4, 2016. https://oversight.house.gov/wp-content/uploads/2016/02/Statement-of-Howard-Schiller-2016-02-04.pdf.

[185] Khot UN, et al. Nitroprusside and Isoproterenol Use after Major Price Increases, *New England Journal of Medicine*, August 10, 2017. http://dx.doi.org/10.1056/NEJMc1700244.

increases on existing drugs. While drug manufacturers have increased some prices by multiple hundreds or even thousands of percent, hospitals report that the 10 to 20 percent increases on widely used generic drugs often have a greater impact on their budgets given the high volumes of these drugs that hospitals purchase. Increasingly, our members report that high launch prices and increased spending due to drug shortages are new challenges they face, as well as budget pressures associated with the ancillary service costs associated with highly complex and potent drugs.

High Launch Prices

Drug manufacturers are increasing the launch prices for new drugs. These prices are the basis for negotiations with purchasers. Examples of recent launch prices include:

- Talz (Eli Lilly), used for treating psoriasis, costs $50,000 a year.[186]
- Keytruda (Merck), used for treating melanoma, costs $152,400 a year.[187]
- Kymriah (Novartis), used for treating leukemia, costs $475,000 for a course of treatment.[188]
- Spinraza (Biogen), used to treat spinal muscular atrophy, costs $750,000 for the first year of treatment and $375,000 per year thereafter.[189]

Drug Shortages

Drug shortages also are a major contributor to increases in drug spending. Medications that experience shortages are largely injectable products that are off patent and have few suppliers; shortages typically arise from quality concerns that cause a halt to production. If a product has few competitors, this disruption cannot be absorbed by other companies and demand outpaces supply. This not only results in a shortage, but also causes prices to rise. For drugs with a sole manufacturer, shortages are exacerbated – since there is no alternative, clinicians must scramble to find the drug or compound the drug in cases where it is possible. They also may recommend an alternative (often less effective) therapy, if one exists. This, in turn, can result in higher spending because manufacturers often capitalize on the situation by increasing the price of the alternative therapy. For example, a 2017 study that examined how drug prices change during supply

---

[186] Waxman, H. et.al, "Getting to the Root of High Prescription Drug Prices: Drivers and potential solutions," *Commonwealth Fund*, Jul 2017. http://www.commonwealthfund.org/~/media/files/publications/fund-report/2017/jul/waxman_high_drug_prices_drivers_solutions_report.pdf?la=en.

[187] Szabo, L., "As Drug Costs Soar, People Delay Or Skip Cancer Treatments," *National Public Radio*, Mar. 15, 2017, https://www.npr.org/sections/health-shots/2017/03/15/520110742/as-drug-costs-soar-people-delay-or-skip-cancer-treatments.

[188] Sagonowsky, E. "At $475,000, is Novartis' Kymriah a bargain—or another example of skyrocketing prices?" *FiercePharma*, August 31, 2017, https://www.fiercepharma.com/pharma/at-475-000-per-treatment-novartis-kymriah-a-bargain-or-just-another-example-skyrocketing.

[189] Picci, A., "The cost of Biogen's new drug: $750,000 per patient," *CBS News*, December 16, 2016. https://www.cbsnews.com/news/the-cost-of-biogens-new-drug-spinraza-750000-per-patient/.

disruptions[190] found that after quality-control issues forced a manufacturer of glycopyrrolate – an injectable agent commonly used before surgery to reduce secretions – to suspend production, the remaining manufacturer increased the price of its product by 855 percent. The list price remained at the new level even after production capacity was restored.

Ancillary Costs

Many new drug therapies are highly potent and come with significant side effects. A recent example is Kymriah, a new blood cancer drug using "CAR-T cell therapy" through which patients' own genes are extracted, modified and reinjected to kill leukemia cells. The potential side effects require extensive ancillary services to monitor patients and prevent infections and other adverse events for a prolonged period of time.

According to the FDA, "Treatment with Kymriah has the potential to cause severe side effects. It carries a boxed warning for cytokine release syndrome (CRS), which is a systemic response to the activation and proliferation of CAR T-cells causing high fever and flu-like symptoms, and for neurological events. Both CRS and neurological events can be life-threatening. Other severe side effects of Kymriah include serious infections, low blood pressure (hypotension), acute kidney injury, fever, and decreased oxygen (hypoxia). Most symptoms appear within one to 22 days following infusion of Kymriah. Since the CD19 antigen is also present on normal B-cells, and Kymriah will also destroy those normal B cells that produce antibodies, there may be an increased risk of infections for a prolonged period of time"[191] (emphasis added).

While these services do not directly increase the cost of the drug, they do impact the overall cost of care.

Hospitals' Approach to Reducing Drug Costs

Hospitals and health systems are committed to ensuring patients receive high-value care. Hospital pharmacists continually work to reduce the costs of drug therapies in order to maintain and expand access to care. Specific examples of approaches taken by hospitals include:

- Identifying equally effective and safe alternative therapies that may be less costly;
- Ongoing monitoring of pricing changes to anticipate upcoming needs;

---

[190] Davies, B., Hwang, T., and Kesselheim, A., "Ensuring Access to Injectable Generic Drugs — The Case of Intravesical BCG for Bladder Cancer," *New England Journal of Medicine*, April 13, 2017.

[191] Food & Drug Administration, "FDA approval brings first gene therapy to the United States," August 30, 2017. https://www.fda.gov/NewsEvents/Newsroom/PressAnnouncements/ucm574058.htm.

- Improving inventory management, including by changing how and where medicines are stocked and how they are delivered to clinicians;
- Reducing waste by identifying safe approaches to splitting excessively large single dose vials into multiple doses; and
- Compounding therapies in-house.

Despite these efforts, increased drug spending remains a challenge and one which we believe requires legislative and regulatory intervention. We urge Congress and the Administration to support patients and providers by taking immediate action to reign in the rising cost of drugs, including by passing the Creating and Restoring Equal Access to Equivalent Samples Act (CREATES Act) and protecting the 340B Program. We also offer a broader set of comprehensive solutions in Appendix B.

The CREATES Act

Generic drugs are one tool for reducing drug prices, as they increase competition after the monopoly enjoyed by drug manufacturer ends when a drug's patent expires. The CREATES Act targets two forms of anticompetitive behavior that are being used to block and delay entry of generic drugs. The first is known as sample-sharing. This occurs when brand-name drug companies refuse to sell samples of their product to potential generic competitors so the generic company cannot perform testing to show that its product is bioequivalent to the brand-name product, a prerequisite for approval by the FDA. The second involves participation in a shared safety protocol. This occurs when brand-name manufacturers whose products require a distribution safety protocol refuse to allow generic competitors to participate in that safety protocol, which is needed to gain FDA approval. The CREATES Act allows a generic drug manufacturer facing the sample-sharing delay tactic to bring an action in federal court for injunctive relief, such as to obtain the sample it needs. The bill also authorizes a judge to award damages to deter future delaying conduct. We urge Congress to pass the CREATES Act.

The 340B Program

Congress created the 340B program to permit safety-net hospitals that care for communities with a high number of low-income and uninsured patients "to stretch scarce Federal resources as far as possible, reaching more eligible patients and providing more comprehensive services."[192] Section 340B of the Public Health Service Act requires pharmaceutical manufacturers participating in Medicaid to sell outpatient drugs at discounted prices to these health care organizations. For 25 years, the 340B program has been critical in helping hospitals expand access to lifesaving prescription drugs and

---

[192] https://www.hrsa.gov/opa/index.html.

comprehensive health care services to communities across the country with a high number of low-income and uninsured individuals, *at no cost to the federal government.*

Given the increasingly high cost of pharmaceuticals, the 340B program provides critical support to help hospitals' efforts to build healthy communities. In 2015, the 340B program accounted for only 2.8 percent of the $457 billion in annual drug purchases made in the U.S. However, hospitals were able to use those savings to support many programs that are improving and saving lives.[193]

Thirty percent of the hospitals that serve 340B communities are located in rural communities. Nearly 50 percent of those hospitals' communities significantly exceeded the minimum Medicare disproportionate share hospital (DSH) adjustment percentage of 11.75 percent, which is the qualifying threshold for the 340B program. In fact, one-fifth of these hospitals have a Medicare DSH adjustment percentage of more than 25 percent. Many 340B hospitals are financially vulnerable, and in 2015, one out of every four hospitals had a negative operating margin.[194]

The 340B program enables these hospitals to serve their communities by reinvesting savings from reduced drug pricing into programs that benefit their patients, particularly their vulnerable patients. In 2015, 340B hospitals provided $23.8 billion in uncompensated care.[195] Examples of programs provided by 340B hospitals include:

- Financial assistance programs for patients unable to afford their prescriptions;
- Provision of clinical pharmacy services, such as disease management programs or medication therapy management;
- Increased access to other medical services, such as obstetrics, diabetes education, oncology services and other ambulatory services;
- Establishment of additional outpatient clinics to improve access to care;
- Community outreach programs; and
- Free vaccinations for vulnerable populations.

In addition, an examination of hospital services illustrates that 340B hospitals provide access to essential services to their communities:[196]

- Nearly two-thirds of 340B hospitals provide trauma care.
- Three-quarters of 340B hospitals provide pediatric medical surgical services.
- Nearly all 340B hospitals have obstetrics (OB) units.

---

[193] Assistant Secretary for Planning and Evaluation, "Issue Brief: Observations on Trends in Prescription Drug Spending," March, 2016. https://aspe.hhs.gov/system/files/pdf/187586/Drugspending.pdf and The Health Resources and Services Administration, "FY 2018 Justification of Estimates for Appropriations Committees," https://www.hrsa.gov/sites/default/files/hrsa/about/budget/budget-justification-2018.pdf.

[194] AHA 2015 Annual Survey Data.

[195] AHA 2015 Annual Survey Data.

[196] Ibid.

- Approximately two-thirds of 340B hospitals provide psychiatric services.
- 42 percent of 340B hospitals provide substance abuse or dependency services.
- 58 percent of 340B hospitals have Neonatal Intensive Care Units (NICUs).
- Nearly all 340B hospitals provide breast cancer screening.

The 340B program is under threat, especially as a result of a recent change in Medicare payment policy that reduces by nearly 30 percent, or $1.6 billion, Medicare payments to certain hospitals for outpatient drugs purchased under the 340B program. Cuts of this magnitude will negate the intent of the program, reducing resources that hospitals use to expand access to care and services to vulnerable communities. We urge Congress to pass H.R. 4392, which would prevent these cuts from going into effect and reducing critical health care resources in vulnerable communities.

Conclusion

We appreciate the opportunity to provide these comments and support the Committee's efforts and attention to examining the issue of the drug supply chain and the cost of medications. We remain deeply committed to working with Congress, the Administration and other health care stakeholders to ensure that all Americans can access the drug therapies they need to lead healthy, happy and productive lives.

Mr. BURGESS. Thank you, Mr. Nickels.

Dr. Harmon, you're recognized for 3 minutes to summarize your opening statement, please.

STATEMENT OF GERALD HARMON

Dr. HARMON. Thank you, Chairman Burgess, Ranking Member Green, distinguished members of the subcommittee.

I am Gerry Harmon. I am a practising family physician from Parleys Island, South Carolina, and Chairman of the AMA Board of Trustees.

I think we can all agree that our goal is to ensure patients have access to the right medication at the right time. I want to speak to the physician's role of prescribing the most appropriate treatment and the challenges my patients and I face.

Affordability in price can indeed be a major barrier, but so are the various administrative hoops that we have to jump through when prescribing medications. Such hoops includes things such as prior authorizations, frequently changing drug formularies, step therapy, nonstandardized forms, all put in place by insurance companies in an attempt to manage costs.

These barriers usually delay treatment for my patients and, clearly, take time away from patient care. As an example, in the few days I've been away from my practice on a trip such as today, I received an email from a long-time patient who has recently changed his insurance coverage. His blood pressure medicine that he's been stable on for years now is not on the new formulary under his new plan and he's down to his last 30 days of therapy. I am going to have to call his pharmacy benefit managers—PBM, request a form and a fax number, fill out the form with some data points and fax it back.

Eventually, I hope to get some ideas from the insurance company and/or the PBM about what types of different medications I might consider or steps I might follow in order to prescribe my patient's medicine. I cannot do this in a standard form or electronically via email. My patient, meanwhile, is at risk for running out of medications or changing to a less effective therapy. Clearly, that's going to endanger his health. He could end up going to the emergency room or having a serious illness such as a heart attack or a stroke, which adds enormous cost to the entire health care system.

Such efforts to maintain cost and value in such an otherwise stable patient are, clearly, misdirected. In another venue, doctors who administer biologic medications to treat certain cancer, rheumatoid arthritis patients face even more costs and challenges than a primary care doctor like myself.

Small community practices in particular are at a disadvantage relative to hospitals and large practices when it comes to requiring biological medications for special patients. Patients usually have to pay a high co-pay for medicine. We've alluded to that in other testimony. It could cost tens of thousands of dollars and the co-pay can be as high as 20 or 30 percent, and that's a bunch of money to my patient population.

When the patients cannot afford the co-pay, the physicians, who must pay for the medicines up front, cannot manage the debt, and the patients are referred to treated in the hospitals or outpatient settings that are much more expensive. And these are just some of the challenges doctors face when helping patients navigate medicines.

What could help physicians like myself? We've offered some opportunities for improvement in our written testimony. There are so many opportunities. We can discuss them almost ad infinitum.

In closing, I would like to thank you. AMA looks forward to working with you on this issue.

Thank you.

[The prepared statement of Dr. Harmon follows:]

TESTIMONY OF THE AMERICAN MEDICAL ASSOCIATION, HEALTH SUBCOMMITTEE, HOUSE COMMITTEE ON ENERGY AND COMMERCE

RE: Examining the Pharmaceutical Supply Chain
Presented by: Gerald Harmon, MD
December 13, 2017

The American Medical Association (AMA) applauds the Health Subcommittee of the U.S. House of Representatives Committee on Energy and Commerce for convening key stakeholders to examine the pharmaceutical supply chain and consider well-crafted and effective public policy solutions that would alleviate the high cost of prescription drugs.[197] It is our goal to ensure that patients have access to and receive the right medical treatment at the right time, and we welcome the opportunity to share with the Subcommittee the steps that physicians take to help patients receive their medically necessary prescriptions or physician-administered drug treatments. Below we briefly outline what the escalating cost and complexity of obtaining these treatments mean for patient adherence, timely access, and health outcomes. The AMA has a large body of policies that address the rising cost of prescription drugs and we look forward to continuing dialogue to seek solutions to improve access, lower costs, and reduce the administrative burdens without stifling innovation.

The Cost to Patients, Physician Practices, and the Health System

Patients are facing mounting costs and administrative barriers to obtaining prescription drugs from a pharmacy or through physician-administered treatments. Patients and physicians often must navigate complex and resource intensive requirements. These are consequential problems that may negatively impact the ability of patients to obtain needed medications in a timely manner and to maintain treatment.

Physicians experience and see first-hand the difficulty and burden high pharmaceutical costs have imposed on their patients, on physician practices, and the broader health care system. The burden, however, is not solely caused by the escalating cost of pharmaceuticals, but the increase in medication utilization management policies due to those higher costs as well. Patients may take greater clinical risks when treatments are cost prohibitive. If patients delay, forgo, or ration their pharmaceutical treatment, their health status may deteriorate. This means patients who cannot afford their medication will eventually require medical interventions in more costly care settings,

[197] Throughout this document the term pharmaceuticals and prescription drugs are referenced—both encompass biologicals and biosimilars as well.

such as emergency departments, when their condition is at a more advanced stage of disease.

The time and expense that physicians and the extended care team, patients, and their caregivers spend complying with documentation requirements is another significant issue that needs to be addressed. Physicians and their staff will typically undertake multiple steps before the patient is able to receive their prescription, including: finding clinically appropriate but more affordable alternatives; identifying and applying for discounts or patient assistance programs; and filing appeals or exception requests continues to divert the finite resources away from direct patient clinical care to a large volume of paperwork, emails, facsimiles, and phone calls. Administrative burdens have also led to increasing delays in medically necessary care. As outlined below, the high cost of pharmaceuticals not only negatively impacts the patient who requires them and cannot afford them, the cost is also passed on to other patients when physicians and the extended heath care team are consumed with repetitive administrative minutiae documenting, often repeatedly, medical need in order to comply with expanding insurer medication management utilization program policies. In addition, the two pincers that patients and physicians are squeezed between—high priced pharmaceuticals and increasingly onerous documentation requirements— continue to erode the physician-patient relationship, as well as lower morale and fuel burn-out among the health care team members.

Two Broad Pathways: Pharmacy-Dispensed or Physician-Administered Pharmaceuticals

While physician practices are varied and patient coverage and preferences differ markedly, there are generally two different ways in which patients receive their prescription drug treatments: pharmacy-dispensed or physician-administered.

First, a physician or other duly licensed clinician prepares a prescription and it is either transmitted electronically, or in some instances, provided to the patient who then takes it to a pharmacy. The physician is not involved in the acquisition or dispensing of the medication, but, as detailed below, this does not insulate physicians and their practices from administrative and other resources costs. The patient then must obtain the medication from a pharmacy. The dispensing pharmacy is responsible for obtaining any applicable payments from the patient and health insurer. For patients who receive a prescription from a clinician, many of the policies, processes, and challenges to ensure they receive and take their medicine are similar across Medicare and commercial insurers. For Medicare beneficiaries this may be a benefit under the Medicare Part D prescription drug benefit. Alternatively, Medicare Part D benefits may be bundled together with inpatient and outpatient covered services in a single private plan (referred to as Medicare Advantage/Part C).

Alternatively, a physician may administer a pharmaceutical treatment to the patient. In this scenario, the physician must obtain, store, prepare, and administer the pharmaceutical. The physician is responsible for seeking reimbursement from any applicable insurer in addition to any applicable patient co-payment or deductible. Patients who have health insurance may have coverage for outpatient care that includes physician-administered pharmaceutical treatments, which, by way of example, for Medicare beneficiaries are covered and paid under the Part B benefit and are often referred to as Part B drugs. Part B drugs are a subset of pharmaceuticals that treat chronic and/or severe illnesses, such as cancer and rheumatoid arthritis, which require much greater physician involvement than a normal prescription that patients obtain from a pharmacy. Part B drugs typically must be injected or infused in a physician's office or outpatient facility, and often require clinical monitoring. Based on a recent U.S. Government Accountability Office (GAO) report, the general payment methodologies for physician-administered drugs vary across public insurers and commercial insurers.

There are different reimbursement systems for the Medicare Part B physician-administered drugs and those covered under Medicare Part D, and these differences are mirrored in the commercial market. The challenges that patients and physicians face are mounting under both pathways, as discussed below. The methods used by commercial and public insurers to cover and calculate payment for medication varies based on whether it is a pharmacy-dispensed or a physician-administered drug. This has implications for the requirements, tasks, and resources that physicians and their staff must expend to ensure that a patient has timely access to treatments.

Pharmacy-Dispensed Pharmaceuticals

With increasing frequency over the past decade, physicians no longer are able to prepare a clinically appropriate prescription for their patient and be reasonably assured that the patient will be able to receive the medication and take it on a consistent basis as prescribed. In 2016, 89 percent of prescriptions dispensed were for generic pharmaceuticals;[198] yet, the savings provided by generic use has been overshadowed by the increase in prices for brand drugs as well as for older, previously affordable, pharmaceutical treatments. These developments have led to a burgeoning number of more restrictive commercial and public insurer prescription drug plan designs and medication utilization management policies.

When prescribing a pharmaceutical for a patient, physicians must consider clinical factors, patient preferences, and other circumstances, as well as the cost to the patient based on variable insurance benefit designs, such as drug formularies. Yet, as discussed

---

[198] *Generic Pharmaceutical Access & Savings in the U.S.*, Association for Accessible Medicines (2017).

below, physicians rarely have readily accessible, accurate, up-to-date information on a patient's coverage and the insurer's utilization policies, along with clinical options and cost, at the point-of-prescribing. Both public and commercial insurers now have a large number of utilization management programs, such as medication step therapy, dosing limits, and prior authorization. The lack of uniformity or consistency places additional strain on a physician practice.

Prior Authorization

Insurers outline in their coverage design that certain pharmaceuticals are subject to the insurer's review and approval before a prescription will be covered, even if it is on the formulary. Typically, a physician and patient learn that prior authorization is required when the pharmacy staff notify them. The physician and clinical staff will then need to provide documentation in the format required by the insurer and meet the insurer's criteria. This will often entail a significant amount of physician, pharmacist, and their extended teams' time. Every insurer has its own forms, criteria, and processes. This lack of standardization exacerbates delays and overall complexity. If an adverse decision is made by the insurer, the physician and staff will often need to assist the patient with filing an exceptions request or an appeal. Both an exceptions request and an appeal involve additional time, delay, and paperwork.

Step Therapy

Insurers have developed formularies of certain covered pharmaceuticals that require a patient to try a less expensive drug to ascertain whether it is effective before a more costly alternative will be covered. This step therapy requirement may not be known to the patient or physician in advance. The pharmacy staff will typically notify the patient and physician practice after the prescription is transmitted through e-prescribing or provided by the patient to the pharmacy. This, in turn, will require additional clinician and staff time (for both the physician practice and the pharmacy) to determine whether the alternative medication is appropriate based on the particular medical needs of the patient. If it is not, the physician will, after consulting with the patient, submit an exceptions request or appeal requiring the submission of additional documentation. In addition, it may require a subsequent patient visit and more time to assess the effectiveness of the treatment including submitting documentation to satisfy the insurer that the less expensive alternative was not effective for the patient. Step therapy "shifts clinical decision-making away from physicians and toward centralized policies that define treatment steps for patient populations based on the potential for more cost-effective care."[199] Evidence is lacking that step therapy approaches improve patient outcomes. Rather, step therapy can "delay access to the most efficacious therapies, potentially trades

[199] Does A 'One-Size-Fits-All' Formulary Policy Make Sense? Adrienne Chung, Joanna MacEwan, Dana Goldman. *Health Affairs Blog.*

prescription spending for time and hospital costs to patients and providers," and "fail-first policies, as their name suggests increase the risk of dangerous side effects."[200]

Quantity and Dosing Limits

Increasingly, insurers are placing quantity and dosing limits on certain pharmaceuticals that are part of the covered formulary. Certain drugs may be limited to the amount that a patient may be prescribed per prescription for a certain time period. For example, one insurer limits patients to 30 tablets per prescription for levothyroxine per 30 days. Physicians may have to navigate the appeals or exceptions process for the patient, delaying necessary treatment and absorbing additional time and resources. In addition, insurers may alter the dose that they will cover midway through treatment, which can cause confusion and potentially life-threatening consequences for patients.

The foregoing can create significant barriers for patients by delaying the start or continuation of necessary treatment and negatively affect patient health outcomes. The very manual and time-consuming processes used in these programs place excessive burdens on physicians, the health care team, and pharmacies, and divert valuable resources away from direct patient care. Commercial and public health insurers tout the benefits of these programs to drive value. This comes, however, at the cost of delayed or denied patient care and wasted time and increased inefficiencies on the part of physicians and other clinical staff.

The most appropriate course of treatment for a given medical condition depends on the patient's unique clinical situation and the care plan developed by the physician in consultation with his/her patient. While a particular pharmaceutical might generally be considered appropriate for a condition, the presence of comorbidities or patient intolerances, for example, may necessitate an alternative treatment. The failure to account for this can obstruct proper patient care. Too often, insurer utilization management programs do not allow for flexibility, including the timely overriding of step therapy requirements and appeal of prior authorization denials. Physicians and their patients do not have rapid, standard appeals processes for negative prescription drug utilization management program decisions or other needed exceptions. Too many insurers still do not provide physicians with direct access, such as a toll-free number, to a provider of the same training and specialty/subspecialty for discussion of medical necessity issues.

Health plans and pharmacy benefit managers (PBMs) may also change their formularies at any point during a patient's plan year to remove one pharmaceutical in favor of another. This means that the patient may be forced to switch to a drug that is less effective, and it also is highly unlikely the patient receives a cost discount when the change is made. This switch may destabilize a patient or it will require additional resource expenditure by the physician and extended health care team to file an exceptions

---

[200] Id.

request and/or to file an appeal. As a result, last year the AMA launched a grassroots campaign and website, TruthinRx.org, the goal of which was to expose the opaque process that pharmaceutical companies, PBMs and health plans engage in when pricing prescription drugs and to rally grassroots support to call on lawmakers to demand transparency. To date, over 150,000 individuals have signed a petition to members of Congress in support of greater drug pricing transparency.

Finally, there is considerable variation between utilization review entities' prior authorization criteria and requirements and extensive use of proprietary forms. This lack of standardization is associated with significant administrative burdens for physicians and the extended health care team, who must identify and comply with each public and commercial insurer's unique requirements. Furthermore, any clinically based utilization management criteria should be similar—if not identical—across clinical utilization review entities.

The foregoing are just some of the onerous aspects of helping a patient obtain a prescription written by their physician or other duly authorized prescriber on the health team. The negative impact on physicians and patients of such policies that have been applied by insurers to pharmaceuticals (as well as devices and medical services and procedures) has prompted the AMA–along with a growing number of national medical specialty societies and state medical associations— along with the American Hospital Association, the American Pharmacists Association, and other stakeholders to call upon health plans, benefit managers, and any other party conducting utilization management, as well as accreditation organizations, to apply Prior Authorization and Utilization Management Reform Principles (Reform Principles) developed by these stakeholders. The Reform Principles include a number of recommended solutions.

Physicians are looking for the tools that would help their patients and their care teams to make the right clinical decision that meets patient clinical and coverage needs and personal preferences. There are promising examples that the AMA has committed to exploring and advancing. A recent publication on *The Impact of Information Technology on the Diffusion of New Pharmaceuticals,* which is part of a National Bureau of Economic Research Working Paper Series, found that physicians with information about generic drug availability and patient insurer formulary data at point-of-prescribing will prescribe more generics. The researchers combined data on prescriptions and use of a point-of-care electronic pharmaceutical reference database for over 125,000 individual U.S. physicians. They found that physicians who relied upon the reference database prescribed a significantly more diverse set of products, were faster to begin prescribing new generic drugs, and had a greater propensity to prescribe generics in general. Interestingly, the researchers found that physicians using the reference database were not faster to prescribe new branded drugs. The researchers concluded that the results suggested improvements to physician information access could have important implications for the costs and efficiency of medical care. It is clear that transparency among plans to aid global databases that are well-designed and clinically validated and updated could reduce administrative burdens and increase value.

Physician Administered Pharmaceutical Treatments

The challenges associated with securing authorization or complying with applicable utilization policies of commercial and public health insurers discussed above concerning pharmacy dispensed drugs apply as well for physician-administered pharmaceuticals. In addition, physicians must comply with additional state and federal laws, regulations, and standards related to the professional licensing, acquisition, storage, preparation, administration, and disposal (when applicable) of physician-administered pharmaceuticals.

In addition, physicians must have compliance and training programs for staff along with adequate staffing. All of the foregoing factors are relevant when considering the methodologies employed by Medicare and other public and commercial insurers to reimburse for physician-administered pharmaceuticals. Larger practices and hospital outpatient departments are able to leverage economies of scale for acquisition, overhead, and compliance savings that smaller, community-based physician practices with established relationships with patients often cannot.

In 2016, the GAO reported that compared to Medicare, other public insurers generally paid rates that were the same or lower than Medicare payment for physician-administered pharmaceuticals.[201] In the Veterans Choice Program the Veterans Health Administration reimburses providers at negotiated rates that, in general, cannot exceed, and are, according to the GAO, usually equal to, Medicare's rate. State Medicaid plans under fee-for-service reimburse providers at their acquisition cost, as defined by the state. The GAO found that states often define acquisition costs at Medicare's rate. Finally, the GAO noted that, in contrast to Medicare, two commercial insurers often had higher than Medicare's rate. GAO found when interviewing the two commercial insurers that it could be the case that the Medicare payment rates are used as a benchmark for negotiation and the final commercial insurer rates are often above the Medicare rate. The GAO found that insurers' pharmaceutical utilization management and cost-containment approaches for physician-administered pharmaceuticals also varied. The GAO used as an example that certain insurers may be able to leverage purchasing power to negotiate lower payment rates.

As the Medicare program serves as a benchmark for other public and commercial insurers, the following summarizes the current responsibilities and challenges that physician practices face under the Medicare Part B program for physician-administered

---

[201] *Physician-administered Pharmaceuticals: Comparison of Insurer Payment Methodologies* (GAO, August 1, 2016).

pharmaceuticals. Currently, Part B drugs are set at the Average Sales Price (ASP) +6 percent. The ASP is defined as the volume weighted average manufacturer sales price net of all rebates, discounts, and other price concessions. Pharmaceutical manufacturers that participate in the Medicaid Drug Rebate Program (MDRP) are required to submit ASP sales prices and volume to CMS quarterly for each pharmaceutical. CMS then uses this data to calibrate the ASP rates in a subsequent quarter, with a two-quarter lag (i.e., first quarter sales are the basis for third quarter ASP payment rates). Under budget sequestration, however, Medicare is required to make a two percent reduction in its 80 percent share of covered charges, so that the actual rates are ASP+4.3 percent today.

Pharmaceuticals paid under Medicare Part B generally fall into three categories: (1) pharmaceuticals furnished incident to a physician's service in the office or HOPD; (2) pharmaceuticals administered via a covered item of durable medical equipment; and (3) other categories of pharmaceuticals explicitly identified in the law. Physicians purchase the pharmaceuticals directly from manufacturers and distributors, and Medicare reimburses physicians for the cost of the pharmaceuticals. A separate payment is made for administration of the pharmaceutical.

The ASP is an average, so nearly half pay more than average and nearly half pay less. Physicians who pay more than average, often small practices or rural providers, start at a disadvantage with this methodology. The rebates and discounts that ASP incorporates typically are only secured by hospitals and other large purchasers, which has over time reduced the ASP and created tremendous financial pressure on physician practices (small and mid-size) because they are not able to negotiate such discounts, nor do they have the financial reserves to benefit from prompt pay discounts. In addition, some beneficiaries may not be able to meet their 20 percent copayment, which then falls to the practice as debt. Another pressure is the two quarter lag time for ASP payment rates to reflect current prices—the fluctuation in price may be significant enough that physicians face losses. Furthermore, physicians can also be reimbursed inaccurately due to prompt-pay discounting programs where discounts negotiated between the manufacturer and the distributor are included in the calculation of the ASP, but not passed through to physicians decreasing their margins for reimbursement. In contrast, hospital outpatient departments (which are more expensive sites of service for Medicare) are often able to obtain pharmaceuticals below the existing reimbursement rate.

It is already the case that many smaller practices have had to refer cancer and other patients who need chemotherapy and other expensive life-saving drugs to hospital outpatient departments, thereby undermining continuity of care and creating burdens for frail and medically compromised patients. A study by the Moran Company puts the shift in chemotherapy services for Medicare patients at 30 percent between 2005 and 2011. Data from the Medicare Payment Advisory Commission came to a similar conclusion, specifically noting that Medicare Part B drug expenditures in hospital outpatient departments grew at 20 percent a year between 2009 and 2012 compared to five percent a year in physician offices. Studies by Moran, Milliman, and Avalere all have found that this shift increases costs to both the insurers and patients. A 2012 study by Avalere concluded that after adjusting for patient risk the average total cost of care for chemotherapy patients was about 24 percent higher in the hospital outpatient department than in a physician office. It found that the cost of chemotherapy in the hospital outpatient department exceeds costs in the office by 42 percent to 67 percent, with the cost of the drug itself coming in at 25 percent to 47 percent higher in the hospital outpatient department.

For small physician practices, opportunities to select between pharmaceutical treatments can be limited. Physicians often have little flexibility to choose between different pharmaceuticals, either because the patient's condition will dictate use a particular drug treatment, or because eventually they are going to have to use each of the options. As noted by MedPAC, in oncology, the appropriate medication regimen for a particular patient depends not just on the type of cancer but on the stage and other variants. Some of the pharmaceuticals are given together. Some are given sequentially; as the efficacy of the first choice drug wanes, a second and then potentially a third one will be used. Cancer drugs in particular are toxic, requiring special inventory management and safe handling by specially trained personnel which is another cost.

When physicians are not able to offer physician-administered pharmaceuticals, the gains that could be realized from the various innovation initiatives for breakthrough drugs will be undermined by payment methods that forces physicians to refer to practices that do not have an established relationship with the patient, so the most appropriate targeted treatment can be received. Fragmentation of care for patients faced with serious health challenges can contribute to poor outcomes.

Conclusion

The AMA thanks the Subcommittee for this hearing and for careful consideration of the cost and administrative burdens associated with rising pharmaceutical costs. We welcome the opportunity to work closely with the Subcommittee moving forward.

Mr. BURGESS. Thank you, Dr. Harmon.

Mr. Hoey, you're recognized for 3 minutes, please, to summarize your opening statement.

STATEMENT OF B. DOUGLAS HOEY

Mr. HOEY. Thank you, Chairman Burgess, and Ranking Member Green and members of the subcommittee for conducting this hearing and for the invitation to testify.

I am Douglas Hoey, CEO of the National Community Pharmacists Association. NCPA represents America's community pharmacists including the owners of 22,000 independent community pharmacies.

More than any industry segment, independent pharmacists are in underserved rural and urban areas. Local pharmacists are the medication experts on the health care team and, importantly, to consumers nationwide. These health care professionals are easily accessible.

Pharmacists increase health care quality and decrease its costs by optimizing safe and effective medication use. Over the past few years, CMS has been testing new payment and care models across hundreds of community pharmacists and to date, nearly 300,000 patients have been enrolled. Early findings suggest high patient satisfaction, improved outcomes, and reduced overall health care spending with reductions of greater than $1000 a year for those patients who received high clinical intervention. To achieve that future promise, however, systemic barriers must be overcome. We believe intermediary parties, pharmacy benefit manager middlemen, are increasing pricing complexity and contributing to higher prescription drug costs.

Since their inception, PBMs have morphed from claims adjudicators into little known and largely unregulated corporations, and despite their immense market influence, PBMs are not subject to industry-wide regulation nor do they have an obligation to always put their clients' interests above their own. Opaque PBM practices that require increased transparency including PBM-retained rebates and spread pricing, generic drug reimbursement schemes and pharmacy direct and indirect remuneration, or DIR, fees.

And I will expand on our members' current number-one concern, which are DIR fees. Now, these fees are assessed on pharmacies months after a prescription is filled. CMS has identified concerns from the rapid growth in DIR fees including higher beneficiary costs, accelerating patients into the donut hole, and the shifting of liability for Part B costs from plan sponsors to CMS.

In the recently released Medicare proposed rule, CMS explicitly states they are considering requiring all price concessions from pharmacies to be reflected at the point of sale.

NCPA strongly supports this approach. CMS estimates this would result in significant patient savings at the pharmacy counter, as well as overall savings over a 10-year period.

In conclusion, it makes financial sense for Congress to demand increased true transparency into the prescription drug marketplace for all taxpayer-funded prescription drugs, and to fully utilize the expertise of the community pharmacist to identify potential savings.

Thank you.

[The prepared statement of Mr. Hoey follows:]

Statement for the Record: The National Community Pharmacists Association (NCPA), United States House of Representatives, Energy and Commerce Committee, Subcommittee on Health, Hearing: "Examining the Drug Supply Chain," December 13, 2017

Chairman Burgess, Ranking Member Green and Members of the Subcommittee:

Thank you for conducting this hearing on the pharmaceutical supply chain and how the delivery system may contribute to the rising costs of prescription medications. In this statement, NCPA would like to present our thoughts on the cost savings that can be realized by fully utilizing the services of the pharmacist and also how we believe an intermediary party— Pharmacy Benefit Manager (PBM) "middlemen"— in the supply chain are increasing complexity and contributing to escalating drug costs. NCPA represents America's community pharmacists, including the owners of more than 22,000 independent community pharmacies. Together they represent an $80 billion health care marketplace and employ more than 250,000 individuals on a full or part-time basis.

More than any other segment of the pharmacy industry, independent pharmacies are often located in the underserved and rural areas that are home to many Medicare beneficiaries. In fact, independent pharmacies represent 52 percent of all rural retail pharmacies and there are over 1,800 independent community pharmacies operating as the only retail pharmacy within their rural communities. Pharmacists have more medication-related education and training than any other health care professional. Pharmacists can and do assist patients in optimizing the impact of medications and decreasing patients' costs by providing services focused on safe and appropriate medication use. For example, pharmacists provide medication management services, which are especially important for patients who have complex care plans, take multiple drugs, or have chronic conditions. Additionally, to address hospital readmissions, pharmacists help patients transition between care settings. Pharmacists are the most accessible health care professional but unfortunately, patients do not always have access to pharmacies that are closest to them because certain community pharmacies are excluded from preferred pharmacy networks by Pharmacy Benefit Managers ("PBMs"). Finally, pharmacists do not play a role in determining a patient's financial responsibility for prescription medications that they access through any prescription drug coverage. Ultimately, these amounts are determined by the insurer and the pharmacy benefits manager.

Overly Concentrated and Largely Unregulated PBM Marketplace

Three large companies lead the PBM market – Express Scripts, OptumRx and CVS Caremark – and these three companies collect more than $200 billion a year to manage prescription services for insurance carriers covering 180 million Americans and government programs servicing approximately 110 million more.[202] In addition, the largest PBM has increased its profit per-adjusted prescription 500 percent since 2003.[203] Since their inception, PBMs have morphed from claims adjudicators into little known and largely unregulated corporate giants that exploit their strategic position at the "middle" of nearly all drug transactions in the U.S. to extract profits from the upstream and downstream participants in the drug supply chain while providing questionable value to the ultimate consumer. PBMs are also heavily involved in and reap enormous profits from their involvement in federally supported or subsidized health care programs, like Medicare and Medicaid.

Current Lack of Transparency Regarding PBM Retained Rebates and "Spread" Profits

PBMs serve as the "middlemen" in most of all prescription drug transactions in the United States. They can leverage the number of beneficiaries in a particular plan to negotiate lucrative rebates from pharmaceutical manufacturers. They also formulate pharmacy provider networks that will supply or dispense these drugs to the plans' beneficiaries and in turn, charge the plan sponsor for these products. What most plan sponsors and consumers alike do not realize is that PBMs extract "spread" profits from both activities. PBMs typically claim they pass along approximately 90 percent of these manufacturer rebates to plan sponsors. However, this hinges on what is considered a "rebate." Rebate agreements between PBMs and manufacturers are considered "proprietary" and are not shared with plan sponsors. Also, many contracts allow PBMs to essentially "relabel" rebates. In this way, rebate amounts can be "reclassified" as "formulary management fees," "healthcare data fees" or a variety of other creative monikers. Even in a contract in which the PBM is required to pass along all rebates, these reclassified amounts are not included.

It is also through these activities that PBMs wield immense power in influencing precisely what prescription drug products will be considered "on formulary" or that will be covered by a specific health plan. Typically, the actual drug products selected are

---

[202] *How 'price cutting' middlemen are making crucial drugs vastly more expensive, available at* http://www.latimes.com/business/hilzik/la-fi-hiltzik-pbm-drugs-20170611-story.html.

[203] Investor's Business Daily, Nov. 21, 2016, *available at* http://www.investors.com/politics/commentary/a-sick-calculation-about-prescription-drugs/.

chosen by the PBM to garner the greatest amount of rebate dollars. In addition, this "rebate game" has attracted a great deal of attention lately and it has come to light that the proliferation of these rebates is causing drug manufacturers to offset their payments to PBMs by raising the list prices of medications.

This dynamic is also extremely troubling considering the fact that in today's health care marketplace – in which many consumers receive prescription drug coverage under high-deductible plans— patient cost-sharing amounts for medications are based off these artificially inflated "list prices." Patient cost-sharing is a percent of the 'invoice' or retail price, not the net or rebated price. The Center for Medicine in the Public Interest confirmed this dynamic and specifically provided that rebates as percent of total price growth have increased ten-fold since 2011.[204]

In addition, the amount that the PBM reimburses a pharmacy for dispensing a drug is not the same amount that the PBM "charges" the plan for the same drug. The PBM "marks up" the cost, charging the plan more than the pharmacy is reimbursed, keeping the difference as pure profit. It is precisely these hidden spread amounts that should be disclosed.

PBMs typically enter into contracts in which they will assume no fiduciary duty to employers or plan sponsors, which means that the PBM has no affirmative duty to disclose the fact that certain plan benefit designs may financially enrich the PBM or the fact that the PBM may be profiting from the sale of claims data derived from that plan sponsor. Ultimately, without any fiduciary obligation, there is no transparency or accountability for PBM conduct.

Cost Savings to Health Plan Sponsors Could be Realized with Increased PBM Transparency

The vast sums of money that PBMs are making by virtue of the drug spend of a particular plan should not be "proprietary" information on the part of the PBM. Instead, this information should belong to the plan. These disclosures could easily be protected by confidentiality agreements to address possible PBM concerns about such information weakening their negotiating stance with manufacturers. If plan sponsors have a clearer picture about the amount of money that is being made by their vendor by handling the plan's business, this may provide them with a greater ability to negotiate more competitive contracts in the first place.

---

[204] Robert Goldberg, *Drug Costs Driven by Rebates*, Center for Medicine in the Public Interest, *available at* http://bionj.org/wp-content/uploads/2015/11/drug-costs-driven-by-rebates.pdf.

Lack of Transparency in Generic Drug Reimbursement

In today's marketplace, generic drugs currently comprise approximately 86 percent of all prescriptions dispensed in the United States.[205] Given this fact, it is somewhat surprising that there is no standardized method for determining how pharmacies are reimbursed for generic drugs. PBMs create and maintain "Maximum Allowable Cost" or MAC lists that set the upper limit or maximum amount that a PBM/plan will pay for most generic drugs. Pharmacies are not provided any insight into how drug products are selected to be put onto this list or how exactly these prices are determined or updated. In short, contracted pharmacies have zero insight or transparency into the MAC process and sign contracts without having any idea of the rate at which they will be reimbursed for most of the prescriptions they fill. In response to PBM secrecy surrounding the creation and maintenance of these lists, at least twenty-six states have enacted legislation to try to compel greater transparency into this system. The PBM industry in general has vigorously opposed these efforts and in fact is currently engaged in litigation with several individual states that have sought to compel compliance.

PBM Industry Largely Unregulated

Given the immense market influence that PBMs exert, one would expect these entities to be subject to the same type of comprehensive regulation that is currently required of commercial health insurers. However, PBMs are not subject to industry-wide regulation like what is generally required of commercial health insurers. There are no federal laws or regulations that are specific to the PBM industry. Instead, PBMs face a patchwork of regulations at the state level that are designed to curtail some of the more onerous PBM business practices such as abusive PBM audits of pharmacies and requirements related to timely MAC updates. However, even in states that have been able to pass these limited reforms, PBMs typically resist complying and have recently filed lawsuits against states.

Explosion of Pharmacy "DIR Fees" in the Medicare Part D Program Are Increasing Costs to Consumers and the Medicare Program

Pharmacy direct and indirect remuneration ("DIR") fees are effectively clawback fees assessed on pharmacies retroactively months later, rather than deducted from claims

---

205 PhRMA, *The Reality of Prescription Medicine Costs in Three Charts*; May 27, 2014, *available at* http://www.phrma.org.catalyst.the-reality-of-prescription-medicine-costs-in-three-charts.

on a real-time basis at the point-of-sale. Earlier this year CMS identified several concerns resulting from the rapid growth in pharmacy DIR fees[206]. First, beneficiaries face higher cost-sharing for drugs and are accelerated into the coverage gap or "donut hole" phase of their benefit. Second, more beneficiaries reach the catastrophic phase of the benefit, for which CMS incurs approximately 80 percent of the cost (HHS Office of Inspector General has noted[207] that these catastrophic costs have tripled in recent years - from $10 billion in 2010 to $33 billion in 2015 – driven by pharmacy DIR fees). Third, liability for Part D costs is increasingly being shifted from Part D plan sponsors to CMS.

These findings were reinforced and bolstered by a report earlier this year by a leading actuarial firm commissioned by NCPA.[208] In addition, MedPAC recently warned[209] that, because of DIR, the gap between gross and net drug prices has grown 20 percent annually from 2010-2015 and that "plan incentives [are] not aligned with beneficiary and Medicare."

By utilizing tactics such as pharmacy DIR fees, the Part D plan sponsor or its PBM often receives additional compensation after the point-of-sale that serves to change the final cost of the drug for the payer, or the price paid to the pharmacy, for the drug.

The point-of-sale price/"negotiated price" recorded on Prescription Drug Event ("PDE") records is extremely significant. It is used to calculate beneficiary cost-sharing and to adjudicate the Part D benefit. Any fees or payment that are made after the point-of-sale are not reflected in the negotiated price but rather are reported to CMS separately.

Many beneficiaries and caregivers rely on the online Medicare Plan Finder to evaluate and choose a Part D plan. However, the data displayed on Medicare Plan Finder are based on point-of-sale prices. The vast proliferation of DIR and post point-of-sale price concessions have rendered this drug price information grossly inaccurate.

Fortunately, CMS is acutely aware of DIR fees and their impact on Part D beneficiary and program costs. In the recently released Medicare proposed rule, "Contract Year 2019 Policy and Technical Changes to the Medicare Advantage, Medicare Cost Plan, Medicare Fee-for-Service, the Medicare Prescription Drug Benefit Programs, and the PACE Program," CMS explicitly states they are considering requiring all price concessions from pharmacies be reflected in the negotiated price that is made available at the point-of-sale and reported to CMS on a PDE record, even when such concessions are contingent upon performance by the pharmacy. NCPA strongly supports this approach. It would give independent community pharmacies greater predictability about their net reimbursement rates so they can make more informed operational decisions. In addition, it would not preclude any pay-for-performance arrangements

---

[206] CMS, *Medicare Part D – Direct and Indirect Remuneration, available at* https://www.cms.gov/newsroom/mediareleasedatabase/fact-sheets/2017-fact-sheet-items/2017-01-19-2.html.

[207] HHS Office of Inspector General, *High-Price Drugs Are Increasing Federal Payments for Medicare Part D Catastrophic Coverage, available at* https://oig.hhs.gov/oei/reports/oei-02-16-00270.asp.

[208] *The Impacts of Prescription Drug Direct and Indirect Remuneration under Medicare Part D*, Feb. 2017.

[209] *Payment and plan incentives in Part D*, April 7, 2017.

between the Part D Plan/PBM and the pharmacy. Contrary to what the PBM industry has stated about this approach, CMS estimates that reflecting all pharmacy price concessions at the point-of-sale would result in significant beneficiary savings in cost sharing (at the pharmacy counter) as well as an overall savings (taking into account both premium amount and cost sharing amounts) over ten years.

Conclusion

In conclusion, the prescription drug marketplace continues to grow at an alarming pace. Large mergers continue to be announced every day while at the same time healthcare costs – and particularly prescription drug costs – are at an all-time high. The current business climate seems to be one in which market power is increasingly concentrated in an ever-shrinking number of corporate entities. The overly concentrated and largely unregulated PBM industry exerts immense influence over how prescription drugs are accessed by the majority of Americans. Given the fact that the federal government is the largest single payer of health care in the United States,[210] it makes financial sense for Congress to demand increased transparency into this aspect of the prescription drug marketplace in order to identify potential savings. In addition, Congress could enact common-sense legislation to address the proliferation of PBM-generated pharmacy "DIR" fees to lower out-of-pocket costs to Part D beneficiaries and reduce federal government Medicare Part D spending.

Mr. GUTHRIE [presiding]. Thank you. The gentleman's time has expired and I recognize Mr. Mitchell for 3 minutes for your opening statement.

STATEMENT OF DAVID MITCHELL

Mr. MITCHELL. Thank you.

Chairman Burgess, Ranking Member Green, Chairman Walden, members of the committee, I am honored to be here today.

I am David Mitchell and I am founder of Patients for Affordable Drugs. We are bipartisan. We focus on policies to lower prescription drug prices. We don't accept funding from any organizations that profit from the development or distribution of prescription drugs.

---

[210] Troy, Tevi D., *How the Government As a Payer Shapes the Health Care Marketplace*, American Health Policy Institute, 2015.

More importantly for today, I have an incurable blood cancer called multiple myeloma and prescription drugs are keeping me alive, literally. Right now, my treatment is 5 hours of infusions, carry a price tag of $450,000 this year. I am very grateful to the science and research communities for these drugs, and because my disease is incurable, it finds its way around drugs. It mutates. I need innovation of new drugs if I am going to stay alive. This is not theoretical for me. It's literally life and death.

But my experience has taught me one irrefutable fact, and that is that drugs don't work if people can't afford them. Since our launch in February, we've built a community of almost 20,000 Americans from every state. Patients tell us terrible stories of skipping doses, cutting pills in half, even declaring bankruptcy, because of the price of their drugs. They're scared, they're angry, and they need help.

I am going to highlight a few policy solutions for the drug supply chain. First, however, it is critical to note that prices set by drug corporations with government-granted monopolies are at the headwaters of the pricing problem.

When retail prices set by drug corporations go up, all the players in the system make more money—drug manufacturer, PBMs, doctors, hospitals. The people hurt are patients, consumers, taxpayers, and employers who foot the bill.

But the drug supply chain downstream is also a big part of the problem. Here's a patient perspective on some elements. One, we should allow Medicare to directly negotiate lower prices for patients. Every other developed country in the world does this. We should, too.

We need increased transparency throughout the supply chain. Three pharmacy benefit managers control almost 80 percent of the market and negotiate in secret, leaving consumers, taxpayers, and policymakers in the dark.

Co-pay coupons and patient assistant programs are phony charities. They are designed to do one thing. That is keep prices high. They are not charity. They are marketing. According to City Research, for every $1 million spent on charitable donations, drug corporations reap as much as $21 million in return. We should lower drug prices and make co-pay coupons unnecessary.

Finally, we have to ensure that patients pay based on rebated, not list, prices and that patients with insurance don't pay more than they would if they paid cash.

Gag clauses should be outlawed. I am extremely encouraged that members on both sides of the aisle are here today focusing on drug pricing because, in my experience, the most enduring legislative solutions have come with bipartisan action.

Thank you.

[The prepared statement of Mr. Mitchell follows:]

Statement of David E. Mitchell, Founder, Patients for Affordable Drugs, *before the* U.S. House of Representatives, Subcommittee on Health of the Energy and Commerce Committee, "Examining the Drug Supply Chain," December 13, 2017

Chairman Burgess, Ranking Member Green, Members of the Subcommittee: I am honored to be here today.

Section 1. Background and Introduction

My name is David Mitchell. I am the Founder of Patients For Affordable Drugs. We are a bipartisan, national patient organization focused on policies to lower drug prices. We don't accept funding from any organizations that profit from the development or distribution of prescription drugs.

More importantly to today's hearing, I have an incurable blood cancer, and prescription drugs are keeping me alive. Several days ago, I received five hours of drug infusions that carry a price tag of more than $20,000 every time I get them. I've had them 22 times over the course of the year. So, $450,000 worth of drugs are keeping me upright.

I am very grateful to the science and research communities in our country for these drugs. And because my disease is incurable, I need innovation and new drugs if I am going to live as long as I hope to. This is not theoretical for me—it is life and death.

But my experience as a cancer patient has taught me one irrefutable fact: Drugs don't work if people can't afford them.

Section 2. Patients Are Crying out for Help

Since our launch in February, we have built a community of almost 20,000 Americans across every state.

Dalia Hunter from Texas wrote, "I've got Rheumatoid Disease. My monthly drug cost, after insurance, is somewhere from $700-$1,800 a month. There is no way to afford this so I've gone without these meds. Who knows what kind of permanent damage has been done to my joints."

There are thousands of people like Dalia, who tell us devastating stories of skipping doses, cutting pills in half, and even declaring bankruptcy because of the prices of their drugs.

People are scared and angry, and they need help.

A September Harvard poll showed that 4 in 10 Americans want lowering prescription drug prices to be Congress' top priority.

Sixty four percent of Americans, including a majority of Democrats, Independents, and Republicans, listed lowering drug prices as their top health care priority, according to a Kaiser Health poll.

The message we hear from patients is simple. They understand that drug corporations have monopoly pricing power. Patients and taxpayers know the prescription drug pricing system in the U.S. is rigged against them. They want leaders in Washington to fight to lower the price of drugs and get something done.

This is a central health care issue that impacts millions of people every day. We agree with President Trump: "Drug companies frankly are getting away with murder." And drug companies are not the only ones who take advantage of patients' pocketbooks.

Section 3: The Supply Chain Is Part of the Problem

Prices set by drug corporations with government-granted monopolies are at the headwaters of the problem we face.

But the drug supply chain downstream is also part of the problem.

When retail prices set by drug corporations rise, all players in the system make more money – drug manufacturers, PBMs, doctors, and hospitals. The people hurt are patients, consumers, taxpayers, and employers who foot the bill.

There are steps we can take to help Americans struggling under high drug prices.

Here is a patient perspective on some of the important issues in the supply chain and what can be done about them:

- Allow Medicare to negotiate lower costs for patients. The government grants drug manufacturers a monopoly for up to 12 years. Medicare negotiations would help balance that monopoly pricing power. Below is a chart that demonstrates why we need negotiations – especially for brand drugs – the fastest growing sector of health spending.

Prices for Brand-Name Prescription Drugs Doubled Between 2008 and 2016

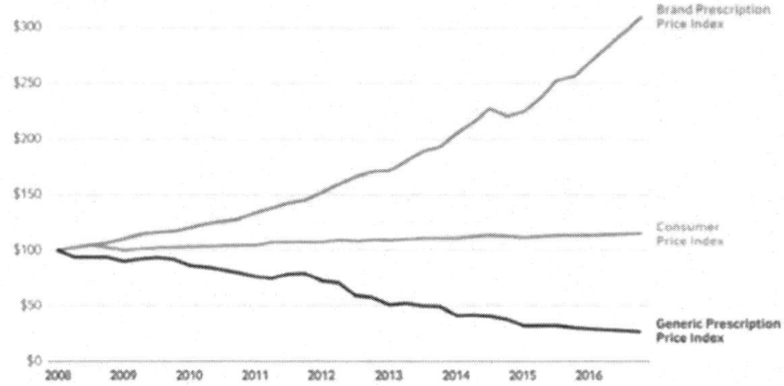

Source: Kaiser Family Foundation analysis of data from Express Scripts 2015 Prescription Price Index.

- Increase transparency throughout the drug supply chain. Three pharmacy benefit managers control about 75 percent of the drug market. PBMs negotiate deals in secret, leaving consumers and policymakers in the dark. Americans can't tell if these corporations provide value in the form of rebates for patients or if they keep rebates to increase profits. We do know the combined operating profit of the three largest PBMs was $10.1 billion in 2015, up 30% from 2013.
  Increased transparency would help consumers better understand drug prices. As recommended by the National Academies of Sciences, Engineering, and Medicine, Congress should require PBMs to disclose drug discounts and rebates, so we can ensure reductions in prices reach patients. The recommendation avoids specific disclosures that PBMs claim would inhibit their negotiating success. Instead, the report recommends that PBMs make quarterly disclosures at the national drug code level. We support this change.
- Follow the Trump Administration's lead to allow Part D Medicare beneficiaries to pay out-of-pocket costs based on rebated – not retail – drug prices. Right now, Medicare Part D beneficiaries pay out-of-pocket costs based on retail prices of drugs. Everyone else in the system – employers, insurers, the government – pays based on rebated prices. The Trump Administration requested feedback on changes so patients get the benefit of the rebate price. We encourage Congress to support such a change. Congress should also cap patient out-of-pocket costs at the catastrophic level. With drugs costing $20,000 per month, the catastrophic costs can be crushing.
- Ensure patients with insurance don't pay more than they would if they paid cash. Supply chain contracts often forbid pharmacists from telling insured consumers that they could pay less if they paid cash rather than use insurance cards. These gag clauses are wrong and should be outlawed.

- Use caution around outcomes-based pricing arrangements. First, it is important to distinguish between value-pricing and outcomes-pricing. Value-pricing is conducted by organizations like the Institute for Clinical and Economic Review, the American Society of Clinical Oncology, and the National Comprehensive Cancer Network. They examine the value of a new drug to patients and serve as one input for negotiations by private parties and the Veterans Administration. Value-pricing can be a useful tool.

  Outcomes-based pricing is different. It ties reimbursement of a drug to its effectiveness. While this sounds attractive, it's a disaster for patients. Outcomes-pricing in general stipulates that if a drug fails, the drug company will provide a refund. But that system contains a major flaw. It does not lower drug prices; it allows drug companies to keep prices high. Drug companies have the clinical data that tell them how many patients react positively to a drug and how many will fail. Rather than lower prices, drug companies will simply raise the price of a drug to compensate for failures. Furthermore, it is not clear any refunds will make their way to patients. It is also not clear how to use such a process for drugs like insulin where patients react differently as individuals and drug companies may want to claim user error if the patient doesn't do everything right to manage their disease.
- Work for lower prices instead of making patients rely on assistance programs and copay coupons. Copay coupons and patient assistant programs are phony charities designed to do one thing: keep prices high. One MS patient called them band-aids—dirty, infected band-aids. They are not charity—they are marketing. According to Citi Research, for every $1 million spent on charitable donations, drug corporations reap as much as $21 million in return. We should lower drug prices and make copay coupons unnecessary.
- Investigate the insulin market. Three insulin manufacturers command 80 percent of the market for this lifesaving drug. Together, the companies raised prices more than 300 percent in the past ten years – for a drug invented in 1923 and for which the patents were sold for $3. The prices move in lockstep and people with diabetes suffer at the hands of what can only be called an insulin cartel. Democratic and Republican members in the House are already looking into the insulin market. We encourage Congress to look into anti-competitive behavior and possible price-fixing by Eli Lilly, Novo Nordisk, and Sanofi.

Section 4: Bipartisan Action to Restore Balance Is Possible

In conclusion, our health care system should maximize affordability and accessibility of drugs while ensuring a robust R&D pipeline and fair profits for companies all along the supply chain. That balance has been lost. The system encourages high prices that benefit big players.

Consider this story from Jon Pavlus of Worland, Wyoming: "I've had diabetes for 52 years and in the last 6 years I've watched my insulin prices go from $6.75 a vial to $375 a vial. I can't afford this. I need help!"

We hope to work with Congress to lower drug prices and let Americans focus on living healthy and productive lives rather than struggling with the rising cost of medicines they depend on.

I am extremely encouraged that members on both sides of the aisle are focused on these issues. In my experience, the most enduring legislative successes in our country have come with bipartisan action.

Mr. BURGESS. Thank you, Mr. Mitchell, and I want to thank the entire panel for their testimony and we will move into the question/ answer portion of the hearing.

We'd like to recognize the gentleman from Oregon, Mr. Walden, chairman of the full committee, 5 minutes for questions, please.

Mr. WALDEN. I want to thank the chairman very much and, again, I want to thank all the witnesses today. You have helped us scratch the surface, get a better understanding from the start to the finish—from the molecular development to the patient who's on a lifesaving drug.

And, obviously, you have also outlined for us differences of opinion about how we achieve more affordable health care and not just—we are looking at this, by the way, not just at the drug chain but across the entire industry of health care. And it is a big one, it is an expensive one, and I know when I go home to Oregon it is on top of everybody's minds. They may complain about their insurance premium or this, that, or the other thing.

But at the end of the day, they all want to know why—you name it in health care—why it costs what it does or they want to know what it costs, because of lack of transparency. You don't even know. There are all these schemes and things and I think we are all trying to get to the bottom of it and my goal is to have an informed process, beginning today, that lets you all make your case.

And I would just be curious, as you all have heard each other talk, and we finished with Mr. Mitchell, who I've met with before in my office, and sorry for what you're going through, obviously, but you make a very compelling case.

You make some pretty strong statements about what needs to be changed and I would like to go to the other end because some of those are targeted at the pharmaceutical companies and see if we can get a response from Ms. Reilly on what Mr. Mitchell said and how we should be guided in this, and if others want to weigh in along the way that would be good as well.

Ms. REILLY. Well, thank you for the question, and I think a lot of what I heard out of David's mouth are things that we do agree with.

For example, today, as I talked about and others talked about, our companies do provide robust discounts and rebates to pharmacy benefit managers and insurers, and unlike almost any other part of the health care system, those rebates and discounts aren't passed back to the patients.

If a patient with a deductible today ends up in the hospital before they reach their deductible, the price they pay is a negotiated price that that insurance company has negotiated on their behalf. It seems strange that if a patient instead needs a pharmaceutical before they reach their deductible, that they're asked to pay a full unnegotiated price for the medicine and don't get the benefit of that discount and actually earn money on every transaction. That doesn't seem right to me and I think that does need to change.

CMS just, earlier this year, posted their new Part D rule. In it, they put a request for information out about the potential for passing through discounts and rebates in the Medicare Part D program. We actually think that's a good first step. Today, the evidence suggests by CMS that PBMs prefer medicines with high list prices and high rebates because for those products they can use those rebate dollars to keep their premiums low and they also put people into catastrophic quicker and passing through——

Mr. WALDEN. Right. So I want to give them a chance to respond to that because I assume they will want to.

So let's go to the insurance plans. You have heard what Ms. Reilly said about consumers paying the full freight here and not being covered by insurance and no negotiation. Is that accurate? Is there something we should do about that?

Mr. EYLES. So thank you, Chairman Walden, for the opportunity. What I would say is health plans negotiate on behalf of their members and consumers every single day across all parts of the supply chain, whether it be providers or drug manufacturers.

To put this into context, I think you probably heard some of the statistics thrown around that 90 percent of the prescriptions are generic that are filled in this country. So that means about 10 percent are filled through retail—that are brands. Not all of those brands offer rebates. There's a large number of brands that don't offer rebates. So really we are trying to focus on a much smaller problem when the bigger problem really comes back to the price.

Using Ms. Reilly's example earlier of insulin of $400 a vial, a decade ago that vial was only about $90. Right now, if prices of insulin increased only by the consumer price index rather than much, much higher rates, we'd only be paying about $100 per vial, all right, if you're just following inflation. We wouldn't be having this discussion about rebates——

Mr. WALDEN. So——

Mr. EYLES [continuing]. If it didn't start with the price.

Mr. WALDEN. So who can tell me why that insulin is the price it is today?

Ms. REILLY. I would say, Chairman Walden, the net price of insulins have not changed all that significantly. What has changed is the levels of discounts and rebates that are being demanded in part because it is an extremely competitive market.

As I mentioned before, insurance companies, PBMs, in the Part D program, for example, they like high list prices that come with high rebates because they can then use those rebates to keep their premiums low, attract patients to their health care plan. Unfortunately, what the problem is is they're not sharing those rebates and discounts back with patients as they do if a patient ends up in the hospital or uses a physician and that's what needs to change.

Mr. WALDEN. All right. My time has expired. We didn't get to the PBM's view of this. I hope we do, coming forward, because this is the debate. Because at home the constituents say why is insulin $400 when it used to be a hundred dollars or whatever the number is, And that's repeated time again, whether it is EpiPen or whatever. We can't answer that either because I am not sure there is a good answer.

So with that, Mr. Chairman, I've exhausted my time and I, again, appreciate your willingness to have this hearing and yield back.

Mr. BURGESS. Chair thanks the gentleman. Gentleman does yield back.

The chair recognizes the gentleman from Texas, Mr. Green, 5 minutes for questions, please.

Mr. GREEN. Thank you, Mr. Chairman.

A Harvard study found that there are more than three-quarters of the public believe that name brand prescription drugs are too high and an issue primarily driven by price increases in the absence of additional competition. Biologics represent the majority of these high-priced drugs representing 7 out of the 10 highest grossing pharmaceutical products in 2015.

A landmark 2014 Rand study also estimated that biosimilars could save as much as $40 billion through 2024 in the United States alone, and we have another study from IMS Health opening markets to biosimilar competition health care systems could realize savings of more than 10 billion euros in the E.U. alone between 2016 and 2020. The cumulative savings over the next 5 years in the E.U. and the United States would be 49 billion in euros.

Mr. Davis, Mr. Merritt, do you agree that we should support policies to encourage a workable pathway for biosimilars as we in Congress do encourage bringing these product online and encouraging uptake by physicians and plans for their patients? Mr. Davis first.

Mr. DAVIS. Congressman, thank you for your question.

The short answer is yes, we represent biosimilar manufacturers today in addition to generic manufacturers, and as you stated, biosimilars hold the potential for so much promise in terms of increasing access and realizing savings because they will provide competition to the increasingly costly degree of specialized medicine and personalized medicine moving forward.

There's a couple challenges with respect to making sure that we realize the full potential of biosimilars here in the U.S. market. One is getting them to market, which is why we need to create some Fast Generics Act pass so that our members can actually gain access to the samples to do the pharmacovigilance to apply to the FDA to get biosimilars to the market. And then the second thing we have to look at, and we have to be candid about this, is right now there are eight biosimilars that have been approved by the FDA. There are only three on the market. The other five are tied up in endless litigation.

So if we ultimately want to—we have a lot of catching up to do in terms of you mentioned the E.U. They are light years ahead of us in terms of utilization, access, and savings on biosimilars.

We have the opportunity from a policy perspective to catch up. The Federal Government started scoring savings for biosimilars in 2014 fiscal year. The first one wasn't on the market until September of 2015. So we have more work to do there.

Mr. GREEN. Mr. Merritt.

Mr. MERRITT. And I would agree with what Chip said. Biologics are the future. Specialty products are the future and they're very expensive. They're very great products, as David Mitchell mentioned.

But right now, they're often unaffordable and the key is competition. Biologics already have 12 years of exclusivity. We'd like that to be down to seven so we can get competition started faster.

We'd like these drugs to have the same name the way generics do with brand drugs on the regular market and a host of other things because without competition, you're not going to have savings and if you have more and more brand protection for every little minute change you make and if litigation ties these up for years and years, for a month, a couple of months, a year of being tied up in litigation can cost consumers billions of dollars. And so we are very aligned with the generics on this.

Mr. GREEN. Mr. Chairman, I believe that our government's approach to approving and integrating biosimilars in our health system would impact overall potential for competition and access to more affordable life changing drugs for patients. Let's hope we can continue to support this developing market so that patients can realize the value and benefit of such treatments.

Mr. Eyles, the complexity of the drug supply chain is hard to overstate as evidenced by all 10 of our witnesses this morning. They've been in the growing chorus calling for greater transparency in the drug supply chain.

Some states have already taken action. California recently enacted legislation that would require reporting of certain price hikes and legislation that would be introduced in both the House and the Senate—that has been introduced would create a similar federal requirement.

What we've already seen is some good actors taking meaningful steps to increase transparency. For example, Sanofi and Janssen have agreed to disclose their drug price increases each year. Sanofi also announced it would put limits on how much it will increase drug prices. But as you note in your testimony that more could be done to encourage open and straightforward price setting and high-light the need for disclosure of intended launch price.

Could you discuss further why the disclosure of intended launch price would be helpful to insurers and how you believe such a disclosure be operationalized?

Mr. EYLES. Thank you, Ranking Member Green.

Yes, we've been very supportive of greater transparency into really both when it comes to launch prices and price increases.

While we are not supportive of controlling prices, we think it is important to have more information out there in the public domain about exactly how prices are set. Right now, pharmaceutical prices are set in the black box.

When a new product gets launched with a price of $475,000 no one really understands how that got set.

Mr. GREEN. Well——

Mr. EYLES. We think ahead of time, having additional visibility into how prices get determined by the manufacturer and then price increases over time, particularly those on higher cost drugs and those that exceed certain thresholds, it'll be important to understand other parts of the health care system have oversight and controls on them.

For example, insurers have to report all of the inputs into their rates before they get approved. We are not looking to have specific approval of drug prices but we do think it is important to have greater transparency and greater dialogue around how are prices being set up front.

Mr. GREEN. Well, Mr. Chairman, thank you. I know I am over time.

But transparency always works and, like you said, it works in other parts of the health care delivery system. So thank you for the time.

Mr. BURGESS. Gentleman yields back. Chair thanks the gentleman. The chair recognizes the gentleman from Kentucky, Mr. Guthrie, vice chairman of the Health Subcommittee. 5 minutes for your questions, please.

Mr. GUTHRIE. Thank you very much. Thanks for everybody being here today, and it is really a great day to start this process. I was invited not long ago to the White House with the majority leader and we met with the President. I want to tell you, we walked away with the President wanting action on this issue. He's very focused on it. I think this is the beginning of a process that I hope will lead to an action as we move forward.

I have some prepared questions but I will get back to what the chairman said. I don't think we ever got a really good answer.

If insulin is a competitive product and it was $90 10 years ago and it should be $100 if you just went through the standard inflation, why is it $400? It's got to be somewhere between here and here it has increased in price and maybe, Mr. Merritt, you'd like to address that.

Mr. MERRITT. Yes. And this happens with a lot of drugs, but you see it a lot in insulin is there are insulin products but they have new methods of administration—actually some better methods of administration and that creates a whole new patent protection for these products.

And so that is how the prices go up and, again, on a very basic point, drug makers can charge whatever they want for a product. That's not saying a price is right or wrong but it has nothing to do with anybody at this table except for the drug manufacturers.

All that we can do is get the biggest rebates possible, the biggest discounts possible, pass it on to the plans and employers and have them use it to reduce premiums, cost sharing, or whatever each plan wants to do.

But just the fact that we don't control the prices, that they have patent protection with minor changes in the products, again, making the products better, that's what gives them that pricing power.

Mr. GUTHRIE. So the insulin—so Ms. Reilly, that would—so innovation has come from PhRMA. Therefore, you have invested the research dollars so you're recapturing those resources dollars, therefore it is four times what it was?

Ms. REILLY. Well, Mark is correct that there have been significant advancements in insulin. We now have long-acting insulins. We have an insulin that's injectable with pens and other things.

But, again, I would say the list price of the medicine is not what the manufacturer retains, and in the case of the insulin marketplace, there are multiple competing products.

What manufacturers have retained over the last 5 years has been stable or declining and part of the reason for that is we do have PBMs that are buying these medicines that, again, CMS, MedPAC, and others have demonstrated that what they prefer is a high list price and a high rebate.

That lowers the net price considerably. The rebates on average in the insulin market space are 65 percent.

Mr. GUTHRIE. Well, who sets the list price then? For what the PBMs have to charge, who sets the list price?

Ms. REILLY. Well, and I want to respond to something that both Mark and Matt said with regard to the list price. The list price is not set in a vacuum.

Our companies have to engage with PBMs and insurance companies every day in determining the list price and their preferences, quite honestly, matter significantly. And they matter to the extent that if they want a high list price with a high rebate and they're telling a company when they control a hundred million lives, an individual one, that is their preference if that product is to get on formulary.

Commonly, PBMs pick and choose amongst insulins and they say to a company, if you don't give me the price I want, you're off my formulary. And if you are buying on behalf of a hundred million Americans, more than countries like France and Germany, the leverage they exert is significant.

Mr. GUTHRIE. So would you argue your market price is the list price less rebate? You know that going in——

Ms. REILLY. Yes. Yes.

Mr. GUTHRIE [continuing]. Therefore, you have to set a higher list price to get the market price that you think you need to cover your—same way with biologics?

Ms. REILLY. Just to stay flat. Yes.

Mr. GUTHRIE. To stay flat.

Mr. MERRITT. If I could just jump in for a second, it would be an anti-trust violation for those discussions to ever happen. Those discussions don't happen. Manufacturers set the price according to however they want to move their products, whatever they think they need to do. PBMs have zero input into that. Health plans have zero input into that.

Of course, we get the biggest rebates that we can, but remember, this is a chicken and egg thing. If the price goes up, we are going to get a bigger rebate because our clients, Matt's companies and others are going to demand us to get bigger and bigger discounts. But the——

Ms. REILLY. I would argue——

Mr. MERRITT. No, I am not done yet. But the list prices are the list prices, and that is a drug maker thing. It has nothing to do with——

Mr. GUTHRIE. Well, let me——

Mr. BUCSHON. Mr. Chairman, I—Mr. Chairman——

Mr. GUTHRIE. Not—let me——

Mr. BUCSHON. He interrupted her testimony.

Mr. GUTHRIE. I am going to let you finish your thought.

Then——

Mr. MERRITT. Yes. That's what I am saying. It's just a basic thing. I think sometimes you can try to over complicate the whole issue of supply chain.

Supply chain is just how you distribute products. Every industry uses them. They're not exotic. They all use rebates.

Mr. GUTHRIE. I got about 40 seconds. Yes, let me go back to——

Ms. REILLY. I would say you have to ask the question that if our revenue is flat or declining in the space of insulin and the list price is increasing? It's benefiting everyone that's paid off of the list price including the PBMs and the health plans.

Mr. GUTHRIE. So the argument the rebate doesn't go to the consumer?

Ms. REILLY. No, it does not get passed——

Mr. GUTHRIE. Do you have an answer for that, Mr. Merritt?

Mr. MERRITT. It does. It goes to the client who may use it to reduce the cost of that particular drug—the cost sharing, or more commonly it is used to reduce overall.

Mr. GUTHRIE. I guess I will have Administrator Eyles and AHIP. So the rebate does go to the consumer?

Mr. EYLES. They go to people who purchase health insurance coverage. Yes, they go to everyone. That's right. So when you look at filings that insurance companies have to file with every state department of insurance, there are specific lines dedicated to pharmaceutical rebates and when rates get approved those rebates are taken into account. There are different——

Ms. REILLY. I would argue that's a perversity of insurance.

Mr. GUTHRIE. Time is expired. I wish I had more time with that but——

Ms. REILLY. Right. The purpose of insurance is for healthy to subsidize the sick. We are evolving to a system where the sick are subsidizing the healthy through rebates.

Mr. BURGESS. Gentleman yields back his time. Chair thanks the gentleman.

The chair recognizes the gentleman from New Jersey 5 minutes for questions, please.

Mr. PALLONE. Thank you, Mr. Chairman.

I have long believed that one critical component of the successful drug supply chain is a robust generic manufacturing presence and market.

Generics can continue to play a role in fostering increased competition and affordable access to medications, which is why I've continuously worked to provide generics with a level playing field and supported increased assistance and incentives including most recently through the FDA Reauthorization Act as a way to encourage a strong generic presence in our pharmaceutical market.

So I wanted to ask Mr. Davis a couple questions. In your testimony you noted that generics operate under a very different business model than brand drug manufacturers.

Can you further discuss how the business model for generic drugs is different than brand drugs and the different considerations generic drug manufacturers take into account when making product development decisions?

Mr. DAVIS. Thank you, Ranking Member Pallone, and thank you for your leadership on ensuring a level playing field. I am happy to address that.

The debate that you just heard between the branded industry and the PBMs and the insurers on rebates as a percentage of list price and discounts are for 11 percent of all prescriptions in the United States.

It is not the generic business model. So if there is one thing I leave this committee with today it is to think of generics differently than the way you think about policy that impacts the branded industry.

We are a commoditized, not monopolized industry. As a result of that, the way the supply chain actually leverages driving prices down to where we are in 16 consecutive months of price deflation is by combining their resources and leveraging their purchasing ability where there are now three wholesaler retail pharmacy consortiums that are controlling 90 percent of the generic supply chain.

So you have three suppliers who are driving the prices down lower than they have ever been before in the generic marketplace and as a result of that they are moving increasingly toward what are called single-sourcing contracts meaning they want to partner or contract with one generic company to fill a majority of their portfolio of purchasing needs.

As a result of that, what we have seen is, quite frankly, an unsustainable supply chain for generics moving forward, if in fact we can ensure that there is robust competition on the buyer side in addition to the seller side.

In 2000, there were approximately 200 wholesalers on the market. Today, there are three that control 90 percent of the supply chain. The buyer side is three.

We are still 20 to 30 competitive generic manufacturers all competing for that business, and economics will dictate over time that you will see more consolidation on our side in an effort to level out that negotiating table.

Mr. PALLONE. All right. I want to ask two more questions.

You talked about how generic manufacturers operated in this commodity style market as a result of the multiple manufacturers marketing the same product.

But do you want to explain a little better the role that plays in bringing the generic drug to market?

Mr. DAVIS. Happy to do so. You have——

Mr. PALLONE. And then I've got one more question.

Mr. DAVIS. Sure. You have a situation, Congressman, where the ability for a generic manufacturer, when you actually get to what's called commoditized pricing in the generic marketplace, a decade ago it took eight, nine, or ten generic competitors to get to 80 to 85 percent off the reference for the originator price.

You get there now as soon as three, four, or five generic entrants, which is why the FDA commissioner has prioritized not just the first generic application at FDA but the first, second, and third.

Our companies have to make decisions in a commoditized market that has varying price fluctuation upward and downward about what the sustainability is of the competitive market in any therapeutic area. So that's a significant factor in determining if they go to market once they get approved and if they stay on the market once they are approved.

Mr. PALLONE. All right. Then lastly, let me just ask briefly about the rebates. We've heard quite a bit of debate about the appropriateness or value of rebates in the drug supply chain.

So what role, if any, do rebates play in the negotiations a generic drug manufacturer undertakes with payers and how does reimbursement traditionally work for generic drugs?

Mr. DAVIS. Thank you for that. It's an important distinction. As I said, for 89 percent of the prescriptions in the U.S. that are generic, the traditional rebate model by and large does not apply.

Generic companies are reimbursed in many ways based upon two things: their ability to meet that wholesaler demand with the three who control 90 percent of the market.

By saying can you meet our volume requests and are you willing to meet the price that we are actually going to tell you we are going to pay for that product—let's take generic Crestor, for example, rosuvastatin—and if you don't—and if you're not willing to offer it at 10 cents a capsule, one of your 19, 20, or 21 other competitors that are also marketing that will, and we will cut you out.

So it is really about volume and ability to keep your price as low as possible. So it is an example of the market actually working.

Mr. PALLONE. All right. Thanks a lot, Mr. Davis.

Mr. BURGESS. Gentleman yields back. The chair thanks the gentleman.

The chair recognizes the gentlelady from Tennessee, Mrs. Blackburn, 5 minutes for questions, please.

Mrs. BLACKBURN. Thank you, Mr. Chairman.

I appreciate that, and I appreciate the discussion that we are having here this morning on this issue. I will say I am a little surprised. There's a lot of finger pointing that is going around.

But I will tell you all, I think there is more than enough blame to go around for what we see transpiring in the marketplace and with the high cost.

And listening to you all, I will tell you there is absolutely—it confirms to me why so many of my patients—my constituents will say as a patient who takes something regularly, they have tried to find other options in the marketplace—programs like GoodRX or I know there are several others—because they are very frustrated.

And Mr. Mitchell, I appreciate the concerns that you bring to bear as a patient and someone who is using something. This is an issue that we need to address, and we need your best efforts in solving this.

So I am going to focus on not things in the past, but as we move forward. And let's put our attention there. And for each of you on the panel—and we are going to start with Ms. Reilly and work all the way down—what change would you like to see in the market-place or what change in law should we make to make certain that, as Chairman Walden said, we are focused on access, delivery, and the cost of these pharmaceuticals to patients.

Now, you are only going to have about 30 seconds. So Mr. Merritt, listen—make that good and concise for me. OK. Ms. Reilly, you are on. Let's go right down the panel.

Ms. REILLY. Great. I would say two things. The first, as I mentioned before, passing through those robust discounts and rebates that totalled over $100 billion last year back to patients. That would lower patient drug costs immediately.

The second, which is more of a mid-to longer-term option, is moving our system towards one where-which moves towards a value-based system away from volume. Let's reward companies that deliver medicines that are delivering the outcomes that patients and payers want.

Mrs. BLACKBURN. Thank you. Mr. DILENGE. Thank you.

I mentioned at the outset that we are part of a coalition with insurers, PBMs, and others, and one of the ideas is in fact exactly what you were talking about in terms of patient information.

We need to empower patients. Right now, they do not have good information about their choices. They don't know about their formularies. Their formularies are constantly changing throughout the year.

Their prices are changing, their co-pays, their co-shares. If they had more access to good information they'd be able to find cheaper medicine.

Mrs. BLACKBURN. OK. Time's up.

Mr. DAVIS. Congresswoman, thank you.

There are three things that we would recommend. The first is to repeal the misguided Medicaid penalty on generic drugs. It was passed in the fall of 2015 as part of the balanced budget agreement.

It actually punishes generic manufacturers in the circumstances where they don't take a price increase, and serves as a disincentive.

Pass the CREATES Act, as I mentioned earlier, and include biosimilars in the coverage gap for Part D to ensure a robust biosimilars market, moving forward.

Ms. GALLENAGH. Thank you.

As wholesalers, we don't actually take positions on transparency or on pricing issues. But I would say that our members would support anything that examines greater competition in the market-place and better access for patients.

Mrs. BLACKBURN. OK.

Mr. MERRITT. I agree with a couple things that were said before. Value-based contracting would be great. The patent reforms that Chip and the generics industry have talked about, and also something that we haven't talked about and may not come up today but electronic prescribing.

We'd like doctors to be able to look at the formularies before they prescribe the drugs so patients aren't surprised at the pharmacy as they can choose the least expensive option available.

Mr. EYLES. Solutions that bring more competition through generics and biosimilars. That's the first thing. That's very important.

The second is greater price transparency, both about how prices get set and how prices are increased, and we'd agree that it's important to also move towards value-based pricing and outcomes-based pricing.

Mr. NICKELS. I would agree with a number of the things that have been said already—greater competition, greater transparency. I would agree on the CREATES Act as a piece of legislation that should move forward and, of course, as I mentioned in my statement, protecting the 340B program.

Dr. HARMON. I would tell you that not only is Mr. Mitchell the formal patient representative. All of us in the room are either patients or caregivers for patients. So we all wear that same appellation.

As a provider, as a physician, what I would like to see is transparency. It's been alluded to. That's not just a buzzword. It needs to be a reality and I need to eliminate these administrative hassles that interfere with delivering care for my patients. Thanks.

Mr. HOEY. I have three suggestions. One would be the transparency with spread pricing. That's what the pharmacy has paid and what the employer is charged, which are two different things. The employers charged more. The second would be pharmacy DIRs at the point of sale or prohibiting pharmacy DIRs altogether, and then the third would be eliminating the conflicts of interest that exist between a price giver and a price taker.

So they're giving prices but they're also taking a price, and there is an immense conflict of interest. Thank you.

Mr. MITCHELL. I would focus on promoting competition and making Hatch-Waxman work as intended. That means no more pay-for-delay. There's a bipartisan bill to do that now.

The CREATES Act is an incredibly important bipartisan bill. It would save more than $3 billion. That is important. But all elements of patent abuse that extend patents beyond what you intend with our laws should be addressed to promote competition because competition lowers prices.

Mrs. BLACKBURN. You all did a great job staying under the time limit. I thank you all.

And as I yield back, I will just say listen to what you said. Transparency, competition—basically, focusing on the patient and those are worthy goals.

I thank you for the hearing and I yield back.

Mr. BURGESS. Gentlelady yields back. Chair thanks the gentlelady. Chair yields to the gentlelady, Ms. Matsui from California, 5 minutes for questions, please.

Ms. MATSUI. Thank you, Mr. Chairman.

High drug prices are really at the top of the mind of our constituents and we've seen recent examples of extreme bad actors raising prices purely for profit motives.

Congress does need to review and better understand drug pricing to ensure that we are incentivizing research and innovation and development of new drug treatments and cures without creating loopholes that can be taken advantage of.

Drug pricing is particularly complicated because it is not transparent to the public and because drug companies often end up with monopolies, which we all know can drive up costs. We need an approach that focuses on the patient and the cost to the health care system, which will be tethered by ensuring that there is sufficient competition in the market place.

Where there is more than one option for a drug or treatment, costs tend to be driven down. As we move toward precision medicine, we move away from multiple treatment options per person.

So this is something we will only have to grapple with more and more. I know we talked about this. Let me follow up here.

Ms. Reilly, when drug companies set the initial list price for the drug from which all of the components of the price follow, do manufacturers also publish or make available how they determine the list price?

Ms. REILLY. Well, companies—and to be honest, as PhRMA we don't engage with our companies in terms of how they price their products. We can't for anti-trust reasons.

However, many companies have talked about their philosophies with regards to how they price their product and they look at a number of factors.

They look at the prevalence of the disease. They look at existing treatments that are already in the market.

Ms. MATSUI. How about the research and development costs that the company has done?

Ms. REILLY. Research and development is a cost of doing business that, obviously, has to be recouped. But companies really are focusing on the value that a given medicine is bringing to market and the list price that we come up with is very much negotiated with the purchasers of the product.

A PBM or insurance company does not have to cover our product. In fact, some proudly talk about the fact that they exclude certain products from formularies if they don't get the price that they want. So they're not done in a vacuum.

Ms. MATSUI. All right. Let me switch here.

Dr. Harmon, when a doctor prescribes a drug, how often do they know how much it will cost a patient?

Dr. HARMON. Representative Matsui, they really only know if they do it a lot, because if I de novo prescribe a drug I have no idea. You heard it from some of the other panelists.

Increase transparency on drug pricing and availability and formulary would greatly enhance my ability to adequately and accurately prescribe the right treatment for the right patient at the right time.

Ms. MATSUI. So when doctors are familiar with certain drugs that they prescribe, they know to recommend to their patient if they have two generics that do the same job as a named drug.

Do you tend to use this price information in a systemic way or anecdotally from what they hear from the patients?

Dr. HARMON. Systemically. I try to be an evidence-based prescriber. So I deal with my medical literature and up-to-date treatments that are made available to me. I make that decision, Congresswoman Matsui. But also 99 percent of the time I write on my prescription blank or I sent the electronic prescription substitution authorized.

Ms. MATSUI. OK.

Dr. HARMON. Generics are available. Rarely do I prescribe the brand name. The only exception is if I know that their insurance plan ahead of time will authorize the brand and actually have a better affordability to the patient than a similarly priced generic.

Ms. MATSUI. OK. Thank you.

I want to ensure that we continue to encourage innovation and development of new cures and the ability to profit as part of that when you are in such a risky business.

But I think the profit has gotten way out of control in many cases. I want to make sure the potential for profit is truly incentivizing innovation, not just lining investors' pockets.

Mr. DiLenge. What are examples of biologic companies that are innovating but also keeping prices low?

Mr. DILENGE. I think the vast majority are, and so we've seen, particularly over the last couple years but we've seen incredible market competition in biologics, not necessarily by biosimilars.

I agree with Chip on some of his comments there. But among branded biologics there is intense competition. In fact, the time to entry for the second biologic in a class has dropped dramatically.

And so what you are seeing is a lot of great competition and the second and third products are coming in usually cheaper than the first.

Ms. MATSUI. OK.

Mr. DILENGE. So we are seeing a lot of good competitive market dynamics in biologics.

Ms. MATSUI. Well, I would say so, but I think when you increase more competition and eliminate the monopolies, because there are still some loopholes and ways for players along the chain to take advantage of this system with our without competition.

So do you see—I guess Mr. Mitchell—do you see policy solutions that encourage innovation but close loopholes?

Mr. MITCHELL. Can you pose that question again, ma'am? I didn't hear it.

Ms. MATSUI. OK. Do you see policy solutions that encourage innovations but close loopholes?

Mr. MITCHELL. I think, most importantly, that we want to incentivize companies to invent new drugs and not invest time and money to milk money out of old drugs, and that's why I place the emphasis in what I said to the lady from Tennessee on closing patent loopholes——

Ms. MATSUI. Right.

Mr. MITCHELL [continuing]. That allow them to get more time beyond that which you intend under Hatch-Waxman instead of focusing their attention on developing new drugs, making more innovation.

Ms. MATSUI. All right. Thank you very much.

Mr. DILENGE. Ms. Matsui, if I just may respond real quick, I think it's important to emphasize that the time to market for generics has stayed the same for two decades.

So the idea that there is all this patent evergreening and that innovators are getting all these new patents and pushing out the time for generics the data just doesn't support that. Thank you.

Ms. MATSUI. OK. Thank you. I yield back.

Mr. BURGESS. Gentlelady yields back. Chair thanks the gentlelady.

The chair recognizes the gentleman from Texas, Mr. Barton, 5 minutes for questions, please.

Mr. BARTON. Thank you, Mr. Chairman and Ranking Member Green, for holding this hearing. We have established the number of witnesses we can have on one panel because there is no more room.

[Laughter.]

So we know that the number now is 10. This committee has jurisdiction over quite a bit of the U.S. economy.

The three most complicated issues we deal with in terms of pricing are the price of gasoline—when it's up everybody's mad at us, the price of prescription drugs, which we are talking about today, and the price of cable TV. And I may be using a misnomer for cable TV. It may not be cable TV anymore.

But of those three, the one that is most complicated and the most byzantine pricing mechanism is drugs. I take six prescription drugs every day.

I had a heart attack 6 years ago and I have high blood pressure and so I take six drugs. I couldn't tell you what those drugs cost. My insurance company pays it. I pay a little bit of a deductible so I know what my deductible is when I get them filled every three months. I get a 90-day supply.

Some of them are Plavix or Plavix, Lisinopril, Lipitor. Those are some of the name brands, and I think everything I am taking now is a generic. I don't believe I use any of the name brands.

So it's good to have this hearing. I hope we learn something from it. It would be nice if we could come up with a simplified system for drug pricing and perhaps this hearing will begin that.

My specific questions are going to deal with the pricing of biosimilars. Now, Congresswoman Eshoo and I worked together several years ago to get a biosimilar title in what's now called the Affordable Care Act and there is just—it's been one rocky ride trying to get biosimilars to the marketplace.

And recently Congresswoman Eshoo and I led a letter that 48 other members signed asking them to have a separate code at CMS for biosimilars.

Mr. Davis, you represent both the generic drug companies and the biosimilar drug companies. You mentioned in your written testimony that biosimilars are more complicated, difficult to develop than traditional drugs. Could you expand on that briefly, please?

Mr. DAVIS. Sure, Congressman. Thank you for the question.

Biosimilars are a subset of biologics. So the reverse engineering process associated with biosimilars is heavily science weighted and much more expensive over time.

So development programs for biosimilars can cost $150 million to $400 million in advance of filing the application. So what we need to recognize is that there are similarities in terms of the value that competition from biosimilars will present to traditional biologics in the market once they get there that is akin to the traditional small molecule versus generic competition that we've seen for years in the branded side.

At the same time, we do need to recognize that they are a different class of drug and as a result of that, through the leadership of you, Congresswoman Eshoo, and others, be able to have a pathway established here in the U.S. as part of the Affordable Care Act through BPCIA.

That pathway, as was suggested earlier, has not gone as smoothly as possible and there are several policy reasons why we are where we are, not the least of which was the potential to have different J codes for the originator product and all of the competitors in a separate one at CMS.

Because of the leadership of this committee, CMS has announced a plan change to that as of January 1. So thank you for that as well.

Another solution that would increase the uptick in interest on the part of our members to make the investments they need to bring biosimilars to market will be making sure that biosimilars are treated like biologics in the Part D coverage gap.

So it's actually our members asking to be held to the 50 percent discount to make sure that the value that biosimilars from a pricing perspective doesn't get lost as people go through the Part D program.

Mr. BARTON. Mr. DiLenge, as Mr. Davis just said, CMS has announced that they're going to reverse their earlier policy and assign a separate HCPCS code for each biosimilar rather than have a single payment rate.

Do you believe that this promotes a more vibrant and sustainable market for biosimilars and hopefully over time reduces prices?

Mr. DILENGE. Absolutely. We need to be able to incentivize for the reasons that Mr. Davis said. You need to really incentivize the biosimilar marketplace differently than you would a traditional generic marketplace.

And so while you have all the generics in the same code and that works for that marketplace, it does not work for biosimilars. It won't spur the investment.

I talked earlier today about the investment that's required for all types of innovation but biological innovation in particular is very, very expensive and you need to have the right incentives, and the Federal Government, the way they code—it sounds really arcane, coding, but it actually does impact what investors think about going into markets.

Mr. BARTON. OK. Thank you, Mr. Chairman.

Mr. BURGESS. Gentleman yields back. Chair thanks the gentleman.

Chair recognizes the gentleman from Oregon, Dr. Schrader, 5 minutes for your questions, please.

Mr. SCHRADER. Thank you, Mr. Chairman. Very good hearing. Probably should have a follow-up, given the breadth of the group in front of us here.

At the outset, I am not someone that blames the pharmaceutical industry or the supply chain for the problems we are seeing. This is just an outgrowth of industry developments and the innovation that's out there, as pointed out, a lot of the starts on these innovative drugs fail—90 percent failure rate.

That's not generally a good business model. But these guys do it because they care about the marketplace and there, hopefully, is a profit to be made at some point in time. I would remind everybody that pharmaceuticals are not the highest cost in our health care system. But at the same time, they are one of the fastest rising costs and my guess is they will continue to increase in cost because of the tremendous excitement and innovation in precision medicine. It's wonderful.

As a little old country veterinarian that I had to do and I now look at as almost a barbaric kind of way are going to be so refined that people will not have some of the great side effects that we see today in the marketplace.

But having said that, we are also stewards of the taxpayer dollar and as things get expensive and we have this wonderful opportunity in this country and hearing everybody talk about innovation that's now occurring in particular in this country that's great.

But we have to be able to afford things, and therefore we have to ask some tough questions and hopefully work on how do we all together make this medication at least slightly more affordable to the taxpayer and, frankly, to folks in the individual marketplace also.

So having said that, Mr. Davis, can you talk to me a little bit about the REMS issue and restrictive access abuse—that sort of thing. Why, in particular, do we need an effective enforcement mechanism to address that?

Mr. DAVIS. Congressman, thank you for the question and I would be remiss if I didn't start by thanking you for your leadership on this issue as well as Congressman Welch.

It's important because—let me start with—REMS was created in 2007 as part of the reauthorization for the prescription drug user fee program then, and REMS, in terms of ensuring patient safety is a very important program.

The original statute—the authorizing statute—also said that REM should not be used for the unintended consequences of delaying competition from generics.

The challenge we have is that's exactly what, in many instances, it is being used for and the reason that there is no remedy for it is because there is no sufficient enforcement mechanism in the authorizing legislation from 10 years ago, and there have been constant efforts on the part of generic manufacturers in 2012 as part of the first generic user fee agreement that coincided with the reauthorization of the PDUFA.

They came very close. There was a provision in the Senate version that actually would have remedied this issue. It's 5 years later and it still exists. And if you want a robust biosimilars market and you want to make sure that competition gets to market sooner rather than later, claiming patient safety issues that have never been documented after the FDA certifies generic manufacturers will appropriately handle the samples they need to do the pharmacovigilance is just an excuse to prolong monopolies beyond their intended effect.

Mr. SCHRADER. All right.

Mr. Merritt, talking about PBMs, I remember a day 20 years ago when they were the godsend, if you will, to reducing drug prices and having someone knowledgeable deal with the panoply of drugs that are out there and getting it.

I would like to think that still exists, obviously, or people wouldn't be using you. There is a supply and demand. The reason they use PBMs is because they think they're getting value.

Some insurers had moved away from that a little bit here very recently and everyone talks nowadays about this black box, and given the fact that you guys have to talk about some of the rebates when you are reporting to Part D and CMS.

Is there a way to inject some transparency in what you do without giving away proprietary information in the private insurance market?

Mr. MERRITT. Yes. That's a great question.

Yes, Medicare Part D is a great example because consumers have transparency. They choose their plans. They can see what the premiums are, what the cost sharing is, what the drug selection is of every plan, which is why you have 90 percent satisfaction with Medicare Part D.

I agree with something Dr. Harmon said. It would be nice if there was that transparency in the doctor's office so people weren't surprised—the physician, the pharmacist, and the patient—as to what a drug actually costs a patient because Lori is correct, the cost sharing is different for different plans because different plans have different goals and different populations.

So if there was electronic prescribing and doctors and patients seeing what the actual out-of-pocket costs were in the doctor's office I think that would really help.

Mr. SCHRADER. Very good. Well, I've got a ton of questions probably like everybody else here and I appreciate all the participants on the panel.

I guess, Mr. Chairman, it'd be nice maybe to have a work group at some point in time, work with all our participants, the patient groups also, about what are some of the best solutions because I don't think there is a silver bullet here that's going to require everyone to get in the boat together and figure out how do we make sure we still have the most vibrant innovative pharmaceutical market in the world that is increasingly doing amazing things, from my perspective.

Thank you, Mr. Chairman. Yield back.

Mr. BURGESS. Chair thanks the gentleman. Gentleman yields back.

Chair recognizes the gentleman from Illinois, Mr. Shimkus, 5 minutes for questions, please.

Mr. SHIMKUS. Thank you, Mr. Chairman.

This is a great panel. Appreciate you all being here. I would recommend that we break it down. There's too many—because I think all of us want to talk to each one of you.

I know you can all come and visit with us but to have that interaction. Some of you are going to get lost in the shuffle and we apologize for that.

I've spent a lot of time in this health care arena on orphan drugs, on antibiotic resistance. So and I, like some of my colleagues, understand the 90 percent failure rate, understand the R&D.

We want to make sure there is a return. We are the innovators in the world but we just have to be careful.

And then we've got these—how do you provide lifesaving drugs to a small population that you can't get a return just from selling that drug to that individual. So that's all part of this debate.

The antibiotic thing, which Gene Green and I have worked on, we are floating tradeable vouchers somehow, having the company get some way to get a return on that so that they can have a ready-made supply of something which you, hopefully, don't have to use. Can you imagine asking a company to have something on the shelf that you hope you don't use?

So that's why you all are there for the right reason, trying to make the system work. I really do appreciate it.

This transparency debate is also key. It gets us frustrated and you just talk about drug prices in a hospital setting, but the hospital has a federal mandate called EMTALA—emergency room. Anybody can go.

High cost—how do they balance that versus an outpatient clinic that doesn't have that mandate of that service? I think you always win with being transparent and then you help educate the consumer, and then the consumers say, well, that's why I have to pay a little bit more because, shoot, the hospital's paying for this emergency room access, which they have to do.

So health care is a most challenging and frustrating payment process that we have and many years I tried to stay off this committee because I didn't want to deal with it. They kept throwing me back on so I am stuck with it.

[Laughter.]

But I really want to talk to one provision too that I hear. I want to go to the local pharmacist. I think one provision that just really gripes me is this clawback issue.

So here's what happens. Doctor gives a prescription to a patient. A patient goes to a pharmacist. They pay the transaction or the insurance, and then months later tell me what happens. It's hard to believe.

Mr. HOEY. You're leading right up to it, Congressman, exactly to the punch line. So months later, the money that the pharmacy collected from the consumer is taken back by the insurance plan, or the PBM.

So for——

Mr. SHIMKUS. And the drug probably has already been consumed.

Mr. HOEY. Hopefully it's worked and that patient is doing fantastic on it. But the payment is still in play.

So the pharmacy basically is forced to act like a mule to take the money from the patient and then that money is clawed back from the pharmacy to the health plan or the PBM.

Mr. SHIMKUS. Can someone tell me why? Can someone defend that practice? Do you really want to try?

Mr. MERRITT. No. No, we don't defend the practice. It's an outlier behavior. It's something that is outlier behavior in the industry and we understand frustrations on that. And to the degree it exists, it exists rarely and hopefully more rarely in the future.

Mr. SHIMKUS. Well, when our local pharmacists come to see us, especially the community-owned small ones, they show us. They show us the bill.

They show us the receipt, so I hope that people are listening to the hearing and saying, we got to fix this. Because it's just not right to offer a service, pay the cost and then for someone else later on to say, oh, you got to give us money back because whatever parameter. It's not truth in advertising.

It's not truth in billing, and I am tired of it. I really am—and I hope it gets fixed.

With that, Mr. Chairman, I am going to yield back before I get more angry.

[Laughter.]

Mr. BURGESS. The chair thanks the gentleman. The chair would remind the gentleman that he was the ranking member of this sub-committee when we were in the minority and I was down on the first row. So he's got a lot of time in service here.

[Laughter.]

Chair recognizes the gentlelady from Colorado, Ms. DeGette, 5 minutes for questions, please.

Ms. DEGETTE. Thank you, Mr. Chairman.

Over the last 6 months, as many of the these panelists know, I've been working with Congressman Tom Reed, who is my co-chair of the Diabetes Caucus on what's going on with insulin prices around drug pricing.

And what we've learned across the whole drug chain is that there is a lack of transparency, which we've been talking about a lot in the hearing today, and we've also learned that there is a lot of finger pointing, which we've also seen in this panel today.

It's kind of good. It's frustrating to have 11 witnesses but you hear all of that. And so I want to kind of focus on this issue of the complex web of financial and contractual relationships between the players here with the idea that maybe we can get to some more transparency and the ultimate goal being to help the patients.

Ms. Reilly, I heard you talking about your view of how the market is working in your opening statement and I agreed with almost everything you were saying but you left one thing out and the thing you left out is why the price of insulin is $400 to begin with.

Now, I know there are a lot of different delivery systems. There's a lot of different kinds of insulin. We've moved away from the animal insulin. We don't have a generic yet, although that's coming soon, et cetera, et cetera. But some would say it's not just the other players. PhRMA has a role in this, too.

So I want to ask you and two other witnesses a very simple question as we go forward, and that is this. Will PhRMA, AHIP, and PCMA each agree to work with your member companies to share information with us about your contract with other supply chain players including sharing specific examples of contract terms?

Obviously, I don't want to undermine confidentiality. But until we know what the contract terms are it's really hard for us to get that transparency.

Yes or no, Ms. Reilly.

Ms. REILLY. Well, we as——

Ms. DEGETTE. Yes or no would work.

Ms. REILLY. I don't have access to those contracts, Congresswoman.

Ms. DEGETTE. Can you work with your members to try to get us that information?

Ms. REILLY. You could probably work independently with them.

As a trade association, we cannot be privy to confidential information.

Ms. DEGETTE. You're not going to help.

OK. Mr. Merritt, can you help us with that?

Ms. REILLY. It's a violation of anti-trust.

Mr. MERRITT. Yes. Yes.

Ms. DEGETTE. OK. And Mr. Eyles, can you help us with that?

Mr. EYLES. Yes.

Ms. DEGETTE. OK.

Now, I was listening with great interest to Mr. Guthrie's questions about the PBMs and I want to ask you a couple of questions, Mr. Merritt, about this because I heard you say that the rebates always go back to the consumers.

But I know from my investigation they don't always go back to the consumers in the form of lower drug prices. Isn't that correct? Yes or no.

Mr. MERRITT. Well, yes in the sense that—— Ms. DEGETTE. Thank you.

Mr. MERRITT. No, but we give the rebates to the plans and then they sometimes——

Ms. DEGETTE. Right. But they don't always go back in the form of lower drug prices.

And so I want to ask you sometimes the PBMs actually make money off of the rebates paid by the pharmaceutical companies. Is that correct?

Mr. MERRITT. That totally depends on the client. The client—— Ms. DEGETTE. But it could happen, right?

Mr. MERRITT. If the client wants that to be that way. Ms. DEGETTE. Yes. That answer is yes.

Now, my understanding is that some of your member clients pass some but not always all of the rebates onto their insurance or employer clients. Is that correct?

Mr. MERRITT. It's determined by the insurer but——

Ms. DEGETTE. Right. That's correct. Some do, some don't.

Mr. MERRITT. A hundred percent of the big employers requires

100 percent pass-through of those rebates.

Ms. DEGETTE. But not everybody, right? Not everybody?

Mr. MERRITT. Probably because they don't want to.

Ms. DEGETTE. Right. Yes. OK.

Is it true that PBMs sometimes make money off administration fees paid by pharmaceutical companies that are separate from rebates?

Mr. MERRITT. There are different fee agreements and there are different ways that we have to work——

Ms. DEGETTE. And so the answer to that is yes, too, isn't it? I am sorry?

Mr. MERRITT. Yes.

Ms. DEGETTE. Thank you.

Now, do your member companies sometimes include price protection clauses intended to insulate PBMs from drug price increases in your contracts with pharmaceutical companies?

Mr. MERRITT. They're intended to insulate our clients from price increases.

Ms. DEGETTE. And so that answer is yes, right?

Mr. MERRITT. Well, our clients. So I guess it would be that was there to insulate our clients from price increases. They want those there.

Ms. DEGETTE. OK. Member companies sometimes include price protection clauses intended to insulate PBMs from price increases in contracts in pharmaceutical companies—yes or no?

Mr. MERRITT. I guess it would be no.

Ms. DEGETTE. OK. Do these price protection clauses sometimes allow your member companies to make additional money through clawbacks when a drug's price increases?

Mr. MERRITT. I am not aware of that in the clawbacks.

Ms. DEGETTE. Yes. So if a drug price increases they can get clawbacks. Ms. Reilly, you were nodding.

Mr. MERRITT. Oh, I see.

Ms. REILLY. Well, I was—yes, I actually have a document right here and it states Express Scripts has more than 90 percent of brand manufacturer contracts include price protections.

Ms. DEGETTE. Can I get a copy of that?

Ms. REILLY. Absolutely.

Ms. DEGETTE. And Mr. Chairman, I would like to put that into the record.

Mr. BURGESS. Without objection, so ordered.

[The information appears at the conclusion of the hearing.]

Ms. DEGETTE. OK. Mr. Chairman, as you can imagine I have many more questions and I apologize for making you answer yes or no. We have 5 minutes.

I am going to submit these to the witnesses and I thought the idea that Mr. Schrader had to have a task force is an excellent idea.

Thank you. I yield back.

Mr. BURGESS. Chair thanks the gentlelady. The gentlelady yields back.

The chair recognizes the gentleman from Ohio, Mr. Latta, 5 minutes for questions, please.

Mr. LATTA. Well, thank you very much, Mr. Chairman, and to our panel, thanks very much for being here today. It's been a very, very interesting discussion we've been having this morning.

Several years ago, I sponsored the legislation on track-and-trace, from making sure that we don't have adulterated counterfeit drugs entering the market. So this has been a really fascinating hearing that we've been having today.

And I am also working on legislation right now to modernize and reform the FDA's OTC monograph system. I would like to talk a little bit more about that to see how we examine ways to modernize the regulatory infrastructure of prescription drugs.

As members, I believe we should always be looking for avenues to reduce burdensome regulation, foster innovation, spur competition, and provide certainty for consumers and businesses.

And as we go forward, how can Congress help modernize the regulatory infrastructure at the FDA in order to bring these new medicines to market in a quicker manner? Because we had the hearing earlier this fall that was really fascinating to see how long it's been going back to 1972 when you are looking at 45 years.

So Ms. Reilly, if I could ask you, what can we do as members as we look at legislation to help modernize this infrastructure at the FDA?

Ms. REILLY. That's a great question, and I would congratulate this committee on recent passage of the Prescription Drug User Fee Act, PDUFA and GDUFA as well, because that's a significant step forward in terms of modernizing the agency. I also think Commissioner Gottlieb has done a number of things on his initiative to move this in the right direction.

There are a handful of areas that I think still need further work. Combination products—EpiPen has come up on a number of comments here before and I think more needs to be done to ensure that when we have combination products, be it auto injector products like EpiPen that you have got two different parts of the agency that need to work more closely together so that we can spur competition, get those products to market sooner.

I think innovative clinical trial design is another area. As was mentioned before, the medicines that are coming to market are very different than the medicines that came 20 years ago. And so we need to modernize clinical trial design and the regulatory tools that are used to review those products as well.

And then I would say we need to continue to advance prescription-focused drug development. Having the patient at the center through the process of the Food and Drug Administration is vitally important but ensuring that patients I also heard as reimbursement decisions and coverage decisions are equally as important.

Mr. LATTA. Thank you.

Mr. DiLenge or—and Mr. Davis, would either of you like to comment on ways in which the FDA modernization or increased generics on the market would also help benefit our consumers and the patients out there?

Mr. DAVIS. Congressman, thank you for the question.

Yes, and then first I would second the recommendations that Ms. Reilly made. I think relative to the generic market, again, the leadership of this committee to pass the user fee agreement for the generics, we are only in. really, at the beginning of our sixth year of the user fee program with the FDA. The brands had a 20-year head start in many ways.

So that system is much more refined. I think there is a shared both commitment and responsibility between our sector and the agency to make sure that we are driving as much effectiveness and efficiency through the generic and biosimilar approval processes.

A simple example is first cycle approvals for generic applications historically have been very, very low—abysmally low. Under the leadership of Dr. Gottlieb, that has already begun to change.

Mr. LATTA. Let me ask you this. Why has this been so, you know, dismal in the past? What has caused that?

Mr. DAVIS. Quite frankly, I think if you look back I would certainly say on behalf of our members through the first GDUFA implementation the first 5 years engagement between the FDA and the industry in the first couple of years as the Office of Generic Drugs probably could have been more robust and mutually productive.

By the time the FDA started having goals—associated timeline goals associated with approving ANDAs, they were well on their way to have already built OGD.

The aggressive timelines in GDUFA II—8 months for a priority review, 10 months for a standard ANDA—will go a long way towards enhancing competition, getting ANDAs approved and then getting that competition out to the market.

Mr. LATTA. Mr. DiLenge, would you like to comment?

Mr. DILENGE. I would just completely agree with that. You know, we've learned a lot on the innovator side about how you improve first cycle approvals by the FDA. That is critical to getting even more brand-to-brand competition in the marketplace.

We are doing that now on the innovator side. The generic industry, I think, can learn a lot from what we went through over the last 20-plus years of GDUFA and really learn with the new GDUFA how they can interact with the agency in a better way to get more generic drugs through the process quicker on the first tray.

Mr. LATTA. Thank you very much, Mr. Chairman. My time is about to expire and I yield back.

Mr. WALDEN. Would the gentleman yield?

Mr. DAVIS. If I could just add one follow-on comment?

Mr. LATTA. Go ahead.

Mr. DAVIS. It's critically important for us to get more ANDAs approved earlier. Then we also need to make sure that there is a market where those holding those licenses will go to the market and not be tied up in endless delay through patent filings, extensions, evergreenings, and product topping as well.

Where Tom and I would disagree is that is increasingly a significant issue that's keeping generics and biosimilars from the market.

Mr. DILENGE. And we do respectfully disagree with that. There is really no data to show that.

Mr. LATTA. Thank you. And now, Mr. Chairman, my time has expired and I do yield back.

Mr. BURGESS. Your time expired a long time ago. But I do need to recognize the chairman for an informational message.

The chairman is recognized.

Mr. WALDEN. Thank you, and with the indulgence the committee, I know a couple of members have asked about we need to have a work group. We need to have some sort of rump group to address this issue.

Consider yourself on it if you are on the Health Subcommittee. That is the job of this committee. That is the job of other sub-committees that are looking at other things. The O&I Sub-committee is looking at 340B issues, about to issue a report.

But this is where we are going to do regular order right here on the Health Subcommittee to look at the issues that you all are helping us get a better handle on, and I think there may be an opportunity to come back after the 1st of the year and continue this discussion.

It, I am sure, isn't the most fun thing for all of you to be at the same table together but it sure helps us, have you each go back and forth and tell us your points of view.

And so I appreciate the committee's indulgence. But the notion we are going to have a splinter group go off and do something, put a nail in that one because this is the splinter group.

This is the Health Subcommittee. This is the Energy and Commerce Committee and we are going to go through regular order to get the answers that will work for consumers.

With that, I yield back, Mr. Chairman.

Mr. BURGESS. I thank the chairman for the observation. This is indeed the smoke-filled room.

The chair recognizes the gentlelady from California, Ms. Eshoo, 5 minutes for questions, please.

Ms. ESHOO. Thank you, Mr. Chairman, and I want to thank Chairman Walden for the comments that he just made because it's important that the work not only begin here but that the Members are responsible for shaping a policy around what we are discussing, which is so important.

I want to thank all the witnesses, all ten of you. Because I've listened to most—just about every—well, everything since we began, it's a good exercise to just sit still and to listen to the questions that are asked and the answers that are given.

Here are my observations. Number one, and I am proud of this— the United States of America and its genius has produced lifesaving drugs not only for people in the United States but for people around the world.

So the research, the development that comes out of both the biotechnology industry, the pharmaceutical industry are really very, very important and I am proud of the work that I've done over the years to help advance that.

I am a firm believer in it. The other observation I have is if we were starting from scratch and you all designed the system that you are here to talk about today, it really sounds like a Rube Goldberg plan, I have to tell you.

And I don't blame any one of you. You have told your story. You're sticking to your story. But the fact of the matter is is that it's not working well at all and it's not healthy to have the antipathy in the country against you.

It's a very unhealthy thing. It really is, because on the one hand, people need the drugs. We had members speak to their own conditions and what they need to take.

So this is crying out for reform. This is crying out for reform. And I think what I would just put you all on notice on—about is that we are going to reform. We need to reform. We have to answer to our constituents.

We have to answer for what the costs are in the system that we oversee. The Federal Government is the major player and payer in the United States of America when it comes to health care.

So there is going to have to be some give and take on these issues. Mr. Davis, I just want to say something about REMS. Yes, it put into place in 2007 and it was put into place to protect patients. You know that.

Now, the FDA is the one that identifies the issues that need to be identified relative to safety and it's why we have REMS. One of the drugs that comes to mind is sodium oxybate, commonly called the rape drug.

So you said some things about REMS that I don't think are really accurate because the safety relative to these drugs that are very, very dangerous if they get into the wrong hands—that we all need to gather around that. That's a must.

That's not a Republican issue, a Democratic issue. It's there for a very good reason because those drugs, as I said, if they fall into the wrong hands it's dangerous.

I want to thank pharmacists. I have to tell you, in my community in California and Silicon Valley it's very difficult to find a small druggist anymore. They're gone. They're gone. They're gone. It's all the big guys now.

And I am not saying that they may not be doing a good job for people to get their prescription drugs. But I can't name one small druggist anymore, including a cousin of mine that was in the business his entire adult life.

So that says something about money because money is part of the business, and I think that that's a real loss in my communities and I guess communities in different parts of the country.

And to our friend at the end of the table, I think that you are a walking advertisement for the good things we did in the ACA because you would not be covered for anything in terms of what you are going through were it not for the reforms of the insurance industry that we took on in order for you to be covered and at least have peace of mind that you have coverage and that the lifetime limit caps were lifted as well because of the horrendous costs that pile up very quickly when you are dealing with what you are dealing with and I wish you well.

I really wish you well, and thank you for bringing together people on a bipartisan basis. We need you to work with us and congratulations on not being dependent on the money of anyone that's involved in the industry because it then actually, I think, diminishes or brings questions to the effort.

So thank you to all of you and those are my observations. But I think that they more than hint at the work that we need to do because this is—if there were a chart that was brought into the hearing room today, starting with the top—research, development, and then where it goes and who's involved at every level—it would outdo Johnny Carson's roadmap that he used to point to.

So thank you, Mr. Chairman, and I look forward to being a part of the solution at this committee relative to the cost of drugs in our country.

Mr. BURGESS. Gentlelady yields back. Chair thanks the gentlelady.

The chair recognizes the gentleman from New Jersey, Mr. Lance, 5 minutes for your questions, please.

Mr. LANCE. Thank you very much, Mr. Chairman, and my thanks to the panel.

Ms. Reilly, CMS recently announced in a proposed Part D rule that it wants to require Part D sponsors to pass through a portion of manufacturer rebates and pharmacy price concessions at the point of sale.

What is the ideal way in which you think this should function?

Ms. REILLY. Well, thank you for the question and I think it is important and this is an important step I think that CMS is asking for information on this very issue.

I think when Part D was originally designed the notion was just that, that the discounts and rebates that are negotiated—and they are significant in Part D—they're larger than in the commercial marketplace—find their way back to patients at the point of sale.

Today, those dollars are used by health plans and not disagreeing with keeping premiums low as an important goal. We believe, however, in work that we've done that not only could discounts and rebates get passed back to patients, that we could do it in a way that actually saves the government money—upwards of $20 billion over 10 years if we are able to pass those discounts back to patients because it will delay the time in which a patient enters the catastrophic phase of the benefit where the government picks up a large share of the cost and it will also lower the amount that the government is paying for low-income subsidies.

I think the proposal that was put forth in the CMS request needs some fine tuning. They talk about pass-through of discounts through a class of medicines.

We think it actually would work better if it was done on an individual product basis because, quite honestly, companies are not all that interested in providing greater rebates if they're going to be enhancing their competitors.

Confidentiality is important, I think, to make this work. But I would argue this is a good step forward and could be transformational into changing some of the misaligned incentives that exist in the system today that, again, as CMS has previously noted, encourages insurers to pick drugs with high list prices and high rebates.

We want them competing on delivering drugs that provide the best value at the lowest net price and this is a good step in that direction.

Mr. LANCE. Would anyone else on the panel like to comment? Yes, sir.

Mr. MERRITT. You do see some point of sale rebates happening in the commercial market where you have the whole health plan want to say, hey, look, we will raise premiums slightly in order to do that.

We are seeing that happen there. In Medicare it's difficult because CMS has noted this would raise cost to taxpayers by about $80 billion and would increase premiums for patients. And the reason that happens is because Part D reimburses plans based on the premiums, and if the premiums go up so does the cost to the government.

And so I think when you think about point-of-sale costs you shouldn't think about it in terms of reducing costs overall. It doesn't reduce costs overall.

It just shifts costs to taxpayers if it's done wrong in Medicare and from healthy people to sicker people who need the medications and that's a policy decision as to how CMS wants to approve it— look at it.

One thing CMS said is if they do approach this, they want to do it in a cost-neutral way. I think that's the thing that we are working on right now is trying to figure out how that would even happen.

Mr. LANCE. Thank you. Yes, sir.

Mr. HOEY. Congressman, we would say that the rebates allow for shell games to be played and because of the rebates those are often an unreliable—we do support pass through to the point of sale.

However, we believe that it enables shell games if it's not properly monitored and already we are starting to see rebates being relabeled.

So what was a rebate yesterday is no longer a rebate. It's an administrative fee. It's some different category so it doesn't fall into that rebate bucket.

So there is a lot of shapeshifting going on that further complicates the pricing of the product.

Mr. LANCE. And whose responsibility should it be to make sure that that does not continue to occur? Does that require a statutory change or purely a change from the executive branch, in your judgment?

Mr. HOEY. I think it would require a statutory change for that to happen. I do not think that the—that CMS—I can't speak for them, of course, but I don't know that they would say they have the regulatory authority to really police that.

Mr. LANCE. Mr. Mitchell, you wanted to comment? Mr. MITCHELL. Yes, Congressman, if I may, please.

I just want to bring it back to the patient impact of those out-of-pockets paid on retail rather than rebate. The 12 highest out-of-pocket costs for drugs on Medicare Part D annually range from $4,400 a year to almost $12,000 a year.

This really hurts people whose median income is around $26,000 a year. We need to fix something in the system and the proposal from the Trump administration to allow the point-of-sale price paid by patients to be based on rebate if not retail is a good step in the right direction.

It will move some money around unless you change benefit design. But we think the tradeoff is great to help people who are bearing the greatest burden and spread it a little more, even though it may have a slight premium impact.

Mr. LANCE. Well, thank you. I got through one of five questions and I am already over time.

I yield back. Thank you.

Mr. BURGESS. Chair thanks the gentleman.

The chair recognizes the gentlelady from Illinois, Ms. Schakowsky, for 5 minutes for questions, please.

Ms. SCHAKOWSKY. Thank you for holding this hearing today, Mr. Chairman.

I think it's long overdue that this subcommittee and committee work on skyrocketing drug prices.

AARP reported that in 2015 the average drug price was $13,000 per drug for a year's supply and that's almost a quarter of the median U.S. household and four-fifths of the average Social Security benefit.

Now, of course, not all of that money is out-of-pocket costs. But somebody ends up paying.

Mr. Eyles, I want to ask you a question. Does the insurance industry have meaningful input into the list price?

Mr. EYLES. No. We don't have any input into the list price.

Ms. SCHAKOWSKY. And does the insurance industry have any information about what the various factors that go into it including how much spending goes to research and development?

Mr. EYLES. No, that's not reported.

Ms. SCHAKOWSKY. So let's take Sovaldi for a minute. Gilead bought Sovaldi for about $11 billion, investing zero dollars in R&D, and made about $11 billion in year one by jacking up the list price to $84,000 per treatment—per cure, really.

We learned this from Dr. Gerry Anderson, professor of public health at Johns Hopkins University. Dr. Burgess hosted him at a round table. And according to a Senate investigation, we found out that Sovaldi's business model was to reach about 20 percent of the people with Hep C. There's one out of five people who might be able to afford it, and that includes people on Medicare. If their co-payment would be $5,000 they probably couldn't afford it. And the rest of the people, well, too bad.

We talked a bit about insulin. Mr. Eyles mentioned the decade increase. What I had was about 300 percent including the percent—including the period, by the way, that Alex Azar, who is now nominated to head HHS, was at Eli Lilly. And we know the names of people who died because they could not afford to get the insulin they needed.

So this business model, this idea that we can just jack up prices past what people can afford, I wondered if our consumer could speak to that for just a minute.

Mr. MITCHELL. Well, it's not just insulin. Insulin prices have gone up 300 percent over the past 10 years and it's because we have an oligopoly that controls the price of insulin. They move their prices in lockstep and they increase prices because they can.

But you should also look at other drugs like multiple sclerosis drugs.

They have increased 500 percent in price from 2004 to 2017, and when PhRMA says actually, our treatments are lowering cost of care, in 2004 the drugs accounted for 50 percent of treatment costs for multiple sclerosis but in 2017 they account for 75 percent of treatment costs.

The drug I was on for 5 years called Revlimid, made by a company called Celgene, increased its price this year by 20 percent. This is a drug that was invented in the 1950s and which is being kept off of generic is preventing a generic.

Ms. SCHAKOWSKY. Excuse me, so is your point that there was no additional research and development. The price just went up?

Mr. MITCHELL. The price just went up. That's all. Thank you, Congresswoman.

Ms. SCHAKOWSKY. Thank you. I appreciate that.

I want to get to the issue of rebates. Pharmaceutical companies talk on TV during these ads that are ubiquitous—if you can't afford your drug come to us and maybe we can help you and my office, we take advantage of that.

But I wanted to ask, really, yes or no, Ms. Reilly, do drug companies get a tax break for those rebates?

Ms. REILLY. For the donations, yes.

Ms. SCHAKOWSKY. For the donations. So if you set a list price that is up here and then you have a rebate to make it cheaper for some, is it the difference between the list price and the rebate that is considered a donation?

Ms. REILLY. I would have to get back to you on that. I am not sure how that——

Ms. SCHAKOWSKY. But it could be as much as $100 billion because that's what you were saying was about the donation. You said $100 billion.

Ms. REILLY. No, no, no.

Those aren't donations. A hundred billion dollars are the rebates that our companies provide in terms of discounts for insured patients, right. That's totally separate from patient assistance programs that help patients that lack insurance. That's a totally different issue.

Ms. SCHAKOWSKY. How much is that money and—well, I am over time. I would like to know how much goes into those programs and——

Ms. REILLY. I would be happy to——

Ms. SCHAKOWSKY [continuing]. How much of a tax break companies get for lowering the price.

I yield back.

Mr. BURGESS. Gentlelady yields back. Chair thanks the gentlelady.

Chair recognizes the gentleman from Virginia, Mr. Griffith, 5 minutes for your questions, please.

Mr. GRIFFITH. Thank you all for being here. I have to tell you, though, you all have raised my blood pressure today. Everybody is saying that this is the problem and that's the problem and the bottom line is we have our working group, as the chairman said, which is going to be this subcommittee.

I believe you all need a working group. Because if you all don't solve this we are going to come in and come up with an answer and it may not be an answer that you end up liking.

Now, one of the things I've heard today that I do like is transparency, and I understand Mr. Mitchell needs the manufacturers of the drugs, biologicals, whatever—needs a consumer patient advocate, needs the insurance companies out there—we all need that.

We need our doctors. We appreciate that. Love my pharmacists. As you all know, I really think they're front line folks for health care and most people, at least in districts like mine that are mostly rural, they've known their pharmacist for years. They trust their pharmacist. They want their pharmacist's input, and we appreciate that.

But here's the question. Without transparency, Mr. Merritt, I can't figure out for the life of me why the insurance companies can't deal directly with the manufacturers and the pharmacists and what value is it that you are adding?

Because what we've got is a big black box, and we dump the drugs in and we got people pointing fingers. And I am not going to ask you because that's a question we are going to have to answer another day. I only have 3 and a half minutes left. That'll take hours.

But what I am seeing and what the public sees is we've got this big black box called a PBM. They're saying they have to raise their prices so they can then give you a bigger discount and sometimes Mr. Eyles and the insurance companies like that and sometimes you like it and sometimes you get rebates back and sometimes you take money from the pharmacists back after they've already filled the prescription, or the insurance company does.

But it all comes back. For the life of me, if we don't get some transparency in there—and there must be something you are adding to the system and I look forward to you telling me after the meeting in a written form what that is.

But I think we have to have some transparency so the average citizen in the United States understands why it is that you all are up here pointing fingers at one another and it comes back in big part to what's going on inside that big black box called the PBMs.

Now, that being said, on the clawback, as I call it, or DIR fees, as you know, Mr. Hoey, I have a bill in along with my friend, Mr. Congressman Welch, and we've introduced a bipartisan bill that would put an end to this retroactive collection fees from pharmacies.

And it's interesting because we heard Mr. Merritt earlier say that's an outlier. But when I hear from pharmacists in Pennington Gap and in Pulaski and in Salem and in all the small towns in my rural district with 29 jurisdictions that they're having a problem with this, I think it must be the big boys and all of my small pharmacies are the outliers who are getting hit by this. Has that been your experience?

Mr. HOEY. DIR fees are prevalent across every pharmacy that we know of that does business with Medicare Part D, which is every pharmacy. So DIR——

Mr. GRIFFITH. So it's not an outlier, from your perspective?

Mr. HOEY. No. The consumer co-pay clawbacks, I would not call them an outlier. Those are really one PBM that's doing the most damage there.

But DIRs is across the board. It's suffocating independent pharmacies and it leads to some of the consequences that the congresswoman from California alluded to.

Mr. GRIFFITH. And it's interesting because they apparently do this analysis on Part D. I've been reading through the CMS rule analysis and at one point they say, our analysis of Part D plan payment and cost data indicates that in recent years,, DIR amounts Part D sponsors—that would be the insurance companies—and their PBMs actually received have consistently exceeded bid projected amounts and in another part of that analysis it says that that means it goes to their profit line.

Mr. Mitchell and the consumers out there aren't seeing all that in those savings. That's going to profit. Does that happen a lot, Mr. Hoey?

Mr. HOEY. Oh, absolutely. So the DIR fees—I think the CMS analysis from January show that DIR—over $80 billion have been paid in DIR fees over the last 6 years. And so where those DIR fees are going, some of them may be going to lower premiums.

Maybe——

Mr. GRIFFITH. And I suspect some of them are going to lower premiums.

Mr. HOEY. But some of it may not be going to that.

Mr. GRIFFITH. But here's the problem that the American public sees and if I've heard about it I know others have and those may ask questions about it as well and that is I've heard stories—and they're anecdotal and people don't want me to use their names and so forth—where they've gone to their pharmacist.

The pharmacist has told them this is how much it's going to cost and as I think it was Mr. Mitchell testified people are cutting their drugs in half or not taking all their doses they're supposed to, and the pharmacist will say, well, if you pay cash and don't use your insurance you can actually get it cheaper.

Because of all the finger-pointing going on down on this end of the table as to who's made the prices go up, you are actually better off to deal outside the system and just buy it for cash. Have you found that to be true?

Mr. HOEY. That is correct in some cases, and the pharmacies that do that are taking their business life in their own hands.

Mr. GRIFFITH. I understand that. That's why I can't talk about it.

Mr. HOEY. Yes, sir.

Mr. GRIFFITH. Can't talk about it much. So here's the bottom line, folks. If that doesn't say that there is something stinking in Denmark, nothing else does.

We are going to have to work on it and that's why you see Democrats and Republicans upset today.

I yield back.

Mr. GUTHRIE [presiding]. Gentleman yields back.

The chair recognizes Mr. Sarbanes from Maryland for 5 minutes for questions.

Mr. SARBANES. Thank you, Mr. Chairman. Thank the panel.

I want to thank in particular Mr. Hoey for your testimony and for the work of the association. I agree with just about everything that my colleague just finished saying and I hope, as many members have emphasized today, that the message is getting through that on a bipartisan basis we are kind of reaching the end of our tether.

And a lot of it just has to do with trying to catch smoke when it comes to how this pricing works. We have the whole chain represented here, I gather, and I listened to all your testimony as I was navigating the traffic coming in from Baltimore this morning.

So I did listen carefully, and I guess, Mr. Hoey, I would be interested—anybody else who wants to volunteer—but transparency is a word we hear over and over and over again.

What are the two or three things—not to set you up in direct opposition with Mr. Merritt but what are the two or three things in terms of more transparency on the part of the PBMs that you would predict the PBMs would scream the most about if those provisions were put in place?

Mr. HOEY. We've talked about some of them as far as the rebates. That would certainly——

Mr. SARBANES. Yes.

Mr. HOEY [continuing]. Cause, I think, a great deal of consternation. I think also there—on the generic side—and Chip mentioned earlier that 90 percent of the prescriptions are generic and there are very few rebates for those 90 percent. However, they're sort of a de facto rebate that the PBM industry has created.

One of those is through the consumer co-pay clawbacks that we talked about. As we indicated, it's not every PBM that does that but it's about a third of the market. The second is on the MAC prices. So a MAC price is on the generic side and what the PBM does is they set a ceiling for that generic price. That ceiling can vary from pharmacy to pharmacy, from day to day, from hour to hour. So the pharmacy actually has no idea what it's going to be paid for a generic product at any time.

In fact, when the consumer walks in for a prescription, the consumer often doesn't know what they're going to pay for that generic price, for that generic prescription, the pharmacist has no idea, and really, the only entity with the perfect information is in the middle and that's the PBM.

And until the PBM tells the pharmacy what to charge the consumer, the pharmacy has no idea what they're going to be paid and then what to charge the consumer. And furthermore, with DIR prices now, not only does the pharmacy not know until it processes that prescription, but it still doesn't know until months later when more money is clawed back from it.

So those practices make it almost impossible to run a small business and to predict cash flow, to invest in capital, and to hire employees.

Mr. SARBANES. I appreciate it. I can't help but see an analogy when we talk about how the prices can change from hour to hour and, frankly, as the PBMs would say that their role is critical and satisfying on demand need for drugs and the more I listen to it the more it sounds much like the discussion we have of the purchase and pricing of electricity.

We've been doing a lot of hearings in this committee on electricity—modernizing the grid, how purchasing of electricity has these middle operators that have to assemble the resource and then sell it up the line and so forth.

So that, to me, is a powerful analogy and, frankly, where it gets my head, just to send a shudder through the panel here today, is to the idea of regulation approaching a kind of utility regulation when you come—when it comes to drugs, which are needed by just about every American at some point in their life. This is something that traffics in the public space when you look at it that way.

So this is where I come from, and somebody on the Republican side said that if the drug supply chain can't be improved then we may start out in a place that you don't like.

But that's where my head is, and with that I yield back.

Mr. BURGESS [presiding]. Gentleman yields back. The chair thanks the gentleman.

Chair recognizes the gentleman from Florida, Mr. Bilirakis, 5 minutes for questions.

Mr. BILIRAKIS. Thank you, Mr. Chairman. I appreciate it. Thanks for holding this hearing and I thank the panel as well.

Quite a few of my constituents bring this up to me when I am home on the weekends—what about the importation of drugs from Canada? Are they safe? Is it an idea that has merit?

Why don't we start with Ms. Reilly, please.

Ms. REILLY. I think there is, unfortunately, a misnomer that importing drugs from places like Canada—our belief is that often-times, particularly when people go on the internet and they think they're buying a drug from Canada it often is not coming from Canada.

In fact, in the past when the FDA did its investigation and ordered drugs from so-called Canadian internet pharmacies found that over 80 percent of them were coming from countries all over the world and many of those were not the medicines that they purported to be.

Is it fair to say that if I walked into a Canadian drug store today to purchase a medicine would it be safe? Yes, it would.

But the Canadian market is 10 percent of the U.S. market and has repeatedly said that they don't intend nor will be responsible for supplying the U.S. drug market.

The idea of importation raises significant concerns from a safety perspective. We've heard from every FDA commissioner, both administrations going back for over 20 years.

Trying to guarantee the safety of medicines that are coming in from all over the world is near impossible and would jeopardize a supply system today that has been remarkably safe for Americans.

Mr. BILIRAKIS. How about Mr. DiLenge? Do you want to comment on that?

Mr. DILENGE. Yes. First of all, I agree, obviously, with everything that Lori said but let me add another dimension to this, which is by importing what are you importing? You're importing basically price controls on American intellectual property that other governments have imposed through their negotiations of drug prices.

They don't negotiate the foreign governments. They impose prices because they're single purchasers, and what they are doing is, because I talked about it earlier, that vast majority of innovation is occurring in the United States.

They are basically imposing price controls on American intellectual property. It should be investigated as an unfair trading practice—and we encourage that the Trump administration is trying to look at this, finally, as a trading practice problem.

Mr. BILIRAKIS. Anyone want to weigh in? Maybe there is an opposing view.

Mr. DAVIS. Congressman, I would just add from the generic perspective, and I respect and agree with the safety concerns that both Republican and Democratic administrations have found through the FDA commissioners, there is a practical effect with respect to generics.

Because we have a more robust market-based competitive environment for generics here in the U.S., generics cost less in the U.S. than they do in Canada as a market basket. So it begs the question why would you be importing something that's more expensive there?

Mr. BILIRAKIS. OK. Thank you. I will move on to the next question.

Mr. Merritt and Mr. Hoey, CMS recently published their 700-page proposed rule for Medicare Part D for calendar year 2019. One component was their proposed implementation of the drug management program for at-risk beneficiaries from the Comprehensive Addiction Recovery Act of 2016—and that was my provision.

This drug management program, or lock-in, as we call it, is used in Medicare—of course, Medicaid programs and private insurance currently.

Have you had a chance to review the regulations and what are your thoughts on CMS's proposed implementation? We'll start off with Mr. Hoey.

Mr. HOEY. Yes, Congressman, we have had a chance to take a look at that and overall we support the way the Part D lock-in program is structured.

We would contrast that on the Medicaid program the prescriber and the pharmacy that the patient is locked into is chosen by the beneficiary and that's not the situation with Medicare. In the Medicare plan it would be assigned by the plan. So we are concerned about that freedom of choice from the consumer.

Also, with the Medicaid plan it's administered by the state, and the Medicare program it would be administered, again, by the plan. So we are concerned about that.

And lastly, we would be concerned by—since the Medicare plan is administering it, any situation where the patient would be locked into a plan that also owns pharmacies or they're locked into their own mail order pharmacies.

Mr. BILIRAKIS. OK. Fair enough. Mr. Merritt.

Mr. MERRITT. Sure. The key with protecting at-risk patients is to make sure that they're going to one doctor and one pharmacy and those two medical professionals are communicating.

The challenge in the past has been doctor shopping and other addiction-related behaviors in which people are dying. It's a real epidemic.

The challenge we see at our first look at this is there are too many processes where you can't simply work with a particular pharmacy in a local area to a beneficiary and that they have 6 months essentially to work the system and not be at any particular pharmacy and we think for the at-risk patients—not for all patients, not for all drugs—but for at-risk patients on things like opioids, that's a recipe for disaster.

In 6 months people can literally lose their lives, and the whole goal of this program, I think, is patient safety and I think that's what the president has been talking about, too. We do appreciate your leadership on this, though.

Mr. BILIRAKIS. Sure. Absolutely. Thank you. I look forward to working with you in the future and get it right because if we are not safe nothing else matters as far as that is concerned.

Well, I don't have any more time, unfortunately. Mr. BURGESS. Gentleman's time has expired.

Mr. BILIRAKIS. Does anyone want to add something—— Mr. BURGESS. No. The gentleman's time has expired. Mr. BILIRAKIS. All right. All right. All right.

[Laughter.]

Mr. BURGESS. The chair recognizes the gentleman from Missouri, Mr. Long, 5 minutes for questions, please.

Mr. LONG. Ahead of Peter? OK. I didn't realize that.

Thank you all for being——

Mr. BURGESS. I thank the gentleman for pointing that out. But Mr. Welch is not on the subcommittee. Do I have that correct? And as a consequence, we will hear from subcommittee members first.

So you are recognized for 5 minutes.

Mr. LONG. I appreciate it. Thank you. Now that I have one minute left——

[Laughter.]

In 1966 there was a movie, "Ten Little Indians" and when I look at our ten witnesses here today, all these folks were invited to a luxury mountaintop resort where they started getting knocked off one by one from an unseen source. Nobody knew if it was one of them or who did it.

So I am thinking that if we had you all go off for the weekend and come back, whichever one of you comes back next week you'd have the perfect response to all of this and we could get this deal settled.

But it's like Morgan said, everybody's blood pressure gets raised on this. But if you think that we are the ones to come up with a solution, I hope that we can figure out something between then and now.

Let's see. Mr. Merritt, I am given to understand that Express Scripts—one of your members or your members is the only or one of the only PBMs that have implemented a comprehensive opioid solution.

I myself have three friends that I grew up with that have all lost children within the last few years to this opioid crisis and to combat the devastating impact of opioid abuse, which includes, according to this, a 7-day fill, enhanced fraud, waste, and abuse prevention with providers and pharmacies as well as disposal bags for medication waste.

Can you tell us a little bit more about this program and when your other member companies will be initiating similar programs?

Mr. MERRITT. Well, let me talk about it as an industry as a whole, and I do really appreciate those moves by Express Scripts.

I think what we see is that we are able to identify or the PBMs are able to identify people who are at risk. You can look at people who try to get the same scripts filled at multiple pharmacies, have gone to the same doctor to try to get multiple prescriptions.

You can track drug stores that have unusual dispensing patterns or—which aren't many but they do exist—and then providers or physicians who have unusual practices of prescribing and with that information you can identify at-risk people.

It really is important to do the most important thing with any addiction is to limit the supply and have monitoring, as we were just talking about with Congressman Bilirakis, of medical professionals.

And, again, this is not for regular people who don't have a problem. This is for at-risk people on particular drugs. Express Scripts has done a lot on that regard. We do see that happening in the industry more.

We are supporting electronic prescribing legislation right now, which would require these drugs to be electronically prescribed by physicians to a certain pharmacy so that safety could be improved. But, you know, we do see our industry taking a lot of good strides in this.

Mr. LONG. In my state of Missouri we don't have a drug registry. We are, I think, the only state that doesn't have it. Our governor has tried to implement that but it hasn't really gotten off the ground.

We are down in the southwest—at least my district, southwest corner of the state joining Arkansas, Oklahoma, and Kansas, and the doctors that work the late shift on

Friday night and Saturday night in these ERs, folks will come up from Arkansas, Kansas, over from Oklahoma—we are very close to all those states—and their Dr. White is always retired. Dr. White retired in Arkansas and I really need my opioids.

So they'll come in and they'll want to get their prescription filled.

Well, guess what? That doctor has got two choices. He can fill that prescription or, according to Obamacare where you have to rate your physicians, the doctor can say, I am not going to fill this prescription for this guy.

I know that he's addicted to it and he needs help but he doesn't need me to prescribe this. So he doesn't fill it then the guy rates him down on his rating and then he's no longer able to—so it's a huge problem.

So anything that you can share that you can help us with in that regard. Like I said, being the only state that doesn't have the registry it's—and being right down in the corner where you get three other states that all do and all the folks come in on the weekends, Friday, Saturday night, fill up the ER begging these doctors for their opioids.

Ms. Reilly, real quickly, some call for government negotiation in Part D, framing the issue as if there is no competition in the marketplace or negotiation happening now when nothing could be further from the truth.

Can you tell us about the current role in negotiating the Part D program and how that's been responsible for bringing down prescription drug costs?

Ms. REILLY. Absolutely. I think Part D has been the model of success with regards to competition. Today, as I mentioned before, those three large pharmacy benefit managers, they buy on behalf of 70 percent of all prescriptions in this country and they move their market leverage whether they're buying on behalf of Medicare beneficiaries are those in the commercial market to put additional cost pressure. They've done it in such a way where we've had high beneficiary satisfaction. Costs of the program are half of what they were expected to be when Medicare Part D passed and premiums have been low. In fact, there was an amendment offered in this very committee to try and set premiums at a price of around $50. That's never even gone into effect. We've never had an average premium that high. I think that speaks to the testament of the private market where there is a significant amount of competition.

We talked earlier today—I think the evolution of the Part D program is to ensure that that robust competition and those rebates that are collected get passed back to the beneficiary to lower patient out-of-pocket costs.

Mr. LONG. OK. Thank you.

And Mr. Chairman, I don't have any time but if I did I would yield it back.

Mr. BURGESS. Chair thanks the gentleman. Gentleman yields back.

We have been in this hearing a long time and my goal is to proceed without taking a break because then we will have votes on the floor in a little while and they'll want to have to then delay things.

But if anyone does need to take a quick break if you will just do so quietly and then join us back and I think the committee would understand.

So with that, I will recognize Mr. Bucshon of Indiana 5 minutes for questions, please.

Mr. BUCSHON. Thank you, Mr. Chairman.

Mr. Nickels, you seem kind of lonely there. No one has asked you any questions so I figure I might as well do that.

[Laughter.]

Mr. NICKELS. Thank you.

Mr. BUCSHON. Yes. You mentioned 340B. It's a program that I support. I have a lot of rural hospitals that really depend on it.

But I am concerned about the dramatic expansion of the program since the Affordable Care Act, and I want to make sure that the program is being used for its original intent.

And in that vein, I want to first remind everyone what the definition of a grantee is so that we know what the question is. Grantee eligible for 340B include black lung clinics, comprehensive hemophilia diagnostic treatment centers, federally qualified health centers, Native Hawaiian health centers, Ryan White HIV/AIDS program grantees, et cetera. You understand what grantees means.

So what I would say is in the interest of making sure that the program is being used for its original intent, would you be supportive of reporting requirements for hospitals similar to what 340B grantees are required to support, such as providing the number and percentage of individuals who are dispensed or administered 340B drugs disaggregated by insurance status, and the aggregate amount of reimbursement received for drugs purchased under 340B and/or provide contracts that would verify that a hospital meets the legal criteria for 340B eligibility?

Mr. NICKELS. Thank you very much for the question, and to your point, 340B is a very important program to your hospitals, to rural hospitals throughout the country.

It's worth noting that the expansion of the 340B program, which occurred in 2010, did expand largely to rural hospitals, to children's hospitals, and to cancer hospitals. So the dramatic increase has been because of the additional——

Mr. BUCSHON. Fair enough. Approximately half the hospitals in America are participating at this point, right?

Mr. NICKELS. Right. Right. Right. Many of which——

Mr. BUCSHON. Which means half the hospitals in America must be in rural areas.

Mr. NICKELS. Well, actually almost half are in rural areas. That's correct.

Mr. BUCSHON. Yes. OK.

Mr. NICKELS. But also remember that cancer hospitals, children's hospitals, and then DSH hospitals also qualify for the program. So it's more than just rural.

Mr. BUCSHON. So the question is, it seems to me if grantees, the ones I described, have—and it's complicated, I understand that— have requirements to justify their participation in 340B that it would only seem fair that pretty much every participant in the program should be able to show that they're benefiting low-income citizens, hospitals that can't buy expensive cancer medicine.

And so the question stands. Do you all support that type of a change? Because right now, as you probably know, in the law it doesn't really prescribe that you have to justify where the money that you save is going and the reality is, in order to make sure, from our standpoint, that the program is being utilized properly we need that information.

Mr. NICKELS. Right. So you are correct. The eligibility for the program is in statute and not based on anything else. So there is subsets of my membership those are the ones who qualify.

Having said that, we think they should all continue to qualify, but I do agree that further transparency in terms of where the dollars go is something we are certainly willing to discuss with the committee. We've been discussing it with HRSA for many years.

Mr. BUCSHON. Right. That's the point—you are discussing it for many years but we are not getting to an end point. So the question is it's yes or no. You support transparency and this type of thing or you don't.

I understand the strategy if you don't support it is to draw this out for—until we give up and decide not to try to change the law. It's an up or down question to me.

I am all about transparency. I was a heart surgeon before. I asked my hospital that I worked at once, hey, what's the actual cost to do—a patient comes in, goes to the cath lab, gets a cath, goes to the OR, I do a three-vessel bypass surgery, what's the cost, and they said, well, we can't tell you that. And, honestly, they probably couldn't, necessarily.

So I am all about transparency. If the consumer knows, if the public knows, what's wrong with that?

Mr. NICKELS. Right. No, I would say we are certainly in favor of increased transparency, but not in favor of changing the statutory qualifications for the program that would result in rural hospitals being thrown off the program.

Mr. BUCSHON. Well, that's not what we are trying to accomplish. Mr. NICKELS. But if you want to talk about transparency——

Mr. BUCSHON. It's the hospitals in rich suburban areas that are participating, that are buying up medical practices outside of their urban area and then adding all of those practices of the 340B program that I am concerned about.

Mr. NICKELS. Right. And, again, those hospitals though still do have to qualify for the program based on the definition.

Mr. BUCSHON. OK. Fair enough.

Mr. NICKELS. But I do want to answer your question, which is yes, we are willing to discuss transparency and try to work on that with you.

Mr. BUCSHON. All right. Fair enough.

I yield back.

Mr. NICKELS. Thank you.

Mr. BURGESS. Chair thanks the gentleman. Gentleman yields back.

Chair recognizes the gentleman from North Carolina, Mr. Hudson, 5 minutes for questions, please.

Mr. HUDSON. Thank you, Chairman Burgess and Ranking Member Green, for holding this important hearing today. Thank you for all the witnesses. I know we've been here a long time. I've gone to the bathroom four times. I haven't seen you all get up. So congratulations on your fortitude.

[Laughter.]

But I do really appreciate this discussion. I had hoped that today we could start peeling back the onion a little bit on this complex issue of the drug supply chain and really start the process of finding solutions and I think we've really taken a really good step in the right direction. I think there has been some great discussion back and forth. I know it is a challenge to have ten folks at one table.

But I think the ability to have this exchange has been really helpful, certainly for me, and I am excited to continue to work on this, Mr. Chairman.

I would pose this first question maybe to the whole panel and whoever is interested in jumping in. But as more and more patients gravitate toward this issue that's been discussed several times today about people moving toward low-premium high-deductible plans, due to the high cost of insurance plans available today. Patients need to be educated on how to best utilize these plans.

Numerous studies have come out recently that show patients are not engaged in normal shopping behaviors such as discussing cost of service, comparing cost and quality services, or negotiating the price of services. Because patients are responsible for the full cost of their health care before they meet their deductible, expensive treatments during the deductible period can result in patients not adhering to their treatments, resulting in worse outcomes.

My question to whoever would like to answer this is what are you doing to educate patients on the tools available to them to lower their out-of-pocket costs specifically as it relates to drug treatments before they meet their deductible.

So, I don't know—Mr. Eyles, I am sure you want to——

Mr. EYLES. Sure, Congressman. Thanks for the question because it's a really important one, particularly how we engage patients and then consumers so that they have the information that they need.

And our members are committed to developing the tools. Most of them have very robust web-based tools so that people can go on, understand whether their physician is in network or not, what the differences are between formularies, co-payments, what qualifies for being covered before the deductible.

So at least for most individuals preventive services are covered before the deductible with no cost sharing so that people can go and get their annual physicals and understand what's available to them.

One of the challenges that we have, for example, with high deductible plans that are paired with a health savings account—and, again, our members are very supportive of that—are some limitations on the ability to cover services that would be defined as preventive ahead of time. So we think there are some important modifications that we could make to HSAs to improve them, make them better.

But our members are committed to having very robust tools so that people understand cost, quality, and the status of their providers.

Ms. REILLY. I would just also add, and I would agree with Matt's comment about the need for a clarification in the IRS guidance to ensure that to the extent employers and others what to be able to offer a high-deductible plan with a health savings account that they can offer preventative services, things like diabetes medicines before the deductible.

I think the other important piece is we know from all of the literature that patients pick a plan based on premium price, and the lower the premium the higher the likelihood they gravitate towards those plans.

What they don't often realize is by signing up for a low-premium plan they're signing up for a plan with a deductible that may be as high as $5,000 and that they will be responsible for all of the costs until they hit that point.

One of the things that we pushed the previous administration on is to develop an out-of-pocket calculator similar to what exists in Medicare Part D where an individual can enter the information what drugs am I on, what physician do I use, so that they can get a real-life calculation in terms of what their costs are going to be depending on the plan that they pick.

We don't really have that yet today for the exchange plans and I do fear that oftentimes people end up buying plans which are not in their best interest, that aren't going to cover the medicines they need, where their doctor is not in-network, and that's a problem and needs to be improved, and transparency that allows patients to make better choices should absolutely be paramount.

Mr. HUDSON. Mr. Hoey, did you want to jump in or anybody else? Mr. MITCHELL. I would just add those are both good ideas. I had a patient contact me over the weekend who's taking an expensive subcutaneous drug for her cancer. The price went up $1,400.

She said, I can't get anyone to explain to me why. I don't know who raised my price—my doctor, my insurer, the drug company. All of what Ms. Reilly just said needs to be done but there needs to be a way for patients to get their questions answered.

It could be online. It could be on the phone. But the system is impenetrable for us and somehow something that approximates what happens in other industries where customer service is important needs to manifest itself on drug pricing.

Mr. HUDSON. Anybody else want to jump in?

Mr. HOEY. As far as at the counter that's one area where pharmacists—we are sort of a rare breed in that we know the cost of the drug in some cases. We don't know when we are going to get paid but we know the cost of the drug and we know the therapeutic effectiveness of it.

So we can often help the patient, kind of guide them through, especially when they're hitting prior authorizations that Dr. Harmon mentioned or some of the other hurdles that they hit at the counter. We can sometimes help them with that, especially in those high-deductible plans.

Mr. BURGESS. The gentleman's time has expired.

Mr. HUDSON. Guess I should have paid better attention, Mr. Chairman. I apologize.

Thank you for the answers.

Mr. BURGESS. Well, the only reason I interrupt is the gentleman from Georgia, who has been very, very patient, and the gentleman from Georgia is recognized for 5 minutes for questions.

Mr. CARTER. Thank you, Mr. Chairman, and thank all of you for being here today.

Mr. Merritt, I will start with you. Quite often, pharmacists are complaining about the fact that they're being threatened for mailing or delivering drugs by the PBMs because the PBMs own their own mail order pharmacies.

As you well know, pharmacies get contracts from PBMs unless it's a closed network and they can either accept that contract and the terms of that contract or they can't.

If they accept it, then they can service the patient. If they don't, then they can't service the patient and that's what they're left with.

Just a yes a no answer, if you will, Mr. Merritt—do you agree that pharmacists should be able to tell patients that if they pay cash for a medication they can get it cheaper? Yes or no.

Mr. MERRITT. Yes.

Mr. CARTER. You do agree with that? Then why is it that these contracts that I referred to earlier have gag clauses in it where it says that if the pharmacist indeed lets the patient know that if they pay cash it'll be cheaper, that they could be kicked out of this contract and that contract can be terminated?

Why is that? Can you explain that to me? If indeed, as you have said earlier, you are in favor of transparency, why are the gag clauses in there? Can you explain that to me?

Mr. MERRITT. I don't know, and we as an industry don't defend that practice at all. So, we want people to pay the lesser of and in fact almost all the plans work together. The PBMs work together with what's called lesser of logic so that automatically the person will pay the less.

Mr. CARTER. Then why are the gag clauses in there? Why are they in there if you truly want to take care of the patient, if you truly want them to get their medication why is the pharmacist running the risk of being kicked out of the plan if they offer this information to the patient?

Mr. Hoey, do you ever get any of your members complaining of this?

Mr. HOEY. All the time. Our members are intimidated and most of the time will refuse to go on the record because of basically a business death penalty if they're caught talking to media, talking too much.

Mr. CARTER. Mr. Merritt, during the years 2010 through 2015 CMS has said that DIR growth and rebate growth has grown 22 percent per year whereas the Part D gross drug costs have only increased 12 percent.

Can you explain why that difference is there? Why the DIR has grown 22 percent but the Part D drug costs have only grown 12 percent? Is there a reason for that?

Mr. MERRITT. Well, DIR—direct and indirect remuneration—is an important discounting tool in Medicare Part D. The federal——

Mr. CARTER. Can you explain why that difference exists? If the Part D costs have only increased 12 percent, why have the DIR fees increased 22 percent?

Mr. MERRITT. Remember that—sure, and I understand. The PBMs—we get the discounts where we can. We pass them back to the plans and the plans use them as they see fit.

Sometimes usually they want to reduce premiums. They want to reduce overall cost sharing. It depends on their individual strategy.

Mr. CARTER. And how far do these clawbacks of these DIR fees go? Are you aware? How far back do they go? Because I can tell you that my wife's pharmacy in March got a bill for $10,337 that went back not 5 months but 5 years.

Now, let me ask you about that. Those DIR fees, did you credit the government or the consumer with that? Did you go back those 5 years and credit the government? Because what happens is this.

We got a Part D program that has, as you well know and everyone on this panel well knows, has a doughnut hole in it. Mr. Mitchell, I am sure you are in this. I am sure you have Medicare. You pay so much until you get in that doughnut hole, then you have to start paying for it. That means that everyone out here who buys drugs has to start paying for it if you are on Medicare. And when you charge those higher prices—the list prices we've been referring to it as—that pushes people into the doughnut hole even more.

Now, listen. It gets even better, folks. What happens next is that when you get pushed out of the doughnut hole, guess who starts paying for it then? The taxpayer. All of us. We get to share in it.

My question to you, Mr. Merritt, are you sharing that? Are you sharing that with CMS to let them know, hey, you need to credit them back with this? Are you?

Mr. MERRITT. Yes. CMS is aware of the DIR. They see all this information and they've been very clear——

Mr. CARTER. So when my wife's pharmacy got hit for the $10,337, this PBM went back and credited CMS with that and went back to the patient and said, oh, you shouldn't have been in the doughnut hole that quickly—we are going to go back and reimburse you that? So I just want to know because she's going to ask me tonight about that $10,337.

I mentioned it was $10,337 because that's how much it was, and Mr. Hoey, have you had any other of your members who have experienced these type of things?

Mr. HOEY. Both on the retroactive. We had a call this week from a member in the Midwest who went back 5 years, six figures on DIRs. Had another one just this year, also in the Midwest, one pharmacy taken back over $100,000 in DIRs from, really, three different plans.

Mr. CARTER. OK. The last thing I will say is this. All of you said we need more transparency and I will tell you, Mr. Merritt, I pulled out your mission statement earlier today and it says pharmacy benefit managers reduce prescription drug costs and improve convenience and safety for consumers. Reduce prescription drug costs.

Mr. MERRITT. Right.

Mr. CARTER. How is that working out for everybody? If it were working out we wouldn't be here now. If it were working out then we wouldn't have had a 1,553 percent increase in prescription drug costs since PBMs started—1,553 percent increase.

Mr. MERRITT. CMS said the growth was 1 percent last year.

Mr. CARTER. Mr. Merritt, transparency is the key. The most immediate, the most significant impact that we can have on drug prices is to have transparency.

Thank you, Mr. Chairman, and I yield back. Mr. BURGESS. Chair thanks the gentleman.

Chair recognizes the gentleman from Vermont. Not on this sub-committee but we welcome you today and you are recognized for 5 minutes for questions.

Mr. WELCH. Thank you very much and thank you for having this hearing. I thank the panel. It's very helpful.

First of all, this hearing is not about the value of the pharmaceutical industry. They create life-saving and pain-relieving drugs. It is not about trying to stifle innovation. Everyone on this panel wants to support that.

It is about the lack of restraint and the pricing power that the pharma industry has that is resulting in immense heartache for families, and you can create a life-extending pain-relieving drug. But if you kill taxpayers with the price then it's not accessible.

So I want to talk a bit about that. First of all, my colleagues have talked about transparency. That's essential. The opaqueness of the market works for the benefit of the folks pricing it.

Ms. Gallenagh, you said at the very beginning that the whole chain down the line starts with the list price, correct? And I think a number of people on the panel agreed with that. The pharma companies establish the list price, correct?

Ms. GALLENAGH. Yes.

Mr. WELCH. They have no restraints on what they can do?

Ms. GALLENAGH. I would say that the constraint is only our negotiation which, again, our net price is not what we earn, right, the list price.

Mr. WELCH. Let me ask you this. Just get some things established here.

When a company creates a product it gets a patent, correct?

Ms. GALLENAGH. Correct.

Mr. WELCH. And it gets a period of exclusivity.

Ms. GALLENAGH. Correct.

Mr. WELCH. It has a monopoly over that product for a period of time?

Ms. GALLENAGH. It can sell that particular product. It doesn't prohibit competing products that have the same effect, for example.

Mr. WELCH. That particular product——

Ms. GALLENAGH. But we see significant competition well before patent——

Mr. WELCH. Do you have a problem answering the question?

Ms. GALLENAGH. No, I am just trying to clarify.

Mr. WELCH. That product for which you got a patent is something over which you control the price, correct?

Ms. GALLENAGH. We control the price in negotiation with the purchaser of the product. Correct.

Mr. WELCH. And the price that you set is based upon meeting obligations to shareholders in a return on profit, correct?

Ms. GALLENAGH. It is based on a number of factors—the value the medicine provides and the like, yes.

Mr. WELCH. Is it the case that at the end of that patent period that it is something given by public policy as incentive for doing the research any of your member companies have used legal maneuvers to extend that period of original exclusivity in the patent?

Ms. GALLENAGH. It's impossible to extend the length of a particular patent. The current system works this way as a result of Hatch-Waxman.

Mr. WELCH. Hold on a second. Have you ever heard the term evergreening?

Ms. GALLENAGH. I have heard the term evergreening. Of course. Mr. WELCH. And evergreening is extending the life of the control.

Is that correct?

Ms. GALLENAGH. No. Evergreening the——

Mr. WELCH. Has a company in your organizational group, ever paid another company in return for not bringing their competing product to the market?

Ms. GALLENAGH. Companies have entered into what's known as a patent settlement wherein a generic company is trying to enter the market before the expiry of a patent.

Mr. WELCH. According to you?

Ms. GALLENAGH. Excuse me?

Mr. WELCH. According to your company. If you pay somebody off not to bring their competing product to market, then you enjoy——

Ms. GALLENAGH. The generic company——

Mr. WELCH. —the pricing power of that exclusivity perk.

Ms. GALLENAGH. The generic company is trying to bring a product to market prior to the patent expiring. There is——

Mr. WELCH. Isn't there an argument over whether the patent period is a set period in time.

Ms. GALLENAGH. Absolutely.

Mr. WELCH. Exactly. So——

Ms. GALLENAGH. And it cannot be extended beyond that.

Mr. WELCH. It doesn't take a genius to figure out when that period is up. It's called looking at a calendar, right?

Ms. GALLENAGH. Correct. But drug——

Mr. WELCH. OK. So are you familiar with a recent effort by Allergan where they took their products and paid the Mohawk Indian tribe to take, "ownership," as I understand it, as a way of having better defenses against competition?

Ms. GALLENAGH. Yes, I am familiar with that and they used that through a process called inter partes review.

Mr. WELCH. Can you give me any other example in the entire economy of the United States where the owner of a valuable intellectual property would pay someone else to take ownership of that product?

Ms. GALLENAGH. That has been used in other—universities have used that, yes. It has happened.

Mr. WELCH. And give me a specific example.

Ms. GALLENAGH. I can get back to you on it. But I know there are universities that have——

Mr. WELCH. You don't have a specific example now?

Ms. GALLENAGH. I will get back to you. I know it exists.

Mr. WELCH. Is there anyone here who can justify a practice where a seller of a product, like a pharmacy, after selling it, 5 months, 6 months, or a year later has to rebate under a DIR? Can anyone justify that? Anyone—business model would it work with that situation?

Ms. GALLENAGH. If I understand your question, if you are asking whether discounts and rebates are common in industries then I would say absolutely. It is very common for industries to discount and rebate their products. That's not uncommon.

Mr. WELCH. All right. So the situation that you've been describing your company could work with if that happened to the pharmacy or if that happened to pharma?

Ms. GALLENAGH. Different issue than what's happening in the pharmacy. Absolutely.

Mr. WELCH. So you justify what's happening to pharmacists?

Ms. GALLENAGH. No, I don't justify what's happening in the pharmacy. Absolutely not.

Mr. WELCH. All right. Sir, please.

Mr. DAVIS. Congressman, I just wanted to add for a clarifying point around the patents, you are right, and to the point that was made, a finite period of time as to when an individual patent is supposed to end.

There is no such limitation on the number of patents filed on a product to extend its monopoly beyond the main ingredient patent that was originally filed and the best example of that is Humira, which generates the most revenue of any product in the U.S. and in the world at $16 billion per year.

In the 3 years leading up to the main ingredient expiry on that drug, that manufacture filed 50 new patents on that product. So even if they were ultimately struck down, that company continues to enjoy a monopoly while litigation ensues and that is why it is so important to maintain the IPR process in addition to the court process that we have in federal court.

Mr. WELCH. Yield back. Thank you.

Mr. BURGESS. Gentleman's time has expired. Chair thanks the gentleman.

And I think we've been through the entire subcommittee with the exception of your chairman so I am going to recognize myself 5 minutes for questions, and I may not take all 5 minutes because most of the information has been put out in front of the public today.

I want to underscore what Mr. Griffith's line of questioning started with and the recent publication from the National Academy of Sciences on "Making Medicines Affordable: A National Imperative," in the preface of that report, which is lengthy, but in the preface they make the statement that public concern has reached a tipping point, and they go on to cite several examples that may have caused that tipping point to have been reached.

But going further, they say those examples have had a sufficient impact on the health of citizens such as to attract sustained public attention and concern.

A September 2017 survey of adult American priorities for Congress through the end of the current year found lowering prescription drug prices to be the highest ranked above minimum wage, reducing the deficit, rebuilding the nation's infrastructure, reducing taxes, or any other of the six items considered.

So Mr. Griffith's point well taken and this has been a very informative panel. I want to thank all of you and I know there have been some differences of opinion. We expected that. In fact, we welcome that.

Mr. Griffith's admonitions that there may be solutions that you— you are smarter about this stuff than we are by a lot and you may have solutions that you can arrive at, not necessarily individually but in collaboration.

And I would just submit to you that those solutions may well be better than anything we or a federal agency can impose. But I guess the other side of that is if we are not moving towards some solutions to this problem then there likely will be some type of action, perhaps not by this subcommittee this year, perhaps not by this subcommittee next year, but there will be action taken— whether it be by agency or legislatively.

Now, Mr. DiLenge, I am going to switch gears a little bit. I do want to ask you because some of your written testimony is actually fascinating—Mr. Nickels, in his testimony, gave us a list of several medications that were very high in price and one of them was Keytruda and a drug that was developed for malignant melanoma, and the United States president who was president when I was in medical school—Jimmy Carter—publicly disclosed in July of 2015 that he had metastatic melanoma to his liver and his brain. And, of course, I thought the next story in that sequence was a state funeral.

However, a year later, he's speaking at the Democratic Convention. A year ago or a little bit less than a year ago he was at President Trump's inauguration. It is a fantastic story—that when Jimmy Carter was elected president I was in medical school. That story would not have happened.

Can you speak to that?

Mr. DILENGE. Yes. It's just one example of so many incredible miracles. There's no other word for what happened with Jimmy Carter.

Mr. BURGESS. It's a gift. It's a gift.

Mr. DILENGE. It's a miracle, and that is what the hard men and women who worked in our companies, and again, let me remind you all these are mostly start-up companies.

They are trying to raise capital every day. I will give you one quick story of one of our companies right on the cusp of success— started in 2002, has raised $4 billion in public and private investment and partnerships with larger companies.

It spent about $2.5 billion so far in R&D. It is hoping to get its first approval of a dramatically important drug next year from the FDA, and that's after 15 years, OK, of every day working. They've had setbacks. They've had to reduce their staffs because it's been hard to raise capital throughout that whole time period.

This is the reality of what this body does. When it makes public policy it is directly impacting the investment decisions that are being made in companies like this one every day—can we afford to get that capital, to advance that R&D, to get to the next Keytruda. That's exactly what is at stake here.

Mr. BURGESS. And I don't want people to become discouraged from hearing this from the information that we've gotten in this hearing. I am optimistic.

There have been people in my office just very recently, one with a potential gene therapy for a specific type of blindness and one with a therapy for hemophilia. Hemophilia, for crying out loud.

This was never something that I thought when I was in training that day we would ever see and it will have a profound impact on Mr. Eyles' business because of the ramifications. And these individuals also were talking about how do we prepare the—whether it's CMS or private insurance—how do we prepare the payers for what is in development because, again, I consider it a gift to humanity that they are providing.

Yes, there is going to be cost associated with that, with one of these therapies that we're talking about it was a one-time therapy so a lot of research and development costs will have to be recouped on that one injection or one treatment—whatever it is.

Mr. DILENGE. And I can I just add that, our industry has been criticized over the years for basically wanting people to be addicted to drugs, right, that we just want chronic conditions and we don't ever want to cure people, we just want to keep them on drugs for the rest of their life.

These new biotech miracles are actually going to cure people and a lot of them is maybe one-time injections of gene therapy. And that is why when you look at the pricing of those it's going to be shocking. Let's be honest about that. But the value that they deliver is far beyond those prices.

Mr. BURGESS. And some of us have urged to allow the things that are in development—to allow discussions with CMS and payers before the FDA approval just because of the——

Mr. DILENGE. Thank you for your work on that, sir. Mr. BURGESS. Because it is so important.

And Mr. Merritt, you mentioned something in your response to a question. I found it intriguing. I've been a big advocate of physician drug monitoring programs or prescription drug monitoring programs, I guess I should say, the PDMPs. I know it's another layer we put on your life, Dr. Harmon. Apologize about that.

But it is useful to know if someone is getting multiple prescriptions. But then you alluded to that with the data that you have available you can know who is at risk even before they might be identified as a risk to themselves or family or their physician.

So that's pretty powerful information, and I don't know if there is a way for you to share with the person who is providing the care.

But I hope we can find a way that your claims data or whatever we would call it can actually have a profound beneficial impact on what has become a national crisis.

So, perhaps we will enter into more discussions about that. But that was an intriguing thought that you gave us today and I appreciate that.

So once again, thanks everyone, for being here.

Mr. Green, did you have any concluding thoughts?

Mr. GREEN. No, Mr. Chairman.

Mr. BURGESS. Anything else to add for the record?

I want to thank all of you for your testimony and remind members that there are—oh, wait.

I need to submit statements for the following for the record: the American Pharmacists Association, Senior Care Pharmacy Coalition, Coalition for Affordable Prescription Drugs, National Multiple Sclerosis Society, Express Scripts, Alliance for Transplants and Affordable Prescriptions.

[The information fappears at the conclusion of the hearing.]

Mr. BURGESS. Pursuant to committee rules, I remind members they have 10 business days to submit additional questions for the record. I ask the witnesses to submit those responses within 10 business days of the receipt of those questions.

Without objection, the subcommittee is adjourned.

[Whereupon, at 1:15 p.m., the committee was adjourned.]

[Material submitted for inclusion in the record follows:]

December 12, 2017

The Honorable Greg Walden
Chairman
Committee on Energy & Commerce

The Honorable Frank Pallone
Ranking Member
Committee on Energy & Commerce

Dear Chairman Walden and Ranking Member Pallone:

AARP commends the House Energy and Commerce Committee for holding this hearing entitled "Examining the Drug Supply Chain." Addressing the rising cost of prescription drugs is an ongoing priority for AARP members and all older Americans, regardless of party. Older Americans use prescription drugs more than any other segment of the U.S. population, typically on a chronic basis. In fact, on average, older Americans take 4.5 prescription drugs every month.[211]

As launch prices of prescription drugs continue to skyrocket[212] and manufacturers are consistently increasing the prices of existing products[213], older Americans are struggling to afford the drugs they need. According to a recent AARP Rx Price Watch report, the retail price of specialty drugs widely used by older Americans increased by an average of 9.6 percent in 2015 - the largest increase since at least 2006. In 2015, the average annual cost for one specialty drug used on a chronic basis was $52,486, which is slightly less

---

[211] Medicare Part D enrollees take an average of 54 prescriptions per year, or 4.5 different prescription drugs per month. Medicare Payment Advisory Commission (MedPAC), *June 2016 Report to the Congress: Medicare and the Health Care Delivery System* (Washington, DC, MedPAC, June 2016).

[212] E. Silverman, "Cancer Drug Prices are High at Launch and Stay That Way," STAT News, May 2, 2016; D.M. Hartung, D.N. Bourdette, S.M. Ahmed, and R.H. Whitham, "The Cost of Multiple Sclerosis Drugs in the US and the Pharmaceutical Industry," *Neurology* Vol 84(21): 2185-2192.

[213] http://www.aarp.org/rxpricewatch.

than the median U.S. household income, more than twice the median income for Medicare beneficiaries, and more than three times the average Social Security retirement benefit.[214] Moreover, a 2016 AARP Price Watch Report found that 97 percent of brand-name drugs widely used by older Americans experienced a price increase above inflation in 2015.[215] These trends helped push U.S. prescription drug spending to a record high of $425 billion in 2015, with expectations that such spending will surpass $600 billion by 2020.[216]

Rising prices not only affect seniors' pocketbooks, but are large drivers of the growing cost of Medicare and other health programs. In 2015, Medicare Part D spent $137.4 billion on prescription drugs, an increase of 13 percent compared to 2014; and Medicare Part B spent $24.6 billion on prescription drugs, an increase of 14 percent compared to 2014[217]. Affordability is a growing concern for many older Americans. A 2016 survey of the 50+ population found that over 80 percent believe that prescription drug prices are too high, and nearly 90 percent think it is important for politicians to support efforts to reduce prescription drug prices.[218]

AARP stands ready to work with this committee to reduce the price of drugs, including improving our drug delivery system. However, we strongly believe that we need to have an honest discussion of how drugs are priced when they first come to the market, and how those prices increase over time. If prescription drugs continue to come to market with exorbitantly high prices, and those prices continue to increase beyond the rate of inflation each year, patients will struggle to afford the drugs they need no matter how efficient the drug delivery system is.

AARP supports a number of critical reforms that will lower prescription drug costs and increase competition. Those reforms include:

- Price Negotiation: Unlike private insurance plans, Medicare cannot negotiate prescription drug prices with pharmaceutical companies. AARP supports enabling the HHS Secretary to use the bargaining power of Medicare's 55 million beneficiaries to negotiate for lower prescription drug prices.

---

214 S.W. Schondelmeyer and L. Purvis, "Rx Price Watch Report: Trends in Retail Prices of Specialty Prescription Drugs Widely Used by Medicare Beneficiaries, 2006 to 2015," AARP Public Policy Institute, September 2017.

215 S.W. Schondelmeyer and L. Purvis, "Rx Price Watch Report: Trends in Retail Prices of Brand Name Prescription Drugs Widely Used by Medicare Beneficiaries, 2006 to 2015," AARP Public Policy Institute, December 2016.

216 IMS Institute for Healthcare Informatics, *Medicines Use and Spending in the U.S.: A Review of 2015 and Outlook to 2020*, April 2016.

217 https://www.cms.gov/Newsroom/MediaReleaseDatabase/Fact-sheets/2016-Fact-sheets-items/2016-11-14.html.

218 L. Mehegan and L. Skufca, "2015 Survey on Prescription Drugs," *AARP Research*, April 2016.

- Prohibit Anticompetitive Pay-for-Delay Agreements: AARP supports prohibiting patent settlement agreements between brand name and generic drug manufacturers that delay the availability of less-expensive generic drugs, costing the US billions of dollars.
- Close the REMS Loophole: FDA-required Risk Evaluation and Mitigation Strategies (REMS), structured plans for handling drugs associated with known or potential risks that may outweigh the drugs' benefits, are increasingly being abused to block generic or biosimilar manufacturers' access to samples of reference products. Since these samples are needed to develop generic and biosimilar products, such behavior effectively halts generic and biosimilar product development. Left unchecked, these unnecessary delays could cost consumers, government programs, taxpayers, and the health care system billions of dollars annually. AARP supports legislation that would close this loophole.
- Importation: AARP believes that we should reduce barriers to global price competition by allowing for the safe importation of lower priced but equally effective drugs. There is no reason for Americans to continue paying the highest prescription drug prices in the world.
- Drug Price Transparency: AARP supports legislation to require greater price transparency when drug manufacturers implement unreasonably high price increases.
- Part D Rebates: By reducing spending on prescription drugs under Part D, both taxpayers and Part D enrollees will benefit. AARP supports requiring drug manufacturers to provide Medicaid drug rebates for prescription drug dispensed to low-income Part D enrollees. This change alone could save $145 billion over ten years, according to the Congressional Budget Office (CBO).[219]
- Biologic Drugs: AARP supports reducing the market exclusivity period for brand name biologics from twelve years to seven years. This change would help get less expensive generic versions of biologics on the market sooner, yielding billions of dollars in savings over the next ten years.[220]
- FDA drug approval process: AARP believes extra market exclusivity and expedited approval should only be granted in extremely limited circumstances and only for innovations that meet an unmet medical need or substantially improve upon existing therapies. Any efforts to expedite FDA approval processes should ensure that patient safety remains paramount.

---

[219] CBO, *Options for Reducing the Deficit: 2017 to 2026*, December 2016.
[220] CBO, *Proposals for Health Care Programs-CBO's Estimate of the President's Fiscal Year 2017 Budget*, March 2016.

We appreciate the Committee's attention to the important issue of high prescription drug prices and we hope to work together to enact reforms that make drugs more affordable for older Americans and taxpayers.

Sincerely,

Joyce A. Rogers
Senior Vice President, Government Affairs

HOUSE ENERGY AND COMMERCE SUBCOMMITTEE ON HEALTH HEARING: EXAMINING THE DRUG SUPPLY CHAIN, STATEMENT FOR THE RECORD SUBMITTED BY: EXPRESS SCRIPTS, DECEMBER 13, 2017

At Express Scripts, we believe in practicing pharmacy smarter. We put medicine within reach of tens of millions of people by aligning with our customers, taking bold action, and delivering patient-centered care to make better health more affordable and accessible.

Headquartered in St. Louis, Express Scripts is the nation's largest stand-alone pharmacy benefit manager (PBM). We manage drug benefits for more than 80 million Americans, including those in health plans, union-sponsored plans, state employee health plans, and public purchasers, including TRICARE, Medicare Part D, and Medicaid. Our services include providing network-pharmacy claims processing, home delivery pharmacy care, specialty pharmacy care, benefit-design consultation, drug utilization review, formulary management, and medical and drug data analysis services.

Express Scripts drives unique solutions to address rising prescription drug prices. As published in our 2016 Drug Trend Report[221], the average list price for the most commonly used brand drugs increased 10.7 percent in 2017. Due to the tools that Express Scripts implemented in plans covering employees and their families, per-person spending last year on prescription drugs increased just 3.8 percent – 26.9 percent less than the 5.2 percent increase in 2015. Aligned with the best interests of our clients and patients, we are committed to doing whatever it takes to provide the best care and value.

One tool traditionally used by PBMs is negotiating rebates with brand manufacturers and leveraging formulary placement. Claims that PBMs benefit from higher drug prices are entirely false: plan sponsors decide how rebate dollars are directed, and they use rebates to lower premiums and cost sharing for patients in those plans. In fact, Express Scripts' clients receive 89 percent of the rebates the company negotiated with drug

---

[221] http://lab.express-scripts.com/lab/drug-trend-report.

manufacturers. Express Scripts retains the rest in a fully transparent manner for doing our job to bring down drug costs.

Our job at Express Scripts is to make sure our patients, and our clients who provide them a pharmacy benefit, are getting medicines at the lowest net cost. The simple fact is that the manufacturer is solely responsible for setting the list price for a brand drug and for increasing that list price. Rebates do not raise drug prices. Drugmakers raise drug prices, and they alone can lower them.

Not all drugs are rebated, and yet brand manufacturers have raised the price on these drugs as well. For example, list prices for oral oncology medications[222], which are not rebated or discounted to any significant extent, have doubled between 2011 and 2016, from $20 per unit to $40 per unit. Looking at the 39 medications on the market in 2010, between 2010 and 2016:

- Six had 100 to 200 percent inflation;
- One had inflation greater than 300 percent;
- One had inflation greater than 800 percent.

Additionally, the following list of prescription drugs that receive **no rebate** have experienced significant price growth in 2017:

Drug Name	Indication	Manufacturer	2017 YTD Price Increase
BANZEL	Seizures	Eisai Inc.	24.2%
EFFEXOR XR	Depression	Pfizer Inc.	19.2%
FIRAZYR	Hereditary Angioedema	Shire US Inc.	9.0%
IMBRUVICA	Cancer	Janssen Pharmaceuticals Inc	8.4%
ISENTRESS	HIV	Merck & Co. Inc.	7.9%
LIPITOR	High Blood Cholesterol	Pfizer Inc.	18.2%
MENOPUR	Infertility	Ferring Pharmaceuticals	11.9%
ORKAMBI	Cystic Fibrosis	Vertex Pharmaceuticals Inc.	5.0%
PREZISTA	HIV	Janssen Pharmaceuticals Inc./Johnson and Johnson	7.9%
PROGRAF	Transplant	Astellas Pharma US Inc.	14.2%
PULMOZYME	Cystic Fibrosis	Genentech, Inc.	7.0%
STRIBILD	HIV	Gilead Sciences Inc.	7.3%
TRIUMEQ	HIV	ViiV Healthcare	7.9%

[222] http://lab.express-scripts.com/lab/insights/industry-updates/the-cost-of-hope-5-things-to-know-about-the-cost-of-cancer-drugs.

Express Scripts supports policies that lower the price of prescription drugs by promoting competition in the marketplace and accelerating approval of generic drugs and biosimilar therapies. We are proud that our generic fill rate is more than 80 percent. Competition is the key to containing drug prices, and we look forward to working with the Committee on policies to achieve that goal.

Beyond rebates and formulary placement, Express Scripts has led the industry in developing value-based payment solutions in our SafeGuard Rx program that can further address high-cost specialty drugs. Mechanisms such as indication-based pricing, outcomes-based pricing, remote patient monitoring, and early discontinuation reimbursement lower costs for drugs treating diabetes, Multiple Sclerosis, certain cancers, inflammatory diseases, and pulmonary conditions. Value-based reimbursement programs are implemented more easily in commercial markets, and solutions to regulatory barriers in public programs are currently being explored.

Finally, Express Scripts is now offering innovative solutions for consumers and patients who experience high drug costs due to being either uninsured or insured under a high deductible plan. Inside Rx is a new, partially owned subsidiary that leverages Express Scripts' purchasing power to expand affordable access to brand and generic medications for patients in need. Largely focused on the uninsured, InsideRx provides significant discounts averaging 40 percent on 68 commonly used prescription medications at the point-of-sale, resulting in an average savings of $81 per prescription.

Similarly, Express Scripts will be launching SmartShare Rx[223] in January 2018, a point-of-sale rebate solution that plan sponsors may choose to provide to their members while they are in the deductible phase of their pharmacy benefit.

Express Scripts is also committed to improving drug price transparency for patients and doctors. Express Scripts has partnered[224] with Surecripts to provide real-time information to physicians and patients at the time of prescribing through the patient's Electronic Health Record (EHR), including patient-specific cost sharing for that prescription drug. This information will allow patients to receive the most appropriate, cost-effective medication.

Thank you for the opportunity to share information on the market-based solutions Express Scripts has developed to address further prescription drug costs. We thank the Committee for addressing this complex but crucial topic for American patients and families, and we hope to continue to be a resource to the Committee in its work on the drug supply chain.

---

[223] http://lab.express-scripts.com/lab/insights/industry-updates/sharing-smarter.

[224] http://lab.express-scripts.com/lab/insights/drug-options/healthcare-connectivity-improves-healthcare-itself.

December 13, 2017, American Pharmacists Association Statement for the Record, to the House Energy and Commerce Committee, Subcommittee on Health Hearing: "Examining the Drug Supply Chain"

As drugs become more and more expensive, complex, and personalized, the need to optimize their impact also increases. Pharmacists have more medication-related education and training than any other health care professional. Yet, despite their expertise and accessibility, pharmacists are often an underutilized health care resource in helping to address medication costs by improving the impact, and therefore, value of medications. The American Pharmacists Association (APhA), and our members appreciate the opportunity to provide our comments on the important role pharmacists play in patients' lives as you examine the drug supply chain in our country.

Founded in 1852 as the American Pharmaceutical Association, APhA represents 64,000 pharmacists, pharmaceutical scientists, student pharmacists, pharmacy technicians, and others interested in improving medication use and advancing patient care. APhA members provide care in all practice settings, including community pharmacies, hospitals, long-term care facilities, community health centers, physician offices, ambulatory clinics, managed care organizations, hospice settings, and the uniformed services.

Cost versus Value

In order to get the greatest benefit from medications, patients must understand how to use their medications safely and effectively. Pharmacists are the medication experts on the patient's health care team. Pharmacists today graduate with a Doctorate of Pharmacy degree, which requires six to eight years to complete. Pharmacists can and do assist patients in optimizing the impact of medications and decreasing patients' costs by providing services focused on safe and appropriate medication use. For example, pharmacists provide medication management services, which are especially important for patients who have complex care plans, take multiple drugs or have chronic conditions. Additionally, to address hospital readmissions, pharmacists help patients transition between care settings.

Unfortunately, despite the fact that many states and Medicaid programs are turning to pharmacists to increase access to health care and address medication-related costs, Medicare Part B does not cover the services pharmacists can provide. Pharmacists arc trained to do more than place medication in a container and while 91% of Americans live within five miles of a community pharmacy[225], many of our Nation's seniors are medically underserved. Pharmacists are an underutilized health care resource which can positively affect the impact and value of medications, beneficiaries' care[226] and the entire Medicare program.

APhA strongly believes H.R. 592, the *Pharmacy and Medically Underserved Areas Enhancement Act,* is a proposal that will improve patient care, health outcomes, value of medications,[227] and consequently, the viability of the Medicare program. Introduced by Representatives Brett Guthrie and G.K. Butterfield, H.R. 592 has 240 bipartisan cosponsors. Similar legislation obtained 297 cosponsors in the 114th Congress.

The legislation will enable Medicare patients in medically underserved communities to better access health care through state-licensed pharmacists practicing according to their own state's scope of practice. In medically underserved communities, pharmacists are often the closest health care professional and accessible outside normal business hours. Helping patients receive the care they need, when they need it, is a common sense and bipartisan solution that will improve outcomes and reduce overall costs.

The importance of medication-related services cannot be overstated, especially in the Medicare program. Medications are the primary method of treating chronic disease and are involved in 8o percent of all treatment regimens. Moreover, the United States spends nearly $300 billion annually on medication-related problems, including nonadherence.[228] Accordingly, not only will S.109 increase beneficiaries' access to health care, it will help improve their outcomes-particularly those impacted by medications. APhA appreciates the support by nearly all Committee members for the *Pharmacy and Medically Underserved Areas Enhancement Act* and urges its swift passage to allow pharmacists to deliver these vital sentences as providers in medically underserved areas.

APhA also encourages the Committee, when considering policy changes, to look beyond isolated components of health care to determine cost and value. Because health coverage is frequently analyzed by the benefit type such as inpatient, outpatient, and drug coverage, a patient's overall services, costs and outcomes may never be reviewed comprehensively. Policies cannot continue to consider drug and medical coverage, and their related costs and outcomes, separately if we are to achieve true value in health care. Current coverage and payment policies related to prescription drugs place incentives on

---

[225] NCPDP Pharmacy File, *ArcGIS Census Tract File*. NACDS Economics Department.

[226] CMS. *Evidence Supporting Enhanced Medication Therapy Management. Center for Medicare and Medicaid Innovation*. 2016. Available at: https:1/innovation.cms.gov/Files/x/mtm-evidencebase.pdf.

[227] *See* Avalerc Health. Exploring Pharmacists' Role in a Changing Healthcare Environment. May 2014. Available at: http: //avalerc.com/expertise/life-sciences /insightsIexploring-pharmacists-role-in-a-changing-healthcare-environment Also, *See* Avalere Health. Developing Trends in Delivery and Reimbursement of Pharmacist Services. October 2015. Available at: /http://avalere.com/exnertise/managed-care /insights /new-analysis-identifies-factors-that-can-facilitate-broader-reimbursement-o.

[228] New England Healthcare Institute. *Thinking Outside the Pillbox: A System-Wide Approach to Improving Patient Adherence for Chronic Disease*. August 2009. Available at: http://www.nehi.net/nublications/lz-thinking-outside-the-pillbox-a-system-wide-apnroach-to-imnro\ing-patient-medication-adherence-for-chronic-disease/view.

the short-term, focusing on cost containment for the product rather than weighing the overall clinical benefit to the patient and the impact to their medical costs. Breaking down the many silos within our health care system will help address that $300 billion dollars spent on medication-related problems-many of which are preventable.[229]

Importation Detracts from Value-Based Care

Broader importation laws will hinder the progress made to move U.S. health care delivery and payment towards value, as opposed to volume, and further fragment care. Because Canadian pharmacists may only fill prescriptions written by Canadian prescribers, expanded importation policies will encourage Americans to seek care from foreign prescribers and pharmacists, whose systems and standards are not integrated into, or consistent with, U.S. systems or care. Value- based care models and other efforts to produce savings and promote quality, such as outcomes-based reimbursement, will be more difficult to measure and optimize if patients are allowed to receive care outside the model's mechanisms to drive results.[230] Moreover, because of the implementation of outcomes-based payment, U.S. health care providers and facilities may be unjustly penalized due to the actions of foreign providers or patients' reactions to non-FDA approved medications.

Other negative events can result from broadened importation, such as increased adverse events and decreased medication adherence, as practitioners may make care decisions based on a patient's incomplete medical and medication profile. Pharmacist-provided services that help patients optimize medications, such as medication therapy management covered under Medicare Part D, may lose their value as medication reviews will likely not be comprehensive. APhA consistently emphasized the value of pharmacist-provided care services, noting that pharmacists' roles extend well beyond the dispensing of a medication. Patients benefit significantly when they have a relationship with a pharmacist.[231,232,233,234,235] The pharmacist-patient relationship will be seriously undermined if importation of non-FDA approved drugs is permitted.

---

229 Ibid.

230 Centers for Medicare & Medicaid Sen;ces, (May 2016). CMS Quality Measure Development Plan: Supporting the Transition to the Merit-based Incentive Payment System (MIPS) and Alternative Payment Models (APMs), available at: https//www.cms.gov/Mcdicare/Ouality-Initiatives-Patient-Assessment-Instruments /Value-Based-Programs/MACRA-MIPS-and-APMs/Final-MDP.pdf, last accessed: May 23, 2017.

231 Phatak, A., Prusi, R., Ward, B., Hansen, L.O., V\7illiams, M.V., Vetter, E., Chapman, N. & Postelnick, M. (2015). Impact of pharmacist involvement in the transitional care of high-risk patients through medication reconciliation, medication education and post-discharge call-backs (IPITCH Study), *Journal of Hospital* Medicine, 11(1), 39-44.

232 McCullough, M.B., Petrakis, B.A., Gillespie, C., Solomon, J.L., Park, A.M. & Ourth, H. (2016). Knowing the patient: A qualitative study on care-taking and the clinical pharmacist-patient relationship, *Research in Social and Administrative Pharmacy,* 12(1), 78-90).

Thank you again for the opportunity to provide our perspective regarding the important role that the pharmacist plays in the drug supply chain.

THE SENIOR CARE PHARMACY COALITION, STATEMENT FOR THE RECORD, BEFORE THE UNITED STATES HOUSE OF REPRESENTATIVES, ENERGY AND COMMERCE COMMITTEE, HEALTH SUBCOMMITTEE, "EXAMINING THE DRUG SUPPLY CHAIN," DECEMBER 13, 2017

The Senior Care Pharmacy Coalition (SCPC) welcomes the opportunity to present this statement for the record before the United States House of Representatives Energy and Commerce Committee, Health Subcommittee, as part of its hearing, "Examining the Drug Supply Chain." SCPC commends the Chairman and Ranking Member for their focus on the pharmaceutical pricing and supply chain. As the only Washington-based organization exclusively representing the interests of long-term care (LTC) pharmacies, we suggest that the LTC pharmacy sector is a meaningful ecosystem through which to understand the pharmaceutical distribution chain, and particularly the invidious efforts of Pharmacy Benefit Managers (PBMs) to siphon billions of dollars out of that system at a cost to consumers and the federal government alike.

There are many actors in the prescription drug markets – brand manufacturers, generic manufacturers, PBMs, wholesalers, group purchasing organizations (GPOs), Pharmacy Services Administrative Organizations (PSAOs), chain pharmacies, independent pharmacies, specialty pharmacies, home infusion pharmacies, LTC pharmacies, mail order pharmacies, Medicare, Medicaid, private insurers and of course consumers (including Medicare and Medicaid beneficiaries). Given that its members are active participants in the distribution chain, and based upon years of analysis, SCPC believes that PBMs, together with their corporate siblings in horizontally and vertically integrated conglomerates, play a negative and damaging role in the supply and payment chain. For that reason, our remarks focus on PBM conglomerates.

In Section I we provide important context concerning the LTC pharmacy sector. Section II describes the PBM industry, and the ways in which the three largest PBMs in the market today have created an "oligopoly" that harms patients, pharmacies and the

---

233 Braaf, S., Rixon, S., Williams, A., Lieu, D. & Manias, E. (2014). Pharmacist patient medication communication during admission and discharge in specialty hospital settings: implications for person centered healthcare, *The International Journal of Person Centered Medicine*.

234 Schuessler, T.J., Ruisinger, J.F., Hare, S.E., Prohaska, E.S. & Melton, B.L. (2015). Patient satisfaction with pharmacist led chronic disease state management programs, *Journal a/Pharmacy Practice,* 29(5), 2015.

235 Mossialos, E., Courtin, E., Naci, H., Bcnrimoj, S., Bam)', M., Farris, K., Noyce, P. & Sketris, I. (2016). From "retailers" to health care providers: Transforming the role of community pharmacists in chronic disease management, *Health Policy.* 119(S), 628-639.

federal government. Section III, focuses in more detail on how PBM pricing and contracting policies impact both consumers and independent LTC pharmacies. Finally, in Section IV, we conclude with recommendations for further Committee and legislative actions.

Before addressing the details, we share with the Committee the findings of the Pacific Research Institute (PRI), which earlier this year conducted a comprehensive review of the literature surrounding PBMs and their business practices.[236] PRI concluded that PBMs "[c]reate pricing uncertainty by incentivizing higher list prices for medicines that enable large rebates and discounts (which are particularly valuable for PBMs)," and which result in:

- The large discrepancy between list prices and transaction prices caus[ing] higher patient co-pays than necessary (co-pays typically depend on list prices);
- For Medicare Part D beneficiaries, the higher list prices and higher co-pays ... push[ing some] patients into the coverage gap ("donut hole") faster;
- Impos[ing] large, and often unknown, fees that creat[ing] substantial revenue uncertainty and volatility, which are particularly problematic for small, LTC and specialty pharmacies;
- Increas[ing] PBMs' share of the gross expenditures at the expense of pharmacies and manufacturers; and
- Through control of the drug formularies, impos[ing] undue influence on the medicines patients can access.

We address these issues in detail below, and urge the Committee to explore these issues as it investigates the drug distribution chain.

LTC Pharmacy Context

The SCPC and its Members: SCPC's members serve about 700,000 residents daily in skilled nursing and assisted living facilities across the country. Our members represent 75% of all independent LTC pharmacy companies.[237] As described below, given the

---

[236] Dr. Wayne Winegarden, *The Economic Costs of Pharmacy Benefit Managers: A Review of the Literature*, Pacific Research Institute (March 2017), available at www.pacificresearchinstitute.org.

[237] SCPC defines "independent LTC pharmacies" as those LTC pharmacies that are not part of a corporate family that includes a pharmacy benefits manager (PBM). SCPC believes that there are inherent conflicts of interest between pharmacies and PBMs, such that common ownership necessarily results in anticompetitive behavior. The largest LTC pharmacy company, Omnicare (which is not an SCPC member), controls roughly 50% of the LTC pharmacy market, with more than 1,000 independent LTC pharmacy companies serving the remainder the market. Omnicare is a wholly owned subsidiary of CVS Health, which also owns Caremark, the largest PBM in the country, as well as Coram, the largest home infusion company, and CVS specialty, the largest

utilization of drugs in LTC settings, LTC pharmacy represents between six and eight percent of the prescription medication spend in the country.

The LTC Sector: LTC pharmacies serve nursing homes, assisted living facilities, and other group and residential settings. LTC pharmacy differs substantially from retail pharmacy. LTC pharmacies are "institutional" or "closed door" pharmacies, which means they are not open to the public and do not sell convenience items as do retail pharmacies. Rather, they contract with LTC facilities and congregate care settings or payer intermediaries to provide pharmacy services to residents in those facilities or settings.

There are four fundamental differences between retail and LTC pharmacy:

1) Retail pharmacies sell myriad products beyond medications to consumers, but as "closed door" operations, LTC pharmacies do not face consumers. For many retail pharmacies, dispensing medications is a "loss leader," with financial success based on sale of convenience items. LTC pharmacies do not have this option. They succeed or fail based entirely on dispensing medications and providing a wide array of services required by statute, regulation and professional responsibility.
2) The clinical responsibility of retail pharmacies ends when the patient leaves the pharmacy with a prescription. The clinical responsibility of LTC pharmacies is continuous and extended, from the time the pharmacy receives a prescription until the patient's transition from a LTC facility to home or another setting is complete.
3) Retail pharmacies dispense the vast majority of medications in 30-day bottles.[238] To meet legal requirements and to ensure the safe dispensing of medications to the patients that they serve, LTC pharmacies dispense prescriptions in specialized, "single unit dose" packages. In other words, the LTC pharmacy dispenses medications by individual dose specific to each patient for each medication administration (or "med pass") at the facility. LTC pharmacies employ sophisticated dispensing technology at both the pharmacy and the LTC facility to improve efficiency and reduce medication errors. LTC pharmacies also dispense and deliver prescriptions to patients 24-hours per day, 7 days a week,

---

specialty pharmacy. For a more extensive discussion of the anticompetitive market impact CVS Health has on drug prices, Medicare Part D beneficiaries, Medicare program costs and LTC pharmacies, *see infra at* 6-7.

[238] It is noteworthy that yet another example of the undue and adverse impact of PBMs and the corporate conglomerates of which they are a part, overall corporate strategy pushes consumers in the community away from retail pharmacies and toward mail-order pharmacies because mail-order pharmacies are less expensive to operate and have higher profit margins than retail pharmacies. For example, as the *New York Times* reported only four days ago, Caremark, the largest PBM in the country and a subsidiary of CVS Health, charges consumers more for a prescription dispensed in a CVS retail pharmacy (another subsidiary of CVS Health and the largest retail pharmacy chain in the country) than the same prescription dispensed by CVS' mail-order pharmacy (yet another subsidiary of CVS Health and the second-largest mail-order pharmacy in America). "Prescription Drugs May Cost More With Insurance than Without It," *New York Times* (December 9, 2017), available at https://www.nytimes.com/2017/12/09/health/drug-prices-generics-insurance.html.

365 days per year. LTC pharmacies pre-position "emergency kits" in nursing homes and other care facilities. LTC pharmacies reconcile prescriptions for opioids and other controlled substances at least daily and often by med pass. Finally, at least monthly and usually more frequently, LTC pharmacies review every patient chart (called Drug Utilization Review) and otherwise manage each care setting transition to ensure medication continuity between sites of care.[239]

4) Retail pharmacies receive payment before patients receive prescriptions; LTC pharmacies often provide medications before payers have confirmed payment. In retail, the pharmacy confirms payment from insurers and receives patient co-payments before giving patients medications. For LTC pharmacies, requirements that medications be delivered to patients within as little as two hours following receipt of a prescription or chart order, coupled with the insurance company/PBM's requirements to assure that prescribed medications are "on formulary" and professional and legal obligations to assure that patients receive clinically appropriate medications, often requires that LTC pharmacies release prescriptions for delivery to facilities before confirming payment. In some cases, as many as 30% of prescriptions leave the pharmacy before payment is confirmed.

The complexity of LTC patient conditions also distinguishes LTC pharmacy from retail pharmacy, and underscores the value LTC pharmacies deliver through their services to patients. The average resident in a skilled nursing facility (SNF) is a woman in her mid-80s suffering from multiple chronic conditions, has mild to moderate dementia who takes 13 prescription medications each month.[240] In assisted living facilities, the average number of prescriptions per patient is even higher. As a result, pharmacy services – not simply dispensing medications – are crucial to the quality of care for patients and increasingly important in preventing adverse events like re-hospitalizations, patient falls, polypharmacy complications, medication-induced dementia and other adverse drug reactions, thereby improving the quality of care and reducing Medicare expenditures.

The Department of Health and Human Services (HHS), through the Centers for Medicare and Medicaid Services (CMS), heavily regulates LTC pharmacies under the Medicare and Medicaid programs. The Medicare and Medicaid Requirements of Participation for skilled nursing facilities (SNFs) and nursing facilities (NFs) contain detailed Pharmacy Services requirements.[241] LTC facilities that participate in Medicare

---

[239] These activities are listed in and required by the *Medicare Prescription Drug Program Manual* (the Part D Manual), Chapter 5, Section 50.5.2.

[240] Managed Health Care Associates, Inc., *MHA Independent Long Term Care Member Study at 27* (2017).

[241] The Part D Manual, Chapter 5, Section 50.5.2.; 42 C.F.R. § 483.5 and .60 (requirement that nursing homes provide specialized medication services); *See* Centers for Medicare and Medicaid Services, State Operations Manual (Publication No. 100-07), available at https://www.cms.gov/Regulations-and-Guidance/Guidance/Manuals/Internet-Only-Manuals-IOMs-Items/CMS1201984.html. The major pharmacy-related bases for violation citations (F-Tags) include: F-Tag 309: Quality of Care; F-Tag 329: Unnecessary Drugs; F-Tag 332-

and Medicaid contract with independent LTC pharmacies to satisfy those requirements, which include specialized packaging, unit dose packaging, and delivery within specified time periods depending on the medication and the urgency of a particular prescription.

Most importantly, LTC pharmacies must provide consulting pharmacy services on an ongoing basis. They are part of the care management team for every patient in a facility, and must conduct periodic drug regimen reviews of patients, participate with facility staff in medication reconciliation and be on-site at every facility at least once every month. In addition, the Medicare Part D Manual lays out specific requirements for pharmacies to qualify as LTC pharmacies eligible for participation in Part D networks. LTC pharmacies must comply with a far more extensive array of statutory and regulatory requirements than retail pharmacies.

Part D is the largest single payer for patient medications in LTC facilities. Medicare Part A is the second-largest payer, with Medicaid Part B and a small amount of Medicaid the other primary payers. In 2015, SCPC sponsored a report which Avalere prepared describing the LTC pharmacy marketplace and major policy challenges the sector faces.[242]

The PBM Marketplace: A Classic Oligopoly Harming Patients, Pharmacies, and the Federal FISC

Who Are the PBMs?

Three PBMs – Caremark, ExpressScripts and Optum – process nearly 75% of all prescriptions dispensed in America. For LTC pharmacies, these three PBMs process more than 90% of all prescriptions. Such a high degree of market concentration is the very definition of an oligopolistic marketplace.[243] Moreover, each of the three major PBMs is part of a corporate conglomerate that has gained significant control over multiple, interdependent markets in the drug distribution chain – not just the PBM market, but also the health insurance, wholesale and pharmacy (retail, LTC, specialty, home infusion and mail order) markets - through acquisitions both horizontal and vertical and through exclusionary conduct, all of which has accelerated dramatically over the past three years.

333: Medication Errors; F-Tag 425: Pharmacy Services; F-Tag 428: Medication Regimen Review; and F-Tag 431: Storage, Labeling, and Controlled Medications. Note that the term "long-term care facilities" does not, under federal law, include assisted living facilities.

[242] Available at http://seniorcarepharmacies.org/wp-content/uploads/2015/10/Avalere_LTC_Pharmacy-the-Evolving-Marketplace-and-Emerging-Policy-Issues.pdf.

[243] *See FTC v. H.J. Heinz Co.*, 246 F.3d 708, 724 (D.C. Cir. 2001) (recognizing that "[i]t is a central object of merger policy to obstruct the creation or reinforcement by merger of such oligopolistic market structures."). *Cf. United States v. Densply Int'l*, 399 F.3d 181, 187 (3d Cir. 2005) (market share of 75-80% was "more than adequate to establish a prima facie case" of market power.").

1) UnitedHealth Group owns Optum Health, the country's third-largest PBM. UnitedHealth is the largest health insurer, largest Medicare Advantage (Part C) Plan sponsor, largest Medicare Part D Plan sponsor and largest Medi-Gap insurer in America. Within the last ten days, UnitedHealth Group agreed to buy the DaVita Medical Group unit, continuing the accelerating trend of vertical and horizontal integration of health care businesses. Optum will take control of DaVita Medical Group's nearly 300 clinics and half-dozen outpatient surgical centers.
2) ESI, Inc., owns Express Scripts, the country's second-largest PBM. It also owns the largest mail-order pharmacy in America. Through Econodisc Contacting Services, ExpressScripts is a co-owner of one of the three GPOs that purchase 91% of all generic medications purchased in the United States.[244]
3) CVS Health owns Caremark, the country's largest PBM. CVS Health is the largest interlocking horizontally and vertically integrated health care insurance/PBM/provider/pharmacy conglomerate in the United States. The company owns the nation's largest retail, LTC and specialty pharmacy chains. The company also owns among the nation's largest mail order and home infusion pharmacies. It operates walk-in medical clinics co-located with CVS retail pharmacies inside Target department stores. CVS Health currently offers its own Part D plans under the brand name "SilverScript." CVS Health will be providing PBM services to Anthem, which insures 19 million Americans, as soon as 2019. CVS Health recently announced its intention to acquire Aetna, the country's third-largest health insurer. CVS Health also is a co-owner of Red Oak, another of the three GPOs that together purchase 91% of all generic medications sold in America.[245]

Such arrangements have created inherent incentives for these large PBMs to favor their own corporate affiliates and exclude competitors, and allow them the power to extract significant sums from today's diffracted drug distribution system.

At a recent hearing before the Federal Trade Commission, Dr. Neeraj Sood of the University of Southern California (USC) Schaeffer School presented a thorough analysis of the PBM sector, and how PBMs are achieving excessive profits.[246] Dr. Sood's analysis effectively demonstrates the adverse impact of the PBM sector on patients, unaffiliated

---

[244] Chester (Chip) Davis, Jr., Association for Accessible Medicines, presentation to FTC & FDA workshop, "Understanding Competition in Prescription Drug Markets: Entry and Supply Chain Dynamics" (Nov. 8, 2017)); *see also National Academy of Sciences Report* at 55.

[245] *Id.*

[246] Neera Sood, Ph.D., Professor and Vice Dean for Research, Sol Price School of Public Policy, University of Southern California, presentation to joint FTC-FDA Workshop, "Follow the money: The flow of funds in the pharmaceutical distribution system," (Nov. 8, 2017), available at https://www.ftc.gov/system/files/documents/public_events/1255653/understanding_competition_in_prescription_drug_markets_workshop_slides_11-8-17.pdf (Slide 74-105).

payers, pharmacies and free market competition. However, his analysis *understates the impact on the LTC pharmacy sector.*

His analysis is based on the three largest publicly traded companies in each channel of the drug distribution chain – manufacturers, wholesalers, GPOs, PBMs and pharmacies. None of the three largest pharmacy chains operates a LTC pharmacy. Dr. Sood notes that the three major PBMs control 75% of all prescriptions; for LTC pharmacy companies, these three companies control a significantly higher 90%+ of all prescriptions. Finally, since nearly half of the LTC pharmacy market is composed of smaller, independent LTC pharmacies, the disproportionate market power these PBMs wield in other markets becomes both overwhelming and necessarily anticompetitive in the LTC pharmacy arena.[247]

Rebates, DIR Fees, and PBM Profits

PBM representatives claim that their role in the drug distribution chain is one of negotiating drug discounts on behalf of purchasers (large employers, health plans, and others) to drive efficiency into the drug distribution system.[248] While that claim may have been true 10 or 20 years ago, it is no longer the case. Rather, PBMs today are a destructive force in the drug distribution system, taking profits for themselves at a cost to patients, pharmacies, and the federal government. PBMs do this through two principle practices: first, they negotiate "rebates" from drug manufacturers, but rather than passing those rebates on to consumers (as they claim they do), they retain the vast majority of those rebates for themselves.[249] Second, PBMs have developed a series of opaque and unjustified "fees" that they charge pharmacies (which in turn effectively are required to "pay to be paid"). The Medicare program defines some of these fees as "Direct and Indirect Remuneration" or "DIR," which we address below.

---

[247] By contrast, for example, retail pharmacy is dominated by chain pharmacies like CVS and Walgreens, which affords them greater comparative market power than LTC pharmacies. In addition, these chain pharmacies also participate in the same purchasing groups that purchase 91% of generic medications, underscoring not only their comparatively greater market power than LTC pharmacies, but also the opaque business relationships that create inherent conflicts of interest and strong incentives for conglomerates that own PBMs to use PBMs as a tool to leverage their overall corporate interests at the expense of patients, pharmacies and government payment programs.

[248] *See generally* http://www.pcmanet.org/policy-issues; *see also* Merritt, Testimony before the Senate HELP Committee, October 17, 2017 at 1, available at https://www.help.senate.gov/imo/media/doc/Merritt.pdf.

[249] *See* National Academy of Sciences, Making Medicines Affordable (Dec, 2017) at 16, available at http://nap.edu/24946 ("The most prominent of these intermediaries are the pharmacy benefit managers (PBMs), who interact with prescription drug insurers—and sometimes directly with employers offering health insurance plans—to negotiate prices both with manufacturers and with retail pharmacies. Adding further to the complexity, drug manufacturers very commonly offer price rebates to PBMs, but no meaningful information exists to determine the size of those rebates, what portion of the rebates eventually results in lower prices for patients, or the portion that the PBMs retain as profit"). While the National Academy has been unable to quantify the portion that PBMs retain as profit, CMS has better data related to the Part D program and should be able to provide that estimate to Congress upon request.

PBMs Harm Competition

PBMs today are exacting billions of dollars from the drug supply chain without providing any value for consumers or the federal government.[250] Moreover, their consolidation and vertical integration exacerbate the harm to consumers, government payment programs, pharmacies and free market competition. Examples of anticompetitive practices by PBMs abound, especially in the LTC pharmacy space.

Contract "Negotiations"

PBMs' ability to secure anti-competitive and one-sided contract terms from LTC pharmacies convincingly demonstrates the anticompetitive impact that PBM market consolidation and vertical/horizontal integration. In *Eastman Kodak Co. v. Image Technology Services*, the Supreme Court found that the ability of a firm to raise prices unilaterally constitutes direct evidence of market power.[251] LTC pharmacies must routinely accept contracts with payment formulas that allow PBMs to change prices daily and with no consideration of the prices competitors pay for the same medication and related services. SCPC's members are routinely forced to accept "take it or leave it" contracts which reflect the inordinate market power that PBMs wield in the LTC pharmacy market. (SCPC urges the Committee to consult CMS' Part D Group to learn of examples CMS has had to address for the last decade, and particularly in the last three years during the PBM industry's period of rapid consolidation.) In 2016, Caremark attempted to increase its already disproportionate market power by refusing to negotiate with the largest PSAO representing LTC pharmacies in negotiations for its 2017 contracts on behalf of Part D PDPs. Caremark improperly tried to influence LTC pharmacies to accept its unilateral, pharmacy-by-pharmacy contracts by refusing to honor key provisions of its existing contracts in 2016 unless the pharmacy accepted the unilateral contract for 2017. SCPC informed CMS of this predatory practice, and the agency instructed Caremark to honor its existing contracts.

MAC Pricing – Another PBM Abuse

The Medicare Part D statute allows PDPs/PBMs to use a methodology known as Maximum Allowable Cost (MAC) pricing to establish payment rates for most generics. Under this methodology, the pharmacy does not know the payment rate for any medications at the time a contract is signed because MAC pricing allows the PDPs/PBMs

[250] National Academy of Sciences at 29 ("[t]he profits generated by PBMs...coupled with insurer's profits and the margins on reimbursement for drugs administered in the hospital or outpatient setting ultimately affect the patients and their ability to pay for therapies, and do not increase the incentives to develop new drugs"). *See also* testimony of Lori M. Reilly, Esq. Executive Vice President, Policy, Research & Membership, PhRMA, before the Senate Health, Education, Labor and Pensions Committee (October 17, 2017), available at https://www.help.senate.gov/imo/media/doc/Reilly2.pdf.

[251] 504 U.S. 451, 477-78 (1992).

to change payments on a day-to-day basis, provided that those changes are based on actual and identifiable changes in the marketplace.[252]

In 2015, SCPC asked Avalere to examine 24 million Part D claims for the eight-quarter period ending March 31, 2015 and, in part, to determine whether there is any relationship between PBM rate changes for commonly prescribed generics and identifiable marketplace changes. The results are deeply troubling. The resultant report, issued in November 2015, demonstrates there is no apparent relationship between changes in the amount a PBM pays for a medication and actual changes in the marketplace.[253]

For example, in April 2014, Omeprazole was the most commonly prescribed medication in America's nursing homes. On April 2, ExpressScripts paid about $1.22 for the cost of the medication. The next day, April 3, ExpressScripts paid about $0.58 for the cost of the same medication. Two weeks later, on April 15, ExpressScripts paid about $0.14 for the cost of the same medication. By contrast, for the entire month of April 2014, Caremark's payment for the same medication varied from $0.14 to $0.18. Optum paid a consistent $0.22 for Omeprazole every day of the month.

Either major PBMs have dramatically disparate access to market information or something other than marketplace changes are driving day-to-day payment changes. The latter seems far more plausible, particularly given PBMs' desultory compliance with a CMS regulation requiring that PBMs report information about payment rate changes under MAC pricing and the marketplace changes justifying each rate change. When confronted by Rep. Doug Collins (R-GA) during a hearing of the Regulatory Reform, Commercial and Antitrust Subcommittee of the House Judiciary Committee, witnesses from Caremark and ExpressScripts were unable to provide any explanation for, much less identify specific marketplace changes to justify, these day-to-day variations within an individual PBM or between PBMs.[254] They did acknowledge, however, that PBMs managed multiple formularies with differing prices for the same medication on the same day, with all payment rates calculated using the MAC pricing methodology. If MAC pricing truly were based on identifiable marketplace changes, then differing prices for the same medication on the same day by the same PBM simply due to different formularies logically could not occur. The most obvious explanation is unilateral price manipulation, another hallmark of an oligopolistic marketplace.

---

[252] *See also* Forbes, Reform Pharmacy Benefit Managers (PBMs) To Improve Pharmaceutical Affordability (March 7, 2017) (noting inefficiency and impact of MAC prices).

[253] The Avalere report is available at: http://seniorcarepharmacies.org/wp-content/uploads/2015/11/20151116_SCPC-MAC-Pricing-Analyses_FINAL.pdf and was introduced by Rep. Collins during a Judiciary Committee hearing.

[254] The subcommittee hearing occurred on November 17, 2015, and was the third in a series of hearings on the state of competition in the health care marketplace. This specific hearing concerned "[t]he State of Competition in the Pharmacy Benefit Manager and Pharmacy Marketplaces." Https://judiciary.house.gov/press-release/regulatory-reform-subcommittee-to-hold-third-hearing-on-the-state-of-competition-in-the-health-care-marketplace/.

The regulation in question requires that PDPs, through their respective PBMs, report price changes and identify the marketplace changes justifying such changes weekly, and that they provide the reports in formats that are user-friendly for pharmacies. 42 C.F.R. § 423.505. PBMs have honored this regulation in the breach, such that no useful or user-friendly data has been reported to CMS since the regulation became effective in January 2016. We urge the Committee to examine this issue as well.

DIR – PBMs' Unjustifiable Fees

PBMs process LTC pharmacy claims under Part D. In recent years, PBMs have imposed and continue to impose a surprising and growing array of fees on LTC pharmacies. These fees have little market-based justification; rather, they represent yet another example of PBMs wielding undue oligopolistic power to the detriment of consumers, government payers, LTC pharmacies and free market competition.

PBM fees fall primarily into three categories: claims processing (or "point-of-sale" fees), "Direct and Indirect Remuneration" or "DIR" fees (post-point-of-sale clawbacks) and "quality" or "performance" fees (also post-point-of-sale). PBMs also regularly create and impose new fees without prior notice or explanation to LTC pharmacies, and no recourse for the LTC pharmacies but to "pay" the fees.[255] PBMs charge LTC pharmacies a claims processing fee ranging from $0.25 to $1.00 per claim. A substantial majority of claims are processed on a computer-to-computer basis, and LTC pharmacies submit hundreds of millions of Part D claims annually. There simply is no market-based justification for such exorbitant fees, and policy analysts often overlook point-of-sale fees like claims processing fees in discussing the impact PBM practices have on the marketplace.

With respect to DIR fees, CMS recently concluded that PBMs ***do not*** pass these fees on to consumers or reduce Medicare expenditures on Part D; not only are the fees pure profit for the PBMs and PDPs, but they actually and routinely misrepresent them to CMS: "[o]ur analysis of the Part D plan payment and cost data indicates that in recent years DIR amounts Part D sponsors and their PBMs actually received have consistently exceeded bid-projected amounts." 82 Fed. Reg. 56240 (November 15, 2017). DIR fees have no clear market justification. Rather, they serve simply to drive up costs to the federal government, consumers and pharmacies to benefit PBMs' bottom lines.[256]

---

[255] "Payment" of these fees is a misnomer, since PBMs typically subtract fees from future payments, making it even harder for LTC pharmacies to contest or even obtain explanations of fees before PBMs take monies from LTC pharmacies.

[256] In the retail context, a corollary to these "clawbacks" through DIR fees, consumers often would pay less for prescription medications if they paid out-of-pocket rather than if they rely on insurance coverage, because the co-pays the insurers charge (as negotiated and administered by PBMs on behalf of health plans) are greater than the out-of-pocket cost for the consumer. "Prescription Drugs May Cost More With Insurance Than Without It," note 3, *supra*. As a consumer quoted in the article states: "It just doesn't seem right…I just feel that the pharmaceutical industry and the health care industry are pulling these numbers out of thin air." The nexus between the pharmaceutical industry and the health care industry for consumers is the PBM industry,

PBM's Unconvincing Effort to Mask DIR Fees as "Quality" Holdbacks

With respect to "quality" fees, one example illustrates how PBMs and their corporate parents manipulate the system to impose fees on LTC pharmacies that not only increase profits for the PBMs but also increase profits for their corporate siblings. LTC pharmacies contract with assisted living facilities ("ALFs") to provide prescription medications and pharmacy services to facility residents.

In some of its contracts with LTC pharmacies that serve ALFs, ExpressScripts imposes a post-point-of-sale "quality fee." The quality fee is calculated such that the higher the percentage of 90- day prescriptions dispensed, the higher the score on this "quality" metric and the lower the fee imposed on LTC pharmacies. LTC pharmacies generally do not dispense in quantities greater than 30-day supplies, and various payment programs strongly encourage - and in some cases require – that the dispensing cycle be shorter. In particular, the Medicare program requires that brand name drugs be dispensed to nursing home patients in supplies no greater than 14 days.

More importantly, the longer the dispensing period, the greater the likelihood of patient non-compliance, particularly in environments like ALFs where residents are responsible to administer their own medications. The ExpressScripts "quality" metric in fact is inversely related to quality. It is directly related, however, to the percentage of mail-order prescriptions dispensed because mail-order pharmacies typically do dispense for 90 days. With ESI owning not only the ExpressScripts PBM but also the largest mail-order pharmacy in America, and with mail-order a realistic alternative for ALF residents to obtain prescription medications, this quality fee seems to be nothing more than naked exploitation by the PBM to benefit its affiliated mail-order business. It appears that Caremark may have created a new fee imposed on LTC pharmacies beginning in 2017 that is based on the same principle and, of course, Caremark's corporate parent, CVS Health, also owns one of the nation's largest mail order pharmacies.

Summary

As clearly documented throughout the National Academy of Sciences Report,[257] all of these fees are opaque to consumers, LTC pharmacies and even the Medicare program itself. CMS' recent report underscores the need for transparency with respect to all of the fees and charges PBMs impose seemingly at whim on LTC pharmacies, particularly given the demonstrable and adverse impact on consumers, government payment programs and free market competition.

The National Academy's first recommendation is that PBM transparency be mandated to understand the dollars that PBMs are retaining relative to their value:

---

which of course is just a part of megalithic and oligopolistic conglomerates that are, in fact, pulling numbers out of thin air, a practice which Congress should stop immediately.

[257] Report at 16, 50, 160.

> Potentially, this represents the largest opportunity among the committee's recommended actions. Transparency would help bring the margins of PBMs and 340B hospital and clinic plans toward a range that is more commensurate with the value they deliver. It might also lower prices from the biopharmaceutical companies. And transparency likely will reduce bad behavior and abuse in the market. Participants in the markets will perform better. If properly structured, this would pass savings on to patients. Importantly, it would not inhibit investments in research and development.[258]

We urge the Committee to pursue PBM transparency – for the benefit of consumers, for the Part D program, and for pharmacies as well.

The PBMs' Trifecta: Excess Profits for PBMs, Harm to Consumers, Medicare & Pharmacies, and Damage to the Free Market

In its' January 19, 2017 analysis, CMS clearly demonstrated how PBM practices increase costs to consumers and the federal government. More specifically, for Part D beneficiaries who pay co-pays and deductibles (i.e., Part D beneficiaries who are not dually eligible for both Medicare and Medicaid), CMS analysis conclusively demonstrates that PBM practices result in higher out-of-pocket costs for beneficiaries. The analysis also confirmed that PBMs approve certain medications in part to force Part D beneficiaries through the "donut hole" in Part D coverage. There are two reasons for this: (1) the more, and more expensive, the medications a beneficiary takes, the greater the revenue and profit for the PBM; and (2) the sooner the beneficiary reaches the donut hole, the greater the revenue and profit for the PBM and PDP because the federal government's share of overall payment for prescription medication increases to 85% once a patient enters the catastrophic layer of Part D coverage.[259] For PBMs, this is the trifecta – they retain the rebates and DIR fees which go directly to the bottom line, consumers are pulled through coverage layers of the Part D program quicker without PBMs having to share savings, and beneficiaries hit the Part D "catastrophic" coverage level sooner, reducing PBMs payment for beneficiaries and increasing federal costs to offset the PBM savings.

PBMs also unduly and improperly harm pharmacies in the process by exacting unjustified DIR fees, which also go directly to the bottom line. Indeed, CMS's January findings were further sharpened in its recent Part D Proposed Rule, where CMS (referring to PBMs as "sponsors") more deeply analyzed how PBMs (mis)manage DIR fees and demonstrated how the PBMs keep these fees as profit, rather than use them for any

---

[258] Report at 160.

[259] *See,* e.g., htpps://www.cms.gov/Newsroom/MediaReleaseDatabase/Fact-sheets/2017-Fact-Sheet-items/2017-01-19-2.html.

legitimate purposes. In the Proposed Rule, CMS noted: "only a handful of plans have passed through a small share of price concessions to beneficiaries at the point of sale. Instead, because of the advantages that accrue to sponsors in terms of premiums…the shifting of costs, and plan revenues, from the way rebates and other price concessions applied as DIR at the end of the coverage are treated under the Part D payment methodology, sponsors may have distorted incentives, 82 Fed. Reg. 56336, 56419 (Nov. 28, 2017).

CMS is not the only entity to reach this conclusion; Dr. Sood concluded both that PBMs earn excess profit and that PBMs contribute to higher drug costs.[260] Further, a recent analysis by the Wakely Group evaluated the budgetary impact of legislation pending in Congress to eliminate DIR fees under Part D contracts. The Wakely Group analysis concluded that the legislation would save the Medicare program more than $3 billion over 10 years.[261] The necessary corollary to this conclusion is that DIR fees currently cost the Medicare program money, thereby increasing the cost to the federal government for prescription drugs under Part D.

Consumer choice is also restricted by PBMs, although few consumers are aware of these restrictions. PBMs negotiate formularies based primarily on the rebates (for brands) and discounts (for generics) they and the plans they represent will earn. Thus, financial incentives for PBMs and PDPs determine the medications to which insureds will have access, rather than clinical considerations and the medical needs of an individual patient. Essentially, PBM and PDP profit, not patient quality or out-of-pocket cost, determines the medications to which enrollees have access.

The result is twofold. Some consumers will receive less than optimal medications to treat their clinical conditions. Others will face higher prices for clinically optimal medications. In either case, consumers are adversely affected – either with inferior quality of care or higher out-of-pocket costs.

Finally, LTC pharmacies clearly suffer from the unfair exploitation of market power detailed in Section II. This is not merely a threat to competitors, but it will increase costs to both consumers and the Part D program. As independent LTC pharmacies are forced out of the market by predatory pricing and practices, market concentration increases and prices inevitably increase as well.

Recommendations

The issues and concerns raised at the Committee's hearing and in this written statement justify Congress taking a hard look at the PBM sector, and revisiting some of

---

[260] https://www.ftc.gov/system/files/documents/public_events/1255653/understanding_competition_in_prescription_drug_markets_workshop_slides_11-8-17.pdf (Slides 91-96).

[261] Available at http://www.ncpa.co/pdf/wakely-report.pdf.

the assumptions that Congress has made over the past decades when enacting Medicaid reforms and the Part D program.

The Part D program began as a free market exercise, but has become an oligopolistic market benefitting only PBMs and the corporate conglomerates of which they are a part. Legislation is needed to enact PBM reforms, and require that PBMs not abuse their market position to the detriment of consumers, pharmacies or the federal fisc.[262]

First, Congress should consider legislation requiring PBMs to pass through all rebates. On November 16, 2017, CMS issued a Proposed Rule that sought public input on several suggested approaches to compelling PBMs to pass all rebates on to Part D beneficiaries. The Subcommittee could accelerate development and consideration of such legislation by holding a hearing specifically focused on these issues.

Second, Congress should enact pending legislation designed to eliminate or severely restrict the use of DIR fees and to require greater transparency regarding PDP and PBM pricing and practices. *See,* e.g., H.R. 1038 (addressing DIR fees); H.R. 1316 (addressing PBM transparency).[263] Once again, the Subcommittee could accelerate consideration of pending legislation with a hearing focused specifically on these concerns.

Third, the Subcommittee should hold a follow up hearing to evaluate how PBMs and the corporate conglomerates of which they are a part exploit undue market power in to the detriment of consumers (including Part D beneficiaries), the Medicare program and the free market. As part of that hearing, we recommend the Committee closely scrutinize the proposed CVS Health acquisition of Aetna in the context of the market power and leverage the corporate conglomerates – particularly CVS Health – have been able to develop.

Finally, the Subcommittee should refer related issues to the House Judiciary Committee for further investigation and evaluation from the perspective of the adverse impact on competition and the shocking degree to which the Medicare Part D program, and America's health care system, has become a creature of ever-larger oligopolistic corporate conglomerates rather than a free and fair marketplace.

---

[262] *See also* Forbes, To Improve Pharmaceutical Pricing, Reform PBMs And Fix Health Care's Systemic Problems (April 4, 2017).

[263] CMS has also sought comments in its recent Part D Proposed Rule on ways in which PBMs could be required to share rebates and DIR fees with consumers at the point of sale, rather than keep rebates and DIR fees as PBM profits. 82 Fed. Reg. 56336, 56419 (Nov. 28, 2017). We encourage the Committee to work with the Agency to expand upon the Agency's ideas and to require PBMs to pass through the rebates, as Congress and CMS originally intended when the Part D Program was created. Unfortunately, the CMS approach to pharmacy fees is misguided. As explained more fully in the statement, PBM pharmacy fees are nothing more than exploitation of undue oligopolistic market power to the detriment of pharmacies more so than consumers. The appropriate market correction regarding pharmacy fees is eliminating them altogether, as various bills pending in both the House and Senate propose.

Conclusion

SCPC thanks the Subcommittee for its focus on the drug distribution chain, and how PBMs drive higher prices and higher out-of-pocket costs. We welcome the opportunity to work with the Subcommittee in the future, and applaud further efforts by the Subcommittee to investigate and legislate in this area so we can return to the free market principles that underlie the nation's laws and the Part D program.

Alan Rosenbloom
President & CEO

Coalition for Affordable Prescription Drugs, Statement for the Record, U.S. House of Representatives, Committee on Energy and Commerce, Subcommittee on Health, December 13, 2017

The Coalition for Affordable Prescription Drugs (CAPD) Appreciates the Opportunity to Submit the Following Statement for the Record

The Coalition for Affordable Prescription Drugs (CAPD) represents a diverse group of large employers, labor unions, health plans, public sector employees and retirees, and other stakeholders who partner with pharmacy benefit managers (PBMs) to help manage costs so that they can continue to offer affordable, accessible health and drug benefit coverage to their employees and members.

We appreciate Dr. Burgess's convening of this hearing on the very real impact rising drug prices have on patients, employers, taxpayers, and our health care system. A new study shows that Americans believe that lowering drug prices should be a top priority for Congress.[264]

An important fact in the debate over high drug prices is this: drug manufacturers - and drug manufacturers alone - set the price for prescription medicines.

We are fortunate to live in a time of unprecedented medical breakthroughs. Manufacturers are developing treatments and cures for diseases like Hepatitis C that improve and extend the lives of patients. We all want patients to have access to these medicines, but the innovative power of these medicines is rendered moot when patients are unable to afford them because of the price set by manufacturers.

---

[264] https://www.politico.com/f/?id=00000160-2734-d0c8-a9eb-2ff71c200000.

The most impactful change to make medicines more affordable for patients would be for manufacturers to price medicines responsibly. Yet, manufacturers' prices continue to rise,[265] increasing by more than nine percent in 2016 alone, following double-digit increases every year since 2012.

Year	List price increase
2012	10.0%
2013	11.4%
2014	13.7%
2015	12.0%
2016	9.2%

It is important to realize that the prices set by manufacturers are the starting point. Pharmacy benefit managers (PBMs) use their size and scale to negotiate the lowest net price for prescriptions and drive down costs on behalf of employers, unions and other health care purchasers.

Despite drug manufacturers setting higher and higher prices, pharmacy benefit managers have kept the net prices that their clients pay steady, increasing only 3.5 percent the same year[266] that manufacturer list prices rose 9.2 percent. That difference represents savings for PBM clients – the employers, unions, retirement plans and government programs that provide health care coverage to 266 million Americans[267]. More than 90 percent of these savings are passed on to employers and unions and are used to lower out of pocket costs and premiums for employees and members.

In addition to delivering savings through negotiations with drug manufacturers, PBMs support better health outcomes and help reduce health care costs through other strategies. Clinical expertise helps ensure the safest, most effective and affordable medications are dispensed, which in many cases is a generic drug. Patient-focused tools and programs also help to improve medication adherence, which is critically important to the nearly 50 percent of Americans with at least one chronic disease.

However, one of the most significant barriers to medication adherence is high out of pocket costs. When drug prices increase, patient co-pays and premiums follow suit. The reality is this: if manufacturers set prices at more responsible levels – and increased them only at sustainable rates – potentially life-saving medicines would be more accessible to the patients that need them.

Fortunately, greater focus is being placed on the prices that drug manufacturers set and the implications that ripple through the system as a result. As Gerard Anderson,

---

265 http://www.imshealth.com/en/thought-leadership/quintilesims-institute/reports/medicines-use-and-spending-in-the-us-review-of-2016-outlook-to-2021.

266 http://www.imshealth.com/en/thought-leadership/quintilesims-institute/reports/medicines-use-and-spending-in-the-us-review-of-2016-outlook-to-2021.

267 https://www.pcmanet.org/wp-content/uploads/2016/11/ROI-on-PBM-Services-FINAL.pdf.

Professor of Medicine at Johns Hopkins University School of Medicine, testified[268] to the Senate HELP Committee in June, "Many people have argued that the list price is irrelevant because few entities actually pay the list price. However, the list price is often used to determine the amount of cost sharing that many patients will pay. Since the list price is the only price that is publicly announced, it becomes the basis for many cost-sharing agreements. Thus, patients are harmed when the list price goes up."

Ensuring greater access and affordability will also depend on fostering greater competition. Facilitating faster reviews of generics and biosimilars, identifying off-patent drugs with little or no generic competition, and ending anti-competitive practices that keep safe, effective alternatives off the market are also key to managing rising drug costs for patients. A competitive environment ensures that PBMs can effectively negotiate on behalf of their partners, ensuring access to needed medications and, at the same time, bending the cost curve of rising drug prices.

CAPD is grateful for the opportunity to submit this testimony and eager to work with stakeholders to find new ideas and build on existing strategies to help drive progress for employers, employees, retirees, taxpayers – and for America's future.

December 11, 2017

The Honorable Michael Burgess
U.S. House of Representatives
Chairman, Subcommittee on Health
Committee on Energy and Commerce

The Honorable Gene Green
U.S. House of Representatives
Ranking Member, Subcommittee on Health
Committee on Energy and Commerce

Dear Chairman Burgess, Ranking Member Green and Members of the Subcommittee:

Thank you for the opportunity to submit comments to the Energy and Commerce Subcommittee on Health's hearing "Examining the Drug Supply Chain" on behalf of the National Multiple Sclerosis Society (Society). The Society works to provide solutions to the challenges of multiple sclerosis (MS) so that everyone affected by this disease can live their best lives. To fulfill this mission, we fund cutting-edge research, drive change through advocacy, facilitate professional education, collaborate with MS organizations

[268] https://www.help.senate.gov/imo/media/doc/Anderson4.pdf.

around the world, and provide services designed to help people affected by MS move their lives forward.

MS is an unpredictable, often disabling disease of the central nervous system, which interrupts the flow of information within the brain and between the brain and the body. Symptoms range from numbness and tingling to blindness and paralysis. The progression, severity and specific symptoms of MS in any one person cannot yet be predicted, but advances in research and treatment are moving us closer to a world free of MS.

Access to MS medications, including disease-modifying therapies (DMTs), has transformed MS treatment over the last two decades. Today there are 15 FDA-approved DMTs that reduce disease activity and disease progression for many people with relapsing forms of MS, including the recent approval of the first ever therapy for primary progressive MS. These medications are crucial to people living with MS; yet high prices, escalating price increases, a complex and opaque supply chain, growing out-of-pocket costs, and confusing and inconsistent formularies create real barriers between people living with MS and their ability to access the medications they need to live their best lives.

For a person with MS, getting your medication shouldn't feel like a full-time job. Living with MS is already difficult for individuals who often experience cognitive challenges and debilitating fatigue. Barriers for people in getting their medications can come in many forms. One individual described the challenges they encountered with the supply chain to receive their medication; "It took us over a month from the time my MS medication was prescribed to the time it was shipped to me. We had to personally coordinate between the physician's office, the insurance company, the specialty mail order pharmacy our plan requires us to use for this drug, another group our insurance uses to complete prior authorizations, the regular mail order pharmacy for our insurance, and the manufacturer's finance department."

This process does not describe a system that is designed with the patient in mind. Too often, people with MS report significant delays in getting their treatment or changing medications when a treatment is no longer working. These delays may result in new MS activity and added stress and anxiety from having to navigate a complex web of uncoordinated individual (yet increasingly inter-owned) systems, processes and entities to get their treatment.

As there are no easy answer or solutions to this complex issue, the Society's Advisory Committee on Access to MS Medications – comprised of people with MS, family members, health policy experts and healthcare providers – released recommendations (also attached) as a part of the Society's "Make MS Medications Accessible Initiative" (Initiative) to ensure that MS medications are affordable and the process for getting them simple and transparent.

The Initiative calls on all parties involved in the supply chain – pharmaceutical companies, insurance providers, pharmacy benefit managers, specialty pharmacies, health care providers, policy makers, and patients – to work together to address escalating prices and other issues that are creating significant barriers to treatment.

A critical element that is needed to address these barriers is increased transparency from all elements the pharmaceutical system and supply chain-manufacturers, insurers and pharmacy benefit managers. Improving the system will require all parties to be operating from the same level of information. Currently, it is difficult to assess deficiencies in the system and implement solutions because there is a lack of publicly available information. One individual with MS noted the challenges that result from a lack of public information on the cost of a therapy; "I hesitate to go on disease modifying drugs because of the cost. I work in the insurance industry and even if I have insurance coverage, the cost of these drugs is prohibitive and shifted one way or another. There needs to be much more transparency…"

The Society believes Congress can serve a vital role in moving these conversations forward by:

- Investigating the role of intermediaries and roadblocks that impact pharmaceutical prices, access, and quality within the pharmaceutical supply chain, including fees at various points of the supply chain.
- Examining the perverse incentives within the supply chain for manufacturers to charge higher prices and then rebate more extensively. It appears that when this happens, many within the supply chain benefit-except for the patient who may be faced with a higher cost-share per month and/or during a deductible period or Medicare's coverage gap.
- Considering the impact of mergers and consolidations within the health system and supply chain in decreasing competition and limiting choices for consumers (of insurers and distribution options). Do mergers and consolidations meet some of the stated goals of improving health outcomes? Are people with chronic illnesses impacted differently? Are there savings throughout the supply chain and health system due to mergers and consolidations?

Ensuring That the Supply Chain and Health Care System Works for the Patient

The pharmaceutical supply chain is an inherent part of the nation's health care system. For far too long, conversations about ways to improve the entire health system have occurred without input from whom we believe should be at the center of all of these decisions--the patient who relies on medications to live their best lives. We urge the

Committee to schedule a hearing to hear directly from patients on how the health system and pharmaceutical supply chain can better meet their needs.

We believe that the health care system should be simplified and coordinated so that patients can get their medication without stress or delay. The current system is not working for people with MS. In addition to the complexities already mentioned, requirements for individuals to use a particular specialty pharmacy can translate to real-world problems for people with MS. If they are unable to change the delivery date of their medication for instance, or if they're not home—their medication could be left out in the heat/ cold or they may not be able to get an adequate supply if traveling. Disrupted treatment can result in negative health consequences for the person with MS—such as MS exacerbations—and higher costs to the healthcare system.

Overwhelmingly, prior authorization requests are approved for MS medications, so simplifying and streamlining these processes just makes sense. Reducing paperwork and end of year burdens on both people with MS and their healthcare providers is a win for individuals and the health system alike. Large health offices report staff spend 20-30 hours per month on prior authorization, step therapy, appeals and other insurance coverage issues for people with MS.

We call for stakeholders to work together to reduce redundancies in the system to increase efficiency and reduce the burden for the person with MS. The Society has specific recommendations on how to make the health care system work people living with MS:

- Prior authorization should happen before the person with MS leaves the healthcare provider's office.
- A person with MS should have the option to get their medication from multiple pharmacies; requiring a single specialty pharmacy may not work best for that individual.
- Step therapy should make sense, and not result in detrimental delays in accessing appropriate medications. Individuals should not be required to fail on similar mechanisms of action, similar routes of administration or a medication they have failed previously.
- Prior authorization approval should be good for a lengthy time period, including across multiple years, as long as the person is stable on the medication.
- Allow multi-year approvals for patient assistance programs.

It's also important for someone living with MS to get the right treatment and if it's working, be able to stay on that treatment. MS is a heterogeneous disease and medications may work differently for individuals. An individual with MS recently described the worry that results when coverage changes; "I worry the insurance companies or employers will tell the doctors to put me on a less expensive medicine. I do not want to change what is working."

Thank you for the opportunity to provide our perspective on the U.S. supply chain and its impact on people living with MS. We look forward to working with the Committee and all stakeholders as you work to improve the U.S. pharmaceutical supply chain to better serve people living with MS.

Sincerely,

Bari Talente
Executive Vice President, Advocacy
National Multiple Sclerosis Society

MAKE MS MEDICATIONS ACCESSIBLE: RECOMMENDATIONS

Background

Multiple sclerosis (MS) medications have transformed the treatment of relapsing MS over the last 20 years. Yet, many people living with MS cannot access the medications they need. Continually escalating prices are creating significant barriers to treatment, including higher costs, increased stress, and a greater burden for those who already live with a chronic, life-altering condition.

Studies show that early and ongoing treatment with a disease-modifying therapy is the best way to modify the course of the disease, prevent the accumulation of disability and protect the brain from damage due to MS. So why are these life-changing medications too often out of reach for those who need them?

People with MS report high and rapidly escalating medication prices, increasing out-of-pocket costs, confusing and inconsistent formularies (the lists of medications an insurer will pay for), and complex approval processes that stand in the way of getting the treatments they need.

These challenges can cause delays in starting a medication or changing medications when a treatment is no longer working. Delays may trigger new MS activity and cause even more stress and anxiety about the future for people already living with the complex challenges of an unpredictable disease like MS.

It is time for change. People with chronic illnesses need to know that they'll be able to get the life-changing medication they need. The National MS Society is launching our effort to make medications accessible, reflecting the needs of the MS movement and rallying all parties involved — pharmaceutical companies, insurance providers, pharmacy benefit managers, specialty pharmacies, healthcare providers, policy makers, people with

MS and others — to work together to focus on getting people with MS the medications they need to live their best lives.

> Medications can only change lives if people can access them.
>
> Medications and the process for getting them must be: affordable, simple and transparent.

The campaign recommendations were developed by the Society's Advisory Committee on Access to MS Medications, a group comprised of people with MS, family members, health policy experts and healthcare providers. They were informed by extensive stakeholder engagement and feedback, including a survey to gain the perspectives of more than 8,500 people with MS. The recommendations are comprehensive, address the challenges across many stakeholders, and provide the basis for conversations to create change. No single stakeholder has all the solutions; we can only find the solutions together.

Affordable

The high prices of the MS medications make treatment for many people unaffordable and inaccessible. MS disease modifying therapies first entered the market in the 1990s priced between $8,000-$15,000 per year. Newer medications have commonly been introduced to the market costing 25-60% higher than existing therapies.[269]

Today, the average price of the MS treatments has increased nearly 400% since 2004. At the same time, insurance design increasingly moved from co-pays to co-insurance for specialty medications, with co-insurance for MS medications as high as 40%-which could be $2,600 each month. On the health insurance exchanges created through the Affordable Care Act, more than 10% of silver plans have greater than 40% coinsurance for all the MS medications and nearly a third of plans place all covered MS therapies on a specialty tier. Reducing prices and limiting out-of-pocket costs will allow more people to access life-changing medications.

Price

Innovation in MS has changed the lives of many people living with MS. We need innovation to continue, while finding a better balance between innovation and affordability, so that people with MS can get the treatments they need in a timely and affordable way. Pricing medications and determining price increases is a complicated area that requires greater openness and recognition that price does impact access.

---

[269] Hartung DM, Bourdette DN, Ahmed SM, Whitham RH. The cost of multiple sclerosis drugs in the US and the pharmaceutical industry: too big to fail? *Neurology* 2015;84:2185-2192.

> "The medication I am on is administered once every four weeks. It is extremely expensive and causes me to reach my deductible after only 1 dose and my out of pocket maximum after 2 doses. This puts a lot of financial strain on my family. This medication has proven to be very effective for me, but I am strongly considering changing medications due to the financial problems my family is now facing."

Recommendations

- Limit price increases for medications that have been on the market for a considerable time.
- Reduce prices for medications that have drastically increased in price since first entering the market.
- Pricing for new treatments to the MS market should consider research and development costs, the value of the medication from the perspective of people with MS and healthcare providers, how price impacts patient access to medications and other medications on the market.
- Value-based pricing should be explored and must include patient engagement in determining value for a lifelong, chronic disease like MS.

Insurance Plan Design

Specialty medications to treat a chronic disease like MS are expensive, yet crucial for people to live their best lives. A growing body of evidence suggests that higher cost sharing for specialty medications is associated with reductions in use.[270] In a recent study of people with MS and health insurance, those who reported a negative insurance change in the previous 12 months had greater odds of not taking their MS medications.[271] Out-of-pocket costs associated with insurance should not prevent someone from using the medication they and their healthcare provider decide is the best option.

Recommendations

All available medications for a particular disease must not be on a specialty tier with co-insurance.

Out-of-pocket costs should not be so high that individuals skip doses or abandon their medication entirely. Reduction in use and adherence data should be considered when determining out-of-pocket costs.

---

[270] Trish E, Xu J, Joyce G. Medicare Beneficiaries Face Growing Out-of-Pocket Burden for Specialty Drugs While in Catastrophic Coverage Phase. *Health Affairs* 2016: 35(9):1564-1571.

[271] Wang G, Marrie RA, Salter A, Fox R, Cofield S, Tyry T, Cutter G. Health insurance affects the use of disease-modifying therapy in multiple sclerosis. *Neurology* 2016;87:1-10.

Out-of-pocket costs for those with significant health expenses should be spread more evenly throughout the year so these costs are not a disincentive to receiving needed treatment and care.

Market and Regulatory Considerations

Specialty medications do not follow a simple supply and demand economic model. Rather, product uptake is dependent on a complex economic supply chain and formulary design. Financial projections should take these factors into consideration and market expectations should be adjusted accordingly. Minor tweaks to existing products should not be afforded lengthy patent protections. Special incentives and possible regulatory intervention should occur when the free market does not appear to be working. When encouraging competition like generics or biosimilars, it should be recognized that multiple generics are required in the market before price is significantly impacted.

> "Without the financial assistance program, I would not still be on my medication. In 15 years, the same has gone from $585 to $5200 per month. How can they explain that?"

Recommendations

- Incentivize multiple generics or biosimilars for a reference product.
- Increased HHS regulatory oversight of drug classes that do not fit the expectations of a competitive market.
- Eliminate lengthy patent protections for minor tweaks to existing products.

Medicare

People with MS report significant difficulties affordably accessing their medications through Medicare. Cost sharing for brand name medications is increasingly in the form of co-insurance rather than a copayment. In 2016, 31% of Medicare prescription drug plan enrollees have co-insurance for preferred brand medications and 96% have co-insurance for non-preferred brand medications.[272] In 2012, 96% of those on Medicare taking an MS therapy reached the catastrophic coverage limit, and nearly half did so by February.[273] While the trend in other types of insurance is to limit out-of-pocket costs, people on Medicare currently have no limit on their financial burden.

---

[272] Hoadley J, Cubanski J, Neuman T. Medicare Part D in 2016 and Trends over Time. Kaiser Family Foundation, September 2016.

[273] Trish E, Xu J, Joyce G. Medicare Beneficiaries Face Growing Out-of-Pocket Burden.

Recommendations

- Limit the out-of-pocket costs for prescription medications.
- Allow Medicare to negotiate prices for medications.

> "I have had MS since I was 21 and the financial burden has dominated my life. I have been in remission for much of this time (I am now 40) but the overall cost of medical coverage that would cover the cost of my medication, as well as the cost of it, has been an overwhelming driver of my lifestyle and major financial decisions… As a young person, I dreamed of entering the Peace Corps or travelling but could not pursue those dreams as I could lose my medical insurance and not be able to get my medication. I am glad to have my health but the cost of my medication has gone from $700/month to over $5,000."

Simple

Getting your medication shouldn't feel like a full-time job. Living with MS is already difficult for individuals who often experience debilitating fatigue and cognitive challenges. Too often, people with MS report significant delays in getting their treatment and added stress and anxiety from having to navigate a complex web of uncoordinated systems, processes and entities in the healthcare system to get their treatment.

Make the Health Care System Work for the Person Who Needs the Medication

The health care system should be designed for the ease of the person who needs the medication, so they can get their medication without stress or delay. Overwhelmingly, prior authorization requests are approved for MS medications, so simplifying and streamlining these processes just makes sense. Reducing paperwork and end of year burdens on both people with MS and their healthcare providers is a win for individuals and the health system alike. Large health offices report staff spend 20-30 hours per month on prior authorization, step therapy, appeals and other insurance coverage issues for people with MS.

> "I worry the insurance companies or employers will tell the doctors to put me on a less expensive medicine. I do not want to change what is working."

Recommendations

- Prior authorization should happen before the person with MS leaves the healthcare provider's office.

- A person with MS should have the option to get their medication from multiple pharmacies; requiring a single specialty pharmacy may not work best for that individual.
- Step therapy should make sense, and not result in detrimental delays in accessing appropriate medications. Individuals should not be required to fail on similar mechanisms of action, similar routes of administration or a medication they have failed previously.
- Prior authorization approval should be good for a lengthy time period, including across multiple years, as long as the person is stable on the medication.
- Allow multi-year approvals for patient assistance programs.

> "It took us over a month from the time my MS medication was prescribed to the time it was shipped to me. We had to personally coordinate between the physician's office, the insurance company, the specialty mail order pharmacy our plan requires us to use for this drug, another group our insurance uses to complete prior authorizations, the regular mail order pharmacy for our insurance, and the manufacturer's finance department"

Get the Right Treatment to the Right Person

MS is a heterogeneous disease and medications may work differently for individuals. Insurance and pharmacy benefit manager (PBM) coverage of the MS therapies is currently highly variable and based on rebate negotiations rather than expert advice, making it difficult for people with MS to move between plans. More consistency in coverage of MS medications across plans, with allowances for flexibility in finding the right treatment, would help simplify the system for people with MS and healthcare providers, and promote shared decision-making between a person and their healthcare provider. Today, the decision of which medication to use is often based on what's covered rather than what's best for the individual.

Recommendations

- Develop consensus prescribing guidelines, led by the MS healthcare provider community.
- Ensure insurance plan design promotes access to treatments, particularly for those with chronic conditions, with decisions based on medical evidence and patient-centered factors.
- Invest in research like precision medicine and biomarkers, to further understanding of which treatment works best for which individuals.

Stay on Treatment that Works

Once a person with MS finds a medication that works, we should make it simple for that person to stay on their treatment.

Recommendation

- People should remain on a treatment that works for them regardless of changes in medication coverage and insurance plan changes.

Simplify and Coordinate Paperwork and Processes

People with MS should not be overburdened by paperwork or be responsible for coordinating different entities to work together just so they can get their medication. We can simplify and integrate processes so there are no delays in getting medication and the person with MS is not overwhelmed.

> "The medication that I take is roughly $6000 per month, or $200 a day. Thanks to copay assistance from the drug company, my medication is more reasonable, but every January I have to reapply for the assistance and hope that I am approved. It is extremely stressful. I don't understand why a drug that helps people with their disease should or would cost so much."

Recommendations

- Develop a uniform patient assistance application for patient assistance/co-pay programs across the manufacturer and non-profit programs.
- Different entities involved in providing medications must work together to coordinate their interactions to increase efficiency and reduce the burden for the person with MS-including the insurer, pharmacy benefit manager, specialty pharmacy and patient assistance program.
- Reduce redundancies and develop integration in processes across stakeholders.

> "The original medication my doctor prescribed was denied by my insurance company. My doctor felt my MS was very aggressive and wanted to start me on a higher end drug. The insurance company said it was a financial decision for them and denied the first and second drug my doctor tried to prescribe. She was then told what drug I was required to try. My treatment was delayed due to the denials resulting in permanent damage to my foot, leg and hand."

Transparent

There is increased pressure on all health care consumers to make good choices. Yet, people have very little information about price and cost to make these decisions. Just the term "price" can mean several different things. The prices charged for MS medications, the actual cost paid for them, and the impacting decisions between a manufacturer price and a negotiated contract with an insurer or pharmacy benefit manager, are outside of the public realm. People with MS need more information to make informed choices; and we all need greater information to improve the system.

Clarify How Relevant Information Can Be Shared

Sharing of relevant information will allow stakeholders and individuals within the health care system to make better decisions. There are ways we can improve the information flow while keeping patient protections at the forefront.

Recommendations

- Clarify regulations to permit greater pre-approval information sharing between manufacturers and payers.
- Clarify regulations to allow greater information sharing regarding post-approval evidence on clinical and economic outcomes.

Transparency from Manufacturers

Innovation of new and better therapies is crucial and can be costly. People with MS support profitability for pharmaceutical manufacturers, but there must be a better balance between innovation and affordability. People with MS and others want to help find solutions, but to do so they need a greater understanding of research and development and other costs, as well as determining factors in setting price and price increases.

> "I hesitate to go on disease modifying drugs because of the cost. I work in the insurance industry and even if I have insurance coverage, the cost of these drugs is prohibitive and shifted one way or another. There needs to be much more transparency..."

Recommendations

- Greater information and transparency about:
  - How determining factors are used to set prices
  - How price increases are determined, including frequency of increases

- o How prices and price increases support research and development, direct-to-consumer advertising and marketing to healthcare providers
- o Numbers of people assisted and money spent on patient assistance support

Transparency from Insurers and Pharmacy Benefit Managers

For people with MS, the formulary (list of approved medications) is the most important part of their health insurance coverage and a deciding factor in the health insurance plan they choose. Criteria for formulary decisions should be easily available and include factors that are important to people taking these medications.

> "Our insurance decides each year what 6 - 8 MS drugs it will cover. So, while there are 14 available, that is not really an option. We must choose between those actually covered.
>
> In that list there are some that I would never choose so I am left with a choice of three or four options at best. So, it is not patient driven but cost driven."

Recommendations

- Formulary coverage, including cost-sharing, must be easily accessible, understandable and searchable (if online) when people with MS are choosing a plan.
- There must be a significant notification period of any changes in coverage in a single year and between plan years.
- Factors used in formulary decision-making should be transparent, and should include patient-centered factors.

Transparency within the System

The system is driven by rebates, which are negotiations between some parties involved in the supply chain but not all parties. This makes it difficult to understand the true benefit to the person taking a medication.

Recommendations

- The public should be allowed greater understanding of the stakeholders engaged in rebate negotiations, of the factors involved in rebates and the benefits to different stakeholders.
- Rebate benefits should be directly passed on to the person taking that particular medication.

- Greater understanding and transparency of the varying prices across the system and internationally is needed.

Chart: Recommended Stakeholder Action

Many of the recommendations above could be implemented by multiple stakeholders. Some require Congressional or regulatory action, others are best achieved through a change in business practices by one or more stakeholders, and other recommendations could be implemented by business practices or public policy change.

Section	Recommendation	Stakeholder with Ability to Change
Price	Limit price increases for medications on market for a considerable time.	• Pharmaceutical Manufacturers • Policy Makers
	Reduce prices for medications which have drastically increased in price since first coming on the market.	• Pharmaceutical Manufacturers • Policy makers
	Pricing for treatments new to the MS market should consider research and development costs, the value of the medication from the perspective of people with MS and healthcare providers, how price impacts patient access to medications, and other medications on market.	• Pharmaceutical Manufacturers
	Value-based pricing should be explored and must include patient engagement in determining value for a lifelong, chronic disease like MS.	• Government agencies • People with MS • National MS Society • Pharmaceutical Manufacturers • Insurers • PBMs
Insurance Plan Design	All available medications for a particular disease must not be on a specialty tier with co-insurance.	• Department of Health and Human Services • Policy Makers • Insurers • Employers
	Out-of-pocket costs should not be so high that individuals skip doses or abandon their medication entirely. Reduction in use and adherence data should be considered when determining out-of-pocket costs.	• Insurers

(Continued)

Section	Recommendation	Stakeholder with Ability to Change
Insurance Plan Design	Out-of-pocket costs for those with significant health expenses should be spread more evenly throughout the year so these costs are not a disincentive to receiving needed treatments and care.	• Insurers • Employers • Policy Makers
Market and Regulatory Considerations	Incentivize multiple generics or biosimilars for a reference product.	• Government Agency • Policy Makers
	Increased HHS regulatory oversight of drug classes that do not fit the expectations of a competitive market.	• Government Agency • Policy Makers
	Eliminate lengthy patent protections for minor tweaks to existing products.	• Policy Makers
Medicare	Limit the out-of-pocket costs for prescription medications.	• Government Agency • Policy Makers
	Allow Medicare to negotiate prices for medications.	• Policy Makers
Make the Health Care System Work for the Person Who Needs the Medication	Prior authorization should happen before the person with MS leaves the healthcare provider's office.	• Insurers • PBMs • Policy Makers
	A person with MS should have the option to get their medication from multiple pharmacies; requiring a single specialty pharmacy may not work best for that individual.	• Insurers • PBMs • Policy Makers
	Step therapy should make sense, and not result in detrimental delays in accessing appropriate medications. Individuals should not be required to fail on similar mechanisms of action, similar routes of administration or a medication they have failed previously.	• Insurers • PBMs • Policy Makers
	Prior authorization approval should be good for a lengthy time period, including across multiple years, as long as the person is stable on the medication.	• Insurers • PBMs • Employers • Policy Makers
	Allow multi-year approvals for patient assistance programs.	• Pharmaceutical manufacturers • Non-profit assistance programs

Section	**Recommendation**	**Stakeholder with Ability to Change**
Get the Right Treatment to the Right Person	Develop consensus prescribing guidelines, led by the MS healthcare provider community.	• American Academy of Neurology
	Ensure insurance plan design promotes access to treatments, particularly for those with chronic conditions, with decisions based on medical evidence and patient-centered factors.	• Insurers • Policy Makers
	Invest in research like precision medicine and biomarkers, to further understanding of which treatment works best for which individuals.	• Government Agencies • National MS Society • Pharmaceutical Manufacturers • Policy Makers
Stay on a Treatment that Works	People should remain on a treatment that works for them regardless of changes in medication coverage and insurance plan changes.	• Insurers • PBMs • Policy Makers
Simplify and Coordinate Paperwork and Processes	Develop a uniform patient assistance application for patient assistance/co-pay programs across the manufacturer and non-profit programs.	• Pharmaceutical Manufacturers • Non-profit Assistance Programs
	Different entities involved in providing medications must work together to coordinate their interactions to increase efficiency and reduce the burden for the person with MS - including the insurer, pharmacy benefit manager, specialty pharmacy and patient assistance program.	• Healthcare Providers • Insurers • PBMs • Specialty Pharmacies • Patient Assistance Programs • People with MS
	Reduce redundancies and develop integration in processes across stakeholders.	• Insurers • PBMs • Specialty Pharmacies • Patient Assistance Programs
Clarify how Relevant Information can be Shared	Clarify regulations to permit greater pre-approval information sharing between manufacturers and payers.	• Government Agency
	Clarify regulations to allow greater information sharing regarding post-approval evidence on clinical and economic outcomes.	• Government Agency

(Continued)

Section	Recommendation	Stakeholder with Ability to Change
Transparency from Manufacturers	Greater information and transparency about: • How determining factors are used to set prices • How price increases are determined, including frequency of increases • How prices and price increases support research and development, direct-to-consumer advertising and marketing to healthcare providers • Numbers of people assisted and money spent on patient assistance support	• Pharmaceutical Manufacturers • Policy Makers
Transparency from Insurers and Pharmacy Benefit Managers	Formulary coverage, including cost-sharing, must be easily accessible, understandable and searchable (if online) when people with MS are choosing a plan.	• Insurers
	There must be a significant notification period of any changes in coverage in a single year and between plan years.	• Insurers • Policy Makers
	Factors used in formulary decision-making should be transparent, and should include patient-centered factors.	• Insurers • Policy Makers
Transparency within the System	The public should be allowed greater understanding of the stakeholders engaged in rebate negotiations, of the factors involved in rebates and the benefits to different stakeholders.	• Pharmaceutical Manufacturers • PBMs • Insurers • Policy Makers
	Rebate benefits should be directly passed on to the person taking that particular medication.	• PBMs • Insurers • Employers • Policy Makers
	Greater understanding and transparency of the varying prices across the system and internationally is needed.	• Pharmaceutical Manufacturers • Insurers

ALLIANCE FOR TRANSPARENT AND AFFORDABLE PRESCRIPTIONS

House Committee on Energy and Commerce Subcommittee on Health, December 13, 2017. Chairman Burgess, Ranking Member Green, and Members of the Subcommittee:

The Alliance for Transparent and Affordable Prescriptions (ATAP) consists of seventeen patient and provider groups who are concerned about the role of pharmacy benefit managers (PBMs) in the rising cost of drugs. ATAP is funded entirely by membership dues and does not take funding from outside sources. We thank the Subcommittee for scheduling today's hearing entitled "Examining the Drug Supply Chain." ATAP was formed on a shared concern that PBMs play an increasingly harmful role in our supply chain.

PBMs are third-party entities that manage and administer prescription drug plans for payers, including Medicare Parts C and D plans, TRICARE, the Federal Employees Health Benefits Program, employers, and health insurers. Among other functions, PBMs negotiate rebates with pharmaceutical manufacturers and manage drug utilization by beneficiaries. Unfortunately, there is very little transparency surrounding PBMs and their role within the delivery system, nor is there any requirement to pass negotiated savings onto patients.

PBMs allege that they are saving costs through negotiating rebates and discounts, but patients have seen little to no benefit from those "savings." As physicians and patients, we have seen firsthand how out-of-pocket costs have risen year after year, even as patients' ability to access the medicines they need is compromised through restrictive formularies, tiering, and other aggressive utilization management techniques. In fact, the current system seems to encourage manufacturers to increase their list prices—which are just the starting point for negotiations— and yet, patient cost-sharing is often based on those inflated list prices.

We urge you to consider the following policy goals to build a better system:

1) Increase transparency in the rebate system through agreed-upon definitions and public disclosure of price concessions.
2) Reduce patient cost-sharing obligations via flow-through of price concessions.
3) Improve access to treatments through transparent, clinically sound formularies.

Increase Transparency

The current lack of transparency, especially with respect to PBMs, has done little to reduce drug costs. One particularly problematic aspect stems from the reclassification of rebates and discounts received from manufacturers. Since there is currently no industry standard for key terms used in PBM contracts with manufacturers, plan sponsors, and pharmacies, each PBM can define terms on an *ad hoc* basis. Because they are typically only contractually obligated to pass onto plan sponsors a specified portion of manufacturer "rebates," PBMs exploit the non-transparent nature of their contract negotiations with manufacturers to reclassify a portion of the rebates received as "fees" and other designations, allowing them to keep a significant portion of the rebate amount as profit.[274]

Another example revolves around the classification of products as "brands" versus "generics." PBMs are not required to follow Food and Drug Administration (FDA) definitions for what is and is not a "generic" drug. This allows the PBM to define as "generics" products that were not approved pursuant to Abbreviated New Drug Applications (ANDAs) by FDA, which is the generally understood definition of the term "generic." Conversely, it allows the PBM to define as "brands" products that *were* approved pursuant to ANDAs when that is financially beneficial. This lack of definitional agreement enables sleights of hands such as treating single-source generic drugs as brand products when financially beneficial or inflating generic substitution rates for products that were invoiced as brands.[275] For this particular example, the solution is to require PBMs to classify a product as a generic or a brand according to how the product was approved by the FDA, consistently across the product life.

There are other examples of varying treatment of money streams and definitional games and trapdoors. Indeed, in the recent Part D rule[276] released by the Centers for Medicare and Medicaid Services (CMS), the agency notes that variation in the treatment of rebates and price concessions may have a negative effect on the competitive balance under the Part D program. Additionally, the quality of information available to Part D beneficiaries is even less conducive to producing efficient choices when price concessions are treated differently by different Part D sponsors.

Thus, as a first step in improving our current system, Congress must urge the Department of Health and Human Services to establish, with stakeholder input and subject to public comment, agreed upon definitions for terms commonly used in PBM contracts in any prescription drug plan financed by the government. In addition to creating industry standards, this will bring clarity and transparency to the various streams of money flowing to and from PBMs. Once definitional clarity exists, disclosure will be meaningful.

---

[274] "Comparing Pharmacy Benefit Managers: Moving Well Beyond the Simple Spreadsheet Analysis" by David Calabrese, RPh, MHP, Am. Health Drug Benefits, 2008 Jun; 1(5): 9-19.

[275] "When is a brand a generic? In a contract with a PBM." Linda Cahn, *Managed Care* (Sept. 2010), available: https://www.managedcaremag.com/archives/2010/9/when-brand-generic-contract-pbm.

[276] "Medicare Program; Contract Year 2019 Policy and Technical Changes to the Medicare Advantage, Medicare Cost Plan, Medicare Fee-for-Service, the Medicare Prescription Drug Benefit Programs, and the PACE Program."

Reduce Cost-Sharing

Reducing patient out-of-pocket exposure may require different approaches depending on the payer. For example, in Medicare Part D, patient out-of-pocket costs could be calculated at the point of sale based on net prices that take into account rebates and other price concessions. In the Part D rule[277] referenced above, CMS included a Request for Information (RFI), indicating that the agency is considering such a requirement. The agency notes that, in recent years, only a handful of plans have passed through a small share of price concessions to beneficiaries at the point of sale." CMS adds that "sponsors may have distorted incentives as compared to what we intended in 2005."

As a result, the Part D rule contains an RFI related to requiring sponsors to include at least a minimum percentage of manufacturer rebates and all pharmacy price concessions received for a Part D drug in the drug's negotiated price at the point of sale. In other words: CMS is considering whether it should require sponsors to share with Medicare beneficiaries at least some portion of the price concessions negotiated by intermediaries. CMS provides ten-year impact estimates of a forced pass-through of 33%, 66%, 90%, and 100% of manufacturer rebates at the point of sale: *at the lowest point of that range (33%), beneficiaries would save $19.6 billion dollars in their out-of-pocket costs.* While a pass-through policy would increase premiums, that increase is more than offset by the deep reductions in cost-sharing at every level of pass-through. Similarly, the per-member-per-month savings estimates provide by CMS tell us that, at a 33% pass-through, beneficiaries would save $30.33 per month, while, at a 100% pass-through, beneficiaries would save $88.13 per month.

Any argument that the policy would increase premiums is disingenuous as it does not factor in the offsetting impact of the large reductions in cost-sharing: the overall savings numbers calculated by CMS are the result of slight increases in premiums that are more than offset by large reductions in cost-sharing. With regard to requiring that all pharmacy price concessions be used to lower the price at the point of sale, CMS notes that such a policy "would affect beneficiary, government, and manufacturer costs largely in the same manner as discussed previously in regards to moving manufacturer rebates to the point of sale." We strongly support a pass-through policy and will file comments with the agency urging CMS to proceed with such a proposal. Similar policies must be implemented in all prescription drug plans in which the government is a partner.

Improve Access

We understand that formularies and other utilization management techniques are a necessary part of reducing healthcare spending.

---

[277] *Id.*

However, the current system for developing formularies does not seem to be based on sound scientific evidence or accepted clinical guidelines, but rather on the cost of the product to the PBM. As prescribers and patients, we recognize that the formulary placement of a drug is in large part just the result of annual negotiations between the PBM and the manufacturer, and not the result of the latest science or clinical outcomes.

To improve access to medically necessary prescriptions, any PBM involved in administering a prescription benefit plan related to any federal health program should publish up-to-date, accurate, and complete formulary lists. That would provide patients with information on tiering structures and any cost-sharing requirements for each tier, as well as restrictions on how and when the product can be obtained by the patient (such as dose or quantity limits, prior authorization, etc.). In addition, there should be one, single, transparent formulary used by both the PBM and the plan sponsor on whose behalf the PBM administers the prescription benefit to avoid duplicative or conflicting formularies.

In closing, we also urge Congress to require the Federal Trade Commission to closely examine the PBM industry in its current form, as many of the aforementioned problems may be related to market consolidation. Combined, the two largest PBMs cover more than 170 million lives.[278] That is more than three times the size of the entire Medicare program.[279] Such a consolidated market, combined with a lack of transparency, means that PBM contracts with pharmaceutical manufacturers and pharmacies are one-sided and may amount to a "take it or leave it" demand for rebates and fees by the PBMs—with poor results for patients and drug spending in our federal health programs. Any additional consolidation of this industry should be avoided lest we inadvertently make a bad problem worse. To that end, we have urged the Federal Trade Commission to closely scrutinize the recently announced CVS Health acquisition of Aetna.[280] It is highly likely that this level of consolidation in an already consolidated, opaque market will cause far more harm than good for patients.

We thank the Subcommittee for holding this important hearing and hope to be a partner as you examine pharmaceutical access and pricing. This is a crisis we can no longer ignore. For too long, the health of patients – both physical and financial – has suffered due to a morass of middlemen whose only incentive is to protect the bottom line. The good news is: it is not too late to change those incentives in a manner that prioritizes patients.

---

[278] Express Scripts covers 83 million. (Express Scripts Corporate Overview, downloadable at http://lab.express-scripts.com/about.) CVS Caremark covers approximately 90 million. (CVS Health At A Glance, https://www.cvshealth.com/about/facts-and-company-information.)

[279] "An Overview of Medicare" by the Kaiser Family Foundation (April 1, 2016), available: http://kff.org/medicare/issue-brief/an-overview-of-medicare/.

[280] https://www.washingtonpost.com/business/economy/what-the-cvs-aetna-deal-means-for-the-future-of-health-care/2017/12/05/e14a8d18-d907-11e7-a841-2066faf731ef_story.html?utm_term=.dcc383e8c5c8.

We hope to work with the Subcommittee to accomplish just that. Sincerely,

American Association of Clinical Urologists
American Bone Health
American College of Rheumatology
Association of Women in Rheumatology
Coalition of State Rheumatology Organizations
Florida Society of Rheumatology
Global Healthy Living Foundation
Lupus and Allied Diseases Association, Inc.
National Organization of Rheumatology Managers
New York State Rheumatology Society
North Carolina Rheumatology Association
Rheumatology Alliance of Louisiana
Rheumatology Nurses Society
Tennessee Rheumatology Society

U.S. Pain Foundation
Greg Walden, Oregon
Chairman

Frank Pallone, Jr., New Jersey
Ranking Member

One Hundred Fifteenth Congress
Congress of the United States
House of Representatives,
Committee on Energy and Commerce

January 8, 2018

Ms. Lori Reilly
Executive Vice President for Policy,
Research, and Membership
Pharmaceutical Research and Manufacturers of America

Dear Ms. Reilly:

Thank you for appearing before the Subcommittee on Health on December 13, 2017, to testify at the hearing entitled "Examining the Drug Supply Chain."

Pursuant to the Rules of the Committee on Energy and Commerce, the hearing record remains open for ten business days to permit Members to submit additional questions for the record, which are attached. The format of your responses to these questions should be as follows: (I) the name of the Member whose question you are addressing, (2) the complete text of the question you are addressing in bold, and (3) your answer to that question in plain text.

To facilitate the printing of the hearing record, please respond to these questions with a transmittal letter by the close of business on January 23, 2018. Thank you again for your time and effort preparing and delivering testimony before the Subcommittee.

Sincerely,

Michael C. Burgess, MD
Chairman, Subcommittee on Health

cc: The Honorable Gene Green, Ranking Member, Subcommittee on Health

ADDITIONAL QUESTIONS FOR THE RECORD

The Honorable Earl L. "Buddy" Carter

Q: Does your organization support increased transparency into the following aspects of the drug supply chain? Yes or No will suffice.

1. Rebate pass throughs
2. PBM "Spread" Profits
3. Generic Drug Reimbursement Methodologies
4. True price for prescription drug at point of sale
5. Pharmacy Direct and Indirect Remuneration ("DIR") fees

A, #1-5: PhRMA is not opposed to transparency. We understand the need to strike a balance and provide consumers and employers with the kinds of information that will help them make better informed health care decisions. For example, lack of transparency in contracts between employers and PBMs has led many plan sponsors to question the share of rebate savings being passed through, how much the PBM is retaining for administrative fees, and whether the PBM is disclosing and passing on other price concessions, such as savings from price protection rebates.[281]

[281] Midwestern Business Group on Health. Drawing a Line in the Sand: Employers Must Rethink Pharmacy Benefit Strategies. September 2017. https://higherlogicdownload.s3.amazonaws.com/MBGH/4f71512a-e946-4060-

However, we also believe that transparency for the sake of transparency can be a double-edged sword. While the presumption seems to be that all transparency is good and can have a positive impact on the market, the Federal Trade Commission has consistently stated over many years that requiring disclosure of PBM-manufacturer negotiated price information can "undercut vigorous competition on drug pricing" and "undermine competition...between pharmaceutical manufacturers to offer discounts" which could "raise prescription drug prices for consumers."[282]

The Honorable Chris Collins

1. The pharmaceutical manufacturing industry is not a naturally attractive market as without government intervention, it would not exist as know it today. It does not adhere to price taking, product homogeneity, and free entry and exit. Accounting for the economic and societal benefits of developing life-saving medicine, many countries grant this industry with both a patent and market exclusivity period to promote a balance between new drug innovation, generic drug competition, and recouping what would otherwise be sunk costs. And while public perception is critical of pharmaceutical manufacturers, there are unfortunate economic challenges that do not allow for this industry to perform like a competitive market. The nature of policies like the Orphan Drug Act, the GAIN Act, and Title Zl that attempt to make this industry like a competitive market are somewhat paradoxical. Competition, therefore, is achieved over a considerable amount of time.
   a. It is projected that spending will decrease in the next five years as many pharmaceutical products with patent protection are set to expire. As it relates to patent protection and market exclusivity, what current government policies towards manufacturers hinder the balance as described above? What current policies can be strengthened or improved?

A: As your question notes, the U.S. prescription drug marketplace is unique, but competition shapes every stage of the process of bringing new medicines to patients. In the R&D process, companies race to bring to patients the first medicine in a therapeutic class. Once approved, a new medicine typically faces swift competition from other brands in its class. For example, less than a year after market entry of the first in a new class of hepatitis C (HCV) treatments, there were multiple competitors on the market that competed on both price and clinical effects.

9575-b27c6554Scb8/Uploadedlmages/Specialty%20Pharmacy/DMJ_MBGH_Line_in_the_Sand_RV12_9617.pdf.

282 T. Koslov and E. Jex, "Price Transparency or TMI?" Federal Trade Commission, July 2, 2015.

After a brand product is on the market for a limited time, generics may be approved and payers shift nearly all utilization to the generics. As a result, 90 percent of all prescriptions in the U.S. are now filled with generic medicines. The U.S. policy and regulatory framework established under the Hatch- Waxman Act and the Biologics Price Competition and Innovation Act strikes a balance between maintaining incentives for innovation while providing access to generic medicines and fostering biosimilar entry.

As noted, additional incentives have been warranted in certain instances. Specifically, the Orphan Drug Act provides critical incentives to foster private-sector investment in treatments for rare diseases or conditions where it would otherwise be difficult to recover private investments given the limited number of patients affected. Similarly, the GAIN Act has sought to address the need for new anti-infective products, such as antibiotics.

However, in certain areas the existing incentives for innovation may be insufficient. Below we note a few such areas where current policies could be strengthened or improved:

- The existing five-year new chemical entity data protection period that begins upon FDA approval of the new drug does not sufficiently reward investment in small molecule drugs, particularly for the novel and complex drugs currently under development. It provides less protection than in other developed countries and regions-particularly the European Union, where an innovative product receives 10 years of exclusivity before generic approval, and potentially as much as 11. Similarly, the incentives provided by three-year exclusivity for a new use of a previously approved chemical entity have been significantly weakened and do not sufficiently support the types of innovations eligible for such exclusivity. Given the substantial investment required for the studies undertaken to obtain the approvals that lead to three-year exclusivity and the benefit to the public health from such an investment, we believe that FDA can, and should, take additional steps to ensure the proper balance between innovation and competition in this context.
- When patents are considered, patent challenges from generic manufacturers in the form of Paragraph IV filings have been filed more frequently and earlier in the brand- name drug lifecycle, with many as early as four years after launch. The uncertainties of the patent system combined with the growing use of the inter parties review (IPR) process at the Patent and Trademark Office (PTO) could create significant challenges for innovative companies looking to develop new products.

2. Several brokers have touted how expensive some pharmaceutical products are, however, it is not a complete and accurate reflection of the pricing of the product when accounting time, investments made, general manufacturing costs, and the like. (Nor does it differentiate the majority of actors that contribute to the advancement of medical science from the minority of less scrupulous actors that do not.) Some brokers try to steer the conversation about drug pricing that ignore basic facts of economics. While public discussion last year was on Spinraza, not too long ago, it was the hepatitis C cure, Sovaldi, that sparked criticism. Despite its $84,000 price tag, it is much less expensive when compared to traditional treatment models including surgical liver transplants. Between 2012 and 2014, Medicare spent nearly $560 million in Part A and Part B for around 7,000 patients. In 2014, 1,906 patients received a liver transplant and the cost per patient after the first year was $170,485 under Part A and $26,225 under Part B. It is also critical to bear in mind these figures are for HCV patients that qualified for a liver transplant and received one through the waiting list.
   a. It is Congress's responsibility to develop policies that address both societal and economic concerns-not to develop policies that are the result of a public relations campaign. Why do you think we are not having a real discussion on cost-savings in the long term-the upfront $84,000 cost for a less than a year treatment over poor performing and more expensive treatments over time?

A: Most representations of prescription medicine costs are overstated. For example, the $84,000 price for Sovaldi that is often quoted does not back out the sizeable rebates and discounts paid by innovative biopharmaceutical companies to insurers. In 2016, brand biopharmaceutical companies paid over $100 billion in rebates and discounts to government and private insurers overall[283], and it has been publicly reported that rebates and discounts for those HCV cures are currently between 50-60%.[284]

Prescription medicines are often the most cost-effective means of preventing and treating disease. So, while it is true that medicines help patients live longer and healthier lives, in many cases medicines can also shift the treatment paradigm toward prevention by allowing patients to avoid expensive hospitalizations and long-term care. An article in Health Affairs echoed this sentiment and found that just an extra $1spent on medicines for adherent patients with congestive heart failure, high blood pressure, diabetes and high

---

[283] Berkeley Research Group. The Pharmaceutical Supply Chain: Gross Drug Expenditures Realized by Stakeholder. January 2017.

[284] Silverman E. What the 'Shocking' Gilead Discounts on its Hepatitis C Drugs Will Mean. Wall Street Journal. February 4, 2015. https://blogs.wsj.com/pharmalot/2015/02/04/what-the-shocking-gilead·discounts-on-its- h e patitis-c-d rugs-will-mean/.

cholesterol can generate \$3 to \$10 in savings on emergency room visits and inpatient hospitalizations.[285]

3. Within the last few years, some pharmaceutical manufacturers and insurers have entered into agreements that would move the traditional reimbursement model to a pay-for-performance pricing model. Merck has partnered with several insurers on its type II diabetes products, Amgen signed on with Harvard Pilgrim and Cigna with its Repatha, and Sanofi and Regeneron paired with Cigna on Praluent. The benefits are clear for insurers and manufacturers take an "eat your lunch" policy as their product, so to speak, is up to bat.
    a. While your industries are in the beginning stages of the pay-for-performance model, can you share preliminary results and elaborate on how this model may replace the current system and reduce drug spending overall?

A. Pay-for-performance approaches for medicines are increasingly proliferating in the US healthcare system. Only seven of these private sector agreements were announced from the late 1990s to 2013; yet, 16 were announced from 2015 through early 2017, and roughly half a dozen more have been announced since then. These publicly disclosed arrangements are only the tip of the iceberg as some have estimated that five to ten times as many pay-for-performance contracts occur, but are not announced publicly. This growth demonstrates that both insurers and the biopharmaceutical industry are actively working to develop new ways to pay for medicines.

In terms of results, there is initial evidence that payers with pay-for-performance arrangements have lower cost sharing as compared to payers without them, for the same medicines. Payers' support of outcomes-based contracts (another term for pay for performance pricing) show these contracts are achieving the desired results. According to a recent survey conducted by Avalere Health, 83% of payers that have already entered into outcomes-based contracts are considering entering into additional outcomes-based contracts beyond the ones they currently have in place. In addition, of payers surveyed that had entered into outcomes-based contracts, half saw improvements in patient management, 38% saw improvements in patient outcomes, and one-third achieved cost savings. In considering these results, it is important to remember that the types and number of arrangements in the marketplace today are very limited due to outdated regulations that were not designed to accommodate innovative payment approaches. We are eager for policymakers to modernize those rules, which could increase the benefits of these arrangements for patients and the healthcare system.

---

285 Roebuck MC, Lieberman JN, Gemmill-Toyama M, et al. Medication Adherence Leads to Lower Care Use And Costs Despite Increased Drug Spending. Health Affairs. 2011;30(1):99.

4. In December 2016, the Senate Special Committee on Aging released an investigative report on significant price increases in prescription drugs whose patents have long expired. Specifically, out of the thousand or so companies in the US, the Committee evaluated four non-innovators or bad actors-manufacturers that do not contribute to the advancement in medical science and health outcomes.
   a. Following the investigation, the Committee recommended several policies aimed to deincentive certain business models and close loopholes that created certain market failures. As Congress considers policies aimed at increasing competition to rein in off patent drug price hikes, what policies should Congress further explore? This includes policies listed in the Committee report.

A: We applaud the efforts of the Senate Special Committee on Aging to address outlier behavior among companies whose business strategy entails significant price increases on drugs whose patents have long-expired rather than a focus on research and development, investment, and innovation. We further applaud the actions taken by Congress to address such behavior by taking steps to eliminate the backlog in generic drug applications at the Food and Drug Administration (FDA) and to foster competition in the area of drug-device combination products though proposals enacted as part of the 21st Century Cures Act and the FDA Reauthorization Act (FDARA).

PhRMA has also been pleased to see Commissioner Gottlieb take steps to advance and implement several policy proposals that PhRMA has supported, designed to facilitate the entry of additional competitors where there are small patient populations and no patent or exclusivity protections serving as a barrier to entry. However, we would urge Congress to consider additional policies to incentivize generic competition, including awarding regulatory incentives to encourage more than one generic drug manufacturer to enter the market and expanding tax credits for the development and manufacturing of qualified generic drugs. In addition, as suggested in the Aging Committee report, we support proposals to waive ANDA user fees and award priority review vouchers upon approval of generic drugs where the reference drug has no remaining patent or exclusivity protection and no generic competition. We look forward to working with both Congress and FDA on developing additional solutions.

The Honorable Diana DeGette

1. Will PhRMA commit to working with your member companies to share information with my office about your contracts with other drug supply chain players, including sharing specific examples of contract terms?

A: PhRMA does not have any source of information about specific types of deals or negotiations, and cannot comment on individual company pricing decisions or offer insight into this question.

2. Please explain the factors pharmaceutical companies consider when setting the Wholesale Acquisition Cost (WAC) price. To the extent possible, please explain in the context of insulin and/or retail pharmaceutical products that have competing branded products in a therapeutic class.

A: Manufacturer may base WAC pricing decisions on a range of factors including affordability, access, and reinvestment needs for R&D to develop tomorrow's innovative medicines. Rebates are used in private negotiations by manufacturers to gain access to payer formularies and determine level of formulary tier placement. Manufacturers pay rebates as a percentage of the current list price (WAC price) at the time the pharmacy dispenses the medicine to the patient. The manufacturer sets the "list" price of a medicine, but is actually paid the "net" price, which is the amount after rebates and any other discounts and fees have been removed.

In recent years, net prices have been growing much more slowly than list prices. Focusing on list prices alone results in a perception that drug prices are growing at unsustainable rates, when the prices manufacturers actually receive are in fact growing at low single digit rates. According to IMS Institute for Healthcare Informatics, brand net prices grew at just 3.5% in 2016, after taking into account discounts and rebates.

3. Do pharmaceutical companies ever feel pressure to raise list prices in order to be more competitive with PBMs and health plans in terms of formulary placement? To the extent possible, please explain in the context of insulin and/or retail pharmaceutical products that have competing branded products in a therapeutic class.

A: Manufacturer may approach rebate negotiations in a number of ways, and pricing decisions are based on a range of factors including afford ability, access, and reinvestment needs for R&D to develop tomorrow's innovative medicines. PhRMA does not have any source of information about specific types of deals or negotiations, and cannot comment on individual company pricing decisions or offer insight into this question.

4. How do pharmaceutical companies develop life cycle management strategies for their products? To the extent possible, please explain in the context of insulin and/or retail pharmaceutical products that have competing branded products in a therapeutic class.

A. As a trade association, PhRMA does not have access to proprietary company data regarding their life cycle management strategies. Generally, researchers follow the trajectory of the science in developing new treatment options, whether it is for a new medicines or additional research to expand treatments to additional patient populations, other diseases and conditions, or to provide new formulations, dosage forms, or drug combinations/regimens that meet the unmet medical needs of patients. In turn, these innovations may result in improved health outcomes and a reduction in unnecessary hospitalizations for patients. Further, these innovations increase brand-to-brand competition, spur continued innovation, and provide payers with increased leverage in negotiating rebates and other discounts.

For example, continued innovation in insulins has resulted in robust brand-to-brand competition on both price and clinical effects and expanded treatment options for patients to help better manage their disease and avoid costly complications. Advances in insulin therapy include new delivery systems and longer-acting formulations which provide greater flexibility in dosing and easing treatment complexity. Given that fewer than half of Americans treated for diabetes have the disease successfully controlled, advances helping to facilitate patient adherence are remarkably valuable to patients.[286] Importantly, the broad range of long-, short-, and rapid-acting insulins available to patients has also enabled payers to leverage competition to negotiate substantial discounts and rebates on these medicines.[287]

5. Do pharmaceutical companies ever stop offering or restrict access to previous versions of a product once a new/updated version comes out? Has this ever happened in the context of insulin?

A. As a trade association, we are not privy to proprietary information about individual companies' business practices and therefore are not in a position to comment. However, the pharmaceutical market is extremely large with thousands of products on the market. Products may come on and off the market for many reasons reflecting the evolving nature of science and innovation, the changing needs of patients impacting demand, advances made in therapy, as well as removal due to safety issues that cannot be corrected.

6. How do pharmaceutical companies change their marketing strategies for older versions of their products when new versions are approved for marketing?

---

[286] Type 2 Diabetes in the Real World: The Elusive Nature of Glycemic Control Steven V. Edelman and William H. Polonsky Diabetes Care 2017 Aug; https;//doi.org/10.2337/dcl6-1974.

[287] Barrett P, Langreth R.The Crazy Math Behind Drug Prices: Intermediaries that Negotiate to lower Prices May Cause Them To Increase Too. *Bloomberg Businessweek,* June 29, 2017. https://www.bloomberg.com/news/articles/2017 06-29/the-crazy* math-behind-drug-prices· langreth R, Keller M, Cannon C. Decoding Big Pharma's Secret Drug Pricing Practices. *Bloomberg.* June 29, 2016. https://www.bloomberg.com/graphics/2016-drug-prices.

A: As a trade association, PhRMA is not privy to proprietary information about individual companies' marketing strategies and therefore are not in a position to comment.

The Honorable Kurt Schrader

I agree with you that we can't only look at list prices when talking about how much we're paying for drugs. But we can't ignore list prices, either. In Part D, for example, when a beneficiary pays coinsurance in the donut hole, they are stuck paying a percentage of the list price of their drug-sometimes thousands of dollars per year. And the people in catastrophic coverage stage are often on the most expensive drugs, which never receive rebates anyway. How can we demand transparency from PBMs and others joining you at the table-which I agree with-and not demand some transparency from pharmaceutical manufacturers when they set list prices? You made a lot of claims at the hearing about how list prices are set while considering PBM discounts. I think that's fair, but you should be required to show your work. Would you be willing to work with us to create strong transparency standards fort he government to examine that will show how you come to list prices?

A: When considering transparency proposals, it is important to be clear about what the transparency seeks to achieve. For example, it would be helpful if insurers shared more information about their prior authorization rules with consumers who are shopping for health plans. This would help inform patients' choice of plan.

While I agree that list prices affect patient cost sharing today, my concern is that greater transparency into how list prices are set does nothing to reduce patient cost sharing. To help patients, it would be more productive to work on passing through manufacturer rebates to patients or clarifying the rules around what preventive services can be covered pre-deductible by high deductible health plans. Those ideas can improve patient affordability in ways that greater transparency, which could undermine existing beneficial competition, simply does not.

Greg Walden, Oregon
Chairman

Frank Pallone, Jr., New Jersey
Ranking Member

One Hundred Fifteenth Congress
Congress of the Unites States
House of Representatives
Committee on Energy and Commerce

January 8, 2018

Mr. Tom DiLenge
President, Advocacy, Law and Public Policy Division
Biotechnology Innovation Organization

Dear Mr. DiLenge:

Thank you for appearing before the Subcommittee on Health on December 13, 2017, to testify at the hearing entitled "Examining the Drug Supply Chain."

Pursuant to the Rules of the Committee on Energy and Commerce, the hearing record remains open for ten business days to permit Members to submit additional questions for the record, which are attached. The format of your responses to these questions should be as follows: (1) the name of the Member whose question you are addressing, (2) the complete text of the question you are addressing in bold, and (3) your answer to that question in plain text.

To facilitate the printing of the hearing record, please respond to these questions with a transmittal letter by the close of business on January 23, 2018.

Thank you again for your time and effort preparing and delivering testimony before the Subcommittee.

Sincerely,

Michael C. Burgess, MD
Chairman, Subcommittee on Health

cc: The Honorable Gene Green, Ranking Member, Subcommittee on Health

QFR Responses from Tom DiLenge, Biotechnology Innovation Organization

The Honorable Earl L. "Buddy" Carter

Question 1: Does your organization support increased transparency into the following aspects of the drug supply chain?

1. Rebate Pass Throughs
2. PBM "Spread" Profits
3. Generic Drug Reimbursement Methodologies
4. True Price for Prescription Drug at Point of Sale
5. Pharmacy Direct and Indirect Remuneration (DIR) Fees

BIO supports the implementation of transparency measures that would apply across the healthcare spectrum. These measures should be grounded in the goal of improving timely access to information that supports informed patient/provider clinical decision making and health insurance enrollment decisions, and that helps ensure smarter healthcare spending, without distorting market dynamics or harming the innovation ecosystem. When applied to prescription drugs, as one element of the broader system, transparency should facilitate access to medications, while continuing to foster competition and the risk-taking required to deliver on the promise of future treatments and cures.

In particular, these measures should:

- Promote an environment that supports value-based approaches to healthcare delivery and payment that benefit the patient (e.g., enable access to data to facilitate the development and utilization of outcomes-based contracts and other value-based approaches).
- Provide information that is meaningful to healthcare decision makers, and in particular, information that can be used by patients to improve their healthcare clinical and insurance enrollment decision making (e.g., plan-level information on prescription drug coverage and cost-sharing requirements; information regarding available patient support opportunities).
- Provide information to inform patients of provider incentive programs that direct prescribers to adhere to pre-specified care regimens and what form those incentives take (e.g., a direct financial reimbursement from the insurer or hospital system to the provider if his/her prescribing behavior matches pre-determined clinical pathways).
- Promote an understanding of the role and impact of each delivery channel participant on patient care, including the role of manufacturers, wholesalers, pharmacies, PBMs, and payers (e.g., highlight the value created for, distributed across, and extracted from the health care system by each player, and its impact on patient access to needed care).
- Present a holistic picture of the healthcare marketplace and promote a broad definition of value (e.g., ensure that any publicly-released data is presented with appropriate context, including taking into account the role and impact of other relevant stakeholders).

The Honorable Chris Collins

Question 1: It is projected that spending will decrease in the next five years as many pharmaceutical products with patent protections are set to expire. As it relates to patent protection and market exclusivity, what current government policies towards manufacturers hinder the [drug competition] balance as described above? What current policies can be strengthened or improved?

At the outset, it is important to recognize that Congressionally-developed drug market competition policies - such as the Hatch-Waxman amendments have fostered a robust and competitive market for both innovative and generic biopharmaceuticals in the United States. As is noted by the Association for Accessible Medicines, in 2016 the U.S. marketplace for generic medicines represented 89% of all prescription fills the overwhelming majority of medication fills for patients.[288] Even more, the FDA recently announced an Agency record of 763 generic approvals in 2017.[289] Accordingly, the generic share of the U.S. prescription drug market is today among the highest of all industrialized countries. At the same time, the United States continues to be the world's top originator of new innovative medicines and treatments. More new medicines are researched and brought to market in the United States than in the rest of the world combined. By all accounts, efforts to foster *both* generic drug competition *and* the creation of new, original medicines have worked very well.

And, increased competition is not limited to generic entry either. The FTC has noted that "approval of breakthrough or pioneer drug product[s are] increasingly followed by entry of a subsequent branded product. The head start that the breakthrough product has had over subsequent branded products has decreased over the past three decades from 8.2 years during the 1970s to 2.25 years during the 1990s."[290] Unquestionably the competitive environment is thriving.

To be sure, there are areas where improvements might better incentivize future innovative drug development; particularly important in light of how quickly and effectively competitive products come to market today. Such recommendations were the topic of BIO's extensive comments to FDA's 2017 docket on prescription medication market incentives.[291]

Generally, policymakers should be mindful to preserve the delicate balance of rights, obligations, and procedures that has successfully incentivized drug development of both generics and innovators for more than 30 years. In recent years, this balance has increasingly come under pressure. For example, the use of so-called Inter Partes Review

---

[288] *See* AAM/ Generic Drug Access and Savings Report.

[289] The number is almost 1,000 when accounting for temporary approvals.

[290] *See* https://www.ftc.gov/sites/default/files/documents/reports/emerging-health-care-issues-follow-biologic-drug-competition-federal-trade-commission-report/p083901biologicsreport.pdf.

[291] *See* Administering the Hatch-Waxman Amendments: Ensuring Appropriate Balance Between Innovation and Access. FDA Docket Number FDA-2017-N-3615.

(IPR) proceedings for challenging patents administratively in the U.S. Patent and Trademark Office is threatening to undermine the detailed patent litigation and dispute resolution processes that were established for the orderly market entry of generic drugs under the 1984 Hatch-Waxman Act.[292] In another example, it is well-known that the Hatch-Waxman 3- year data exclusivity for new approved pharmaceutical uses, as well as patent protection for new uses of a drug, can frequently be circumvented by generic applicants that label their products only for unprotected uses, even if it is perfectly foreseeable that a large percentage of generic sales will be for protected uses. Such developments are troubling and may need appropriate policy attention.

Additional improvements that could be undertaken by the FDA involve the adoption of a more robust and two-sided policy surrounding labeling updates through the Changes Being Effected process. Doing so would permit both sides of the competitive paradigm - innovators and generics- to participate in the labeling update process with FDA. This would inject much more certainty into the labeling process and enhance the ability of physicians and payers to recognize important labeling information quickly and efficiently.

Additionally, we urge FDA and Congress both to consider new incentives for the development of non-addictive and non-opioid pain management products. Incentivizing these developments could help to significantly reduce dependence on addictive painkillers that contribute to the nationwide opioid epidemic. BIO has developed a suite of proposals aimed at facilitating more development in this area. Considerations like enhanced or streamlined FDA approval pathways for designated products and/or unique market exclusivities could go a long way towards an overhaul in pain treatment in the United States.

Question 2: Why do you think we are not having a real discussion on cost-savings in the long term -the upfront $84,000 cost for a less than a year treatment over poor performing and more expensive treatments over time?

Modern biotechnology is a young industry. But in just a few decades, the entrepreneurs, scientists, researchers and investors working in this field have firmly established themselves at the forefront of medical innovation. Innovation truly saves - not just lives, but real dollars as well. In fact, if biopharmaceutical researchers are able to develop a new medicine that delays the onset of Alzheimer's disease by just five years,

---

292 "Patent Challenges Upsetting Hatch-Waxman Act, Hatch Says" Bloomberg News Oct. 20, 2017 https://www.bna.com/patent-challenges-upsetting-n73014471224/; *see also:* Patent Abuse is Undermining American Health Care, The Hill Oct. 212017, available at http://thehill.com/opinion/healthcare/351701-patent·abuse-is-undermining-american-health-care ("[R]ather than facilitate technology developments, IPR can chill advancements in prescription drugs. According to recent reports, it costs $2.6 billion to bring the average drug to market, only 12 percent of patented drugs receive FDA approval, and just 1in 5 approved drugs cover their R&D costs. These manufacturers have explained that patent predictability is essential for generating investments in new medicines and engaging in beneficial joint endeavors with competitors."); Sen. Chuck Schumer (D-N.Y.) said in a 2015 Senate hearing that "no one anticipated" that IPR would turn out to be such "a run-around for Hatch- Waxman.")

America would save $367 billion in healthcare services by 2050[293]. To meaningfully bend the troubling healthcare cost curve, increased investment in new medicines is essential.

On average, it takes 10-15 years to secure FDA approval of a new medicine, from initial discovery of a potential new molecule or approach, through pre-clinical and clinical programs, and through the FDA regulatory and approval processes[294]. In addition, $2.6 billion is the average cost to develop and secure approval of a new medicine, taking into account all the trial and error and research failures along the way, and the cost of capital; this figure has skyrocketed in recent years, doubling since just 2003[295]. This is partly due to increased regulatory and payer demands for more and better data on drug safety and effectiveness. But it also has much to do with the new era of genomic and personalized medicine.

These new medicines do not treat broad classes of patients in blunt ways. Rather, today we are seeing the development of entirely new ways to treat and ultimately cure disease for targeted patient populations using living organisms. New developments in cellular and gene therapies are using the patient's own cells to develop a medicine tailored specifically for that patient, or use other genetic techniques to repair or replace defective genes causing disease. Biotechnology is tackling the most challenging of problems, and the more we learn about our biology and the basis of disease, the more complex our R&D processes become. Furthermore, while these costs go up and up, the patient populations to be served are becoming more and more targeted, reducing the ability to spread these costs across wide patient populations.

Yet despite their expense, these novel medicines offer tremendous value to patients, our healthcare system, and society overall. This value is often overlooked or deliberately ignored by payers because they tend to operate with a short-sighted, annual budgetary mindset, and may not realize the longer-term value of these medicines due to turnover among their covered beneficiaries. In short, we are paying for 21st century medicines with a 20th century payment system focused on limiting volume and access rather than value. BIO supports efforts by policymakers and stakeholders to re-think the drug payment system, especially for one-time cures or other transformative medicines that may have significant upfront costs but that will reduce other, more expensive healthcare services in the future.

---

[293] Alzheimer's Association, Changing the Trajectory of Alzheimer's Disease: How a Treatment by 2025 Saves Lives and Dollars. Retrieved from https:f/alz.org/documents custom/ALZ Trajectory InfoSheet 01.26.15 Final.pdf.

[294] DiMasi J., Grabowski, H., Hansen, R. Innovation in the Pharmaceutical Industry: New estimates of R&D Costs. Journal of Health Economics, 2016, at pp, 20-33.

[295] Ibid.

Question 3: What would the impact be on innovation and for small startup biotech companies if Congress were to adopt price controls or other non-market based policies, some of which have been suggested today?

The United States leads the world in innovative drug development, benefiting patients and caregivers around the globe by ensuring access to new cures and treatments for a range of diseases. This success is made possible by a number of factors: Outstanding scientists, savvy entrepreneurs and business leaders, a committed investment community and world- class universities and research institutions. But that alone is not enough to succeed in getting new drugs across the finish line-and it is not enough to sustain long-term medical innovation. Many other countries have similar capabilities. Rather what makes the United States stand out is its commitment to a competitive, free market system for drugs that doesn't impose artificial limitations on successful innovations.

Biopharmaceutical innovation needs to able to attract the enormous amounts of private capital required to fund these challenging and incredibly risky endeavors. This in turn depends on a public policy environment that supports innovation and incentivizes such investment. That includes:

- Continued advancement of scientific understanding;
- Strong intellectual property (IP) rights and a reliable system for IP transfer, licensing, and collaboration;
- An efficient and predictable regulatory review process; and
- Transparent payment systems that reward innovation and encourage free-market competition.

Setbacks in any of these areas can cause the entire innovation ecosystem to falter. The challenge can be particularly acute when it comes to capital formation for small companies, which are the vast majority of biopharmaceutical companies and account for 70 percent of the industry's future clinical pipeline. Private investment can flow to, and shift among, many different sectors, and investors will flee areas like biotechnology when they think policy decisions could adversely impact an already risky investment. Remember that the vast majority of drug research companies are not yet profitable, and most of these companies are relying on private investors to fund research into new innovative cures and therapies.

It's also clear that, throughout history, advances in science and drug development in the United States have increased when Congress passed legislation that supports, promotes, and incentivizes the innovation being conducted in the Jab. On the flip side of that, short- sighted policy proposals and heated campaign rhetoric can have a chilling effect on medical innovation and the ability of the industry to attract the investment needed to fund clinical trials and other areas of drug development. The reality is that restrictive or narrow Jaws, regulations and insurance policies can scare away the private investment that is needed to fund biopharmaceutical research and to deliver new cures to patients in need. Without doubt, government-imposed price controls in the largest market in the world would seriously harm investment in the next generation of medical breakthroughs - not just in the United States, but across the globe.

Question 4: While your industries are in the beginning stages of the pay-for-performance model, can you share preliminary results and elaborate on how this model may replace the current system and reduce drug spending overall?

Although BIO does not have specific data regarding the value-based arrangements of certain manufacturers, these models, despite their early stages, hold much promise in terms of promoting value in the marketplace. BIO supports policies that would facilitate a robust marketplace for biopharmaceuticals and, in particular, would facilitate engagement between manufacturers and payors with respect to novel arrangements that may help to ensure patient access to innovative therapies.

Potential regulatory barriers to developing and implementing novel arrangements (e.g., value-based arrangements) should be addressed. Specifically, in order to facilitate the use of value-based arrangements in the United States, Congress should:

- Create legislative carve-outs for Best Price and all other government pricing calculations and requirements as they relate to products sold or transferred under value-based arrangements.
- Require the Centers for Medicare & Medicaid Services (CMS) to work with stakeholders-including manufacturers, providers, patient and caregiver representatives, and payors-to establish parameters through notice-and-comment rulemaking for arrangements that meet this statutory exemption (e.g., value-based contracts that financially incentivize measurable improvements in quality of care and/or positive health outcomes) to allow for the flexibility needed in the evolving value-based arrangements space.
- Either expand existing, or create new, statutory exceptions to the Anti-Kickback Statute to clearly protect innovative value-based arrangements that meet certain requirements (e.g., that promote patient access and pose a low risk of patient or federal healthcare program abuse); or direct the Department of Health and Human Services (HHS) Office of Inspector General to implement such exceptions through the creation of new regulatory safe harbors.

Stakeholders-including policymakers, patient advocates, providers, payors, and manufacturers-also should collaborate to consider laws and regulations impacting the robustness of the broader marketplace, including:

- Exploring tax incentives for early-stage research companies.
- Exploring mechanisms to promote a robust generics market upon expiration of all patents and statutory exclusivities applicable to the innovator product.
- Exploring mechanisms to support a robust biosimilars market, upon expiration of all patents and statutory exclusivities applicable to the innovator product, by attracting a broad range of companies and development programs.

Question 5. Following the investigation, the Committee recommended several policies aimed to de-incentivize certain business models and close loopholes that created certain market failures. As Congress considers policies aimed at increasing competition to rein in off patent drug price hikes, what policies should Congress further explore? This includes policies listed in the Committee report.

BIO has joined with stakeholders across the healthcare spectrum - including insurers, PBMs, employers, and patient groups - in a coalition that developed and supports consensus, market-based reforms to lower drug costs without harming innovation. Through the Council for Affordable Health Coverage[296], BIO and our allies are working to:

- Increase marketplace competition by speeding regulatory approval of more innovative drugs, and promoting greater and faster generic and biosimilar entry once patents and exclusivities for innovator drugs have expired;
- Move towards a drug payment system that is based on value and patient outcomes rather than volume, by removing regulatory and legal barriers that hamper value- based arrangements and communications between innovators and payers;
- Empower patients and providers with more data on drug costs and value to help them make more informed choices; and
- Oppose innovation-killing ideas like price controls, drug importation, or direct government "negotiation" of drug prices in Medicare.

The Council estimates that, if fully adopted and implemented, these reforms could lower national health expenditures by $71 billion a year[297]. This approach also is consistent with the landmark 21st Century Cures Act shepherded through Congress last year by this Committee on a strongly bipartisan basis, as well as this Committee's more recently enacted Food & Drug Administration Reauthorization Act (FDARA). BIO was a strong supporter of both of these bills, which we believe will help expedite the delivery of new innovations to patients in need, while also speeding competition among branded

[296] https:1/www.cahc.netlprescription-drugs/.
[297] Ibid.

medicines and from more generics and biosimilars. We all want to see FDA approve generic drugs as efficiently as possible and for the backlog of generic drug applications to be reduced quickly, More choice and competition is good for patients and the healthcare system overall.

That said, it should be noted that, generally speaking, the United States has a robustly competitive market for drugs, where innovators compete vigorously with one another to produce safer and more effective medicines within the same class, and then compete on price as part of negotiations with powerful, sophisticated, and aggressive commercial middlemen such as insurance companies and pharmacy benefit managers who control patient access to these innovative products. While there are pockets of exceptions to this competitive environment, the reality is that the average innovator drug has a short period of time on the market without competition from other similar products (roughly two years[298]), and nearly nine out of every 10 prescriptions filled in America are for cheaper generic copies of once-branded drugs[299].

Greg Walden, Oregon
Chairman

Frank Pallone, Jr., New Jersey
Ranking Member

One Hundred Fifteenth Congress
Congress of the United States
House of Representatives
Committee on Energy and Commerce

January 8, 2018

Mr. Chester Davis
President and CEO
Association for Accessible Medicines

Dear Mr. Davis:

Thank you for appearing before the Subcommittee on Health on December 13, 2017, to testify at the hearing entitled "Examining the Drug Supply Chain."

---

[298] See "Nearly All Later Entrants to Drug Classes Were in Clinical Testing or Regulatory Review Before First-inCiass Approval," Tufts Center for the Study of Drug Development, November 3, 2015, at http://csdd.tufts.edu/news/complete storv/pr ir november december 2015.

[299] Association for Accessible Medicines. Generic Drug Access & Savings in the U.S. (2016). Retrieved from https;1/accessiblemeds.org/sites/default/files/2017-07/2 017-AAM-Access-Savinqs-Report-2017-web2.pdf.

Pursuant to the Rules of the Committee on Energy and Commerce, the hearing record remains open for ten business days to permit Members to submit additional questions for the record, which are attached. The format of your responses to these questions should be as follows: (1) the name of the Member whose question you are addressing, (2) the complete text of the question you are addressing in bold, and (3) your answer to that question in plain text.

To facilitate the printing of the hearing record, please respond to these questions with a transmittal letter by the close of business on January 23, 2018. Thank you again for your time and effort preparing and delivering testimony before the Subcommittee.

Sincerely,

Michael C. Burgess, MD
Chairman, Subcommittee on Health

cc: The Honorable Gene Green, Ranking Member, Subcommittee on Health

AAM Responses to Questions for the Record - December 13, 2017 Subcommittee on Health Hearing, "Examining the Drug Supply Chain"

The Honorable Earl L. "Buddy" Carter

Does your organization support increased transparency into the following aspects of the drug supply chain? Yes or No will suffice.

1. Rebate pass throughs
2. PBM "Spread" Profits
3. Generic Drug Reimbursement Methodologies
4. True price for prescription drug at point of sale
5. Pharmacy Direct and Indirect Remuneration ("DIR") fees

AAM: Generic drugs are distributed and reimbursed differently than the rebate model associated with brand drugs. For that reason, AAM's members typically have less insight into the mechanisms used by PBMs in negotiations with pharmacies, although these can come into play for some products competing directly with their reference product for formulary placement. Instead, generic drug manufacturers operate in a highly competitive market where the focus tends to be on aggressive price negotiations with wholesalers for generic medicines to reach the market.

Nonetheless, AAM supports CMS exploration of new and innovative ways to ensure patients benefit from the savings created by competition. Under current policy, plans and pharmacy benefit managers (PBM) may see incentives to increase brand rebates rather than giving preferential treatment to a lower-cost generic. In these instances, DIR fees can be spread across the wider beneficiary pool, rather than shared directly with the patient. Providing for patients to receive discounts up front could reduce those incentives and allow the specific patient on the medication to recognize the savings created by generic competition.

The Honorable Gus M. Bilirakis

In your testimony, you mention the problem of the Medicaid penalty for generic drugs. Can you explain how this works on the brand side and why you think it doesn't work on the generic side?

AAM: As you noted, the Medicaid Generic Penalty takes a policy that was designed for the brand drug market, and applies it to a market that operates in fundamentally different ways. While brand companies typically market a small number of high-margin products, many generic manufacturers market hundreds of products with varying levels of profitability or loss. Unlike the brand drug industry, in which a manufacturer sets a price for the drug and the price sees a generally upward price trajectory, generic drugs operate in a highly competitive marketplace where prices fluctuate rapidly.

The problem with applying brand-based Medicaid inflationary penalties to generics is in the use of Average Manufacturer Price (AMP) calculations to measure manufacturer price increase. AMP calculations are reported both monthly and quarterly to CMS, and reflect all sales from a manufacturer *at that time* to Retail Community Pharmacies (RCP). However, because AMP is measured by sales during a set period, it is susceptible to regular fluctuations due to a generic manufacturer's customer mix. In quarters where a product is purchased at lower-volume AMP, calculations can rise despite no underlying change to the price of the product. For brand drugs, the general upward trajectory of the price masks these fluctuations and brands expect regular inflationary penalties. However, in the generic market these fluctuations can create much greater variability and lead to situations in which the generic manufacturer cannot predict when they will be subject to a penalty.

This is why generic manufacturers are now subject to millions of dollars in additional rebates for products *even in the absence of changes in the actual price* of the product. These changes do not necessarily reflect any new price being set by the manufacturer, but may merely reflect new purchasing patterns. This is a direct result of a flawed methodology.

These unpredictable, onerous penalties on often low-margin medicines create significant risk for manufacturers, and make it more challenging for manufacturers to continue participating in those markets. A recent analysis concluded that the penalty would "increase uncertainty, reduce revenues, encourage manufacturers to exit the market and discourage the entry of new manufacturers. The predictable effect of discouraging entry into competitive markets is that product availability will be hampered: shortages will be more likely, and the market forces that lead prices to fall will be dampened."[300] Ironically, the analysis also concluded that the penalty "will not only have little effect on generic prices, but it will also have the unanticipated and unintended consequence of increasing the likelihood of shortages for potentially life-saving generic medicines."[301] Accordingly, we urge Congress to repeal this penalty.

The Honorable Chris Collins

1. The pharmaceutical manufacturing industry is not a naturally attractive market, as without government intervention it would not exist as know it today. It does not adhere to price taking, product homogeneity and free entry and exist. Accounting for the economic and societal benefits of developing life-saving medicine, many countries grant this industry with both a patent and market exclusivity period to promote a balance between new drug innovation, generic drug competition and recouping what would otherwise be sunk costs. And while public perception is critical of pharmaceutical manufacturers, there are unfortunate economic challenges that do not allow for this industry to perform like a competitive market. The nature of policies like the Orphan Drug Act, the GAIN Act and Title 21 that attempt to make this industry like a competitive market are somewhat paradoxical. Competition, therefore, is achieved over a considerable amount of time.
   a. It is projected that spending will decrease in the next five years as many pharmaceutical products with patent protection are set to expire. As it relates to patent protection and market exclusivity, what current government policies toward manufacturers hinder the balance as described above? What current policies can be strengthened or improved?

---

[300] Manning and Selck, "Penalizing Generic Drugs with the CPI Rebate will Reduce Competition and Increase the likelihood of Drug Shortages," September 2017. https://www.accessiblemeds.org/sites/default/files/2017-09/Bates-White-Wh ite-Pape r-Report-CPI-Pe n a lty-09-12-2017. Pdf.

[301] Id.

AAM: While it is true that spending *growth* on medicines is expected to slow over the next five years, overall spending is still expected to grow between 4 and 7 percent through 2021, according to Quintiles·IMS.[302]

This growth is anticipated entirely due to new launches and price increases in the branded pharmaceutical market. At the same time, generic manufacturers face significant price deflation and a great deal of uncertainty surrounding the expiry of brand exclusivities. In short, the balance of Hatch-Waxman has shifted unsustainably toward price growth for branded drugs. To improve balance and promote competition for high-priced brand drugs, Congress should curb anticompetitive practices implemented by brand manufacturers looking to excessively extend market monopolies. This includes stopping abuses to FDA-mandated REMS programs and voluntary restricted distribution networks (enacting the CREATES Act and FAST Generics Act), improving the patent system to prevent branded manufacturers from relying on noninnovative patents and setting up federal reimbursement systems that support patient access to lower-priced generic and biosimilar medicines.

2. In December 2016, the Senate Special Committee on Aging released an investigative report on significant price increases in prescription drugs whose patents have long expired. Specifically, out of the thousand or so companies in the U.S., the Committee evaluated four non-innovators or bad actors-manufacturers that do not contribute to the advancement in medical science and health outcomes.
    a. Following the investigation, the Committee recommended several policies aimed to deincentive certain business models and close loopholes that created certain market failures. As Congress considers policies aimed at increasing competition to rein in off patent drug price hikes, what policies should Congress further explore? This includes policies listed in the Committee report.

AAM: A significant barrier to competition is the challenge faced by many generic and biosimilar manufacturers obtaining the samples needed for generic or biosimilar development. This is a result of the misuse of systems designed to ensure the safety of medicines by certain brand drug companies focused on delaying or prevent competition. Such delays created by misuse, abuse or regulatory failure deserve Congressional attention. In short, if generic and biosimilar development is the subject of anti-competitive behavior, these safe, affordable medicines will never enter the supply chain.

---

[302] May 2017. Quintiles-IMS Institute. "Medicines Use and Spending in the U.S.: A Review of 2016 and Outlook to 2021" available at: https://structurecms-staging-psyclone.netdna-ssl.com/clientassets/dwonk/media/attachments/ 590c/6aa0/6970/2d2d/4182/0000/590c6aa069702d2d41820000.pdf?1493985952.

FDA Commissioner Gottlieb has repeatedly highlighted the abuse of FDA-mandated restricted distribution systems and restricted distribution systems that brand companies create on their own, without any mandate from FDA, to delay or completely prevent generic competition.

This occurs when brand companies, using a Risk Evaluation and Mitigation System (REMS) or their own voluntary "safety" program as an excuse, refuse to sell samples of their products to generic and biosimilar companies so that they can conduct the requisite bioequivalence and other testing. AAM members that have sought to purchase brand products from wholesalers in the supply chain are often informed that the wholesalers' contracts prohibit the sale of the brand product for generic studies. To date, FDA has received more than 150 complaints of specific challenges to obtaining samples.

This abuse injures competition. Commissioner Gottlieb recently testified that:

> Brand companies often have an incentive to refuse to agree to a single, shared system REMS. By prolonging the negotiations over a single, shared system REMS, they further delay generic drug approval and competition. We see prolonged negotiations and inability to agree on the terms of a single, shared system REMS regularly.[303]

Unfortunately, we are concerned that FDA's enforcement authorities as provided in FDA Amendments Act (FDAAA) will not be adequate to fully stem the brand abuses that have become so widespread in recent years. For instance, the civil monetary penalties available under FDA's enforcement authority pale in comparison to the revenue available by impeding generic entry. Center for Drug Evaluation and Research (COER) Director Janet Woodcock, M.D., noted that "fines and everything might simply be considered a cost of doing business because there's so much at stake in delaying generic competition."[304] Also, the FDA's authority to address the brand abuses using voluntarily imposed restricted distribution system are highly limited.

To address this problem once and for all, Congress must pass the CREATES Act, bipartisan and bicameral legislation introduced by Representatives Marino and Cicilline, to prevent the misuse of REMS and restricted distribution schemes to delay generic drug competition. AAM also supports Rep. David McKinley and Rep. Peter Welch's FAST Generics Act.

The cost offailure is significant, and will only encourage anti-competitive practices to grow. In the absence of Congressional action, AAM members today must consider the difficulty involved in obtaining branded drugs when determining which generic development programs to pursue. Where access to brand drugs is subject to restricted

---

303 Gottlieb, Scott. "Antitrust Concerns and the FDA Approval Process," Testimony before the House Committee on the Judiciary, Subcommittee on Regulatory Reform, Commercial and Antitrust Law, July 2017. https://www.fda.gov/NewsEvents/Testimony/ucmS68869.htm.

304 Testimony of Dr. Janet Woodcock at "Generic Drug User Fee Amendments: Accelerating Patient Access to Generic Drugs." Senate Committee on Health, Education, Labor and Pensions, January 2016.

access programs, some AAM members have determined that generic development was not feasible and decided against initiating these development programs. This means that patients and taxpayers lose out on opportunities for affordable access to life-saving medicines and our nation's health care system leaves savings on the table.

The Honorable Frank Pallone. Jr.

At the hearing, there was some discussion about the need for increasing competition in the pharmaceutical market. While not a silver bullet for rising drug prices, I believe competition from generic drug manufacturers is one way to help lower prices and increase access to medications for patients. One barrier this Committee has heard about previously is the use of REMS programs by brand drug manufacturers to delay competition through delaying or preventing generic and biosimilar manufacturers' access to samples of branded drug products. These samples are needed by generic and biosimilar manufacturers to conduct the bioequivalence studies needed for FDA approval.

In 2014, FDA released guidance that was intended to help generic and biosimilar manufacturers access samples by providing a letter noting that FDA has determined that the generic or biosimilar manufacturer's study protocol and safety protections are "comparable" to those required under the brand's REMS.

1. In your testimony, you noted that while "well-intentioned" the draft guidance has not helped to solve the problem of brand drug manufacturer's using REMS to impede competition. Why has FDA's draft guidance and letter process not been sufficient to address access to generic samples?

AAM: As you noted, in 2014, FDA released a draft guidance that attempted to address this issue and to assist prospective Abbreviated New Drug Application (ANDA) applicants in their efforts to acquire the samples necessary to conduct bioequivalence testing.[305] The guidance explained that "FDA is aware of instances in which an Reference Listed Drug (RLD) sponsor has refused to sell drug product to a prospective ANDA applicant," and that the agency would review bioequivalence protocols to "facilitat[e] prospective generic applicants' access to RLD supplies to conduct the testing necessary to support ANDA approval."[306] At the prospective ANDA sponsor's request, FDA will send a letter to the RLD sponsor indicating that the proposed testing contains safety protections comparable to those in the applicable REMS and that FDA will not consider

---

[305] FDA, Draft Guidance, How to Obtain a Letter from FDA Stating that Bioequivalence Study Protocols Contain Safety Protections Comparable to Applicable REMS for RLD, p. 2 (Dec. 2014), *available at* http://www.fda.gov/downloads/Drugs/GuidanceComplianceRegulatoryInformation/Guidances/UCM425662.pdf.

[306] *Id.*

it a violation of the REMS for the RLD sponsor to provide sam pies to the designated potential ANDA applicant.[307]

While AAM appreciates FDA's efforts to address this issue, the draft guidance unfortunately has often not been effective in facilitating the exchange of samples and, in some ways, has even exacerbated the problem. AAM members repeatedly have found that brand companies use the draft guidance to argue that their purported safety concerns regarding providing samples to generic companies are reasonable. Brand companies also have argued that obtaining a letter from the agency approving bioequivalence protocols is a *legal requirement* generic companies must fulfill even though the guidance makes clear that "(r]equesting or obtaining a letter from FDA is not a legal requirement."[308] In addition, AAM members have found that FDA's review time of these protocols can take more than a year. As a result, the draft guidance can provide further incentive for brand companies to refuse to engage with a generic company before FDA reviews its protocol.

Last, even when AAM members obtain a letter from the agency, the guidance does not compel the availability of samples. AAM commends FDA for its efforts to address REMS and restricted access abuses, as well as efforts to publicize these abuses and seek additional support from stakeholders. But there is a limit to what FDA can do on its own. One of the key deficiencies in the current FDC Act is that the penalties available to the Agency to stem the kinds of anticompetitive tactics by the brands are insufficient to effectively deter bad behavior by the brands. Ultimately, FDA lacks the ability to, for example, compel brand companies to sell samples to generic manufacturers. Given the sky-rocketing prices for brand drugs today, every day on the market without generic competition can be worth millions of dollars for brand companies. Therefore, AAM encourages Congress to take immediate action by passing the CREATES Act[309] and the FAST Generics Act.[310] These bipartisan bills would prevent the misuse of REMS and voluntarily imposed safety programs to delay generic drug competition.

2. Commissioner Gottlieb has been very outspoken in acknowledging that brand manufacturers use REMS abuse as a way to delay competition, and in fact, recently called on brand manufacturers to "end the shenanigans." What further actions do you think FDA could take to end the practice of REMS abuse?

AAM: There is a limit to what FDA can do on its own. This is why it is important for Congress to act on bipartisan legislation to prevent the misuse of REMS and voluntary restricted distribution programs to delay generic competition. Until these bills become law, however, AAM believes there are several regulatory steps FDA could take to help

[307] *Id.*
[308] *Id.*
[309] Creating and Restoring Equal Access to Equivalent Samples Act of 2017, S. 974, 115th Cong. (2017).
[310] Fair Access for Safe and Timely Generics Act of 2017, H.R. 2015, 115th Cong. (2017).

reverse this trend and to deter brand companies from abusing the REMS requirements. Again, however, even with these actions, AAM believes this will remain a significant problem until and unless Congress acts to pass legislation to fully stem these abuses. AAM provided a series of specific recommendations to FDA in response to the Agency's Federal Register Notice entitled "Administering the Hatch-Waxman Amendments: Ensuring a Balance between Innovation and Access; Public Meeting; Request for Comments."[311] These comments are attached for your reference.

3. Are there additional tools or authorities that Congress should consider that would help to address the abuse of the REMS program?

AAM: Yes. The CREATES Act and the FAST Generics Act are presently pending before Congress. These bipartisan bills would prevent the misuse of REMS and voluntarily imposed safety programs to delay generic drug competition, and would save billions of dollars benefiting patients and taxpayers alike. We encourage Congress to quickly enact this legislation.

The Honorable Diana DeGette

1. Please describe how incremental innovations and so-called "product hopping" and "evergreening" affect the ability of generic companies to enter the market and build more competition in certain therapeutic classes. To the extent possible, please explain in the context of insulin.

AAM: Incremental changes to branded products are often used for the purposes of extending branded monopolies rather than improving patient outcomes. Branded manufacturers use such changes to shift large patient populations from one branded drug to an incrementally different new one prior to the patent expiry of the legacy product in order to insulate themselves from generic competition. This practice is commonly referred to as "product hopping" or "evergreening." Additionally, branded manufacturers have begun filing large numbers of late-stage patents after the product has already been on the market for a number of years to delay market entry of less-expensive competitor biosimilar medicines. Even though these patents may be of questionable validity, they can create enormous costs for biosimilar manufacturers for who are forced to litigate each patent at significant cost. While AAM does not typically comment on specific products or product classes, or engage in validity analysis of any specific patents, the insulin market

[311] 82 Fed. Reg. 28493 (June 22, 2017) (Docket No. FDA-2017-N-3615).

is certainly largely dominated by a number of branded products without any generic competition.

2. Do Risk Evaluation and Mitigation Strategies (REMS) or limited distribution create barriers to entry for biosimilar insulin products?

AAM is not aware of specific instances in which REMS or limited distribution are barriers to entry for biosimilar insulin products. However, as FDA leaders have noted, there are significant incentives for brand manufacturers to create such barriers. This is why we encourage Congress to enact the CREATES Act and the FAST Generics Act.

Nonetheless, the development and market entry of biosimilar insulin products could face significant challenges unless Congress enacts legislation to place biosimilar medicines on a competitive playing field within Medicare Part D. Because biosimilars are precluded from offering the same 50 percent discount as brands in the Coverage Gap Discount Program, they face significant barriers to gaining formulary coverage and patient uptake. We encourage Congress to quickly include biosimilars in the Coverage Gap Discount Program, which is projected to save money for patients and the Medicare program.

3. Given the FDA's recent focus on competition, what more do you think the agency can do to facilitate competition for medicines like insulin?

AAM: We have heard anecdotally from our members that the insulin market presents unique challenges for generic manufacturers. There are market and regulatory barriers that manufacturers must consider. One notable issue is how FDA will handle the "Deemed to Be a License" guidance required by the Biologics Price Competition and Innovation Act (BPCIA), under which FDA will shift some New Drug Applications currently marketed under the Food Drug and Cosmetics Act to Biologic Licenses under the Public Health Service Act. The agency must ensure that insulin products are handled on a case-by-case basis that allows for substitution of appropriate products when necessary. Additionally, FDA needs to ensure that it reliably and quickly communicates with sponsors of follow-on products to ensure that applications move quickly through the agency.

The Honorable Kurt Schrader

1. One of the main concerns about solutions to REMS and restricted access abuse is the enforcement mechanism. Concerns have been raised about increasing the federal government's authority, whether increasing the government's enforcement

authority will actually be effective and the risk of creating an environment for frivolous lawsuits. Can you help me understand why an effective enforcement is necessary to address REMS and restricted access abuse, and the best way to get at an effective enforcement mechanism?

AAM: The CREATES Act is a narrowly tailored proposal to address the well-documented problem of REMS abuses. It does not establish any new requirements on brand companies. Brand companies need only allow the marketplace to work as it should -without limiting the ability of generic manufacturers to purchase samples at commercially-reasonable, market-based prices. Under the bill, only an affirmative defense that samples are available is necessary by brand companies to prevent litigation.

But delaying generic competition can be incredibly profitable for most brand companies. This is why Center for Drug Evaluation and Research (CDER) Director Janet Woodcock, M.D., noted that "fines and everything might simply be considered a cost of doing business because there's so much at stake in delaying generic competition."[312]

To deter this behavior, the CREATES Act authorizes the court to order a brand company to pay a generic manufacturer a monetary penalty up to the revenues accrued during the pendency of the lawsuit. This penalty would eliminate the brand company's monetary gain from forcing the generic to file suit, and incentivizes the brand company to simply make a reasonable offer to sell the samples in the first place.

Contrary to claims that this would lead to frivolous litigation, we believe the bill would actually lead to less litigation. In too many instances today, private litigation is the only way for generic developers to gain access to brand drug samples. The reality is that these bills would provide clarity to all involved. They would give FDA clear authority to waive a shared REMS requirement. They would give clear enforcement and remedies for generic or biosimilar firms. They would give a clear safe harbor for brand drug firms against frivolous claims- in which they would merely have to show that they did not create barriers to purchase. They would even provide immunity against legal claims for any harm suffered in the development of a generic. In doing so, they would reiterate the original REMS statute- that REMS should not be a barrier to competition.

2. You mentioned increased consolidation in the generic drug manufacturer market. How do you account for this increased consolidation, and how do we combat that to ensure there is maximum competition among generic drugs?

AAM: Today, the generic drug manufacturing industry remains generally fragmented. More than 200 generic manufacturers compete to sell into increasingly consolidated wholesale and pharmacy purchasers. In fact, today, three purchasing groups

[312] Testimony of Dr. Janet Woodcock at "Generic Drug User Fee Amendments: Accelerating Patient Access to Generic Drugs." Senate Committee on Health, Education, Labor and Pensions, January 2016.

account for as much as 90 percent of all generic drug purchasing.[313] As these purchasers move more and more toward single-source contracts for generic drugs, it often creates a dynamic where it is possible that no more than three generic manufacturers may be able to successfully market any given product. This risks future competitive success in the generic market as generic drug manufacturers may be forced to maximize economies of scale and consolidate themselves.

An unfortunate yet foreseeable consequence of fewer generic manufacturers is a significantly increased risk of drug shortages. Evidence suggests that generic drugs are particularly susceptible to drug shortages, potentially related to existing market incentives as well as low reimbursement.[314] Such shortages have a serious effect on patient care. Responding to a series of drug shortages in 2011, FDA Commissioner Scott Gottlieb, M.D., testified before Congress that many such shortages were a direct result of low reimbursement for older, low-margin products and that "many hospitals are being forced to ration key medicines and patients to sit on waiting lists for vital drugs."[315]

Greg Walden, Oregon
Chairman

Frank Pallone, Jr., New Jersey
Ranking Member

One Hundred Fifteenth Congress
Congress of the United States
House of Representatives
Committee on Energy and Commerce

January 8, 2018

Ms. Elizabeth Gallenagh
Senior Vice President,
Movement Affairs and General Counsel
Healthcare Distribution Alliance

---

313 "Fein, Adam, "The 2017-18 Economic Report on Pharmaceutical Wholesalers and Specialty Distributors." October 2017.

314 Stromberg, C. (May 2014). Drug Shortages, Pricing, and Regulatory Activity. National Bureau of Economics Working Paper. htto:Uwww.nber.org/chapters/c13102.pdf.

315 Gottlieb, Scott. "Drug Shortages: Why they happen and what they mean" Testimony before the Senate Finance Committee. December 2011. https:l/www.finance.senate.gov/imo/media/doc/Gottlieb%20Testimony1.pdf.

Dear Ms. Gallenagh:

Thank you for appearing before the Subcommittee on Health on December 13, 2017, to testify at the hearing entitled "Examining the DMG Supply Chain."

Pursuant to the Rules of the Committee on Energy and Commerce, the hearing record remains open for ten business days to permit Members to submit additional questions for the record, which are attached. The format of your responses to these questions should be as follows: (1) the name of the Member whose question you are addressing, (2) the complete text of the question you are addressing in bold, and (3) your answer to that question in plain text.

To facilitate the printing of the hearing record, please respond to these questions with a transmittal letter by the close of business on January 23, 2018. Thank you again for your time and effort preparing and delivering testimony before the Subcommittee.

Sincerely,

Michael C. Burgess, MD
Chairman, Subcommittee on Health

cc: The Honorable Gene Green, Ranking Member, Subcommittee on Health

United States House of Representatives, Committee on Energy and Commerce, Subcommittee on Health, "Examining the Drug Supply Chain," December 13, 2017

Elizabeth Gallcnagh, Senior Vice President and General Counsel
Response to Questions for the Record-January 22, 2018

The Honorable Earl L. "Buddy" Carter

Does your organization support increased transparency into the following aspects of the drug supply chain? Yes or No will suffice.

1. Rebate pass throughs
2. PBM "Spread" Profits
3. Generic Drug Reimbursement Methodologies
4. 4 True price for prescription drug at point of sale
5. Pharmacy Direct and Indirect Remuneration ("DIR") fees

HDA is the national trade association representing primary pharmaceutical distributors-the vital link between the nation's pharmaceutical manufacturers and more than 200,000 pharmacies, hospitals, longM tenn care facilities, clinics and others nationwide. Distributors arc unlike any other supply chain participants- their core business is not engaged in manufacturing and they do not prescribe medicines or dispense to patients nor do they provide coverage for prescription drugs or reimburse for prescription drugs. Their key role is to serve as a conduit for medicines to travel from manufacturer to patient while making sure the supply chain is fully secure, fully functional, and as efficient as possible. Given the role of our members in the supply chain and because of their diverse customer base, HDA does not have an established position as to drug pricing transparency efforts related to other entities in the pharmaceutical supply chain.

The Honorable Diana DcGctte

1. Please explain that type of service model (e.g., direct store delivery, self-warehousing, dock-to-dock, drop shipments) your member companies most commonly used for insulin products.

Pharmaceutical distributors offer a wide array of delivery methods for specialty products, including insulin. Orders are shipped via the most appropriate transportation method depending on order size and service level agreements including small parcel shipments, courier delivery, and less than truckload for large hospital systems or large pharmacies. Manufacturers may mandate that distributors use certain packing types for some products requiring specialty handling.

2. Is the amount your member companies typically pay pharmaceutical manufacturers to acquire drugs typically tied in some way to the drug's WAC price? To the extent possible, please explain the context of insulin and/or retail pharmaceutical products that have competing branded products in a therapeutic class.

Pharmaceutical wholesale distributors will generally purchase brand pharmaceuticals at WAC or WAC with a slight percentage decrease adjustment based on negotiations between the individual wholesale distributor and the manufacturer. WAC represents the manufactured list price, and does not include rebates, prompt pay, or other adjustment in price resulting from proprietary negotiations between the manufacturer and wholesaler. Each WAC is specific to the drug, strength, dosage form, package size, and manufacturer. Company negotiations, volume purchases, discounts, availability from multiple manufacturers and other contract terms and agreements may result in larger price adjustments off WAC particularly related to generic pharmaceuticals. Even after company negotiations the fundamental outcome remains static.

The provisions in our organization's antitrust policy preclude HDA from being privy to, or providing a venue for any discussion about prices and/or the components of prices among members. As members may not discuss pricing, pricing formulas, policies or the terms of their purchase and sales contracts in any HDA sponsored venue, the organization is unable to provide any comments or answer questions about specific drug products, including insulin, their prices or negotiations that take place between member companies and their suppliers and/or customers.

3. Do pharmaceutical companies ever provide your member companies with discounts, additional payments, or other financial incentives to acquire data about the distribution of their products?

In exchange for the variety of distribution and logistics services that primary distributors provide to manufacturers, they charge manufacturers what are referred to as "bona fide service fees" for the provision of these services. Some examples of these core services include inventory handling and inventory management, providing manufacturers With data about where (and in which settings) their products are utilized; verifying downstream customer eligibility to purchase products at pricing established under various programs or contracts between such customers and given manufacturers; and processing relevant chargebacks to manufacturers.

These fees, which are not passed on to the customer, represent fair market value for a bona fide, itemized service actually performed on behalf of the manufacturer that the manufacturer would otherwise perform (or contract for) in the absence of the service arrangement. This model reduces demand volatility-aligning order patterns more closely to actual patient demand and, eliminating artificial demand spikes, allowing for a supply chain that operates more smoothly and predictably.

4. Please explain how drug wholesalers and distributors work with PBMs to ensure access to insulin products.

Pharmaceutical wholesale distributors do not contract with PBMs for rebates related to formulary placement of branded prescription drugs, whether insulin or otherwise. Rather, such relationships exist between pharmaceutical manufacturers and their agents with PBMs and the health plans to which such PBMs provide services. PBM-owned mail order and specialty pharmacies may contract with pharmaceutical wholesale distributors for prescription drug distribution services.

Do your member companies' contractual relationships with PBMs ever extend beyond mail order pharmacy operations? If yes, please provide details on the other types of business arrangements PBMs sometimes have with wholesalers and distributors.

To our knowledge, no. As noted above, pharmaceutical wholesale distributors do not contract with PDMs for rebates related to formulary placement of branded prescription drugs. PBM owned mail order and specialty pharmacies may contract with pharmaceutical wholesale distributors for prescription drug distribution services.

Greg Walden, Oregon
Chairman

Frank Pallone, Jr., New Jersey
Ranking Member

One Hundred Fifteenth Congress
Congress of the United States
House of Representatives
Committee on Energy and Commerce

January 8, 2018

Mr. Mark Merritt
President and CEO
Pharmaceutical Care Management Association

Dear Mr. Merritt:

Thank you for appearing before the Subcommittee on Health on December 13, 2017, to testify at the hearing entitled "Examining the Drug Supply Chain."

Pursuant to the Rules of the Committee on Energy and Commerce, the hearing record remains open for ten business days to permit Members to submit additional questions for the record, which are attached. The format of your responses to these questions should be as follows: (1) the name of the Member whose question you are addressing, (2) the complete text of the question you are addressing in bold, and (3) your answer to that question in plain text.

To facilitate the printing of the hearing record, please respond to these questions with a transmittal letter by the close of business on January 23, 2018.

Thank you again for your time and effort preparing and delivering testimony before the Subcommittee.

Sincerely,
Michael C. Burgess, MD
Chairman, Subcommittee on Health

cc: The Honorable Gene Green, Ranking Member, Subcommittee on Health

Questions for the Record, Committee on Energy and Commerce, Subcommittee on Health, Hearing entitled "Examining the Drug Supply Chain," December 13, 2017

The Honorable Earl L. "Buddy" Carter

Does your organization support increased transparency into the following aspects of the drug supply chain? Yes or No will suffice.

1. Rebate pass throughs

PBMs are committed to providing rebate transparency and audit rights to their clients that sponsor coverage. On average plans elect to receive 90 percent of rebates negotiated by PBMs,[316] an increasing number require PBMs to pass through all of them. Roughly 46 percent of commercial PBM contracts are negotiated with 100 percent of rebates passed through to plans,[317] and all rebates in the Medicare Part D program are required to be reported to CMS.

2. PBM "Spread" Profits

Some commercial market clients choose to have PBMs retain the spreads between what is negotiated between sponsors and other stakeholders.

3. Generic Drug Reimbursement Methodologies

State Medicaid programs and other sponsors use Maximum Allowable Cost (MAC) lists to incentivize pharmacies and their pharmacy service administrative organization (PSAO) partners to negotiate competitive prices for generic drugs. These are derived from its specific proprietary methodologies and it would be inappropriate to disclose this proprietary information. Any proposal that restricts the ability to place lower cost, generic drugs on a MAC list will increase costs for plan sponsors that use a PBM to manage their drug benefit.

4. True price for prescription drug at point of sale

---

[316] Drug Channels, "Solving the Mystery of Employer-PBM Rebate Pass-Through," January 14, 2016 http://www.drugchannels.neU2016/01/solllinq mysterv-of-employer-pbm-rebate.html.

[317] See, Pharmacy Benefit Management Institute, "PBMI Research Report: Trends in Drug Benefit Design," 2016.

PCMA supports transparency to consumers on cost-sharing so that they can make informed decisions in the marketplace. A recent CMS analysis of the Medicare Part D program found that requiring plans to use manufacturer rebates and pharmacy price concessions at the point-of- sale would raise premiums and increase the burden on taxpayers by $82 billion, while giving brand drugmakers a $29 billion windfall. The fundamental problem is that policies of this nature do nothing to reduce high prices set by manufacturers.

5. Pharmacy Direct and Indirect Remuneration ("DIR") fees

In its January 2017 fact sheet on DIR, CMS describes the process as follows:

- Fees, payments, or payment adjustments made after the point-of-sale that change the cost of Part D covered drugs for Part D sponsors or PBMs must be reported to CMS as Direct or Indirect Remuneration (DIR). DIR results from payment arrangements negotiated independent of CMS, between Part D sponsors, PBMs, network pharmacies, drug manufacturers, and other parties involved in the administration of the Part D benefit. Manufacturer rebates comprise a significant share of all DIR reported to CMS.
- The final plan payments by CMS are, per statute, to be based on the costs actually incurred by Part D sponsors. These actual costs must reflect any applicable DIR. DIR is apportioned only between Medicare and the Part D plan, generally based on the share of the total Part D drug costs that each is responsible for over the course of the payment year.
- Sponsors must also factor into their plan bids an estimate of the DIR expected to be generated. Higher DIR leads to lower bids and, therefore, puts downward pressure on beneficiary premiums.[318]

Pharmacy DIR is part of the confidential and strategic negotiation process between pharmacies and PBMs. This information is reported to the agency by plan sponsors and accounted for as part of CMS' payments to the plan sponsors. Public disclosure of such agreements would cause, according to FTC, tacit collusion by drug manufacturers and pharmacies and raise costs for consumers.

---

[318] https://www.cms.gov/Newsroom/MediaReleaseDatabase/Fact-sheets/2017-Fact-SheeHtems/2017-01-19-2.html.

The Honorable Richard Hudson

While I can see the merits to benefit designs such as a step-therapy system, it also appears they can also delay patient treatments or result in inferior outcomes. To chronically ill patients, many of whom have issues with medication or treatment adherence, disruptions can be costly, both in aggregate terms to the system, and individually when they get sicker. How can you leverage data science and individual patient Information to maintain the merits of these benefit designs while using this targeted information to provide a more tailored service? Are your plans already leveraging ways to do this, and if not, why not?

Step therapy protocols ensure the right patients get the right medications at the right point in the care continuum, at lower net costs. Step therapy protocols are built on both clinical evidence and cost considerations.

Pharmacy & Therapeutic committees, comprising independent clinician experts including physicians and pharmacists, develop evidence-based guidelines used in step therapy, and assure such protocols do not impair the quality of clinical care.

Sponsors and PBMs continually seek better and more detailed evidence on the effectiveness of drugs for all their indications and subpopulations of patients, in an attempt to continuously improve coverage policies, formularies, and management techniques, including step therapy.

Physicians whose patients need specific drugs for clinical reasons may communicate with health plans to demonstrate the patient's need. Most states and Medicare have expedited appeal procedures for emergency and extremely urgent situations where a patient's access to a specific drug must be expedited. PBMs also are able to track which drugs patients have already tried, so long as the patient remains enrolled in a plan served by the PBM.

The Honorable Gus M. Bilirakis

CMS recently published their 700-page proposed rule for Medicare Part D for Calendar Year 2019. One component was their proposed implementation of the drug management program for at-risk beneficiaries from the Comprehensive Addiction Recovery Act of 2016. This drug management program, or "lock-in," is used in Medicaid programs and in private insurance. Have you had a chance to review their regulations and what are your thoughts on CMS' proposed implementation? Are there improvements that need to be made either through regulation or statutory changes?

PCMA supported the passage of the lock-in provisions under CARA and appreciates CMS undertaking the process to implement it. PBMs and Part D sponsors process many millions of prescription drug claims annually. PBMs are in the unique position of being able to identify patterns of potential misuse and abuse by at-risk Medicare beneficiaries. For example, when PBMs process claims for patients with insurance, they can identify at-risk behavior as well as potential doctor and pharmacy shopping. Electronic prescribing and electronic claims processing improves the ability to track these patterns as it also captures cash-paying transactions in addition to prescriptions covered by insurance.

PCMA supports allowing for plan sponsor flexibility to lock the beneficiary into a specific prescriber(s) or specific pharmacy or both, based on the utilization behavior of the beneficiary. However, we are very concerned that the proposal to require a Part D plan sponsor to wait at least six months from the date the beneficiary is first identified as a potential at-risk beneficiary before limiting that beneficiary to a given pharmacy or prescriber for frequently misused and abused drugs, and defeats the purpose of the lock-in program, which is to quickly take steps to reduce medication misuse in the Part D program. Without timely intervention, patients will continue to misuse opioids. In our comments on the proposed rule, PCMA urged CMS to allow for lock-in as quickly as possible once a beneficiary is considered at-risk. Furthermore, it is essential that CMS both preserve the flexibility of the current Drug Utilization Review (OUR) and Overutilization Monitoring System (OMS) programs while also providing flexibility for Part D plan sponsors and their PBMs to develop and implement their lock-in programs.

The Honorable Diana DeGette

1. Please describe whether and how pharmaceutical companies use intellectual property protections as part of your negotiations on rebates. Please explain in the context of insulin and/or retail pharmaceutical products that have competing branded products in a therapeutic class.

In general, drug manufacturers use intellectual property (IP) protections such as patents and market exclusivities to create a temporary monopoly on selling a particular drug or biologic. These IP protections were designed to encourage more research. However, the system has come to be abused by manufacturers. In the case of insulin, drug manufacturers have continually adjusted formulations, creating insulin analogs that are easier to use and less likely to trigger dangerous low blood sugar episodes. These new formulations also serve to provide drug manufacturers with new IP protections and preserve the manufacturers' monopolies. This practice of making slight product changes to preserve monopoly protections is called evergreening, and it keeps brand prescription drugs under patent protection so other drugmakers cannot copy formulas and offer lower-cost versions.

2. Please describe how patient assistance programs and discount cards offered by pharmaceutical companies affect PBMs' ability to negotiate rebates. To the extent possible, please explain in the context of insulin and/or retail pharmaceutical products that have competing branded products in a therapeutic class.

The notion of drug manufacturer patient assistance programs can be misleading when used for patients with health insurance. Such practices, including coupon and "free" drug programs, entice insured patients to use higher-cost medications when more cost-effective, clinically appropriate alternatives exist They undermine formulary cost-sharing strategies designed to give patients incentives to use the most cost-effective, clinically appropriate medications. For insured patients whose cost-sharing is paid by manufacturers, those plans-and ultimately, consumers-end up paying manufacturers the full cost of a drug. This formulary subversion is considered to violate anti-kickback statutes and is barred in federal programs, such as Medicare and Medicaid. Ultimately, these types of programs undermine the expert pharmacy benefit management services that sponsors hire PBMs to perform on their behalf, and result in increased health care costs for all Americans. These schemes are carried out by drug manufacturers across most drug classes, including insulin.

3. Are rebates collected by PBMs from pharmaceutical companies and passed onto PBM clients sometimes based on a percentage of list price (WAC) or some modified version of list price (e.g., WAC- or Average Wholesale Price- based formulas)? If yes, is it possible that this rebate structure could put pressure on pharmaceutical companies to raise list prices?

PCMA is not privy to contract negotiations of its members' business, but our understanding is that some contracts are negotiated based on percentage discounts from an industry standard. PBMs manage drug benefits to get sponsors and patients the lowest net cost, recommending benefit and cost-sharing designs that encourage the use of the most cost-effective, clinically appropriate drugs. The pharmaceutical industry introduced rebates as a method for providing price concessions; PBMs would welcome a different way to get to lowest net cost.

PBMs respond to requests for proposals (RFPs) from potential clients, which lay out the payer's terms and conditions. Each plan determines what percentage of rebates it wants the PBM to pass through to it, and how much (if any) it wants the PBM to retain as payment for services. We understand that PBMs offer sponsors inflation protection against manufacturer price increases that also mitigates against PBMs having an incentive for manufacturers to raise their prices.

Each drug manufacturer independently decides the price of its drug. The launch prices of new drugs and price increases of existing drugs bear no correlation to the rebates and discounts manufacturers negotiate with PBMs. There are high-priced drugs with low rebates and lower- priced drugs with high rebates. It all depends on how much direct competition a given drug faces in the market. This data argues against the notion that PBM contracts with manufacturers pressure them to increase prices.

4. Are administrative fees collected by PBMs from pharmaceutical companies sometimes based on a percentage of list price (WAC) or some modified version of list price (e.g., WAC- or AWP-based formulas)? If yes, is it possible that this fee structure could put pressure on pharmaceutical companies to raise list prices?

Again, PCMA is not privy to the details of our companies' negotiations with drug manufacturers or other entities and has not even a general understanding of the basis for administrative fees.

5. When a pharmaceutical company chooses to raise a product's list price above an agreed upon threshold under a price protection clause, can that result in the pharmaceutical company paying an additionalrebate?

The question seems to describe what is called a price protection agreement. Some sponsors request this in order to set a ceiling price for drugs. Typically, when drug prices rise, a rebate is issued for anything that exceeds an agreed-upon price threshold.

In practice, as evidence shows, neither price protection agreements, nor any other kind of price concession negotiated by PBMs drives the list price of drugs. Drug manufacturers set their prices and PBMs can negotiate price concessions to the extent manufacturers' products are substitutable for one another in the marketplace.

Greg Walden, Oregon
Chairman

Frank Pallone, Jr., New Jersey
Ranking Member

One Hundred Fifteenth Congress
Congress of the United States
House of Representative
Committee on Energy and Commerce

January 8, 2018

Mr. Matt Eyles
Senior Executive Vice President and
Chief Operating Officer for Policy and Regulatory Affairs
America's Health Insurance Plans

Dear Mr. Eyles:

Thank you for appearing before the Subcommittee on Health on December 13, 2017, to testify at the hearing entitled "Examining the Drug Supply Chain."

Pursuant to the Rules of the Committee on Energy and Commerce, the hearing record remains open for ten business days to permit Members to submit additional questions for the record, which are attached. The format of your responses to these questions should be as follows: (1) the name of the Member whose question you are addressing, (2) the complete text of the question you are addressing in bold, and (3) your answer to that question in plain text.

To facilitate the printing of the hearing record, please respond to these questions with a transmittal letter by the close of business on January 23, 2018.

Thank you again for your time and effort preparing and delivering testimony before the Subcommittee.

Sincerely,
Michael C. Burgess, MD
Chairman, Subcommittee on Health

cc: The Honorable Gene Green, Ranking Member, Subcommittee on Health

AHIP

The Honorable Earl L. "Buddy" Carter

Does your organization support increased transparency into the following aspects of the drug supply chain? Yes or no will suffice.

1. Rebate pass throughs
2. PBM "Spread" Profits
3. Generic Drug Reimbursement Methodologies
4. True price for prescription drug at the point of sale
5, Pharmacy Direct and Indirect Remuneration ("DIR") fees

AHIP's members have embraced the suggestion of the U.S. Federal Trade Commission (FTC) and the U.S. Department of Justice (DOJ) that "[p]rivate payors, governments, and providers should furnish more information on prices and quality to consumers in ways that they find useful and relevant, and continue to experiment with financing structures that give consumers greater incentives to use such information." Thus, health insurance providers have designed innovative products that use information about cost and quality in their structures and empower consumers to use this information.

AHIP also strongly supports transparency to provide policymakers with information that will help them design solutions to problems impacting consumers, such as the soaring price of pharmaceuticals. The focus of such transparency efforts should be the root of the problem: the list price of prescription drugs. Everything that happens in the drug supply chain follows from and is significantly impacted by the initial decision made solely by the manufacturer of where to set the list price. After that, everything that happens in the drug supply chain is impacted by and will change as a result of the list price due to changes by the manufacturer to that price. As a result, AHIP strongly supports transparency initiatives that give policymakers deeper insights into list prices, helping them better understand not only the *what* but the *why* of such prices.

Of course, any transparency initiative should be guided by the insights of the federal competition agencies, the FTC and DOJ, on when such initiatives benefit consumers and when they harm consumers. The FTC and DOJ have indicated that making granular, non-public information about negotiated prices widely available can lead to higher prices and other consumer harms. Obviously, list prices are not negotiated, so making them transparent docs not implicate this concern. Other initiatives that do implicate non-public, negotiated prices do raise such concerns of harm, and therefore policymakers should proceed with caution to ensure that such efforts do not harm the consumers they are attempting to assist.

The Honorable Richard Hudson

While I can see the merits to benefit designs such as a step-therapy system, it also appears they can also delay patient treatments or result in inferior outcomes. To chronically ill patients, many of whom have issues with medication or treatment adherence, disruptions can be costly, both in aggregate terms to the system, and individually when they get sicker. How can you leverage data science and individual patient information to maintain the merits of these benefit designs while using this targeted information to provide a more tailored service? Are your plans already leveraging ways to do this, and if no, why not?

Health plan benefit designs leverage science by relying on existing evidence on safety and effectiveness. This evidence-based approach to coverage policy and medical management involves a systematic review of the safety and effectiveness of medical interventions, including drugs, devices, services, and procedures. In conducting these reviews, health plans rely on a variety of evidence-based resources, typically following a hierarchy of evidence that gives the most weight to randomized clinical trials. The types of evidence that health plans rely on include, but are not limited to:

- Randomized Clinical Trials (RCTs)
- Specialty society guidelines/best practices
- Current scientific and clinical peer reviewed medical literature o CMS coverage decisions and quality metrics
- Agency for 1-lealthcare Research and Quality (AI-IRQ) guidelines
- United States Preventive Services Task Force (USPSTF) recommendations o Well-designed observational studies
- Expert consensus

Health plan coverage policies are also dictated to some extent by federal and state mandates, as well as employer/client requests. Additionally, health plans periodically review their coverage policies and update them based on new information/evidence, such as FDA safety notices, new drug/device approvals, new scientific/clinical research findings, and updated professional society guidelines.

Health plans have adopted evidence-based medical management tools, including step therapy approaches, to improve care and reduce costs for patients. Step therapy typically involves prescribing a recognized safe and cost-effective drug before the approval of a more complex, costlier, or riskier drug or drug combination. Generic medications, for example, offer significant cost savings without any adverse impact on quality or outcomes. As a result, many health plans encourage prescribers and patients to usc generic medications as a first-line of treatment before progressing to brand-name medications.

This evidence-based approach is complemented by opportunities for providers to communicate any unique needs and/or special circumstances regarding patients that could affect coverage. For example, health plans' step therapy policies can encourage physicians to prescribe a traditional, generic, non-steroidal anti-inflammatory drug (NSAID) for patients. However, if a patient has experienced side effects from the generic medication, the physician can request approval to prescribe the more expensive branded NSAID.

The Honorable Gus Bilirakis

CMS recently published their 700-page proposed rule for Medicare Part D for Calendar Year 2019. One component was their proposed implementation of the drug management program for at-risk beneficiaries from the Comprehensive Addiction Recovery Act of 2016. This drug management program, or "lock-in," is used in Medicaid programs and in private insurance. Have you had a chance to review their regulations and what are your thoughts on CMS' proposed implementation? Are there improvements that need to be made either through regulation or statutory changes?

A HIP has thoroughly reviewed the CMS rule, including the provisions relevant to the lock-in program, and has responded with several suggestions. In general, AHIP supports the approach of implementing limits to access to coverage of opioids, including lock-ins. However, we have several recommendations to ensure that the finalized policy protects Medicare beneficiaries from misuse or abuse of opioids while retaining access to pain medications, reduces the burden placed on sponsors in administering such programs, and ensures the integrity of the Part D program.

- Frequently Abused Drugs- In light of overwhelming evidence that beneficiaries taking opioids in addition to other high-risk medications, such as hypnotic-sedatives and muscle relaxants, are at a higher risk of harm, we recommend that CMS continue to review evidence around the use of such high-risk medications and consider their inclusion into the list of frequently abused drugs when appropriate.
- Exemptions for Beneficiaries- AHIP recommends that CMS provide further clarifications around when and how to apply exemptions for beneficiaries in time for plan inclusion into bid applications. For example, there is a lack of clarity as to when the long- term care exemptions apply (e.g., drug utilization review (DUR), coverage limits) and how to implement the cancer diagnosis exemption.
- Case Management- AHIP believes that the expectation of three prescriber outreach attempts by phone after a written attempt is burdensome and unnecessary. Therefore, we ask that CMS consider a potentially less burdensome approach (e.g., two prescriber outreaches). We also ask for some clarification on potential scenarios where a beneficiary's group of prescribers disagree with each other on a proposed limit, such as a prescriber lock-in.
- Lock-in Programs- AHIP strongly supports the direction of using limits as part of the broader national strategy to stem the misuse and abuse of opioids. However, we have concerns with the proposal to prohibit the use of a prescriber lock-in until 6 months after the beneficiary is identified as being at-risk of misuse or abuse of opioids. We believe that certain facts and circumstances would require that a prescriber lock-in be used immediately instead of being a last-resort option.

We recommend that a shorter waiting period be used instead, as this would provide sponsors with more flexibility in structuring beneficiary protections against misuse or abuse of opioids.

- Beneficiary Preference for a Prescriber or Pharmacy- AHIP supports reasonable rules that honor beneficiary preferences. However, we find the beneficiary's unlimited opportunity to change preferences for prescribers and pharmacies to be problematic and burdensome. We also suggest that CMS consider requiring an at-risk beneficiary to provide a reasonable rationale when requesting a change in prescriber selection in a lock- in program.
- Chain Pharmacies and Group Practices- AHIP understands that sponsors and their contracted PDMs often do not have access to prescriber tax identification numbers (TINs), as they are absent from pharmacy submitted claims. We recommend that CMS re-evaluate the proposed policy of using TINs and offer another more feasible option for those with difficulties in obtaining and working with TINs. We also recommend that CMS re-evaluate its policy for determining chain pharmacies, as identification of which pharmacies share real-time data may be difficult in many situations.
- Termination of a Beneficiary's Potential At-Risk or At-Risk Status- AHIP recommends that CMS allow the sponsor, prior to the expiration of the 12-month period, determine if a continuation is warranted, and if so, allow for extension of the designation for another 12- month period. We believe this flexibility to continue limits without interruption is necessary to best protect against misuse and abuse of opioids.

The Honorable Chris Collins

Within the last few years, some pharmaceutical manufacturers and insurers have entered into agreements that would move the traditional reimbursement model to a pay-for- performance pricing model. Merck has partnered with several insurers on its type II diabetes products, Amgen signed on with Harvard Pilgrim and Cigna with its Repatha, and Sanofi and Regeneron paired with Cigna on Praluent. The benefits are clear for insurers and manufacturers take an "eat your lunch" policy as their product, so to speak, is up to bat.

a. While your industries are in the beginning stages of the pay-for-performance model, can you share preliminary results and elaborate on how this model may replace the current system and reduce drug spending overall?

Given the many challenges with skyrocketing drugs costs, health plans are exploring pay-for-performance models to try to negotiate arrangements that are based on outcomes. Outcomes-based contracting is part of a larger effort to promote quality, value, and accountability. These contractual arrangements provide enhanced financial incentives for drug manufacturers that are contingent on agreed-upon standards for quality care, performance, and health outcomes.

These standards can include appropriate use (drugs being utilized for the right population versus overutilization), performance that matches that observed in clinical trials, as well as objective measures of health outcomes, such as hemoglobin Ale levels. Simply put, it is a contracting arrangement structured around a drug's performance, appropriate use of the drug, and the resulting patient outcomes.

These arrangements are still in the beginning stages, and several barriers must be overcome to achieve widespread adoption. For instance, these arrangements are dependent on the existence of valid and reliable outcome measures, engagement of providers and patients to ensure medication adherence, and implementation of a tracking mechanism to track individual patients' clinical status over time to analyze the intervention's effects and measure success. Medicaid "best price" rules and other regulatory barriers may also inhibit the development of value-based payment strategies.

Despite these challenges, we expect to see more of these arrangements as various stakeholders struggle to find ways to combat the rising cost of drugs. It is important to point out that, while new approaches to payment models that link payment to outcomes may prove an important to tool to help make care, treatments, and technology more accessible to patients, they are not a panacea to the problem of excessively high drug prices nor are they appropriate for many drugs. We need to work together to deliver more affordable drug prices overall by incentivizing real competition, fostering innovation, and creating more consumer choices.

The Honorable Frank Pallone, Jr.

1. At the hearing, you were asked what change in the marketplace or change in the law Congress should consider to ensure that we are focused on access, delivery and the cost of pharmaceuticals to patients. You responded that one such solution would be great price transparency- "both about how prices get set and how prices are increased." You also noted in your written testimony that drug manufacturers should have to provide "appropriate transparency into list price increases."
    a. Will you explain further about what you mean by "appropriate transparency into list prices"?

Pharmaceutical list prices remain a black box, justified by vague assertions of research costs or product value that are belied by the data. The simple facts are that pharmaceutical prices, too often, start at astronomical levels and increase at rates divorced from the cost of inputs, the amount of research involved, or any other reasonable justification. These prices have an enormously detrimental impact on consumers, and policymakers have justifiably sought to understand the way that such prices are set and changed.

While different slates have taken varying approaches to pharmaceutical list price transparency, it is important that such transparency initiatives provide insight into the following areas:

- What is the original list price and how is the list price set? Everything that happens in pharmaceutical markets flows from the original list price. Policymakers need to better understand the process by which list prices are set so that they can ensure balance between the twin goals of: (I) encouraging the development of innovative medicines and (2) ensuring that the monopolies granted by patents and FDA regulations are not being misused to the detriment of consumers.
- What is driving significant list price increases? Policymakers need to understand when list prices increase and why. What is the relationship ofthese list price increases to input cost changes? What is their relationship to research costs? What is the relationship of price increases across products and across manufacturers and what do these mean about competition in pharmaceutical markets?
- What is the relationship between research and list prices? Pharmaceutical manufacturers have typically pointed to research costs as a significant driver of high list prices. What is the nature of this relationship and how does it compare to the relationship of non- research factors such as direct-to-consumer (DTC) advertising, detailing, executive compensation, and profits to list prices? The bottom line is that no direct connection exists between how much a pharmaceutical company spends on research to bring a specific product to market and its list price.

All such initiatives should be informed by guidance issued by the FTC and the DOJ on the ways in which transparency can be beneficial and the ways in which it could lead to competitive harm. As a general matter, disseminating non-public negotiated prices poses a risk of competitive harm and should be avoided. While care should be used to avoid such harm, the FTC and DOJ guidance generally should not pose a barrier to transparency on non-negotiated items, such as list prices, which are the appropriate focus of such transparency initiatives.

b. What specific policy recommendations would you offer to help achieve meaningful transparency in how prices are set and how prices are increased?

We suggest that states pursue transparency legislation following the example of California. At the federal level, as part of the FDA approval process, manufacturers should be required to disclose information regarding the intended launch price, the use of the drug, and direct and indirect research and development costs. Both at the federal and state levels, manufacturers should provide appropriate transparency into list price increases.

2. At the hearing we heard many perspectives on the drug supply chain and how each part of the chain contributes to the end price the consumer pays. In your testimony you noted, "The bottom line is that the original list price of a drug is solely determined and controlled by the drug company-not the market-and it drives the entire pricing process. And if the original list price is high, the final cost that a consumer pays will be high."
   a. Will you further discuss how the list price of a pharmaceutical is determined solely by the drug company and not the market or payers as we heard some allege in the hearing?

Everything that happens in the drug supply chain follows from and is significantly impacted by the initial decision of the manufacturer of where to set the list price. Pharmaceutical list prices remain a black box, justified by vague assertions of research costs or product value that are belied by the data. The simple facts are that pharmaceutical prices, too often, start at astronomical levels and increase at rates divorced of the cost of inputs, the amount of research involved, or any other reasonable justification. After that, everything that happens in the drug supply chain is impacted by and will change as a result of changes by the manufacturer of that list price. As a result, AHIP strongly supports transparency initiatives that give policymakers deeper insights into list prices, helping them better understand not only the *what* but the *why* of such prices.

These prices have an enormously detrimental impact on consumers, and policymakers have justifiably sought to understand the way that such prices are set and changed. These prices are also why health plans and PBMs aggressively negotiate with manufacturers for ways to reduce the impact of these prices, so that they can pass savings onto consumers. These savings negotiated by health plans and PBMs are important, but they are not enough to offset the trend of price hikes on decades-old brand name and generic medications, or six-figure launch prices for new ones.

- When the price of Acthar gel- a drug that was approved in the 1950s- goes from $41 per vial to $42,000 in a few years[319], no amount of discounts can counter a I 00,000 percent price hike.
- An analysis of the leukemia drug, Gleevec, found post-discount price increases of 15 percent per year, every year since 2008[320]. The drug launched in 2001 at $30,000 per year and now costs over $100,000. Yet, Gleevec is the exact same product today in 2017 that it was at launch-no other industry operates in a fashion similar to the pharmaceutical industry.

b. how docs the original list price affect the subsequent prices in each part of the supply chain as the drug moves from manufacturer to the end usc, the consumer? Is there a close relationship between the price the consumer pays at the pharmacy and the manufacturer's list price?

The price that wholesalers, pharmacies, and consumers pay is highly correlated to the original list price set by the drug manufacturer. Wholesalers and some pharmacy purchasing organizations may acquire the drug at a modest reduction off the list price in exchange for volume and/or prompt pay discounts. These discounts are not significant because wholesalers do not influence the "market share" of specific prescription drugs. Wholesalers then take possession of the drug and distribute and resell to pharmacies (e.g., smaller community pharmacies) after a small markup above the discounted wholesale acquisition price. This total cost represents the pharmacy's acquisition cost.

At this point, the consumer enters the process. For individuals who lack health insurance but are prescribed a medication, they often pay the highest prices, especially for branded drugs. Typically, they pay the full list price set by the drug company (or the pharmacy acquisition cost) plus a markup.

By contrast, for individuals with insurance who arc dispensed a prescription drug from a pharmacy in the health plan's network, the pharmacy typically communicates electronically with a PBM, which administers drug benefits under a contract with the health plan. From the PBM, the pharmacy receives confirmation of coverage; whether the drug is subject to any utilization management tools, such as prior authorization; whether there are any potential safety issues, such as quantity limits or drug-drug interactions; the reimbursement amount to be paid by the plan; and the co-payment or co-insurance owed by the consumer. The total payment to the pharmacy is typically based on a negotiated contract rate between the pharmacy and the health plan (or the PBM acting on behalf of the health plan). This contract reimburses the pharmacy for its acquisition cost and provides a dispensing fee.

[319] *ProPublica,* "The Obscure Drug with a Growing Medicare Tab." August 2014.
[320] *The Washington Post.* "A window into one of the most baffling things about drug prices." March 2016.

The amount that the consumer or patient pays depends on several factors: (1) the negotiated rate between the plan and pharmacy; (2) the type of drug (i.e., branded or generic); (3) the plan's benefit design (e.g., co-pay or co-insurance); and (4) where the enrollee is within that benefit design at the time of purchase (e.g., in the deductible period, copayment period, maximum out- of-pocket limit or catastrophic phase for those in Medicare Part D). The pharmacy collects the appropriate cost sharing amount from the consumer and receives the remainder from the health plan or PBM at a later settlement time based on the payment terms under the contract. (The process described above assumes that there are no manufacturer-sponsored drug coupons and/or co-payment cards, where the manufacturer directly pays a large portion of the consumer's cost sharing. These payment schemes are often not operationally transparent to payers, distort an already dysfunctional pricing market, and further complicate a confusing process for consumers.)

Given that the amounts charged by pharmacies for branded drugs reflects the pharmacies' acquisition costs, *these charges are closely correlated to the list price set exclusively by the pharmaceutical manufacturer.* That is why out-of-control drug prices show up at pharmacy counters. It is also why health plans aggressively negotiate with manufacturers for ways to reduce the impact of these prices, so they can pass savings onto consumers. For example, if a health plan's pharmacy and therapeutics committee determines that two or more drugs are therapeutically equivalent and eligible for formulary inclusion, health plans (or PBMs) negotiate with manufacturers for rebates in exchange for plans placing the drugs on a preferred formulary tier and/or waiving utilization management tools, such as step therapy protocols. Since drug costs comprise a significant portion of a health plan's total costs, these discounts, which typically take the form of rebates, reduce the net price of the drug.

Rebate amounts typically are calculated and paid by a manufacturer to a health plan on an aggregate basis, long after an individual prescription is filled by a consumer. Because rebates are extended based on actual aggregated utilization by a specific population, they are often paid to health plans several months after the drug has been prescribed and dispensed and all the data can be reconciled. In designing their plan benefits and developing premium rates in advance of the upcoming coverage year, health plans calculate an estimate of the aggregate rebates they expect to receive. Since drug costs comprise a significant portion of a health plan's total costs, plans may use these estimated discounts to reduce the premiums they charge for the overall benefit. Alternatively, plans may incorporate the estimates into lower point-of-sale pricing for individual drugs that generate the rebates. In discussing rebates, it is important to understand that for some branded drugs and biologics without therapeutic alternatives, manufacturers' willingness to negotiate on price is small or nonexistent, rather, rebates are not commonly found for physician-administered drugs, which account for 30 percent of physician drug spending.[321]

By reducing the net price and cost of drugs through available rebates and discounts, all consumers benefit. The savings are passed on through improvements to benefit packages, reductions in premiums, and/or lower out-of-pocket costs. This represents a broad and direct benefit for millions of consumers whether they get their coverage through Medicare, on their own, or through their employer.

c. Do you believe there can be meaningful action to lower prescription drug prices for the American people and for the taxpayer without reforms to address the manufacturer's original list price?

The problem is the price. Period. Any strategy to reduce pharmaceutical costs for the American people must address that fundamental reality.

d. Would you please identify one of two of the most important reforms that would help address high prescription drug prices that this Committee should be addressing in a legislative hearing?

- Create a Robust Biosimilars Market: Biosimilars offer great promise in generating cost savings for consumers. Some ofthe costliest and most widely-used biologics have been on the market for decades without biosimilar competition. To achieve this promise, it is important to ensure that the FDA promulgates regulations that promote a robust market and ensure providers and patients have unbiased information available to them about the benefits of biosimilars. For example, FDA policies for the labeling, naming, and interchangeability of biosimilars should provide clarity, ensure safety, and avoid unnecessary regulatory hurdles. We also need to address anti-competitive strategies by pharma companies, such as the development of"patcnt estates," and tactics aimed at delaying the availability ofbiosimilars.
- Reduce Rules, Regulation and Red Tape to Generic Entry: To address patent abuses, anti-competitive tactics such as "pay for delay" settlements, "product hopping," and "evergreening" should be prohibited, and the Inter Partes Review (IPR) process through the U.S. Patent and Trademark Office should be preserved. Additional legislation is needed to require brand manufacturers to share information and scientific samples with generic and biosimilar developers to promote the development of these lower cost alternatives.

[321] "Trends in Specialty Drug Benefits," Pharmacy Benefit Management Institute, 2017.

- Publish True R&D Costs and Explain Price Setting and Price Increases: As part of the FDA approval process, manufacturers should be required to disclose information regarding the intended launch price, the use of the drug, and direct and indirect research and development costs. After approval, manufacturers should provide appropriate transparency into list price increases.

3. At the hearing, we touched briefly on the role of third-party programs such as coupons, co-pay card programs, patient assistance programs, or related charitable foundations and the role they may play in the pricing of prescription drugs. In your testimony, you offered recommendations on the actions the Committee should take to address the problem of high drug costs. These recommendations included limiting third-party payment schemes that raise costs, such as drug coupons, co-pay card programs, and related charitable foundations.
   a. Will you discuss further how drug companies are using these programs and why you believe they help to drive up the cost of prescription drugs? How would limiting third- party programs such as drug coupons, co-pay card programs, and related charitable foundations address high drug costs?

Drug coupons, co-pay card programs, and the related charity programs funded by pharmaceutical companies are predominately used to subsidize the patients' share of the treatment cost of branded drugs. This shields patients from directly experiencing the high costs of these drugs, and ultimately removes any incentives for patients to opt for lower cost, therapeutically equivalent alternatives. Meanwhile, health plans and payers must foot the bill for the entire cost of the drug, which gets passed on to consumers and employers in the form of higher premiums.

This significant impact on health care spending was recently assessed by economists at Harvard, UCLA and Northwestern[322]:

> "We study the impact of co pay coupons on branded drugs first facing generic entry between 2007 and 2010 ... We find that coupons increase branded sales by 60+ percent, entirely by reducing the sales of bioequivalent generics. During the five years following generic entry, we estimate that coupons increase total spending by $30 to $120 million per drug, or $700 million to $2.7 billion for our sample alone."

Of further concern, the use of these programs is growing. According to the IMS Institute for Healthcare Informatics, copay cards are used for 8 percent of all branded prescriptions. For some specialty drug classes, that percentage is much higher, as high as

---

322 Dafny, Leemore S., Christopher Ody, and Matt Schmitt. "When Discounts Raise Costs: The Effect of Capay Coupons on Generic Utilization." *American Economic Journal: Economic Policy* 9, no. 2 (May 2017): 91-123.

70 percent for multiple sclerosis and rheumatoid arthritis drugs.[323] A 2014 report by the Office of the Inspector General of HHS noted, "when consumers are relieved of copayment obligations, manufacturers are relieved of a market constraint on drug prices."[324]

Coupons are a tacit agreement from manufacturers that drugs are unaffordable to patients, yet the coupons ultimately serve to increase the overall cost of drugs to the health care system by directing patients to more expensive therapies. In fact, manufacturers are increasingly using these schemes as a strategy to increase the use of expensive branded medications when lower-cost generic alternatives come to market.

The actual dissemination of coupons includes utilizing patient assistance programs (PAPs), either established within a drug manufacturer, often as a 50l(c)(3) private foundation, or through an independent charity. Generally, but dependent on the legal tax filing of the organization, donors to both manufacturer PAPs and independent PAPs can deduct their donations of inventory or cash. The size, funding, and scope of these organizations has grown rapidly in recent years. A 2016 analysis of 2014 Internal Revenue Service (IRS) data found that charitable giving by I 0 large manufacturer patient assistance programs rose from $376 million in 2001 to $6.1 billion in 2014, accounting for 84% of all pharmaceutical giving and one-sixth of all U.S. corporate charitable deductions in 2014.[325] Charitable giving by five of the main independent charity PAPs increased from $2 million in 2001 to $868 million in 2014.

Any Federal or State efforts to limit the ability for these payment schemes to direct patients to higher-cost drugs when a lower-cost, therapeutically equivalent therapy is available would protect individuals from higher costs on the back end due to premium increases. Additionally, federal policymakers should carefully scrutinize the cyclical nature of manufacturer charitable giving to patient assistance programs that may result in increased utilization of specific branded medications. We support the Committee's attention to limiting these market distortions to ensure that consumers have access to high-quality treatments at the most competitive price possible.

b. You mentioned in your testimony that these programs are prohibited in certain federal programs. Is our enforcement of this prohibition robust?

The use of co-pay coupons distributed by manufacturers is prohibited under the anti-kickback statute for individuals with federal health care benefits, including Medicare (including Medicare Part D), Medicaid, TRICARE, and Veterans Health Administration programs. However, private health plans used by individuals in the Federal Employees

---

[323] IMS Institute for Healthcare Informatics, "Medicines Use and Spending Shifts." April 2015.
[324] HIIS, OIG, "Special Advisory Bulletin: Pharmaceutical Manufacturer Copayment Coupons." September 2014.
[325] Austin Frerick, "The Cloak of Social Responsibility: Pharmaceutical Corporate Charity." *TaT Notes,* November 28, 2016.

Health Benefit (FEHB) Program and private health plans offered as Qualified Health Plans (QHPs) under the Affordable Care Act (ACA) are not considered government programs, and those individuals may use co-pay coupons. Also, coupons distributed by independently-run charities are permitted to be used in conjunction with federal health care benefits, even if charities receive cash donations from drug manufacturers.

In September of 2014, the HHS Office of the Inspector General (OlG) released a report from the Office of Evaluation and Inspections (OEl) that reviewed the steps taken by manufacturers to prevent coupon use in concert with federal benefits.[326] Due to the anti-kickback statute, coupons generally include standard language noting that use is prohibited for beneficiaries in federal health programs.

The report found that, of the manufacturers surveyed, manufacturers are not consistently including notices on coupons to inform individuals in federal health care programs that their use is prohibited. In addition, the report found that the use of coupons is not operationally transparent to Medicare Part D plans, "which impedes Part D plans and others from identifying and monitoring the usc of coupons for drugs paid for by Part D.[327] The report also raises the importance of maintaining beneficiary cost-sharing requirements, and the risk of coupons providing short-term financial relief to beneficiaries while ultimately increasing costs to federal health care programs and their beneficiaries.

The report recommends that CMS work with manufacturers and pharmacies to improve the operational transparency of coupon use. This operational transparency is also a significant issue for commercial health plans, and a standard format for identifying coupons in pharmacy claims transactions is needed. Additional CMS guidance and oversight of coupon use in federal health care programs would be welcome, to help both manufacturers, pharmacies, and health plans understand the compliance measures required on the part of manufacturers to ensure that coupons are not being used in violation of the anti-kickback statute.

c. What more can Congress do to address this problem, both in our federal healthcare programs as well as in the private insurance market?

Limiting the ability for these payment schemes to direct patients to higher-cost drugs when a lower-cost, therapeutically equivalent therapy is available would protect individuals from higher costs on the back end due to premium increases. We support the Committee's attention to limiting these market distortions to ensure that consumers have access to high-quality treatments at the most competitive price possible.

---

[326] HHS, OIG, "Manufacturer Safeguards May Not Prevent Copayment Coupon Use for Part D Drugs," September 2014.

[327] Ibid.

We also recommend HHS/CMS be directed to outline a strategy for ongoing assessment and monitoring of these payments schemes. Such an approach should include oversight of the practice of pharmaceutical companies donating to charitable organizations, to ensure that these charities arc operating as intended and that pharmaceutical companies arc not exerting influence over how the charities allocate their funding.

Additional CMS guidance and oversight of coupon use in federal health care programs would be welcome, to help both manufacturers, pharmacies, and health plans understand the compliance measures required on the part of manufacturers to ensure that coupons arc not being used in violation of the anti-kickback statute.

The Honorable Diana DeGette

1. When designing pharmacy benefits and formularies for health plans, how do your member companies balance clinical evidence about various treatment options with contractual guarantees to pharmaceutical companies about formulary placement?

Health plans' pharmacy benefit designs and formularies leverage science by relying on existing evidence on safety and effectiveness. This evidence-based approach to coverage policy and medical management involves a systematic review of the safety and effectiveness of medical interventions, including drugs, devices, services, and procedures. In conducting these reviews, health plans' pharmacy and therapeutics committees rely on a variety of evidence-based resources, typically following a hierarchy of evidence that gives the most weight to randomized clinical trials. The types of evidence that health plans rely on include, but are not limited to:

- Randomized Clinical Trials (RCTs)
- Specialty society guidelines/best practices
- Current scientific and clinical peer reviewed medical literature o CMS coverage decisions and quality metrics
- AHRQ guidelines
- USPSTF recommendations
- Well-designed observational studies o Expert consensus

Health plan pharmacy policies and formularies are also dictated to some extent by federal and state mandates, as well as employer/client requests. Additionally, health plans periodically review their coverage policies and update them based on new information/evidence, such as FDA safety notices, new drug approvals, new scientific/clinical research findings, and updated professional society guidelines.

2. To what extent do your member companies track how rebate dollars passed on by PBMs and pharmaceutical companies are used by health insurance plans?

Rebate amounts typically are calculated and paid by a manufacturer to a health plan (or PBM) on an aggregate basis, long after an individual prescription is filled by a consumer. Because rebates are extended based on actual aggregate utilization of a specific population, they are paid several months after the drug has been prescribed and dispensed and all the data can be reconciled. In designing their plan benefits and developing premium rates in advance of the upcoming coverage year, health plans calculate an estimate of the aggregate rebates they expect to receive.

Since drug costs comprise a significant portion of a health plan's total costs, plans may use these estimated discounts to reduce the premiums they charge for the overall benefit, improve benefit packages, and/or lower out-of-pocket costs. Alternatively, plans may incorporate advance estimates into lower point-of-sale pricing for individual drugs that generate the rebates. By reducing the net price and cost of drugs, all consumers benefit. This represents a broad and direct benefit for millions of customers, whether they get their coverage through Medicare, on their own, or through their employer.

In discussing rebates, it's important to understand the role they play within the broader system for setting the cost of drugs that consumers pay at the pharmacy. For some branded drugs and biologics without therapeutic alternatives, manufacturers' willingness to negotiate on price is small or nonexistent. For generic prescriptions, accounting for 89 percent of dispensed medications, rebates or discounts are not generally offered. Further, rebates are not commonly found for physician-administered drugs, which account for 30 percent of prescription drug spending.

3. Are rebate dollars retrieved from pharmaceutical companies or passed on by PBMs considered under the Medical Loss Ratio (MLR)? If yes, please explain how rebate dollars factor into MLR calculations.

Health insurance providers must provide consumer rebates if they do not meet a set threshold for the percentage of revenue spent on medical claims (generally, 80 or 85 percent depending on the market). Prescription drug rebates are included in the medical loss ratio (MLR) calculation.

The costs for prescription drugs are treated as other health claims, while prescription drug rebates are treated as revenue. Both claims and revenue are reconciled and reported in the second quarter of the year for the previous plan year for a set of products, and insurance providers file MLR reports with HHS at this time. Any rebates owed are distributed in the third quarter and are based on the average MLR ratio over the prior three years.

The Honorable Kurt Schrader

Many of my constituents have complained about increased deductibles, which increases the amount they have to pay out-of-pocket for their drugs. Sometimes they don't have a choice to go to a lower deductible plan. Why have there been an increased number of high- deductible health plans in the market?

Deductibles and other cost-sharing requirements are a common feature of both public and private health insurance coverage. In general, plans that feature higher cost-sharing (including deductibles) tend to have lower premiums while plans with lower deductibles tend to have higher premiums. The use of deductibles and other cost-sharing is an important way for employers and health plans to offer lower products with lower premiums-which is critically important in a competitive and price-sensitive market.

Both premiums and deductibles have been increasing in recent years-reflecting increases in medical and pharmacy trend which, in turn, reflects both the utilization and prices of health care services. In the employer-sponsored market-where over 150 million Americans receive health insurance coverage-the average deductible for single coverage is $1,200. And, about half (45%) of workers covered in large group coverage are enrolled in a plan with a deductible that exceeds $1,000.

Deductibles in the individual market (including on- and off-the exchange marketplace) tend to be higher, which is why implementation of the cost-sharing reduction (CSR) benefit program as intended is so important. For the 2017 plan year, most consumers-over 6 million-benefited from the CSR program which substantially reduce patient cost-sharing (including deductibles) to promote access to needed medical care and prescription drugs. By providing lower-income individuals with lower deductibles and other cost-sharing, the CSR program helps eliminate financial barriers to needed medical care. It is also important to note that all consumers benefit from annual out-of-pocket maximums-which caps patients' out-of-pocket spending to provide protection from catastrophic health care costs.

Greg Walden, Oregon
Chairman

Frank Pallone, Jr., New Jersey
Ranking Member

One Hundred Fifteenth Congress
Congress of the United States
House of Representatives
Committee on Energy and Commerce

January 8, 2018

Mr. Tom Nickels
Executive Vice President for Government Relations and Public Policy
American Hospital Association

Dear Mr. Nickels:

Thank you for appearing before the Subcommittee on Health on December 13, 2017, to testify at the hearing entitled "Examining the DMG Supply Chain."

Pursuant to the Rules of the Committee on Energy and Commerce, the hearing record remains open for ten business days to permit Members to submit additional questions for the record, which are attached. The format of your responses to these questions should be as follows: (1) the name of the Member whose question you are addressing, (2) the complete text of the question you are addressing in bold, and (3) your answer to that question in plain text.

To facilitate the printing of the hearing record, please respond to these questions with a transmittal letter by the close of business on January 23, 2018. Thank you again for your time and effort preparing and delivering testimony before the Subcommittee.

Sincerely,

Michael C. Burgess, MD
Chairman, Subcommittee on Health

cc: The Honorable Gene Green, Ranking Member, Subcommittee on Health

AMERICAN HOSPITAL ASSOCIATION

January 23, 2018

The Honorable Michael C. Burgess, MD
United States House of Representatives

Dear Congressman Burgess,

On behalf of our nearly 5,000 member hospitals, health systems and other health care organizations, and our clinician partners including more than 270,000 affiliated physicians, 2 million nurses and other caregivers- and the 43,000 health care leaders who belong to our professional membership groups, the American Hospital Association (AHA) thanks you for your continued efforts to understand and address the challenge of high and rising prescription drug prices.

As we discussed during the December 2017 hearing on the drug supply chain, the high cost of drugs threatens patient access to care and health outcomes. In this letter, we respond to Congressman Carter's subsequent question regarding whether the AliA's supports increased transparency across several aspects of the drug supply chain. The AHA believes that increased transparency, in conjunction with other policies, will help the U.S. health care system achieve sustainable drug prices. While we generally support transparency in the areas identified, we strongly encourage Congress to focus first on transparency in list prices.

All aspects of pricing along the drug supply chain are based off the initial list price, which is set solely by drug manufacturers. Payers, providers and the public have little information about how drugs are priced, and this information gap challenges payers' abilities to make decisions regarding coverage and pricing of drugs, and often results in mid-year cost increases that providers are unprepared to manage. We specifically encourage Congress to advance transparency in drug prices by:

- Increasing the disclosure requirements drug manufacturers must meet related to anticipated or intended pricing for a drug at the time of application for drug approval. Information should include how research and development contribute to the price of the drug, and
- Issuing consumer and provider-facing reports on drug pricing that can help decision-making regarding a specific drug therapy.

Thank you for the opportunity to provide additional input as you continue your investigation into the challenge of drug prices,

Sincerely,

Thomas P. Nickels
Executive Vice President

Greg Walden, Oregon
Chairman

Frank Pallone, Jr., New Jersey
Ranking Member

One Hundred Fifteenth Congress
Congress of the United States
House of Representatives
Committee on Energy and Commerce

January 8, 2018

Dr. Gerald Harmon
Chair, Board of Trustees
American Medical Association

Dear Dr. Harmon:

Thank you for appearing before the Subcommittee on Health on December 13, 2017, to testify at the hearing entitled "Examining the Drug Supply Chain."

Pursuant to the Rules of the Committee on Energy and Commerce, the hearing record remains open for ten business days to permit Members to submit additional questions for the record, which are attached. The format of your responses to these questions should be as follows: (1) the name of the Member whose question you are addressing, (2) the complete text of the question you are addressing in bold, and (3) your answer to that question in plain text.

To facilitate the printing of the hearing record, please respond to these questions with a transmittal letter by the close of business on January 23, 2018. Thank you again for your time and effort preparing and delivering testimony before the Subcommittee.

Sincerely,

Michael C. Burgess, MD
Chairman, Subcommittee on Health

cc: The Honorable Gene Green, Ranking Member, Subcommittee on Health

American Medical Association

Gerald E. Harmon, MD
Chair, Board of Trustees

January 23, 2018

The Honorable Michael C. Burgess, MD
Chairman
Subcommittee on Health
Energy and Commerce Committee

The Honorable Gene Green
Ranking Member
Subcommittee on Health
Energy and Commerce Committee

Dear Chairman Burgess and Ranking Member Green:

Thank you for the opportunity to testify before the Committee on Energy and Commerce Subcommittee on Health during the hearing entitled, "Examining the Drug Supply Chain," The American Medical Association (AMA) applauds your leadership and efforts to identify and address the factors, policies, and practices that impact access and affordability of medically necessary medication treatment for patients, The hearing was extraordinarily helpful to advancing informed public policy discussions, The AMA looks forward to working closely with you to identify and implement workable solutions.

Below are the AMA's responses to the follow-up questions posed by the Honorable Congressmen Earl L. "Buddy" Carter and Frank Pallone, Jr.:

The Honorable Earl L. "Buddy" Carter

Does your organization support increased transparency into the following aspects of the drug supply chain? Yes or No will suffice.

As outlined in my written testimony, the AMA strongly supports increased transparency. And, based on the hearing testimony, we support increased transparency in light of the complex policies and practices among insurers, distributors, pharmaceutical benefits managers (PBMs), and pharmacies.

1) Rebate pass throughs. *Yes, the A MA strongly supports increased transparency.*
2) PBM "Spread" Profits, *Yes, the AMA strongly supports increased transparency*
3) Generic Drug Reimbursement Methodologies. *Yes, the AMA strongly supports increased transparency.*
4) True price for prescription drug at point of sale. *Yes, the AMA strongly supports increased transparency.*
5) Pharmacy Direct and Indirect Remuneration ("DIR") fees, *Yes, the AMA strongly supports increased tramparency.*

The Honorable Frank Pallone, Jr.

I understand that the *AMA* has been supportive of a ban on direct-to-consumer advertising. Can you explain why your organization and your members support a ban, and how you think a ban could help to address rising drug costs?

The following is the actual language of policies adopted by our House of Delegates (HOD) addressing this issue. The HOD is comprised of every national medical specialty society and state medical association, and has adopted extensive policies on the topic of directed consumer marketing that are the most responsive to the questions posed. In brief during the numerous HOD discussions of policy related to direct-to-consumer marketing, physician delegates regularly cited concerns that such advertising may have some benefits, but noted that such advertising often diverts the very limited time patients and physicians have together to discussions that are not relevant to a patient's diagnosis or to medically necessary and reasonable treatment options. In addition, during the AMA policy development process, physicians have also observed that the drugs promoted through such methods often do not have the same documented risk profiles of more established and often less expensive treatment options. Physician representatives have also noted during these discussions that such marketing may create unrealistic expectations when less expensive albeit equally effective treatments are available. Throughout the policy discussion about the impact on patient health outcomes and the physician-patient relationship, there is a generalized concern that the advertising promotes more expensive, costly treatment alternatives when less expensive alternatives with established risk profiles and evidence of relative efficacy among a larger and more diverse patient population are available.

The specific policies:

Direct-to-Consumer Advertisement of Prescription Drugs

Direct to-consumer advertising may raise awareness about diseases and treatment and may help inform patients about the availability of new diagnostic tests, drugs, treatments, and devices. However, direct-to- consumer advertising also carries the risk of creating unrealistic expectations for patients and conflicts of interest for physicians, adversely affecting patients' health and safety, and compromising patient physician relationships. In the context of direct-to-consumer advertising of prescription drugs, physicians individually should:

(a) Remain objective about advertised tests, drugs, treatments, and devices, avoiding bias for or against advertised products.

(b) Engage in dialogue with patients who request tests, drugs, treatments, or devices they have seen advertised to:

- assess and enhance the patient's understanding ofthe test, drug or device;

- educate patients about why an advertised test, drug, or device may not be suitable for them, including providing cost-ffectiveness information about different options.

(c) Resist commercially induced pressure to prescribe tests, drugs, or devices that may not be indicated

(d) Obtain informed consent before prescribing an advertised lest, drug, or device, in keeping with professional standards.

(e) Deny requests for an inappropriate test, drug, or device.

(f) Consider reporting to the sponsoring manufacturer or appropriate authorities direct-to-consumer advertising that:

- promotes false expectations;
- does not enhance consumer education;
- conveys unclear, inaccurate, or misleading health education messages;
- fails to refer patients to their physicians for additional information;
- does not identify the target population at risk;
- encourages consumer selfdiagnosis and treatment.

Collectively, physicians should:

(g) Encourage and engage in studies that examine the impact of direct-to-consumer advertising on patient health and medical care.

(h) Whenever possible, assist authorities to enforce existing law by reporting advertisements that do not·

- provide a fair and balanced discussion of the use of the drug product for the disease, disorder, or condition;
- clearly explain warnings, precautions, and potential adverse reactions associated with the drug product;
- present summary information in language that can be understood by the consumer
- comply with applicable regulations;
- provide collateral materials to educate both physicians and consumers.

AMA Principles of Medical Ethics. (The Opinions are offered as ethics guidance for physicians and are not intended to establish standard of clinical practice or rules of law.)

Direct-to-Consumer Advertising (DTCA) of Prescription Drugs and Implantable Devices

1. To support a ban on direct-to-consumer advertising for prescription drugs and implantable medical devices.
2. That until such a ban is in place, our AMA opposes product-claim DTC4 that does not satisfy the following guidelines:
   a) The advertisement should be indication-specific and enhance consumer education about the drug or implantable medical device, and the disease, disorder, or condition for which the drug or device is used
   b) In addition to creating awareness about a drug or implantable medical device for the treatment or prevention of a disease, disorder, or condition, the advertisement should convey a clear, accurate and responsible health education message by providing objective information about the benefits and risks of the drug or implantable medical device for a given indication. Information about benefits should reflect the true efficacy of the drug or implantable medical device as determined by clinical trials that resulted in the drug's or device's approval for marketing.
   c) The advertisement should clearly indicate that the product is a prescription drug or implantable medical device to distinguish such advertising from other advertising for nonprescription products.
   d) The advertisement should not encourage self-diagnosis and self-treatment, hut should refer patients to their physicians for more information. A statement, such as "Your physician may recommend other appropriate treatments, 11 is recommended.
   e) The advertisement should exhibit fair balance between benefit and risk information when discussing the use of the drug or implantable medical device product for the disease, disorder, or condition. The amount of time or space devoted to benefit and risk information, as well as its cognitive accessibility, should be comparable.
   f) The advertisement should present information about warnings, precautions, and potential adverse reactions associated with the drug or implantable medical device product in a manner (e.g., at a reading grade level) such that it will be understood by a majority of consumers, without distraction of content, and will help facilitate communication between physician and patient.
   g) The advertisement should not make comparative claims for the product versus other prescription drug or implantable medical device products; however, the advertisement should include information about the availability of alternative non-drug or non-operative management options such as diet

and lifestyle changes, where appropriate, for the disease, disorder, or condition.

h) In general, product-claim DTCA should not use an actor to portray o health care professional who promotes the drug or implantable medical device product, because this portrayal may be misleading and deceptive. If actors portray health care professionals in DTCA, a disclaimer should be prominently displayed

i) The use of actual health care professionals, either practicing or retired, in DTCA to endorse a specific drug or implantable medical device product is discouraged but if utilized, the advertisement must include a clearly visible disclaimer that the health care professional is compensated for the endorsement.

j) The advertisement should be targeted for placement in print, broadcast, or other electronic media so as to avoid audiences that are not age appropriate for the messages involved.

k) In addition to the above, the advertisement must comply with all other applicable Food and Drug Administration (FDA) regulations, policies and guidelines.

3. That/he FDA review and pre-approve all DTCA for prescription drugs or implantable medical device products before pharmaceutical and medical device manufacturers (sponsors) run the ads, both to ensure compliance with federal regulations and consistency with FDA-approved labeling for the drug or implantable medical device product.
4. That the Congress provide sufficient funding to the FDA, either through direct appropriations or through prescription drug or implantable medical device user fees, to ensure effective regulation of DTCA.
5. That DTCA for newly approved prescription drug or implantable medical device products not be run until sufficient post-marketing experience has been obtained to determine product risks in the general population and until physicians have been appropriately educated about the drug or implantable medical device. The time interval for this moratorium on DTCA for newly approved drugs or implantable medical devices should be determined by the FDA, in negotiations with the drug or medical device product's sponsor, at the time of drug or implantable medical device approval. The length of the moratorium may vary from drug to drug and device to device depending on various factors, such as: the innovative nature of the drug or implantable medical device; the severity of the disease that the drug or implantable medical device is intended to treat; the availability of alternative therapies; and the intensity and timeliness of the education about the drug or implantable medical device for physicians who are most likely to prescribe it.

6. That our AMA opposes any manufacturer (drug or device sponsol) incentive programs for physician prescribing and pharmacist dispensing that are run concurrently with DTCA.
7. That our AMA encourages the FDA, other appropriate federal agencies, and the pharmaceutical and medical device industries to conduct or find research on the effect of DTCA, focusing on its impact on the patient-physician relationship as well as overall health outcomes and cost benefit analyses; research results should be available to the public.
8. That our AMA supports the concept that when companies engage in DTCA, they assume an increased responsibility for the informational content and an increased duty to warn consumers, and they may lose an element of protection normally accorded under the learned intermedium doctrine.
9. That our AMA encourages physicians to be familiar with the above AMA guidelines for product-claim DTCA and with the Council on Ethical and Judicial Affairs Ethical Opinion E-9. 6.7 and to adhere to the ethical guidance provided in that Opinion.
10. That the Congress should request the Agency for Healthcare Research and Quality or other appropriate entity to perform periodic evidence-based reviews of DTCA in the United States to determine the impact of DTCA on health outcomes and the public health If DTCA is found to have a negative impact on health outcomes and is detrimental to the public health, the Congress should consider enacting legislation to increase DTCA regulation or, if necessary, to prohibit DTCA in some or all media. In such legislation, eve1y effort should be made to not violate protections on commercial speech, as provided by the First Amendment to the US. Constitution.
11. That our AMA supports eliminating the costs for DTC4 of prescription drugs as a deductible business expense for tax purposes.
12. That our AMA continues to monitor DTCA, including new research findings, and work with the FDA and the pharmaceutical and medical device industries to make policy changes regarding DTCA, as necessary.
13. That our AMA supports "help-seeking" or "disease mvareness1' advertisements (i.e., advertisements that discuss a disease, disorder, or condition and advise consumers to see their physicians, but do not mention a drug or implantable medical device or other medical product and are not regulated by the FDA).
14. Our AMA will advocate to the applicable Federal agencies (including the Food and Drug Administration, the Federal Trade Commission, and the Federal Communications Commission) which regulate or influence direct-to-consumer advertising of prescription drugs that such advertising should be required to state the manufacturer's suggested retail price of those drugs.

Thank you for considering the AMA's testimony and responses to the questions posed.

Sincerely,

Gerald E. Harmon, MD

cc: James L. Madara, MD

Greg Walden, Oregon
Chairman

Frank Pallone, Jr., New Jersey
Ranking Member

One Hundred Fifteenth Congress
Congress of the United States
House of Representatives
Committee on Energy and Commerce

January 8, 2018

Mr. B. Douglas Hoey
CEO
National Community Pharmacists Association

Dear Mr. Hoey: Thank you for appearing before the Subcommittee on Health on December 13, 2017, to testify at the hearing entitled "Examining the Drug Supply Chain." Pursuant to the Rules of the Committee on Energy and Commerce, the hearing record remains open for ten business days to permit Members to submit additional questions for the record, which are attached. The format of your responses to these questions should be as follows: (1) the name of the Member whose question you are addressing, (2) the complete text of the question you are addressing in bold, and (3) your answer to that question in plain text. To facilitate the printing of the hearing record, please respond to these questions with a transmittal letter by the close of business on January 23, 2018. Thank you again for your time and effort preparing and delivering testimony before the Subcommittee. Sincerely,

Michael C. Burgess, MD
Chairman, Subcommittee on Health
cc: The Honorable Gene Green, Ranking Member, Subcommittee on Health

NATIONAL COMMUNITY PHARMACISTS ASSOCIATION

January 22, 2018

Chairman Michael Burgess, MD
Energy and Commerce Subcommittee on Health
United States House of Representatives
Re: Reponses to Questions for the Record Regarding the December 13, 2017 Hearing entitled" Examining the Drug Supply Chain."

Dear Chairman Burgess:

Thank you for holding the December 13, 2017 hearing on Examining the Drug Supply Chain. I was honored to testify on behalf of America's 22,000 independent community pharmacies and provide their perspective on the role they play in our nation's drug supply chain. I am also pleased to provide responses to the Questions for the Record. I have enclosed my responses with this letter.

Respectfully submitted,

B. Douglas Hoey, R. Ph, MBA
CEO
National Community Pharmacists Association

Mr. B. Douglas Hoey, R. Ph, MBA
CEO, National Community Pharmacists Association

QUESTIONS SUBMITTED FOR THE RECORD FOR CONGRESSMAN EARL L. "BUDDY" CARTER

1. We have heard about "clawbacks" being taken at the pharmacy and understand that there may be two different types-one in which the pharmacy collects money from the patient that the plan or PBM takes back from the Pharmacy- and one in which the PBM takes back money from the amount that the pharmacy earns from dispensing a medication. Could you provide more clarity and detail about these two different types of "clawbacks"?

NCPA's Answer. The term "clawback" is often used in the supply chain industry to describe various types of PBM activity. Below, NCPA will discuss two types of clawbacks and suggest alternative language to describe each practice to avoid further confusion.

First, pharmacy direct and indirect remuneration ("DIR") fees are effectively "clawback" fees assessed on pharmacies retroactively months later, rather than deducted from claims on a real-time basis at the point-of-sale when a prescription is dispensed. The clawback here is essentially the PBM's practice of taking back these fees from pharmacies months after the point-of-sale. NCPA primarily refers to these fees as retroactive pharmacy DIR fees. These fees take many forms: preferred network fees, "true ups" to various brand and generic effective rates, and adjustments due to performance compared to other pharmacies in Sponsors' Part D networks based on various contract provisions. Put simply, retroactive pharmacy DIR fees can be almost anything. The retroactive nature of these fees makes it exceedingly difficult for small businesses to operate and maintain a successful business.

In addition, last year the Centers for Medicaid and Medicare Services ("CMS") identified several concerns resulting from the rapid growth in retroactive pharmacy DIR fees.[328] First, beneficiaries face higher cost-sharing for drugs and are accelerated into the coverage gap or "donut hole" phase of their benefit Second, more beneficiaries reach the catastrophic phase of the benefit, for which CMS incurs approximately eighty percent of the cost (The HHS Office of Inspector General has noted[329] that these catastrophic costs that are driven by pharmacy DIR fees have tripled in recent years- from $10 billion in 2010 to $33 billion in 2015). Third, liability for Part D costs is increasingly being shifted from Part D plan sponsors to CMS.

In contrast, copay clawbacks are a PBM practice by which PBMs manipulate copayments to secure additional revenue at the expense of the consumer. In these instances, instead of a traditional co pay, patients are unknowingly paying more than they should at the pharmacy counter. This practice is best explained through an example: the cost of a drug is $11.65, including tax and pharmacist's fee. The patient's copay, however, is $50.00. The PBM requires the pharmacy to use the patient's health insurance and charge the patient the $50.00 capay. The difference between the capay and the actual cost of the drug ($38.35, in this example) is called the "spread." When the spread is taken back by the PBM, this process is often called the "capay clawback." The patient pays the $50.00 capay to the pharmacy and the spread is sent back to the PBM.[330]

2. It is my understanding that many of your member pharmacies serve very rural or urban areas that are underserved by health care providers in general. What are some of

---

[328] CMS, *Medicare Part D-Direct and Indirect Remuneration, available at* https://www.cms.gov/newsroom/mediareleasedatabase/fact-sheets/2017-fact-sheet-items/2017-0l-19-2.html.

[329] HHS Office of Inspector General, *High-Price Drugs Are Increasing Federal Payments for Medicare Part D Catastrophic Coverage, avaUable at* https://oig.hhs.gov/oei/reports/oei-02-16-00270.asp.

[330] NCPA, *The Great Big Prescription Drug Clawback,* May 20, 2016, *available at* http://www.ncpanet.org/newsroom/ncpa's-blog---the-dose/ncpa's-blog---the-dose---2016/2016/05/20/the-great-big-prescription-drug-clawback.

the biggest challenges to your members in terms of remaining open for business and able to serve these patients?

NCPA's Answer. Two of the biggest issues facing independent pharmacies are:1) the lack of transparency regarding PBMs, including PBM spread profits, and generic reimbursement; and 2) patient access to pharmacies in preferred networks.

The PBM Industry is Largely Unregulated

PBM practices outlined in Answer 1 have a massive impact on an independent business' ability to operate and effectively serve patients. Given the immense market influence that PBMs exert, one might expect that these entities would be subject to the same types of comprehensive regulation that is currently required of commercial health insurers. However, PBMs are *not* subject to industry-wide regulation. In fact, there are no federal laws or regulations that are specific to the PBM industry. Instead, PBMs face a patchwork of regulations at the state level that are designed to curtail some of the more onerous PBM business practices such as abusive PBM audits of pharmacies and requirements related to timely Maximum Allowable Cost ("MAC") updates. Unfortunately, even in states that have been able to pass limited reforms, PBMs typically resist complying with no recourse. To this end, there are currently lawsuits filed against two states which attempted to legislatively address onerous PBM business practices.

Second, in today's marketplace, generic drugs currently comprise approximately 86 percent of all prescriptions dispensed in the United States.[331] Given this fact, it is surprising that there is no standardized method for determining how pharmacies are reimbursed for generic drugs. PBMs create and maintain "Maximum Allowable Cost" or "MAC Lists" that set the upper limit or maximum amount that a PBM/plan will pay for most generic drugs. Pharmacies are not provided any insight into how drug products are selected to be put onto these MAC Lists or how exactly these prices are determined or updated. In short, contracted pharmacies have zero insight or transparency into the MAC process and sign contracts without having any idea of the rate at which they will be reimbursed for many of the prescriptions they fill. In response to PBMs' secrecy surrounding the creation and maintenance of these MAC Lists, at least 26 states have enacted legislation to try to compel greater transparency into this system. Unsurprisingly, the PBM industry has vigorously opposed these efforts and is currently engaged in litigation with individual states that have sought to compel their compliance with price transparency laws.

Limited Preferred Pharmacy Networks

---

[331] PhRMA, *The Reality of Prescription Medicine Costs in Three Charts,* May 27, 2014, *available at* http://www.phrma.org.catalyst.the-rea!ity-of-prescription-medicine-costs-in-three-charts.

Finally, with respect to patient access to pharmacies in rural and underserved areas, an overwhelming majority of Part 0 plans have created separate preferred pharmacy networks and many community pharmacies are excluded from these networks. As you have noted, independent pharmacists are the most accessible health care professional with 95 percent of Americans living within five miles of a pharmacy. Unfortunately, patients do not always have access to pharmacies that are the closest to them because certain community pharmacies are excluded from prescription drug plans ("POPs") by PBMs that create closed network provider lists. NCPA believes limiting access to community pharmacies severely thwarts the delivery of beneficial and accessible health care services to patients, and more specifically to some of our most vulnerable populations.

If their local pharmacy is not included in a preferred network, a senior must either switch to a preferred network pharmacy or pay higher co payments or coinsurance to access the local pharmacy of their choice. In rural areas, accessing a preferred pharmacy may require significant travel. In urban areas, CMS recently found that fifty-four percent of preferred pharmacy networks fail to meet standards for access to pharmacies.

In medically underserved areas, local pharmacies are an important part of the health care delivery system where patients can not only access prescription drugs but also receive services like preventative screenings and medication therapy management. Excluding community pharmacies from preferred pharmacy networks takes away choices from seniors and could lead to reduced access to medical services. To protect this important access to health care and to support more providers in POPs, NCPA recommends that community pharmacies in underserved areas be allowed to participate in Medicare Part 0 preferred pharmacy networks if they are willing to accept the contract terms and conditions that other preferred providers operate under. This gives seniors more choice, allows community pharmacies to compete, and preserves access to medical services in underserved areas.

3. There seems to be an assumption that pharmacies play a role in determining the prices that patients pay when they arrive at the pharmacy to fill a prescription under their prescription drug coverage- If this is not the case, could you please elaborate as to exactly who is in control of this process?

NCPA's Answer. Pharmacists are part of the supply chain that interacts directly with the patient and are keenly aware of the frustrations and challenges patients face when dealing with high drug costs. NCPA believes requiring retroactive pharmacy OIR fees to be calculated at point-of-sale is a policy that works to lower cost-sharing for patients, and ultimately save the patient money.

NCPA would also like to point out that examining other activities in the supply chain could lower patient cost. For example, PBMs wield immense power in influencing precisely what prescription drug products will be considered "on formulary" or what will be covered by a specific health plan. Typically, the PBM chooses specific drug products to garner the greatest amount of rebate dollars for its profits. Lately, the PBMs' "rebate game" has attracted a great deal of attention as it has come to light that the proliferation of these rebates is causing drug manufacturers to offset their payments to PBMs by raising the list prices of medications. This dynamic is extremely troubling because in today's health care marketplace in which many consumers receive prescription drug coverage under high-deductible plans-patient cost sharing amounts for medications are based off these artificially inflated "list prices." Patient cost sharing is a percent of the "invoice" or retail price, not the net or rebated price.

This suggests that ultimately rebate dollars are not passed through directly to patients. The Center for Medicine in the Public Interest confirmed this chapter and has specifically stated that rebates as percent of total price growth increased ten-fold since 2011.[332] 1n addition, the amount that PBMs reimburse a pharmacy for dispensing a drug is not the same amount that PBMs "charge" plans for the same drug. PBMs "mark up" the cost of drugs, charging plans more than pharmacies are reimbursed and keeping the difference as pure profit. We believe that these hidden spread amounts should be disclosed to plan sponsors.

4. There has been a lot of discussion around retroactive pharmacy "DIR" fees in the Medicare Part D program and the disruption they are causing particularly in small pharmacies. Could you briefly provide some background and perhaps some potential solutions that could be utilized to ameliorate the problem?

NCPA's Answer. Pharmacy direct and indirect remuneration ("DIR") are fees that are retroactively assessed against pharmacies months after the sale of a prescription, rather than deducted from claims on a real-time basis at the point-of-sale. These fees take many forms: preferred network fees, "true ups" to various brand and generic effective rates, and adjustments due to performance compared to other pharmacies in Sponsors' Part D networks based on various quality measures. Put simply, retroactive pharmacy DIR fees can be almost anything.

The issue with retroactive pharmacy DIR fees is that these fees are not included in the "negotiated price" that is recorded on the "Prescription Drug Event" ("POE"). The point-of-sale price also known as the "negotiated price" that is recorded on the POE records is extremely significant because it is used to calculate beneficiary cost-sharing and to adjudicate the Part D benefit. Any fees or payments that are made after the point-of-sale are not reflected in the negotiated price but rather are reported to CMS separately.

Further, as outlined in Answer 1, retroactive pharmacy DIR fees force beneficiaries to face higher cost- sharing for drugs and progress more rapidly into the coverage gap or "donut hole" phase of their benefit. Second, more beneficiaries reach the catastrophic phase of the benefit, for which CMS incurs approximately eighty percent of the cost (The

[332] Robert Goldberg, *Drug Costs Driven by Rebates,* Center for Medicine in the Public Interest, *available at* http://bionj.org/wp-content/uploads/2015/11/drug-costs-driven-by-rebates.pdf.

HHS Office of Inspector General has noted[333] that these catastrophic costs that are driven by pharmacy DIR fees have tripled in recent years- from $10 billion in 2010 to $33 billion in 2015). Third, liability for Part D costs is increasingly being shifted from Part D plan sponsors to CMS.

A leading actuarial firm reinforced and bolstered these findings in a report earlier this year commissioned by NCPA[334]. In addition, MedPAC has recently warned[335] that because of DIR, the gap between gross and net drug prices has grown 20 percent annually from 2010-2015 and that "plan incentives [are] not aligned with beneficiary and Medicare." By utilizing tactics such as pharmacy DIR fees, the Part D plan sponsor or its PBM often receive additional compensation after the point-of-sale that serves to change the final cost of the drug for the payer or the price paid to the pharmacy for the drug.

To address these concerns, and to help preserve access to independent community pharmacies, one solution would be to require Medicare Part D Plan Sponsors/PBMs to utilize point-of-sale discounts, rather than retroactive pharmacy payment reductions. This approach would also lower beneficiary cost-sharing and reduce Medicare program costs and liability. Finally, this approach would allow the use of pay-for-performance arrangements and encourage true quality incentive programs instead of misaligned programs that blur the line between reimbursement for ingredient cost and pharmacist performance.

5. Some media accounts and legal complaints allege that patients have faced so-called "copay clawbacks." By virtue of these "clawbacks," patients sometimes incur higher cost-sharing than they would without their insurance. Allegedly, the differential is taken by the Pharmacy Benefit Manager. If PBMs are the "experts" in managing patients' drug benefit costs, how can any major PBM allow something like this to become a repeated practice? In your testimony, you stated copay clawback practices are being conducted by "outliers" in the industry. Has the PBM industry taken any steps to remedy this apparent "outlier" situation or is this a systematic practice that has gone unaddressed?

NCPA's Answer. In our members experience, "copay clawbacks" are primarily assessed when a patient has a high deductible commercial health plan. There is one major PBM that assesses the vast majority of these "copay clawbacks." To our knowledge the PBM industry has not taken any steps to remedy this presumed "outlier" activity. Unfortunately, we still hear about examples where the patient is incurring higher cost-sharing by using their health plan/PBM than they would by paying the cash price for the drug. And after the prescription is dispensed the PBM recoups the copay amount from the pharmacy.

---

[333] HHS Office of Inspector General. *High-Price Drugs Are Increasing Federal Payments for Medicare Part D Catastrophic Coverage, available at* https://oig.hhs.gov/oei/reoorts/oei-02-16-00270.asp.

[334] NCPA, *The Impacts af Prescription Drug Direct and Indirect Remuneration Under Medicare Part D,* Feb. 2017.

[335] MedPac, *Payment and Plan Incentives in Part D,* Apr. 7, 2017, *available at* http://www.medoac.gov/docs/default-source/defau!t-document-librarv/payment-and-p!an-incentives-in-part-d-april-2017-for-public.pdf?sfvrsn=O.

6. There have been public reports of PBM's relabeling rebate dollars with another name to retain the value. Do PBM's relabel fees to whatever they prefer such as "formulary rebates" vs. "administrative fees" vs. "price protection rebates"? Do PBM's profit from manufacturer price increases?

NCPA's Answer. It is our understanding that PBMs do relabel rebate dollars with different names and by doing so are able to retain a higher share of the rebate. The higher the manufacturer sets the price of a drug the higher rebate the PBM may be able to retain.

7. Gag clauses were briefly brought up in the hearing. Can you explain how your members are restricted by gag clauses included in the contracts between PBMs and pharmacists? What are some examples of the restrictions on what they can and can't say? Do you have any input on ways in which the pharmacists can ensure their patient is also paying the amount that is in their best interest?

NCPA's Answer. Our members are in effect prohibited from sharing information with their patients regarding the cost of their medications. The real issue is that pharmacies can't share what they are being reimbursed, because that is considered confidential by the PBMs. Combine that with having to charge the patient what the PBM says at point-of-sale, requiring pharmacies to run the claim if the patient presents insurance, and agreeing to overly broad confidentiality provisions (that may incorporate the terms and conditions of the PBM's Provider Manual, which is often hundreds of pages and subject to unilateral revisions by the PBM at any time), and the pharmacy is hamstrung. For example, one of the largest PBMs uses a Pharmacy Provider Agreement that includes the following provisions that highlight the issues:

> Confidentiality: Provider acknowledges and agrees that in the performance of services hereunder, Provider will comply with the Confidentiality provisions set forth in the Provider Manual and as set forth in this Agreement.
>
> Contacting Sponsors or Media: Provider hereby agrees (and shall cause its affiliates, employees, independent contractors, shareholders, members, officers, directors and agents to agree) that it shall not engage in any conduct or communications, including, but not limited to, contacting any media or any Sponsor and/or Sponsor's Members or other party without the prior consent of [PBM].

Violation of any of these provisions or others could very well lead the PBM to terminate the contract with the pharmacy and remove the pharmacy from the PBM's networks, resulting in the inability of the pharmacy to continue to service a significant percentage of its customers.

For patients to pay the amount in their best interest it may be necessary to require health plans/PBMs to explicitly allow pharmacists to inform patients about the cost of the medication or the availability of any therapeutically equivalent alternative medication or alternative method of purchasing the prescription including but not limited to paying a cash price.

8. Does your organization support increased transparency into the following aspect of the drug supply chain? Yes or No will suffice.

- Rebate pass throughs
- PBM "Spread" Profits
- Generic Drug Reimbursement Methodologies
- True price for prescription drug at point of sale
- Pharmacy Direct and Indirect Remuneration ("DIR") fees

NCPA's Answer. NCPA supports increased transparency into the following aspects of the drug supply chain:

- Rebate pass throughs-Yes b. PBM "Spread" Profits-Yes
- Generic Drug Reimbursement Methodologies-Yes
- True price for prescription drug at point of sale-Yes
- Pharmacy Direct and Indirect Remuneration ("DIR") fees-Yes

Question Submitted for the Record from Congressman Gus M. Bilirakis

1. CMS recently published their 700-page proposed rule for Medicare Part D for Calendar Year 2019. One component was their proposed implementation of the drug management program from at-risk beneficiaries from the Comprehensive Addiction Recovery Act of 2016. This drug management program, or "lock-in," is used in Medicaid program and in private insurance. Have you had a chance to review their regulations and what are your thoughts on CMS' proposed implementation? Are there improvements that need to be made either through regulation or statutory changes?

NCPA's Answer. We have reviewed the proposed Medicare Part D rule and the section implementing the drug management program. Our thoughts are the following:

NCPA would like to voice support for CMS' conservative and uniform approach to implement the Comprehensive Addiction and Recovery Act of 2016 provisions in Medicare Part D. NCPA supports the frequently abused drug definition and urges CMS to finalize the proposal to designate opioids, except buprenorphine for medication-assisted treatment {MAT) and injectables, as frequently abused drugs. We also strongly support that this rule supersedes current policy, and sponsors no longer be allowed to implement the current policy for non-opioid medications. This is crucial for consistency and smooth implementation of the drug management program.

NCPA supports the exemption of hospice, cancer, and LTC patients from drug management programs. We ask that in addition to these exempted individuals, CMS also exempt residents of any facility for which frequently abused drugs are dispensed for residents through a contract with a single pharmacy.

This could be accomplished utilizing the NCPDP Patient Residence Field. Our members who provide pharmacy services to those residing in long-term facilities provide services to assisted living facilities (ALFs) in a very similar, if not identical, fashion. This is due to the need ALFs have because many patients are being admitted who would most likely qualify for a LTC facility if it were not for cost- containment measures. To require a resident of an ALF to receive pharmacy services from a provider outside of normal ALF operations is not feasible and leads to disconnects in care.

We strongly support prescriber agreement to implement a pharmacy lock-in and that any notices sent from plan sponsors or PBMs be approved by the Secretary. NCPA feels it is vital that all notices sent to beneficiaries that are approved by the Secretary make very clear that any lock-in program applies only to frequently abused drugs. Our members are concerned that pharmacy lock-ins could be utilized to steer patients unknowingly to a pharmacy for all their drug needs, not just opioids. It is also vital that the notices don't just simply offer beneficiaries a plan sponsor/PBM created list of prescriber(s) and pharmacy(ies) from which to choose. The beneficiary must be able to write in their prescriber and pharmacy of choice and not be limited to a list provided by the plan sponsor/PBM. NCPA also supports CMS' proposal to allow the beneficiary to submit pharmacy preference at any time and asks that this be included in the final rule.

We agree with CMS that the additional reference to beneficiary preference in the context of reasonable access in CARA means that a beneficiary-allowable preference should prevail over a sponsor's/PBM's evaluation of geographic location, the beneficiary's predominant usage of a prescriber and/or pharmacy impact on cost-sharing and reasonable travel time.

Since preference only is to be considered by plans/PBMs when delegating prescriber/pharmacy for purposes of the Part D lock-in program, there must be protections in place for continual access. Our members have relayed to us that a very common scenario with lock-in programs is when the lock-in pharmacy is closed and the patient has no alternative to obtain their medication. In these instances, we have learned of unfortunate hospital admissions. NCPA therefore recommends that there be a back-up plan in place for a beneficiary to obtain medications when their lock-in pharmacy is closed.

The CARA Act provides that an "at-risk" patient may be "locked-in" to a pharmacy chain or group of pharmacies under common ownership and control. Also, if a PDP sponsor determines that a beneficiary's choice of pharmacy is determined to be a contributing factor in that beneficiary's "at-risk" status, the PDP sponsor may re-assign the beneficiary to another pharmacy. We feel strongly that if a PDP sponsor determines that a beneficiary's choice of pharmacy is contributing to his or her "at-risk" status and that pharmacy is part of a group of pharmacies under common ownership or control, the

PDP sponsor may not simply assign that beneficiary to another location of that pharmacy chain.

We urge CMS remain vigilant in ensuring appropriate patient access. We strongly recommend that CMS require plans/PBMs report percentage of times when beneficiary preference is/is not considered and to track which pharmacy the plan/PBM utilizes to override patient preference.

Greg Walden, Oregon
Chairman

Frank Pallone, Jr., New Jersey
Ranking Member
One Hundred Fifteenth Congress
Congress of the United States
House of Representatives
Committee on Energy and Commerce

January 8, 2018

Mr. David Mitchell
President and Founder
Patients for Affordable Drugs

Dear Mr. Mitchell:

Thank you for appearing before the Subcommittee on Health on December 13, 2017, to testify at the hearing entitled "Examining the Drug Supply Chain."

Pursuant to the Rules of the Committee on Energy and Commerce, the hearing record remains open for ten business days to permit Members to submit additional questions for the record, which are attached. The format of your responses to these questions should be as follows: (1) the name of the Member whose question you are addressing, (2) the complete text of the question you are addressing in bold, and (3) your answer to that question in plain text.

To facilitate the printing of the hearing record, please respond to these questions with a transmittal letter by the close of business on January 23, 2018. Thank you again for your time and effort preparing and delivering testimony before the Subcommittee.

Sincerely,

Michael C. Burgess, MD
Chairman, Subcommittee on Health

cc: The Honorable Gene Green, Ranking Member, Subcommittee on Health

The Honorable Earl L. "Buddy" Carter

Does your organization support increased transparency into the following aspects of the drug supply chain? Yes or No will suffice.

1. Rebate pass throughs Yes
2. PBM "Spread" Profits No
3. Generic Drug Reimbursement Methodologies I don't know what this means
4. True price for prescription drug at point of sale Yes
5. Pharmacy Direct and Indirect Remuneration ("DIR") fees. We support a clear and transparent payment system for pharmacies with no gag clauses or clawbacks.

The Honorable Frank Pallone Jr.

I. As we heard at the hearing, so many Members of this Committee have heard from family. friends, and constituents about their personal experiences with rising drug costs. I know I have heard concerns from constituents in my district about treatments and medications being priced out of their reach, leading them to make decisions about whether to fill their prescription in the first place, or whether to forego paying other bills in order to access the medication they need. One of the things that has struck me about the drug pricing conversation is that there are so many different problems happening in the market. For example, high drug prices no longer seem limited to just new blockbuster drugs, we have also seen the prices of some generic drugs rise rapidly.

a. Can you discuss briefly what you and other patients you work with have experienced when it comes to prescription drug prices in the last few years? We've heard from tens of thousands patients from all over the country. Heartbreaking stories of cutting pills in half, skipping doses, going without food, even declaring bankruptcy because of high drug prices. People are hurting. They are angry, and they don't understand how this could be happening to them in the United States of America.

b. In your opinion, what are some of the causes of rising drug prices? Is there a commonality into the circumstances around the different price increases that you have identified? The commonality is that drug companies set prices too high and raise prices without regard for patients or taxpayers. Drug companies get away with this behavior because the industry is given government granted monopolies. And they abuse that power by blocking competition to maintain monopolies far beyond what is intended under the Hatch-Waxman Act. PBMs skim off the top by executing billions of dollars in secret deals. Hospitals and doctors make more money when drug prices rise because they are often paid on a percentage of list price. The system is built to benefit the rich and powerful. The people who suffer under ever-rising prices are patients, consumers, taxpayers, and employers.

c. As this Committee examines potential policy solutions, what policy recommendations would you offer in regards to drug pricing that would offer patients greater relief from increased drug costs?

- Medicare should negotiate directly with corporations over the price of drugs.
- Patent law should be amended to outlaw pay-for-delay, product hopping, REMs abuses, and all other forms of manipulation that wrongfully extend patents and prevents generic competition to lower prices.
- PBMs should be required to conduct their business transparently.
- Drugs developed with taxpayer tunding should be priced so that US patients pay no more for those drugs than people in other developed countries.
- And Congress should require disclosure from drug corporations so patients, taxpayers, and policymakcrs understand how they set prices. For example: how much are drug companies spending on research and innovation? How much for marketing and advertising? How much for manufacturing and distribution?

2. Mr. Mitchell as you know the National Academies of Sciences, Engineering, and Medicine recommended in a recent report that policy makers work to increase financial transparency in the drug supply chain. The report recommends that Congress require insurers and manufacturers to disclose more information about pricing. In your testimony you note that your organization is supportive of increased transparency, and specitically the report's recommendation that PBMs provide quarterly disclosures at the national drug code level.

a. From the patient perspective, what information about the supply chain is publicly available to patients and what is not?

When drug prices rise, it is very hard for patients to find out why prices went up and who is responsible for the increase. That should change. Policy makers and taxpayers should have access to retail drug prices and the average rebated prices. Patients should know if they can pay less by paying cash. We should be able to understand who is making how much money-drug companies, PBMs, insurers, doctors and hospitals. That information is need in the interests of our national health expenditures, and lawmakers need it to make informed decisions about how to set policy.

b. Why do you think that sort of disclosure by PB Ms is the right approach0

Markets work best with information, Patients, consumers, and potential market disruptors cannot make informed choices without information. We need transparency around drug rebates and other charges, how much PBMs keep, how much goes to insurers, and if any money reaches patients and consumers in the form of lower prices or lower premium.

c. Is there other information you think is important for other members of the supply chain to disclose and why do you believe this is beneficial for patients?

Clear disclosure of prices and choices should be made to patients. They should know, for example, if they can pay less by paying cash versus using their insurance.

The Honorable Diana DeGette

1. We understand that your organization collects stories from all over the country about how high drug prices are affecting patients. How often do you hear from patients experiencing a heavy burden due to the cost of their insulin?

A very large percentage of the stories we receive come from insulin users-we estimate around 15 percent. This issue touches Americans of every state, race, religion, job status, and political party. Taking insulin is not a choice- it is a matter of life and death for thousands of Americans across the country.

2. Are there any common themes in patient stories about insulin that Congress should be aware of?

Patients often express frustration. Like me, they do not understand how the price of insulin has risen so dramatically for a drug invented in the 1920s under a patent sold for $3. Patients often mention struggling to afford not only insulin, but all of the other supplies needed. They fear losing insurance and being unable to purchase this drug that is essential for them to live.

3. Have you heard from many patients about their experiences with patient assistance programs (PAPs) run by pharmaceutical companies? Please identify any common themes that you think Congress should be aware of and explain in the context of insulin to the extent that it's possible.

Common comments include:

"[don't qualify for assistance"
"Assistance program funding comes and goes and is unreliable"
"I live in fear that assistance programs will not be there"

Patients should not have to rely on these programs which are not charity but rather are marketing programs of the drug companies. It is estimated that drug companies make as much as $21 million for every one million invested in so-called assistance programs. Insulin should be affordable without patient reliance on company-controlled funding.

4. Options to appeal health plan determinations are often available to patients who are not able to access the specific type of insulin they need. Have you heard from patients who have made appeals to health plans in an effort to get a specific drug? Please describe their experiences and any common themes that you think Congress should be aware of.

Patient appeals can be made. But they too often take too long to be resolved, and insurance plan "rules" often trump patient and physician judgement. It is simple: When a patient and his or her physician report that a given product is not performing for the patient for any reason-outcomes or side-effects-the patient must be able to receive the alternative product.

In: U.S. Drug Supply, Investigational Drugs …
Editor: Emil R. Berg
ISBN: 978-1-53617-442-7

Chapter 2

INVESTIGATIONAL DRUGS: FDA AND DRUG MANUFACTURERS HAVE ONGOING EFFORTS TO FACILITATE ACCESS FOR SOME PATIENTS*

United States Government Accountability Office

ABBREVIATIONS

Federal RTT Act	federal Right to Try Act
FDA	Food and Drug Administration
FDARA	Food and Drug Administration Reauthorization Act of 2017
HBV	hepatitis B virus
HCV	hepatitis C virus
HIV	human immunodeficiency virus
IND	investigational new drug application
IRB	institutional review board

WHY GAO DID THIS STUDY

When investigational drugs show promise for treating serious or life- threatening diseases, patients are often interested in obtaining access to them. Congress included a

* This is an edited, reformatted and augmented version of United States Government Accountability Office; Report to Congressional Requesters, Publication No. GAO-19-630, dated September 2019.

provision in the FDA Reauthorization Act of 2017 for GAO to review actions taken to facilitate access to these drugs.

This chapter describes (1) actions FDA and drug manufacturers have taken to broaden eligibility criteria for clinical trials, (2) actions FDA has taken to facilitate access to investigational drugs outside of clinical trials, and (3) information drug manufacturers have communicated to patients and physicians about access to investigational drugs outside of clinical trials.

GAO reviewed laws, regulations, FDA documents, and manufacturer policies and interviewed FDA officials and a non- generalizable selection of 10 manufacturers and 14 other stakeholders (including patient advocacy and physician organizations). The manufacturers were developing drugs to treat serious or life-threatening diseases, and were selected for variation in company size. GAO also reviewed information that a non-generalizable selection of 29 manufacturers communicated through their websites about access to investigational drugs outside of clinical trials. GAO selected manufacturers for variation in the type of serious diseases their investigational drugs were intended to treat, company size, and other factors.

HHS provided technical comments on a draft of this chapter, which GAO incorporated as appropriate.

What GAO Found

Individuals may access investigational drugs—those not yet approved for marketing in the United States by the Food and Drug Administration (FDA)—by participating in clinical trials conducted by drug manufacturers to test drug effectiveness and safety. FDA has ongoing efforts to help manufacturers identify the circumstances under which they could broaden clinical trial eligibility criteria to include patients who are commonly excluded, such as pediatric patients and patients with impaired liver and kidney function, without compromising study results.

- FDA issued guidance in March 2019 with recommendations on ways manufacturers could broaden eligibility criteria for cancer clinical trials, when clinically appropriate. In June 2019, FDA issued related guidance that applies to a wider range of clinical trials beyond cancer trials.
- One of the 10 manufacturers GAO interviewed reported broadening its eligibility criteria to include more patients, such as those with HIV. Another manufacturer has begun reviewing its eligibility criteria and expects to include adolescents, as appropriate, in future studies—a population that has generally been excluded from trials. However, these and two other manufacturers cited challenges in these efforts. One stated that expanding participation to patients who use other

medications, for example, could adversely affect a study's ability to identify the effects of the studied drug.

Outside of clinical trials, patients with certain medical conditions, who are unable to enroll in a clinical trial, and have no other comparable medical options, may request to obtain access to investigational drugs. This can occur under FDA's expanded access program, or through a 2018 federal law known as "Right to Try." Under either pathway, a patient can only access the investigational drug if its manufacturer agrees to the request. FDA has taken steps to facilitate access to investigational drugs outside of clinical trials, and most manufacturers in GAO's review communicated information to patients and physicians through their websites about how to access their investigational drugs outside of clinical trials. For example:

- Since 2017, FDA took steps to simplify its expanded access program to make it easier to participate. In addition, to address concerns raised by manufacturers, FDA clarified guidance on how it would review data resulting from the program. Seven of the 10 manufacturers GAO interviewed viewed the guidance as an improvement.
- GAO's review of information communicated by 29 manufacturers on their websites found that 23 had policies about accessing investigational drugs outside of clinical trials. At the time of GAO's review, 19 of the 23 stated they would consider individual requests for access, while the other four stated they would not. More than half of the manufacturers stated that if they approve a request, they require additional steps, such as FDA review of the request.

September 9, 2019

The Honorable Lamar Alexander
Chairman

The Honorable Patty Murray
Ranking Member
Committee on Health, Education, Labor, and Pensions
United States Senate

The Honorable Frank Pallone, Jr. Chairman

The Honorable Greg Walden
Republican Leader
Committee on Energy and Commerce
House of Representatives

Before drugs or biologics are approved for marketing in the United States by the Food and Drug Administration (FDA), they are considered investigational.[1] As part of the drug development process, these investigational drugs are tested for safety and effectiveness on humans in clinical trials. When investigational drugs show promise for treating serious or life-threatening diseases or conditions such as metastatic cancer, patients and physicians are often interested in obtaining access to them before they are approved.[2] While some patients may obtain access to these drugs by participating in clinical trials, not all patients are able to participate—for example, because they do not meet the eligibility criteria that manufacturers have established for enrolling in a study.[3] Questions have been raised in recent years about whether clinical trial eligibility criteria are too narrow and exclude patients who are likely to be treated once a drug is approved, and FDA has historically provided guidance to manufacturers to help them consider the circumstances under which they could broaden these criteria without compromising study results or raising ethical issues.[4]

Outside of clinical trials, patients who are unable to participate in the trials, and who have certain medical conditions, such as life-threatening conditions, and no comparable medical options, can seek access to investigational drugs through two pathways: 1) FDA's expanded access program and 2) the federal Right to Try Act (federal RTT Act).[5] Under either of these two pathways, access to the investigational drug can only occur if the drug manufacturer agrees to provide access.

---

[1] See 21 C.F.R. § 312.3 (2018). Drugs are defined to include, among other things, articles intended for use in the diagnosis, cure, mitigation, treatment, or prevention of disease, and include components of those articles. See 21 U.S.C. §§ 321(g)(1)(B),(D). Biologic products (referred to as biologics in this chapter) are materials, such as viruses, therapeutic sera, toxins, antitoxins, vaccines, or analogous products to prevent, treat, or cure human diseases or injuries. See 21 C.F.R. § 600.3(h) (2018). In general, biologics are derived from living sources, such as humans, animals, and microorganisms. For the purpose of this chapter, we refer to drugs and biologics collectively as "drugs."

[2] A disease is characterized by specific signs and symptoms (e.g., Alzheimer's disease) whereas a condition is an unhealthy state (e.g., chronic pain).

[3] Eligibility criteria define the patient population to be studied in a clinical trial. Inclusion criteria specify the characteristics required for participation, such as the stage of a disease. Exclusion criteria specify the characteristics that disqualify patients from participation, such as the presence of comorbidities or being too young or too old.

[4] For example, FDA has issued guidance documents with recommendations to include patient populations in clinical trials that have been typically excluded from participation, such as elderly patients and pregnant women. See Food and Drug Administration, *Guideline for the Study of Drugs Likely to be Used in the Elderly* (Rockville, Md.: November 1989) and *Pregnant Women: Scientific and Ethical Considerations for Inclusion in Clinical Trials Draft Guidance for Industry* (Silver Spring, Md.: April 2018).

[5] See Food and Drug Administration Modernization Act of 1997, Pub. L. No. 105-115, § 402, 111 Stat. 2296, 2365 (authorizing expanded access) (codified as amended at 21 U.S.C. § 360bbb); Trickett Wendler, Frank Mongiello, Jordan McLinn, and Matthew Bellina Right to Try Act of 2017, Pub. L. No. 115-176, 132 Stat. 1372 (2018) (codified at 21 U.S.C. § 360bbb-0a).

Requests to obtain access to investigational drugs through FDA's expanded access program must be reviewed by both FDA and an institutional review board (IRB) in addition to being agreed upon by the drug manufacturer.[6] Some stakeholders—including physician and patient advocacy groups—have criticized FDA's program for being too complex and burdensome to entities involved, which they contend could pose a barrier to individual patients' access to these drugs. However, others argue that FDA is not a barrier because it allows most requests for expanded access to proceed and because factors beyond FDA's program—such as a manufacturer's approval—prevent patients from obtaining access. In 2017, we found that FDA allowed 99 percent of the requests under its expanded access program to proceed. We also found that the agency and other stakeholders had taken steps to simplify and improve the expanded access process.[7] For example, FDA shortened the form required for individual patient requests, and it partnered with the Reagan-Udall Foundation to develop a website—referred to as the Expanded Access Navigator—to help physicians and patients locate drug manufacturers' expanded access policies.[8]

The other pathway for obtaining investigational drugs outside of clinical trials—the federal RTT Act—was established by law in May 2018. This provided another pathway for individuals with life-threatening diseases or conditions to seek access to investigational drugs without a requirement for FDA or IRB involvement.[9] Some stakeholders, including some physicians and medical ethicists, have questioned whether patient safety could be compromised by allowing access to investigational drugs without

---

[6] FDA determines whether to allow expanded access requests to proceed, after which an IRB must approve patients' expanded access treatment plans.
An IRB is any board, committee, or other group formally designated by an institution to review, approve the initiation of, and conduct periodic review of biomedical research involving human subjects. The primary responsibility of an IRB is to ensure protections for human volunteers in clinical trials and that informed consent will be obtained.

[7] GAO, *Investigational New Drugs: FDA Has Taken Steps to Improve the Expanded Access Program but Should Further Clarify How Adverse Events Data Are Used*, GAO-17-564 (Washington, D.C.: July 11, 2017).

[8] The Reagan-Udall Foundation is a non-profit organization that was established by Congress to assist FDA. See 21 U.S.C. § 379dd. The Expanded Access Navigator was launched in July 2017. See Reagan-Udall Foundation, *Expanded Access Navigator*, accessed May 28, 2019, http://navigator.reaganudall.org/. This website complemented a provision in the 21st Century Cures Act that required certain manufacturers to make their expanded access policies publicly available. Pub. L. No. 114-255, § 3032, 130 Stat. 1033, 1100 (2016) (codified as amended at 21 U.S.C. § 360bbb-0). Under this requirement, as amended by the FDA Reauthorization Act of 2017, manufacturers must make their policies publicly available, such as by posting them on a publicly available internet website, beginning on the earlier of (a) the initiation of a phase II or phase III study for a drug or (b) as applicable, 15 days after the drug receives a designation as a breakthrough therapy, fast track product, or regenerative advanced therapy. 21 U.S.C. § 360bbb-0(f) (as amended by Pub. L. No. 115-52, § 610(c), 131 Stat. 1005, 1053).

[9] A number of states have enacted related legislation, referred to as Right-to-Try laws, placing limitations under state law on liability and licensing actions against individuals or entities involved in the care of individuals seeking access to drugs that have successfully completed phase I clinical trials and met other conditions. By May 2018, 40 states had enacted such laws. See National Conference of State Legislatures, "*Right to Try" Experimental Prescription Medicines State Laws and Legislation for 2014–2018*, accessed June 13, 2019, http://www.ncsl.org/research/health/state-laws-and-legislation-related-to-biologic-medications-and-substitution-of-biosimilars.aspx#Right_to_Try.

FDA and IRB review and whether the new pathway will improve access for patients because it does not compel manufacturers to allow access to their investigational drugs.

The FDA Reauthorization Act of 2017 (FDARA) included a provision for us to describe actions taken by FDA and drug manufacturers to facilitate individual access to investigational drugs.[10] This chapter examines

1. actions FDA and drug manufacturers have taken to broaden patient eligibility criteria for clinical trials,
2. actions FDA has taken to help facilitate access to investigational drugs outside of clinical trials, and
3. information drug manufacturers have communicated to patients and physicians about access to their investigational drugs outside of clinical trials.

To describe what actions FDA and drug manufacturers have taken to broaden patient eligibility criteria for clinical trials, we reviewed FDA guidance, reports and other related documents and interviewed knowledgeable FDA officials about the agency's ongoing or planned actions on this topic. We also analyzed information collected through interviews with, or written responses to, questions from a non- generalizable selection of 10 drug manufacturers about any ongoing or planned actions they had to broaden the eligibility criteria for their clinical trials, challenges associated with broader criteria, and other efforts to increase participation in clinical trials. We selected the drug manufacturers to achieve variation in company size and because they were developing drugs or biologics to treat serious or life-threatening diseases or conditions.

To describe what actions FDA has taken to help facilitate access to investigational drugs outside of clinical trials, we reviewed laws, FDA regulations and guidance, and FDA's website and other related documents about FDA's expanded access program and the federal RTT pathway. We also interviewed knowledgeable FDA officials about the agency's ongoing and planned actions related to this topic and a non-generalizable selection of 24 stakeholder organizations to obtain their views on FDA's actions. The organizations included the 10 selected manufacturers noted above; three trade groups representing manufacturers; three patient advocacy organizations; two physician organizations; two public policy research organizations; two organizations that work with manufacturers to facilitate access outside of clinical trials; one organization focused on improving access to investigational drugs through clinical trials; and one physician representing a research organization.

---

[10] Pub. L. No. 115-52, § 610(a)(2), 131 Stat. 1052.

We selected patient advocacy and physician organizations that broadly represented the views of patients and physicians, including those stating they have experience in seeking access to investigational drugs outside of clinical trials. In addition, we selected organizations to provide a range of perspectives regarding FDA's expanded access program and the federal RTT pathway.

To describe what information drug manufacturers have communicated to patients and physicians about access to their investigational drugs outside of clinical trials, we reviewed the websites of a non-generalizable selection of 29 drug manufacturers.[11] We first selected 21 drug manufacturers that were developing investigational drugs or biologics intended to treat 10 serious diseases to achieve variation across several factors.[12] These factors included company size, participation in the Expanded Access Navigator, and whether the manufacturer had an investigational drug or biologic that FDA designated as a breakthrough therapy, fast track product, or regenerative medicine advanced therapy in fiscal year 2018.[13] Two of these 21 manufacturers were among the 10 we interviewed. In addition, we reviewed the websites of the other eight drug manufacturers we interviewed. We conducted our review of manufacturer websites between January 31, 2019, and March 12, 2019, by using a data collection instrument that included a standard set of questions for collecting information on the availability of information, procedures for making a request for access to investigational drugs, and the factors that the manufacturer would consider in evaluating requests. For manufacturers that we determined had not communicated information on their websites about access to investigational drugs at the time of our review, we contacted them to verify this. To supplement our analysis, we reviewed additional information that manufacturers communicated on their websites, such as whether they provided information about access to specific investigational drugs.

We conducted this performance audit from August 2018 to September 2019 in accordance with generally accepted government auditing standards. Those standards require that we plan and perform the audit to obtain sufficient, appropriate evidence to provide a reasonable basis for our findings and conclusions based on our audit objectives. We believe that the evidence obtained provides a reasonable basis for our findings and conclusions based on our audit objectives.

---

[11] Manufacturers are required to make such information "public and readily available, such as by posting such policies on a publicly available Internet website." 21 U.S.C. § 360bbb-0(b).

[12] We selected the following 10 serious diseases: Duchenne muscular dystrophy, Alzheimer's disease, pancreatic cancer, metastatic breast cancer, acute myeloid leukemia, human immunodeficiency virus (HIV) infection, schizophrenia, cystic fibrosis, hemophilia type a or b, and chronic heart failure. We selected these 10 diseases because they are generally recognized as serious and reflect a range of types of diseases (e.g., neurological, viral, psychiatric, cancer).

[13] Manufacturers voluntarily participate in the Expanded Access Navigator by providing links to their expanded access policies posted on their websites. Breakthrough therapy, fast track product, and regenerative medicine advanced therapy designations are used by FDA to expedite the development and review of certain drugs and biologics intended to treat conditions that are generally considered serious.

Background

Clinical Trials

When patients are seeking access to investigational drugs, their first option is to consider whether they can obtain them through participation in a clinical trial. Clinical trials are a step in the drug development process through which a drug manufacturer assesses the safety and effectiveness of its investigational drug through human testing. A clinical trial can take place in a variety of settings (e.g., research hospitals, universities, and community clinics) and geographic locations, and is led by a principal investigator that is typically a physician.

Manufacturers establish clinical trial eligibility criteria to define the patient population to be studied, and only patients who meet those criteria can participate. These criteria can vary depending on the drug being studied and its intended use. Patient eligibility criteria consist of both inclusion and exclusion criteria. Inclusion criteria specify the characteristics of the patient that are required for participation, such as the stage or characteristics of a disease, and typically identify a patient population in which it is expected that the manufacturer can demonstrate the effect of an investigational drug. In comparison, exclusion criteria specify the characteristics that disqualify patients from clinical trial participation and can include factors that could mask the effect of an investigational drug, such as the presence of comorbidities or simultaneous use of other drugs.[14] Certain patient populations, such as children and pregnant women, may also be excluded from clinical trial participation because of ethical reasons.[15]

Drug manufacturers, FDA, and IRBs each have responsibilities as part of the clinical trial process. In order to test an investigational drug on human volunteers in clinical trials, a manufacturer must first submit an investigational new drug application (IND) to FDA. FDA is responsible for reviewing the IND, which includes various components such as the clinical trial protocol that describes the patient eligibility criteria, the medications and dosages to be studied, and other details. In turn, an IRB is responsible for reviewing and approving the clinical trial protocol as well as reviewing the informed consent form for the study.[16] In general, clinical trials that involve human volunteers can begin after FDA has reviewed and allowed the IND to proceed and the IRB has given its approval.

---

[14] A comorbidity is a medical condition beyond the condition an investigational drug is intended to treat.

[15] For example, pregnant women have been excluded because of concerns about the potential for injury to the fetus.

[16] Many institutions (such as research hospitals) have their own IRB to oversee human subjects research conducted within the institution or by the staff of the institution—these are commonly referred to as local IRBs. A physician who does not have access to a local IRB typically uses an independent IRB, which is not associated with any institution.

An investigational drug typically goes through three phases of clinical trials before an application is submitted to FDA for marketing approval.[17] At any point during the clinical trials, FDA could issue a clinical hold on the existing IND that would delay the proposed clinical trials or suspend the ongoing clinical trials. When a proposed or ongoing study is placed on a complete clinical hold, the investigational drug cannot be administered to any human volunteers.[18] Traditionally, the three clinical trial phases are the following:

- Phase I: This clinical trial phase generally tests the safety of the drug on about 20 to 80 healthy volunteers. The goal of this phase is to determine the drug's most frequent side effects and how it is metabolized and excreted. If the drug does not show unacceptable toxicity in the phase I clinical trials, it may move on to phase II.
- Phase II: This clinical trial phase assesses the drug's safety and effectiveness on people who have a certain disease or condition, and typically the assessment is conducted on a few dozen to hundreds of volunteers. Generally, during this phase some volunteers receive the drug and others receive a control, such as a placebo. If there is evidence that the drug is effective in the phase II clinical trials, it may move on to phase III.
- Phase III: This clinical trial phase generally involves several hundreds to thousands of volunteers who have a certain disease or condition and gathers more information about the drug's safety and effectiveness, again while being compared to a control.

If phase III clinical trials are successfully completed, the drug may move on to FDA's review and approval process. When seeking FDA's approval to market a drug in the United States, the manufacturer submits an application to FDA that includes the data from the safety and efficacy clinical trials for FDA to review.[19] Safety data include clinical trial results about a drug's toxicity (e.g., the highest tolerable dose) and adverse events that may result from exposure to the drug. Efficacy data include information on

[17] According to FDA officials, in some cases when a new drug is being tested for a life- threatening condition, the drug development process may be expedited by going through only one or two phases of clinical trials before an application is submitted to FDA for marketing approval. In addition, postmarket studies are required for some drugs that FDA has approved for marketing.

[18] See 21 C.F.R. § 312.42 (2018). A clinical hold may be either a complete clinical hold or a partial clinical hold. Reasons for imposing complete clinical holds can include human volunteers being subject to unreasonable and significant risks of illness or injury from the drug. According to FDA officials, the agency may also place a drug on a partial clinical hold during which the drug cannot be administered to certain types of patients. See Food and Drug Administration, *Guidance for Industry: Submitting and Reviewing Complete Responses to Clinical Holds* (Rockville, Md.: October 2000).

[19] When seeking approval for marketing of a new drug in the United States, the manufacturer submits to FDA a new drug application. See 21 C.F.R. § 314.50 (2018). When seeking approval for marketing of a new biologic in the United States, the manufacturer submits to FDA a biologics license application. See 21 C.F.R. § 601.2 (2018).

whether the drug demonstrated a health benefit over a placebo. FDA reviews the information in the application to either approve or not approve the drug.

FDA's Expanded Access Program

If a patient seeking access to an investigational drug is not able to participate in the drug's clinical trial (e.g., because of the study's eligibility criteria or geographic location), another pathway to potentially obtain access to the drug outside of a clinical trial is through FDA's expanded access program. Under the program, a licensed physician can submit a request for access to an investigational drug for treatment use on behalf of a patient and may do so during or after phase I, II, or III of clinical trials. To allow access to an investigational drug under the program, FDA must determine that a patient has a serious or immediately life-threatening disease or condition and has no other comparable medical options, among other criteria.[20]

FDA's goals for the program are to facilitate the availability of investigational drugs when appropriate, ensure patient safety, and preserve the clinical trial development process.[21] FDA is responsible for determining whether to allow individual requests to proceed to treatment once the manufacturer has agreed to provide access.[22] If FDA allows the request to proceed, an IRB must approve the clinical treatment plan that is submitted as part of the individual request and review the informed consent form.[23] The licensed physician treating a patient under expanded access would be required to report to FDA any unexpected serious adverse reactions that occur during treatment for which there is a reasonable possibility that the drug caused the reaction.[24]

The Federal RTT Act

In 2018 the federal RTT Act established another pathway through which patients may potentially obtain access to investigational drugs outside of clinical trials. To be eligible under the law, a patient must have been diagnosed with a life-threatening disease or condition, have exhausted approved treatment options, and be unable to participate in a clinical trial involving the investigational drug.[25] Obtaining access to investigational

---

[20] See 21 C.F.R. § 312.305(a) (2018).

[21] FDA's expanded access program includes options through which requests can be submitted for individual patients or for groups of patients. This chapter focuses on individual patient requests. For more information about the broader expanded access program, see GAO-17-564.

[22] For individual requests, physicians can submit FDA Form 3926 (the Individual Patient Expanded Access Investigational New Drug Application) or FDA Form 1571 (the Investigational New Drug Application).

[23] See 21 C.F.R. § 312.305(c)(4) (2018).

[24] See 21 C.F.R. § 312.32(c) (2018).

[25] Pub. L. No. 115-176, § 2(a), 132 Stat. 1372 (codified in pertinent part to 21 U.S.C. § 360bbb-0a(a)(1)).

drugs through the federal RTT Act primarily requires the involvement of the manufacturer and treating physician. Similar to FDA's expanded access program, treatment can only proceed if the drug manufacturer allows the patient access to its drug. Under the federal RTT Act, the manufacturer is responsible for providing to FDA an annual summary of any use of its drugs under this pathway that includes information on any known serious adverse events.[26] The treating physician is responsible for requesting access to the investigational drug for the patient and for obtaining written informed consent from or on behalf of the patient if the manufacturer agrees to provide access. Eligibility of an investigational drug for patient use through this pathway is based on certain criteria, including that the drug has completed phase I clinical trials, the manufacturer has not discontinued clinical development of the drug, and the drug has not been placed on a clinical hold.[27] Unlike FDA's expanded access program, the federal RTT Act does not require the FDA or an IRB to review individual requests for access.

Figure 1 shows a summary of the three pathways through which patients may obtain access to investigational drugs.

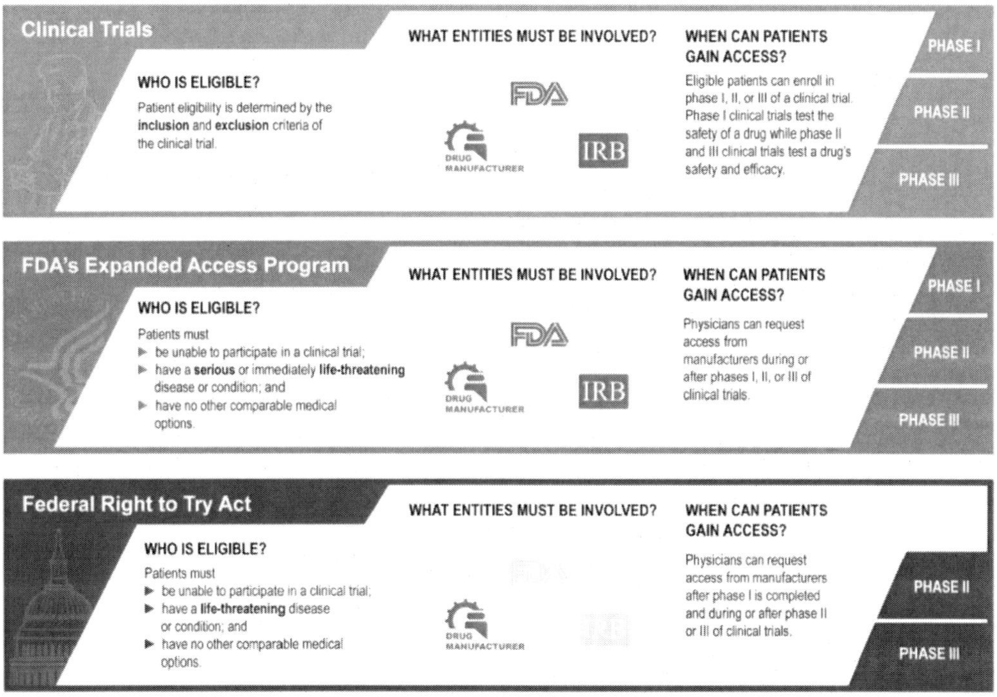

FDA= Food and Drug Administration. IRB = institutional review board.
Source: GAO analysis of FDA information. | GAO-19-630

Figure 1. Access to Investigational Drugs through Three Pathways.

[26] FDA is also responsible for posting an annual summary report on the use of investigational drugs through the RTT pathway on its website.

[27] See Pub. L. No. 115-176, § 2(a),132 Stat. 1372 (codified in pertinent part to 21 U.S.C. § 360bbb-0a(a)(2)).

FDA Issued Guidance to Help Manufacturers Broaden Clinical Trial Eligibility Criteria and Two Manufacturers We Interviewed Took Steps to Broaden Their Criteria

Some patients, such as those with compromised liver and kidney function, have traditionally been excluded from clinical trials. FDA has ongoing efforts to help drug manufacturers identify the circumstances under which they could broaden their eligibility criteria to include such patients without compromising study results. These efforts include issuing recent guidance with recommendations for including certain patients in clinical trials for cancer drugs. Officials from one of the 10 drug manufacturers we interviewed told us they had broadened their eligibility criteria and another one was taking steps to do so, but these officials and others noted challenges to broadening eligibility criteria.

FDA Public Workshop on Broadening Eligibility Criteria

In April 2018, FDA held a public workshop with stakeholders—including drug manufacturers, patient advocacy groups, and government agencies—to discuss ways drug manufacturers and other investigators could safely broaden eligibility criteria for clinical trials and to inform FDA guidance on this topic. In July 2018 FDA publicly released a report summarizing the workshop, in accordance with FDARA.[28] According to the report, stakeholders at the meeting emphasized the importance of broadening clinical trial eligibility, when appropriate, to include more patients who will likely use the drug if it is approved. Stakeholders recommended that investigators ensure that the eligibility criteria for each of their clinical trials are scientifically justifiable, rather than, for example, "copying and pasting" a narrow set of criteria from a prior study without considering if the exclusions are valid for scientific reasons. According to the report, this practice can unnecessarily limit eligibility for certain patients. While stakeholders commented that assessing whether eligibility criteria are scientifically justifiable may require additional time and resources, they emphasized it could lead to the removal of unnecessarily restrictive eligibility criteria and thereby increase participation among patient populations that have been typically excluded from clinical trials, such as pediatric patients and patients with compromised liver and kidney function.

[28] FDARA required that FDA, in coordination with other stakeholders, convene a public meeting to discuss clinical trial inclusion and exclusion criteria and make a report on the topics discussed at the meeting available on FDA's website. See Pub. L. No. 115-52, § 610(a)(1), 131 Stat. 1051 (codified at 21 U.S.C. § 360bbb note). See Food and Drug Administration, *Public Workshop: Evaluating Inclusion and Exclusion Criteria in Clinical Trials* (Silver Spring, Md.: August 2018).

FDA Guidance on Eligibility Criteria

In March 2019, FDA issued four new draft guidance documents and finalized one guidance document with recommendations for drug manufacturers to broaden clinical trial eligibility criteria for drugs that treat cancer. The guidance recommends that manufacturers include certain patient populations that have typically been excluded from participation.[29] The patient populations are adolescents; pediatrics (children and adolescents); patients with human immunodeficiency virus (HIV), hepatitis B virus (HBV), or hepatitis C virus (HCV) infections; patients with brain metastases (i.e., cancer that has spread to the brain); and patients with compromised kidney, heart, or liver function, or who have a history of (or concurrent) cancer. According to FDA, the guidance documents are intended to help drug manufacturers and other investigators broaden cancer trial eligibility criteria. This will help improve patient access to investigational drugs and ensure that the results from the clinical trials are generalizable to patients likely to use the drugs once they are approved. In addition, FDA officials have noted that including broader patient populations in clinical trials can lead to new information in a drug's labeling, which will help communicate the safe and effective use of these drugs. Table 1 provides a summary of each of the five guidance documents.

In June 2019, FDA issued draft guidance for manufacturers on broadening clinical trial eligibility criteria, in accordance with FDARA.[30] The guidance applies to a wider range of clinical trials beyond cancer trials and includes recommendations to broaden eligibility criteria and considerations for the use of clinical trial designs and other methodologies to help facilitate patient participation.[31] For example, FDA recommends that manufacturers examine each exclusion criterion to determine if it is needed to help assure the safety of trial participants or to achieve the study's objectives. If not, the manufacturer should consider eliminating or modifying the criterion to expand the study population as well as tailoring the exclusion criteria as narrowly as possible to avoid unnecessary restrictions to the study population.

---

[29] See Food and Drug Administration, *Considerations for the Inclusion of Adolescent Patients in Adult Oncology Clinical Trials, Guidance for Industry; Cancer Clinical Trial Eligibility Criteria: Minimum Age for Pediatric Patients, Draft Guidance for Industry; Cancer Clinical Trial Eligibility Criteria: Patients with HIV, Hepatitis B Virus, or Hepatitis C Virus Infections, Draft Guidance for Industry*; *Cancer Clinical Trial Eligibility Criteria: Brain Metastases, Draft Guidance for Industry; Cancer Clinical Trial Eligibility Criteria: Patients with Organ Dysfunction or Prior or Concurrent Malignancies, Draft Guidance for Industry* (Silver Spring, Md.: March 2019). FDA's guidance on the inclusion of adolescent patients in cancer clinical trials is final guidance and its guidance on the inclusion of the other four patient populations is draft guidance. Guidance documents represent FDA's current thinking on a topic. Neither draft nor final guidance documents legally bind FDA or confer legal rights on affected individuals. See 21 C.F.R. § 10.115 (2018). According to FDA, this guidance is intended to assist stakeholders who are responsible for the development and oversight of clinical trials.

[30] See Pub. L. No. 115-52, § 610(a)(3), 131 Stat. 1052 (codified at 21 U.S.C. § 360bbb note). Food and Drug Administration, *Enhancing the Diversity of Clinical Trial Populations—Eligibility Criteria, Enrollment Practices, and Trial Designs, Draft Guidance for Industry* (Silver Spring, Md.: June 2019).

[31] The draft guidance applies to both demographic populations (e.g., sex, race, age) and non-demographic populations (e.g., patients with organ dysfunction, comorbidities).

Table 1. Summary of the Food and Drug Administration's (FDA) Guidance on Including Certain Patients in Cancer Clinical Trials, March 2019

Patient population	Summary
Pediatric patients	FDA recommends that drug manufacturers consider including pediatric patients in adult cancer trials, in part, to prevent delays in the development of and access to potentially effective new cancer drugs for this population. For example, FDA specifies that children aged 2 to 11 should be considered for inclusion. The guidance recommends that they should be considered for inclusion when there is evidence from adult studies demonstrating that children will likely respond to a drug in a way similar to adults, and when there are no concerns about the potential for toxicity related to severe effects on growth and development.
Adolescent patients	FDA recommends that drug manufacturers consider including adolescents aged 12 to 17 in adult cancer clinical trials, in part, because some cancers found in adolescent patients are similar in biology to those found in adults. For example, the guidance recommends that adolescents should be considered for inclusion in early phase cancer clinical trials if they have cancers that have relapsed and after some initial evidence from adult studies is obtained about a drug's toxicity and effect on the body (e.g., how it is absorbed).
Patients with human immunodeficiency virus (HIV), hepatitis B virus (HBV), or hepatitis C virus (HCV) infections	FDA recommends that drug manufacturers consider including patients with HIV, HBV, and HCV infections in cancer trials, in part, because HIV and HBV infections can be chronically managed, and HCV infections can be cured with certain anti-viral drugs. For example, the guidance recommends that eligibility criteria for patients with cancer and concurrent HIV infection should focus on patients' immune system functioning and use of drugs to treat HIV. To illustrate, the guidance recommends that patients with a history of certain AIDS-defining infections should be eligible if they have not had the infection within the past 12 months.
Patients with cancer spread to the brain	FDA recommends that drug manufacturers consider including patients with cancers that have spread to the brain in cancer trials, in part, because there is an increasing incidence of patients living with cancers that commonly spread to the brain (e.g., breast and lung cancer). For example, the guidance recommends that patients who have active cancer that has spread to the brain be included in cancer trials, as long as the treating physician has determined that the patient does not require immediate treatment for their central nervous system disease.
Patients with compromised organ function	FDA recommends that drug manufacturers consider including patients with compromised kidney, heart, and liver function in cancer trials, in part, because there is an increasing number of such patients given the increasing life expectancy in the general population. For example, the guidance recommends that as data on a drug's toxicity and other effects on the body (e.g., how it is absorbed) become available during drug development, eligibility criteria should be revised to include patients with compromised organ function where safe parameters regarding dosage adjustments have been determined.

Source: GAO summary of FDA documents. | GAO-19-630

Note: FDA's guidance on the inclusion of adolescent patients in cancer clinical trials is final guidance and its guidance for the other patient populations is draft guidance.

Two Manufacturers' Efforts to Broaden Eligibility Criteria

Officials from one of the 10 drug manufacturers we interviewed told us they broadened their clinical trial eligibility criteria and another manufacturer we interviewed reported that it was taking steps to do so. These two manufacturers told us they were taking these steps in part because both believe it will facilitate the drug approval process.[32] Officials from one manufacturer stated that they broadened their eligibility criteria by removing exclusions after determining they were not critical to clinical trial designs, including exclusions related to liver function, infections (e.g., HIV), and the use of other medications (e.g., steroids). The officials explained that, since 2015, they have systematically evaluated their eligibility criteria to ensure that they do not unnecessarily exclude patient populations from their clinical trials. Officials from the second manufacturer told us they have begun evaluating whether to remove certain exclusion criteria that they typically use in clinical trials, and added that their efforts are partially in response to FDA's 2018 public workshop report, as described above. For example, the manufacturer is reviewing its exclusion of adolescents in prior clinical trials and officials told us they will likely include adolescents in an upcoming study if they determine that patient safety would not be compromised.

Officials from both manufacturers stated that broader eligibility criteria will allow more patients to access investigational drugs through clinical trial participation. It can also, officials said, help them obtain FDA approval for a drug that extends to a wider range of patients, if the drug is found to be safe and effective. Further, officials from one of the two manufacturers noted that broader eligibility criteria, such as criteria that include patients with infections, could help streamline the process for conducting clinical trials—for example, by eliminating the need to conduct clinical testing to screen for the presence of infections.

Although most drug manufacturers in our review did not report efforts to broaden their eligibility criteria, many noted efforts to address other barriers to clinical trial participation. For example, to address geographic barriers, officials from six of the 10 manufacturers told us they help cover costs for patients to travel to clinical trial sites, such as by reimbursing transportation and hotel costs for patients who travel long distances.[33] In addition, officials from one manufacturer said they completed a pilot clinical trial on diabetes in 2019 that used decentralized trial locations in three states, such as retail health clinics and patients' homes, to help patients overcome challenges with obtaining transportation to trial sites. Similarly, within the next 2 years, another manufacturer is planning to conduct a pilot clinical trial that is fully remote and expects the design to improve patient participation in rural communities.

---

[32] One manufacturer developing drugs to treat rare diseases stated that because of the small number of patients with such diseases, its eligibility criteria are sufficiently broad in order to recruit a large enough sample for a study.

[33] According to FDA guidance, reimbursement for travel expenses to and from a clinical trial site and associated costs such as airfare and lodging do not raise issues of undue influence on the part of drug manufacturers and are generally considered acceptable practice. See Food and Drug Administration, *Information Sheet, Payment and Reimbursement to Research Subjects, Guidance for Institutional Review Boards and Clinical Investigators, accessed June 18, 2019,* https://www.fda.gov/regulatory-information/search-fda-guidance-documents/payment-and-reimbursement-research- subjects.

To address the lack of information about upcoming and ongoing clinical trials that is available to and tailored to patients, two manufacturers launched clinical trial registries in 2015 and 2016, respectively.[34] Officials from one of the manufacturers stated they designed their registry to bridge the gap between the information that patients want about clinical trials (e.g., information targeted to medical conditions that uses basic terminology), and what is available in ClinicalTrials.gov, a federal database that includes information on privately and publicly funded clinical trial studies.[35] Officials explained that ClinicalTrials.gov is, in general, more targeted to physicians.[36]

In addition, to address barriers associated with the mistrust of research stemming from historical events among African-Americans and other communities, one manufacturer has several ongoing efforts to increase the participation of racially and ethnically diverse populations in its clinical trials.[37] For example, the manufacturer conducts workshops to train minority investigators who conduct clinical trials and requires certain clinical trial sites to be located in areas with minority patient populations of more than 25 percent.

Challenges with Broadening Eligibility Criteria

Officials from four of the 10 drug manufacturers we interviewed—including the two taking steps to broaden their clinical trial eligibility criteria—told us broadening eligibility criteria is challenging. They stated that broader criteria must be carefully balanced with the need to collect evidence from a well-defined population. Officials from one manufacturer explained that removing standard exclusion criteria, such as excluding patients who use other medications, could interfere with the success of their clinical trial if those medications make it difficult to identify the effects of the studied drug. In addition, officials from another manufacturer emphasized that determining whether to remove exclusion criteria takes time and resources because it involves additional study, which could slow down the clinical development of a drug.

---

[34] A clinical trial registry is a web-based search tool that helps patients locate information about ongoing clinical trials, including those conducted by manufacturers.

[35] In addition to information about clinical trials, ClinicalTrials.gov includes certain information about the availability of expanded access for investigational drugs.

[36] Officials from eight other stakeholders we interviewed similarly commented that ClinicalTrials.gov uses complex terminology, which can be difficult for some patients to understand.

[37] There have been well-documented cases of abuse of African-American participants in clinical research, such as the Tuskegee Syphilis Study.

FDA Took Several Recent Actions to Facilitate Access to Investigational Drugs Outside of Clinical Trials

FDA Simplified the Institutional Review Board Process and Launched a Pilot Program to Facilitate Access to Investigational Drugs Outside of Clinical Trials

To facilitate access to investigational drugs outside of clinical trials, FDA has simplified its expanded access program's IRB review requirements for individual patient requests.[38] FDA made this change in October 2017, in accordance with a provision in FDARA.[39] This provision addressed concerns that FDA's requirement to convene a full IRB to review an expanded access request could result in delays of approvals because full IRBs may not meet regularly. Under the revised process, FDA now allows for a waiver of the requirement for full IRB review when concurrence is obtained by the IRB chair or another designated member. According to FDA officials, the updated process will help reduce the potential burden for physicians, who are responsible for obtaining IRB approval, while still protecting patients.

In addition, to further simplify its expanded access process for individual patient requests, in June 2019 FDA launched a pilot program called Project Facilitate for oncologists and other health care professionals that treat patients with cancer.[40] According to FDA officials, the pilot program is focused on oncology because the agency receives a large number of individual expanded access requests from oncologists. Under the pilot program, FDA established a new call center that provides a single point of contact where FDA staff are available to answer questions, assist in filling out appropriate paperwork, and facilitate the overall process for requesting and obtaining access to investigational drugs. For example, FDA officials told us that FDA staff may assist oncologists in locating an IRB, if needed. As part of the pilot program, FDA will follow up on individual requests and gather data, such as how many patients received investigational drugs, and if not, why the requests were denied by manufacturers.[41] According to FDA, the agency can use these data to determine how the process is benefiting patients.

---

[38] See Food and Drug Administration, *Expanded Access to Investigational Drugs for Treatment Use—Questions and Answers, Guidance for Industry* (Silver Spring, Md.: October 2017), 5-6.

Under FDA's expanded access program, a licensed physician can request access to investigational drugs for treatment use on behalf of a patient. FDA must approve the request, and if so, the request must be reviewed by an IRB. Our July 2017 report described actions FDA had taken to simplify the expanded access process, such as issuing a new simplified application form for individual requests and finalizing its related guidance.

FDA's expanded access program includes different processes for requests to access a drug for an individual patient and for requests to access a drug for multiple patients.

[39] Pub. L. No. 115-52, § 610(b), 131 Stat.1053 (codified at 21 U.S.C. § 360bbb note).

[40] See Food and Drug Administration, *Project Facilitate*, accessed July 10, 2019, https:// www.fda.gov/about-fda/oncology-center-excellence/project-facilitate.

[41] FDA officials told us the agency's current plan is to obtain such information from the treating physicians or their health care teams.

Twenty of the stakeholders we interviewed were familiar with FDA's simplified IRB review requirements, and of those, 18 told us these updates were helpful for physicians and patients.[42] For example, officials from one drug manufacturer commented that the new IRB review requirements reduce the amount of time it takes for patients to obtain access to investigational drugs, which is especially important for patients who are very sick. In addition, we spoke to 12 stakeholders about FDA's plans for its pilot program, and of those, nine generally had positive views of the agency's planned activities.[43] Officials from one manufacturer explained that the pilot program could help reduce the burden on oncologists seeking access to investigational drugs for their patients through the expanded access program. On the other hand, the officials from this same manufacturer raised concerns about the potential for FDA to intentionally or unintentionally pressure companies to make their investigational drugs available to patients, should FDA have increased involvement with drug manufacturers as part of the pilot program.

FDA Increased Communication about the Expanded Access Program and the Federal RTT Act to Facilitate Access to Investigational Drugs Outside of Clinical Trials

FDA has also taken recent actions to facilitate access to investigational drugs outside of clinical trials by increasing its communication about the expanded access program and the federal RTT Act.

FDA's Increased Communication about the Expanded Access Program

In November 2018, FDA updated the web pages for its expanded access program in response to findings from an external assessment that the web pages were difficult to navigate and contained unclear information.[44] FDA created separate web pages for patients, physicians, and drug manufacturers, and tailored information about the expanded access process to each of these stakeholders. In addition, FDA added a new

---

[42] Of the 24 stakeholders, four were unfamiliar with the updates to the IRB review requirements.

[43] Of the 24 stakeholders, we spoke to 12 about FDA's plans for its pilot program. We became aware of FDA's plans to conduct the pilot program after we completed many of our stakeholder interviews.

[44] See Food and Drug Administration, *Expanded Access*, accessed May 29, 2019, https:// www.fda.gov/news-events/public-health-focus/expanded-access.
To identify ways to improve its expanded access program, FDA commissioned an external assessment of the program in 2017 that included obtaining the perspectives of various stakeholders such as health care providers and drug manufacturers. See Food and Drug Administration, *Expanded Access Program Report* (Silver Spring, Md.: May 2018).

web page with information that is commonly requested by physicians and patients, such as the instructions for completing the form for submitting individual requests and definitions of keywords associated with the expanded access process (e.g., IRB, informed consent).

In addition, in October 2017, in response to a recommendation in our July 2017 report, FDA clarified its guidance for drug manufacturers on how the agency reviews adverse events that occur under FDA's expanded access program.[45] In the 2017 report, we found that some drug manufacturers were concerned that use of adverse event data may influence FDA in making final approval decisions, and that this possibility could contribute to a manufacturer deciding not to grant patients access to their drugs through the expanded access program. In response, we recommended that FDA clearly communicate how the agency will use adverse event data from expanded access use when reviewing drugs and biologics for approval.[46]

FDA's updated guidance states that FDA is not aware of instances in which adverse event information prevented the agency from approving a drug, and that it is very rare for FDA to place a clinical hold on an investigational drug due to adverse events observed during expanded access treatment.[47] The guidance also explains that several factors make it difficult for FDA to link an adverse event to the expanded use of a drug being considered for approval. For example, the guidance acknowledges that the use of investigational drugs though the expanded access program generally occurs outside of a controlled clinical trial setting and patients receiving such drugs may be sicker than patients participating in a clinical trial, making it more difficult to determine whether the use of the investigational drug has led to the adverse event.

In responding to questions about increased FDA communication about the expanded access program, 19 of the stakeholders we interviewed were familiar with FDA's updated expanded access web pages, and of those, 16 told us they were an improvement.[48] Officials from one physician organization stated that the updated web pages were easier to navigate than the previous web pages and presented information about the process more clearly.

Among the 10 manufacturers we interviewed, we found varying views of FDA's updated guidance on the use of adverse event data.

---

[45] See Food and Drug Administration, *Expanded Access to Investigational Drugs for Treatment Use—Questions and Answers, Guidance for Industry* (Silver Spring, Md.: October 2017), 18-19.

[46] See GAO-17-564.

[47] For example, see study examining FDA's use of safety information obtained during expanded access to place clinical holds: Jonathan P. Jarow, Steven Lemery, Kevin Bugin, Sean Khozin, and Richard Moscicki, "Expanded Access of Investigational Drugs: The Experience of the Center of Drug Evaluation and Research Over a 10-Year Period," *Therapeutic Innovation & Regulatory Science*, vol. 50, no. 6 (2016). Also see study examining FDA's use of safety information obtained during expanded access to affect labeling: Jonathan P. Jarow and Richard Moscicki, "Impact of Expanded Access on FDA Regulatory Action and Product Labeling," *Therapeutic Innovation & Regulatory Science*, vol. 51, no. 6 (2017).

[48] Of the 24 stakeholders, officials from three stakeholders told us they were unfamiliar with FDA's updated expanded access web pages. We did not ask the other two stakeholders their views on the updated web pages because of the timing of those interviews relative to the timing of FDA's updates.

- Officials from seven of the 10 manufacturers viewed the updated guidance as an improvement. Officials from one of the seven explained that it contributed to their company's decision to allow access to investigational drugs, when appropriate.
- Officials from two of the 10 manufacturers did not view the guidance as an improvement. Officials from both manufacturers stated that they still had significant concerns about the potential use of adverse event data by FDA to adversely affect the development of their investigational drugs, such as being used to issue a clinical hold. An official from one of the two manufacturers commented that these concerns remained despite FDA's statement in the guidance that it is difficult for FDA to link expanded access use to a particular adverse event. In addition, officials from two other manufacturers who viewed the guidance as an improvement similarly expressed remaining concerns that adverse events could negatively affect the development of their investigational drugs.
- One manufacturer was unfamiliar with the updated guidance.

Further, officials from four of the 10 drug manufacturers we interviewed, including two who viewed the updated guidance as an improvement, said they believed that manufacturers' concerns about this issue may never be fully resolved even with additional FDA guidance.

In other comments related to FDA's communication on its use of adverse events data from the expanded access program, some drug manufacturers we interviewed noted the merits of using efficacy and safety data from the expanded access program to inform FDA's drug approval decisions. Officials from two of the 10 manufacturers told us they believe that FDA's potential use of adverse event data from expanded access use, but not efficacy data, would be unfair. Officials from one of these two manufacturers cited FDA's updated guidance on adverse events as contributing to their view, referring to FDA's statement that it is unlikely that FDA's program would yield data that is useful to FDA in considering an investigational drug's effectiveness.

However, FDA officials told us that efficacy and safety data from the expanded access program have been used to support drug approvals in several instances. For example, in January 2018 FDA approved the drug Lutathera to treat rare tumors in the pancreas and gastrointestinal tract using efficacy and safety data the manufacturer submitted to FDA from a subset of the roughly 1,200 patients who received the drug through the expanded access program. Officials from four of the 10 manufacturers expressed interest in discussing further with FDA how the agency would evaluate efficacy and safety data from the expanded access program and use these data to help support a drug's approval and other regulatory decisions.[49]

FDA's Communication about the Federal RTT Act

In November 2018, FDA launched a new federal RTT web page that outlines both the eligibility requirements for patients interested in seeking access to investigational drugs and the criteria that must be met for an investigational drug to be eligible for use through this pathway.[50] For example, the web page states that patients must be diagnosed with a life- threatening disease or condition to be eligible to access investigational drugs under the federal RTT pathway. Further, the agency plans to issue proposed regulations in September 2019 to implement the federal RTT Act requirement for manufacturers to submit an annual summary to FDA on any use of their investigational drugs under this pathway.[51] The regulations will include a due date for manufacturers to submit the annual summaries as well as information on what they are to contain, according to FDA.

Fourteen of the stakeholders we interviewed were familiar with FDA's new web page on the federal RTT Act, and among those, eight stated that it communicated useful and balanced information for physicians and patients.[52] Officials from the remaining six stakeholders told us they did not find it helpful for physicians or patients. For example, officials from two stakeholders (including one drug manufacturer) commented at the time of our review that the web page could be misleading to some patients if they interpret the federal RTT Act to mean that manufacturers must provide access to their investigational drugs. Both added that FDA should more clearly communicate on the web page that there is no such requirement. In addition, officials from another stakeholder stated at the time of our review that FDA should explain on the web page the agency's role in implementing the federal RTT Act. In May 2019 FDA clarified on its web page that the federal RTT Act does not require manufacturers to provide patients access to their investigational drugs and that FDA's role includes posting a consolidated annual summary report on the use of investigational drugs through the federal RTT pathway.

---

[49] FDA officials told us they discussed the use of data from the expanded access program to support drug approval decisions at a November 2018 meeting that the Reagan-Udall Foundation sponsored for stakeholders, including drug manufacturers. See Reagan-Udall Foundation for the Food and Drug Administration, *Public Meeting Report: Leveraging Real-World Treatment Experience from Expanded Access Protocols* (Washington, D.C.: November 2018).

[50] See Food and Drug Administration, *Right to Try*, accessed June 19, 2019, https:// www.fda.gov/patients/learn-about-expanded-access-and-other-treatment-options/ri ght-try.

[51] See Pub. L. No. 115-176, § 2(a), 132 Stat. 1372 (codified in pertinent part at 21 U.S.C. § 360bbb-0a(d)). This provision also requires FDA to post an annual summary report of the use of investigational drugs under the federal RTT pathway.

[52] Of the remaining 10 stakeholders we interviewed, officials from seven stakeholders told us they were not familiar with the federal RTT web page. We did not ask the other three stakeholders their views on the federal RTT web page because of the timing of those interviews relative to the timing of the launch of the new web page.

MOST SELECTED MANUFACTURERS COMMUNICATED WHETHER THEY CONSIDER REQUESTS FOR ACCESS TO INVESTIGATIONAL DRUGS OUTSIDE OF CLINICAL TRIALS AND CONDITIONS FOR APPROVAL

Most of the 29 drug manufacturers in our review used their websites to communicate to patients and physicians whether they would consider individual requests for access to their investigational drugs outside of clinical trials. Among those that would consider requests, most also communicated the conditions under which they would review requests and grant access.

Manufacturers' Consideration of Requests for Access

Our review of drug manufacturers' websites between January 31, 2019, and March 12, 2019, found that 23 of the 29 manufacturers in our review used their websites to communicate whether they considered individual requests for access to investigational drugs outside of clinical trials.[53] In communicating this information, 19 of the 23 manufacturers stated they were willing to consider requests, while the other four stated they were not considering requests.[54] The remaining six of the 29 manufacturers did not communicate information about whether they would consider requests for access to investigational drugs outside of clinical trials at the time of our review, but officials from all six told us they were in the process of developing content on this topic that they intended to post on their websites.

Information Communicated by Manufacturers that Consider Requests

Among the 19 manufacturers willing to consider requests for access to investigational drugs outside of clinical trials, all communicated on their websites that they required physicians to submit requests on behalf of their patients and provided information on how physicians should submit these requests. In addition, 18 manufacturers communicated an

[53] Manufacturers used a variety of terms to characterize access to investigational drugs outside of clinical trials, such as "pre-approval access," "compassionate use access," and "early access."

[54] Eleven of the 19 manufacturers that stated on their websites that they did consider requests for access also made this information available to patients and physicians on the Reagan-Udall Expanded Access Navigator. See Reagan-Udall Foundation, *Expanded Access Navigator Company Directory*, accessed April 2, 2019, http://navigator.reaganudall.org/company-directory.

estimated time frame within which they would respond to requests.[55] The manufacturers provided additional information, including the following:

- Eighteen communicated information about the type of patient for whom they would consider granting access.
  - Eighteen stated that patients must have a serious or life- threatening disease or condition; have no comparable or satisfactory alternative therapies available; and be unable to participate in a clinical trial to be eligible to obtain access.
  - In addition, 17 stated that the treating physician must determine for the patient seeking access that the risk of taking the investigational drug is not greater than the anticipated benefit.
- Fifteen communicated other factors they would take into account during their review of requests. These factors included the following:
  - Ten stated that the supply of their investigational drugs was a consideration. That is, a manufacturer must have a sufficient supply of the investigational drug to support the drug's clinical development before granting access to patients outside of clinical trials.
  - Five referred to specific drugs to which they would consider granting access when describing the conditions under which they would consider reviewing requests. For example, one manufacturer stated that it would consider requests to access three of its investigational drugs (intended to treat bladder cancer, influenza, and HIV).
- One manufacturer communicated that after its initial review of individual requests, it uses an external advisory committee to further evaluate certain requests and ensure they are evaluated in an ethical and fair manner. The committee, which includes bioethical experts, physicians and patient representatives, makes recommendations to the manufacturer about providing access to individual patients.[56]
- Many of the 19 manufacturers that communicated they were willing to consider individual requests for access stated that after they have approved a request they also required external entities to review the request. These included the following:
  - Thirteen stated they require the relevant regulatory authority to review requests. Of these, six specified that they require FDA to review requests for

---

[55] The type of responses that drug manufacturers indicated they would give within these estimated time frames varied, including an acknowledgement of receipt and a decision about whether to provide access.

[56] In addition, this manufacturer communicated how many patients ultimately were granted access to an investigational drug outside of clinical trials. None of the other 18 manufacturers that communicated information about factors they take into account when reviewing requests also provided information on the number of patients for which they granted access to investigational drugs.

access in the United States. One of these six explained that it required a review by FDA to ensure all available safety data for the investigational drug were considered, and added that FDA is uniquely aware of such safety data.

- Five stated they require the review of a research ethics committee or an IRB.[57]

Information Communicated by Manufacturers that do not Consider Requests

Among the four manufacturers that communicated on their websites they were not considering requests for access to investigational drugs outside of clinical trials at the time of our review, two provided reasons for their decision. Both cited safety concerns; for example, one explained that it wanted to ensure its investigational drugs were administered to patients only through clinical trials where safety could be closely monitored. One also cited limited resources, stating that it chose to focus its resources solely on conducting clinical trials. Both of the manufacturers that provided reasons for not considering requests for access communicated that they will periodically re-evaluate their policies.

AGENCY COMMENTS

We provided a draft of this chapter to HHS for comment and HHS provided technical comments, which we incorporated as appropriate.

We are sending copies of this chapter to the appropriate congressional committees, the Secretary of the Department of Health and Human Services, and other interested parties.

John E. Dicken
Director, Health Care

---

[57] A research ethics committee is a group of individuals who undertake ethical review of research involving humans, applying agreed on ethical principles.

In: U.S. Drug Supply, Investigational Drugs ...
Editor: Emil R. Berg

ISBN: 978-1-53617-442-7

Chapter 3

EVERY PRESCRIPTION CONVEYED SECURELY ACT*

Committee on Energy and Commerce

The Committee on Energy and Commerce, to whom was referred the bill (H.R. 3528) to amend title XVIII of the Social Security Act to require e-prescribing for coverage under part D of the Medicare program of prescription drugs that are controlled substances, having considered the same, report favorably thereon with an amendment and recommend that the bill as amended do pass.

The amendment is as follows:

Strike all after the enacting clause and insert the following:

SECTION 1. SHORT TITLE

This Act may be cited as the "Every Prescription Conveyed Securely Act."

SECTION 2. REQUIRING E-PRESCRIBING FOR COVERAGE OF COVERED PART D CONTROLLED SUBSTANCES

(a) IN GENERAL.—Section 1860D–4(e) of the Social Security Act (42 U.S.C. 1395w– 104(e)) is amended by adding at the end the following:

* This is an edited, reformatted and augmented version of Committee of the Whole House on the State of the Union, House of Representatives, 115th Congress, 2d Session, Serial No. 115–748, dated June 12, 2018.

"(7) REQUIREMENT OF E-PRESCRIBING FOR CONTROLLED SUBSTANCES.—

"(A) IN GENERAL.—Subject to subparagraph (B), a prescription for a covered part D drug under a prescription drug plan (or under an MA–PD plan) for a schedule II, III, IV, or V controlled substance shall be transmitted by a health care practitioner electronically in accordance with an electronic prescription drug program that meets the requirements of paragraph (2).

"(B) EXCEPTION FOR CERTAIN CIRCUMSTANCES.—The Secretary shall, pursuant to rulemaking, specify circumstances with respect to which the Secretary may waive the requirement under subparagraph (A), with respect to a covered part D drug, including in the case of—

(i) a prescription issued when the practitioner and dispenser are the same entity;

(ii) a prescription issued that cannot be transmitted electronically under the most recently implemented version of the National Council for Prescription Drug Programs SCRIPT Standard;

(iii) a prescription issued by a practitioner who has received a waiver or a renewal thereof for a specified period determined by the Secretary, not to exceed one year, from the requirement to use electronic prescribing, pursuant to a process established by regulation by the Secretary, due to demonstrated economic hardship, technological limitations that are not reasonably within the control of the practitioner, or other exceptional circumstance demonstrated by the practitioner;

(iv) a prescription issued by a practitioner under circumstances in which, notwithstanding the practitioner's ability to submit a prescription electronically as required by this subsection, such practitioner reasonably determines that it would be impractical for the individual involved to obtain substances prescribed by electronic prescription in a timely manner, and such delay would adversely impact the individual's medical condition involved;

(v) a prescription issued by a practitioner allowing for the dispensing of a non-patient specific prescription pursuant to a standing order, approved protocol for drug therapy, collaborative drug management, or comprehensive medication management, in response to a public health emergency, or other circumstances where the practitioner may issue a non-patient specific prescription;

(vi) a prescription issued by a practitioner prescribing a drug under a research protocol;

(vii) a prescription issued by a practitioner for a drug for which the Food and Drug Administration requires a prescription to contain elements that are not able to be included in electronic prescribing, such as a drug with risk evaluation and mitigation strategies that include elements to assure safe use; and

(viii) a prescription issued by a practitioner for an individual who—

(I) receives hospice care under this title; or

(II) is a resident of a skilled nursing facility (as defined in section 1819(a)), or a medical institution or nursing facility for which payment is made for an institutionalized individual under section 1902(q)(1)(B), for which frequently abused drugs are dispensed for residents through a contract with a single pharmacy, as determined by the Secretary in accordance with this paragraph.

"(C) DISPENSING.—Nothing in this paragraph shall be construed as requiring a sponsor of a prescription drug plan under this part, MA organization offering an MA–PD plan under part C, or a pharmacist to verify that a practitioner, with respect to a prescription for a covered part D drug, has a waiver (or is otherwise exempt) under subparagraph (B) from the requirement under subparagraph (A). Nothing in this paragraph shall be construed as affecting the ability of the plan to cover or the pharmacists' ability to continue to dispense covered part D drugs from otherwise valid written, oral or fax prescriptions that are consistent with laws and regulations. Nothing in this paragraph shall be construed as affecting the ability of the beneficiary involved to designate a particular pharmacy to dispense a prescribed drug to the extent consistent with the requirements under subsection (b)(1) and under this paragraph.

"(D) ENFORCEMENT.—The Secretary shall, pursuant to rulemaking, have authority to enforce and specify appropriate penalties for non-compliance with the requirement under subparagraph (A)."

(b) EFFECTIVE DATE.—The amendment made by subsection (a) shall apply to coverage of drugs prescribed on or after January 1, 2021.

PURPOSE AND SUMMARY

H.R. 3528, Every Prescription Conveyed Securely Act, was introduced on July 28, 2017, by Rep. Katherine Clark (D–MA) and Rep. Markwayne Mullin (R–OK) to require e-prescribing for coverage of prescribed controlled substances under the Medicare Part D program.

BACKGROUND AND NEED FOR LEGISLATION

The Medicare program serves as the healthcare coverage provider to over 58 million beneficiaries. This number is projected to rise to over 80 million by 2030. In serving the over age 65 population, Medicare accounts for a large share of total opioid prescriptions. In 2016, one out of every three beneficiaries was prescribed an opioid through Medicare Part D. In total, this equates to almost 80 million prescriptions and $4 billion in Medicare

Part D spending. While many Medicare beneficiaries with serious pain-related conditions are being properly prescribed opioids, there is mounting evidence of opioid misuse in the Medicare system. As more seniors and individuals with disabilities come into the program, the challenges of fraud, misuse, and abuse will only increase.

This bill seeks to deter prescription fraud and the diversion of opioids by better securing the prescriptions of controlled substances covered under Medicare Part D by requiring the use of electronic prescribing for such drugs. This bill ensures that prescriptions for controlled substances covered under Medicare Part D are transmitted securely from the prescriber to the dispensing pharmacy and reduces the potential for fraudulent prescriptions.

COMMITTEE ACTION

On April 11 and 12, 2018, the Subcommittee on Health held a hearing entitled "Combating the Opioid Crisis: Improving the Ability of Medicare and Medicaid to Provide Care for Patients" to review legislation related to the opioid epidemic. The Subcommittee received testimony from:

- Kimberly Brandt, Principal Deputy Administrator for Operations, Centers for Medicare and Medicaid Services, U.S. Department of Health and Human Services;
- Michael Botticelli, Executive Director, Grayken Center for Addiction, Boston Medical Center;
- Toby Douglas, Senior Vice President, Medicaid Solutions, Centene Corporation;
- David Guth, CEO, Centerstone;
- John Kravitz, CIO, Geisinger Health System; and,
- Sam Srivastava, CEO, Magellan Health.

On April 25, 2018, the Subcommittee on Health met in open markup session and forwarded H.R. 3528, as amended, to the full Committee by a voice vote. On May 9, 2018, the full Committee on Energy and Commerce met in open markup session and ordered H.R. 3528, as amended, favorable reported to the House by a voice vote.

Committee Votes

Clause 3(b) of rule XIII requires the Committee to list the record votes on the motion to report legislation and amendments thereto. There were no record votes taken in connection with ordering H.R. 3528 reported.

Oversight Findings and Recommendations

Pursuant to clause 2(b)(1) of rule X and clause 3(c)(1) of rule XIII, the Committee held a hearing and made findings that are reflected in this chapter.

New Budget Authority, Entitlement Authority, and Tax Expenditures

Pursuant to clause 3(c)(2) of rule XIII, the Committee finds that H.R. 3528 would result in no new or increased budget authority, entitlement authority, or tax expenditures or revenues.

Congressional Budget Office Estimate

Pursuant to clause 3(c)(3) of rule XIII, the following is the cost estimate provided by the Congressional Budget Office pursuant to section 402 of the Congressional Budget Act of 1974:

U.S. Congress, Congressional Budget Office,
Washington, DC, June 6, 2018.

Hon. Greg Walden
Chairman
Committee on Energy and Commerce
House of Representatives

Dear Mr. Chairman: The Congressional Budget Office has prepared the enclosed document with cost estimates for the opioid-related legislation ordered to be reported on May 9 and May 17, 2018.

If you wish further details on this estimate, we will be pleased to provide them. The CBO staff contacts are Tom Bradley and Chad Chirico.

Sincerely,

Mark P. Hadley
(For Keith Hall, Director).

Opioid Legislation

Summary: On May 9 and May 17, 2018, the House Committee on Energy and Commerce ordered 59 bills to be reported related to the nation's response to the opioid epidemic. Generally, the bills would:

- Provide grants to facilities and providers that treat people with substance use disorders,
- Direct various agencies within the Department of Health and Human Services (HHS) to explore nonopioid approaches to treating pain and to educate providers about those alternatives,
- Modify requirements under Medicaid and Medicare for prescribing controlled substances,
- Expand Medicaid coverage for substance abuse treatment, and
- Direct the Food and Drug Administration (FDA) to modify its oversight of opioid drugs and other medications that are used to manage pain.

Because of the large number of related bills ordered reported by the Committee, CBO is publishing a single comprehensive document that includes estimates for each piece of legislation.

CBO estimates that enacting 20 of the bills would affect direct spending, and 2 of the bills would affect revenues; therefore, pay- as-you-go procedures apply for those bills.

CBO estimates that enacting H.R. 4998, the Health Insurance for Former Foster Youth Act, would increase net direct spending by more than $2.5 billion and on-budget deficits by more than $5 billion in at least one of the four consecutive 10-year periods beginning in 2029. None of the remaining 58 bills included in this estimate would increase net direct spending by more than $2.5 billion or on-budget deficits by more than $5 billion in any of the four consecutive 10-year periods beginning in 2029.

One of the bills reviewed for this document, H.R. 5795, would impose both intergovernmental and private-sector mandates as defined in the Unfunded Mandates Reform Act (UMRA). CBO estimates that the costs of those mandates on public and private entities would fall below the thresholds in UMRA ($80 million and $160 million, respectively, in 2018, adjusted annually for inflation). Five bills, H.R. 5228, H.R. 5333, H.R. 5554, H.R. 5687, and H.R. 5811, would impose private-sector mandates as defined in UMRA. CBO estimates that the costs of the mandates in three of the bills (H.R. 5333, H.R. 5554, and H.R. 5811) would not exceed the UMRA threshold for private entities. Because CBO is uncertain how federal agencies would implement new authority granted in the other two bills, H.R. 5228 and H.R. 5687, CBO cannot determine whether the costs of those mandates would exceed the UMRA threshold.

Estimated cost to the Federal Government: The estimates in this document do not include the effects of interactions among the bills. If all 59 bills were combined and enacted as one piece of legislation, the budgetary effects would be different from the sum of the estimates in this document, although CBO expects that any such differences would be small. The costs of this legislation fall within budget functions 550 (health), 570 (Medicare), 750 (administration of justice), and 800 (general government).

Basis of estimate: For this estimate, CBO assumes that all of the legislation will be enacted late in 2018 and that authorized and estimated amounts will be appropriated each year. Outlays for discretionary programs are estimated based on historical spending patterns for similar programs.

Uncertainty

CBO aims to produce estimates that generally reflect the middle of a range of the most likely budgetary outcomes that would result if the legislation was enacted. Because data on the utilization of mental health and substance abuse treatment under Medicaid and Medicare is scarce, CBO cannot precisely predict how patients or providers would respond to some policy changes or what budgetary effects would result. In addition, several of the bills would give the Department of Health and Human Services (HHS) considerable latitude in designing and implementing policies. Budgetary effects could differ from those provided in CBO's analyses depending on those decisions.

Direct Spending and Revenues

Table 1 lists the 22 bills of the 59 ordered to be reported that would affect direct spending or revenues.

Legislation Primarily Affecting Medicaid. The following nine bills would affect direct spending for the Medicaid program.

H.R. 1925, the At-Risk Youth Medicaid Protection Act of 2017, would require states to suspend, rather than terminate, Medicaid eligibility for juvenile enrollees (generally under 21 years of age) who become inmates of public correctional institutions. States also would have to redetermine those enrollees' Medicaid eligibility before their release and restore their coverage upon release if they qualify for the program. States would be required to process Medicaid applications submitted by or on behalf of juveniles in public correctional institutions who were not enrolled in Medicaid before becoming inmates and ensure that Medicaid coverage is provided when they are released if they are found to be eligible. On the basis of an analysis of juvenile incarceration trends and of the per enrollee spending for Medicaid foster care children, who have a similar health profile to incarcerated juveniles, CBO estimates that implementing the bill would cost $75 million over the 2019–2028 period.

H.R. 4998, the Health Insurance for Former Foster Youth Act, would require states to provide Medicaid coverage to adults up to age 25 who had aged out of foster care in any state. Under current law, such coverage is mandatory only if the former foster care youth has aged out in the state in which the individual applies for coverage. The policy also would apply to former foster children who had been in foster care upon turning 14 years of age but subsequently left foster care to enter into a legal guardianship with a kinship caregiver. The provisions would take effect respect for foster youth who turn 18 on or after January 1, 2023. On the basis of spending for Medicaid foster care children and data from the Census Bureau regarding annual migration rates between states, CBO estimates that implementing the bill would cost $171 million over the 2019–2028 period.

H.R. 5477, the Rural Development of Opioid Capacity Services Act, would direct the Secretary of HHS to conduct a five-year demonstration to increase the number and ability of providers participating in Medicaid to provide treatment for substance use disorders. On the basis of an analysis of federal and state spending for treatment of substance use disorders and the prevalence of such disorders, CBO estimates that enacting the bill would increase direct spending by $301 million over the 2019–2028 period.

H.R. 5583, a bill to amend title XI of the Social Security Act to require States to annually report on certain adult health quality measures, and for other purposes, would require states to include behavioral health indicators in their annual reports on the quality of care under Medicaid. Although the bill would add a requirement for states, CBO estimates that its enactment would not have a significant budgetary effect because most states have systems in place for reporting such measures to the federal government.

H.R. 5797, the IMD CARE Act, would expand Medicaid coverage for people with opioid use disorder who are in institutions for mental disease (IMDs) for up to 30 days per year. Under a current-law policy known as the IMD exclusion, the federal government generally does not make matching payments to state Medicaid programs for most services provided by IMDs to adults between the ages of 21 and 64. Recent administrative changes have made federal financing for IMDs available in limited circumstances, but the statutory prohibition remains in place. CBO analyzed several data sets, primarily those collected by the Substance Abuse and Mental Health Services Administration (SAMHSA), to estimate current federal spending under Medicaid for

IMD services and to estimate spending under H.R. 5797. Using that analysis, CBO estimates that enacting H.R. 5797 would increase direct spending by $991 million over the 2019–2028 period.

Table 1. Estimated changes in mandatory spending and revenues

	By fiscal year, in millions of dollars—												
	2018	2019	2020	2021	2022	2023	2024	2025	2026	2027	2028	2019–2023	2019–2028
	INCREASES OR DECREASES (–) IN DIRECT SPENDING												
Legislation Primarily Affecting Medicaid:													
H.R. 1925, At-Risk Youth Medicaid Protection Act of 2017	0	*	5	5	5	10	10	10	10	10	10	25	75
H.R. 4998, Health Insurance for Former Foster Youth Act	0	0	0	0	0	*	10	21	33	46	61	*	171
H.R. 5477, Rural Development of Opioid Capacity Services Act	0	13	35	58	68	83	27	9	3	3	3	256	301
H.R. 5583, a bill to amend title XI of the Social Security Act to require States to annually report on certain adult health quality measures, and for other purposes	0	*	*	*	*	*	*	*	*	*	*	*	*
H.R. 5797, IMD CARE Act	0	38	158	251	265	279	0	0	0	0	0	991	991
H.R. 5799, Medicaid DRUG Improvement Act[a]	0	*	*	1	1	1	1	1	1	1	1	2	5
H.R. 5801 Medicaid Providers Are Required To Note Experiences in Record Systems to Help In-Need Patients (PARTNERSHIP) Act[a]	0	*	*	*	*	*	*	*	*	*	*	*	*
H.R. 5808, Medicaid Pharmaceutical Home Act of 2018[a]	0	*	–1	–1	–1	–1	–2	–2	–2	–2	–2	–4	–13
H.R. 5810, Medicaid Health HOME Act	0	94	58	62	56	52	48	43	38	32	25	323	509
Legislation Primarily Affecting Medicare:													
H.R. 3528, Every Prescription Conveyed Securely Act	0	0	0	–24	–35	–33	–30	–33	–32	–31	–32	–92	–250
H.R. 4841, Standardizing Electronic Prior Authorization for Safe Prescribing Act of 2018	0	0	0	*	*	*	*	*	*	*	*	*	*
H.R. 5603, Access to Telehealth Services for Opioid Use Disorders Act	0	2	*	*	*	1	1	1	2	2	2	3	11
H.R. 5605, Advancing High Quality Treatment for Opioid Use Disorders in Medicare Act	0	0	0	15	26	24	23	23	10	1	*	65	122
H.R. 5675, a bill to amend title XVIII of the Social Security Act to require prescription drug plan sponsors under the Medicare program to establish drug management programs for at-risk beneficiaries	0	0	0	–6	–7	–7	–7	–8	–9	–9	–11	–20	–64
H.R. 5684, Protecting Seniors From Opioid Abuse Act	0	0	0	*	*	*	*	*	*	*	*	*	*
H.R. 5796, Responsible Education Achieves Care and Healthy Outcomes for Users' Treatment Act of 2018	0	10	25	50	10	5	0	0	0	0	0	100	100
H.R. 5798, Opioid Screening and Chronic Pain Management Alternatives for Seniors Act	0	0	*	1	1	1	1	1	1	1	1	2	5
H.R. 5804, Post-Surgical Injections as an Opioid Alternative Act[a]	0	0	25	30	25	20	10	5	0	0	0	100	115
H.R. 5809, Postoperative Opioid Prevention Act of 2018	0	0	0	0	10	15	20	25	30	35	45	25	180
Legislation Primarily Affecting the Food and Drug Administration:													
H.R. 5333, Over-the-Counter Monograph Safety, Innovation, and Reform Act of 2018[a]	0	0	*	*	*	*	*	*	*	*	*	*	*
	INCREASES OR DECREASES (–) IN REVENUES[b]												
H.R. 5752, Stop Illicit Drug Importation Act of 2018	0	*	*	*	*	*	*	*	*	*	*	*	*

Annual amounts may not sum to totals because of rounding. * = between ¥$500,000 and $500,000. Budget authority is equivalent to outlays.

[a] This bill also would affect spending subject to appropriation.

[b] One additional bill, H.R. 5228, the Stop Counterfeit Drugs by Regulating and Enhancing Enforcement Now Act, would have a negligible effect on revenues.

H.R. 5799, the Medicaid DRUG Improvement Act, would require state Medicaid programs to implement additional reviews of opioid prescriptions, monitor concurrent prescribing of opioids and certain other drugs, and monitor use of antipsychotic drugs by children. CBO estimates that the bill would increase direct spending by $5 million over 2019–2028 period to cover the administrative costs of complying with those requirements. On the basis of stakeholder feedback, CBO expects that the bill would not have a significant effect on Medicaid spending for prescription drugs because many of the bill's requirements would duplicate current efforts to curb opioid and antipsychotic drug use. (If enacted, H.R. 5799 also would affect spending subject to appropriation; CBO has not completed an estimate of that amount).

H.R. 5801, the Medicaid Providers Are Required To Note Experiences in Record Systems to Help In-Need Patients (PARTNERSHIP) Act, would require providers who are permitted to prescribe controlled substances and who participate in Medicaid to query prescription drug monitoring programs (PDMPs) before prescribing controlled substances to Medicaid patients. PDMPs are statewide electronic databases that collect data on controlled substances dispensed in the state. The bill also would require PDMPs to comply with certain data and system criteria, and it would provide additional federal matching funds to certain states to help cover administrative costs. On the basis of a literature review and stakeholder feedback, CBO estimates that the net budgetary effect of enacting H.R. 5801 would be insignificant. Costs for states to come into compliance with the systems and administrative requirements would be roughly offset by savings from small reductions in the number of controlled substances paid for by Medicaid under the proposal. (If enacted, H.R. 5801 also would affect spending subject to appropriation; CBO has not completed an estimate of that amount).

H.R. 5808, the Medicaid Pharmaceutical Home Act of 2018, would require state Medicaid programs to operate pharmacy programs that would identify people at high risk of abusing controlled substances and require those patients to use a limited number of providers and pharmacies. Although nearly all state Medicaid programs currently meet such a requirement, a small number of high-risk Medicaid beneficiaries are not now monitored. Based on an analysis of information about similar state and federal programs, CBO estimates that net Medicaid spending under the bill would decrease by $13 million over the 2019–2028 period. That amount represents a small increase in administrative costs and a small reduction in the number of controlled substances paid for by Medicaid under the proposal. (If enacted, H.R. 5808 also would affect spending subject to appropriation; CBO has not completed an estimate of that amount).

H.R. 5810, the Medicaid Health HOME Act, would allow states to receive six months of enhanced federal Medicaid funding for programs that coordinate care for people with substance use disorders. Based on enrollment and spending data from states that currently participate in Medicaid's Health Homes program, CBO estimates that the expansion would cost approximately $469 million over the 2019–2028 period. The bill also would require states to cover all FDA-approved drugs used in medication-assisted treatment for five years, although states could seek a waiver from that requirement. (Medication-assisted treatment combines behavioral therapy and pharmaceutical treatment for substance use disorders). Under current law, states already cover most FDA-approved drugs used in such programs in some capacity, although a few exclude methadone dispensed by opioid treatment programs. CBO estimates that a small share of those states would begin to cover methadone if this bill was enacted at a federal cost of about $39 million over the 2019–2028 period. In sum, CBO estimates that the enacting H.R. 5810 would increase direct spending by $509 million over the 2019–2028 period.

Legislation Primarily Affecting Medicare. The following ten bills would affect direct spending for the Medicare program.

H.R. 3528, the Every Prescription Conveyed Securely Act, would require prescriptions for controlled substances covered under Medicare Part D to be transmitted electronically, starting on January 1, 2021. Based on CBO's analysis of prescription drug spending, spending for controlled substances is a small share of total drug spending. CBO also assumes a small share of those prescriptions would not be filled because they are not converted to an electronic format. Therefore, CBO expects that enacting H.R. 3528 would reduce the number of prescriptions filled and estimates that Medicare spending would be reduced by $250 million over the 2019– 2028 period.

H.R. 4841, the Standardizing Electronic Prior Authorization for Safe Prescribing Act of 2018, would require health care professionals to submit prior authorization requests electronically, starting on January 1, 2021, for drugs covered under Medicare Part D. Taking into account that many prescribers already use electronic methods to submit such requests, CBO estimates that enacting H.R. 4841 would not significantly affect direct spending for Part D.

H.R. 5603, the Access to Telehealth Services for Opioid Use Disorders Act, would permit the Secretary of HHS to lift current geographic and other restrictions on coverage of telehealth services under Medicare for treatment of substance use disorders or co-occurring mental health disorders. Under the bill, the Secretary of HHS would be directed to encourage other payers to coordinate payments for opioid use disorder treatments and to evaluate the extent to which the demonstration reduces hospitalizations, increases the use of medication-assisted treatments, and improves the health outcomes of individuals with opioid use disorders during and after the demonstration. Based on current use of Medicare telehealth services for treatment of substance use disorders, CBO estimates that expanding that coverage would increase direct spending by $11 million over the 2019–2028 period.

H.R. 5605, the Advancing High Quality Treatment for Opioid Use Disorders in Medicare Act, would establish a five-year demonstration program to increase access to treatment for opioid use disorder. The demonstration would provide incentive payments and funding for care management services based on criteria such as patient engagement, use of evidence-based treatments, and treatment length and intensity. Under the bill, the Secretary of HHS would be directed to encourage other payers to coordinate payments for opioid use disorder treatments and to evaluate the extent to which the demonstration reduces hospitalizations, increases the use of medication-assisted treatments, and improves the health outcomes of individuals with opioid use disorders during and after the demonstration. Based on historical utilization of opioid use disorder treatments and projected spending on incentive payments and care management fees, CBO estimates that increased use of treatment services and the demonstration's incentive payments would increase direct spending by $122 million over the 2019–2028 period.

H.R. 5675, a bill to amend title XVIII of the Social Security Act to require prescription drug plan sponsors under the Medicare program to establish drug management programs for at-risk beneficiaries, would require Part D prescription drug plans to provide drug management programs for Medicare beneficiaries who are at risk for prescription drug abuse. (Under current law, Part D plans are permitted but not required to establish such programs as of 2019). Based on an analysis of the number of plans currently providing those programs, CBO estimates that enacting H.R. 5675 would lower federal spending by $64 million over the 2019–2028 period by reducing the number of prescriptions filled and Medicare's payments for controlled substances.

H.R. 5684, the Protecting Seniors From Opioid Abuse Act, would expand medication therapy management programs under Medicare Part D to include beneficiaries who are at risk for prescription drug abuse. Because relatively few beneficiaries would be affected by this bill, CBO estimates that its enactment would not significantly affect direct spending for Part D.

H.R. 5796, the Responsible Education Achieves Care and Healthy Outcomes for Users' Treatment Act of 2018, would allow the Secretary of HHS to award grants to certain organizations that provide technical assistance and education to high-volume prescribers of opioids. The bill would appropriate $100 million for fiscal year 2019. Based on historical spending patterns for similar activities, CBO estimates that implementing H.R. 5796 would cost $100 million over the 2019–2028 period.

H.R. 5798, the Opioid Screening and Chronic Pain Management Alternatives for Seniors Act, would add an assessment of current opioid prescriptions and screening for opioid use disorder to the Welcome to Medicare Initial Preventive Physical Examination. Based on historical use of the examinations and pain management alternatives, CBO expects that enacting the bill would increase use of pain management services and estimates that direct spending would increase by $5 million over the 2019–2028 period.

H.R. 5804, the Post-Surgical Injections as an Opioid Alternative Act, would freeze the Medicare payment rate for certain analgesic injections provided in ambulatory surgical centers (ASCs). (For injections identified by specific billing codes, Medicare would pay the 2016 rate, which is higher than the current rate, during the 2020– 2024 period). Based on current utilization in the ASC setting, CBO estimates that enacting the legislation would increase direct spending by about $115 million over the 2019–2028 period. (If enacted, H.R. 5804 also would affect spending subject to appropriation; see Table 3).

H.R. 5809, the Postoperative Opioid Prevention Act of 2018, would create an additional payment under Medicare for nonopioid analgesics. Under current law, certain new drugs and devices may receive an additional payment—separate from the bundled payment for a surgical procedure—in outpatient hospital departments and ambulatory surgical centers. The bill would allow nonopioid analgesics to qualify for a five-year period of additional payments. Based on its assessment of current spending for analgesics and on the probability of new nonopioid analgesics coming to market, CBO estimates that H.R. 5809 would increase direct spending by about $180 million over the 2019–2028 period.

Legislation Primarily Affecting the Food and Drug Administration. One bill related to the FDA would affect direct spending.

H.R. 5333, the Over-the-Counter Monograph Safety, Innovation, and Reform Act of 2018, would change the way that the FDA regulates the marketing of over-the-counter (OTC) medicines, and it would authorize that agency to grant 18 months of exclusive market protection for certain qualifying OTC drugs, thus delaying the entry of other versions of the same qualifying OTC product. Medicaid currently provides some coverage for OTC medicines, but only if a medicine is the least costly alternative in its drug class. On the basis of stakeholder feedback, CBO expects that delaying the availability of additional OTC versions of a drug would not significantly affect the average net price paid by Medicaid. As a result, CBO estimates that enacting H.R. 5333 would have a negligible effect on the federal budget. (If enacted, H.R. 5333 also would affect spending subject to appropriation; see Table 3).

Legislation with Revenue Effects. Two bills would affect revenues. However, CBO estimates that one bill, H.R. 5228, the Stop Counterfeit Drugs by Regulating and Enhancing Enforcement Now Act, would have only a negligible effect.

H.R. 5752, the Stop Illicit Drug Importation Act of 2018, would amend the Federal, Food, Drug, and Cosmetic Act (FDCA) to strengthen the FDA's seizure powers and enhance its authority to detain, refuse, seize, or destroy illegal products offered for import. The legislation would subject more people to debarment under the FDCA and thus increase the potential for violations, and subsequently, the assessment of civil penalties, which are recorded in the budget as revenues. CBO estimates that those collections would result in an insignificant increase in revenues. Because H.R. 5752 would prohibit the importation of drugs that are in the process of being scheduled, it also could reduce amounts collected in customs duties. CBO anticipates that the result would be a negligible decrease in revenues. With those results taken together, CBO estimates, enacting H.R. 5752 would generate an insignificant net increase in revenues over the 2019–2028 period.

Spending Subject to Appropriation

For this document, CBO has grouped bills with spending that would be subject to appropriation into four general categories:

- Bills that would have no budgetary effect,
- Bills with provisions that would authorize specified amounts to be appropriated (see Table 2),

- Bills with provisions for which CBO has estimated an authorization of appropriations (see Table 3), and
- Bills with provisions that would affect spending subject to appropriation for which CBO has not yet completed an estimate.

No Budgetary Effect. CBO estimates that 6 of the 59 bills would have no effect on direct spending, revenues, or spending subject to appropriation.

H.R. 3192, the CHIP Mental Health Parity Act, would require all Children's Health Insurance Program (CHIP) plans to cover mental health and substance abuse treatment. In addition, states would not be allowed to impose financial or utilization limits on mental health treatment that are lower than limits placed on physical health treatment. Based on information from the Centers for Medicare and Medicaid Services, CBO estimates that enacting the bill would have no budgetary effect because all CHIP enrollees are already in plans that meet those requirements.

H.R. 3331, a bill to amend title XI of the Social Security Act to promote testing of incentive payments for behavioral health providers for adoption and use of certified electronic health record technology, would give the Center for Medicare and Medicaid Innovation (CMMI) explicit authorization to test a program offering incentive payments to behavioral health providers that adopt and use certified electronic health record technology. Because it is already clear to CMMI that it has that authority, CBO estimates that enacting the legislation would not affect federal spending.

H.R. 5202, the Ensuring Patient Access to Substance Use Disorder Treatments Act of 2018, would clarify permission for pharmacists to deliver controlled substances to providers under certain circumstances. Because this provision would codify current practice, CBO estimates that H.R. 5202 would not affect direct spending or revenues during the 2019–2028 period.

H.R. 5685, the Medicare Opioid Safety Education Act of 2018, would require the Secretary of HHS to include information on opioid use, pain management, and nonopioid pain management treatments in future editions of *Medicare & You,* the program's handbook for beneficiaries, starting on January 1, 2019. Because H.R. 5685 would add information to an existing administrative document, CBO estimates that enacting the bill would have no budgetary effect.

H.R. 5686, the Medicare Clear Health Options in Care for Enrollees Act of 2018, would require prescription drug plans that provide coverage under Medicare Part D to furnish information to beneficiaries about the risks of opioid use and the availability of alternative treatments for pain. CBO estimates that enacting the bill would not affect direct spending because the required activities would not impose significant administrative costs.

H.R. 5716, the Commit to Opioid Medical Prescriber Accountability and Safety for Seniors Act, would require the Secretary of HHS on an annual basis to identify high prescribers of opioids and furnish them with information about proper prescribing methods. Because HHS already has the capacity to meet those requirements, CBO estimates that enacting that provision would not impose additional administrative costs on the agency.

Table 2. Estimated spending subject to appropriation for bills with specified authorizations

	By fiscal year, in millions of dollars—						
	2018	2019	2020	2021	2022	2023	2019–2023
INCREASES IN SPENDING SUBJECT TO APPROPRIATION							
H.R. 4684, Ensuring Access to Quality Sober Living Act:							
Authorization Level	0	3	0	0	0	0	3
Estimated Outlays	0	1	2	*	*	*	3
H.R. 5102, Substance Use Disorder Workforce Loan Repayment Act of 2018:							
Authorization Level	0	25	25	25	25	25	125
Estimated Outlays	0	9	19	23	25	25	100
H.R. 5176, Preventing Overdoses While in Emergency Rooms Act of 2018:							
Authorization Level	0	50	0	0	0	0	50
Estimated Outlays	0	16	26	6	2	1	50
H.R. 5197, Alternatives to Opioids (ALTO) in the Emergency Department Act:							
Authorization Level	0	10	10	10	0	0	30
Estimated Outlays	0	3	8	10	7	2	30
H.R. 5261, Treatment, Education, and Community Help to Combat Addiction Act of 2018:							
Authorization Level	0	4	4	4	4	4	20
Estimated Outlays	0	1	3	4	4	4	16
H.R. 5327, Comprehensive Opioid Recovery Centers Act of 2018:							
Authorization Level	0	10	10	10	10	10	50
Estimated Outlays	0	3	8	10	10	10	41
H.R. 5329, Poison Center Network Enhancement Act of 2018:							
Authorization Level	0	30	30	30	30	30	151
Estimated Outlays	0	12	25	29	29	29	125
H.R. 5353, Eliminating Opioid-Related Infectious Diseases Act of 2018:							
Authorization Level	0	40	40	40	40	40	200
Estimated Outlays	0	15	34	38	39	40	166
H.R. 5580, Surveillance and Testing of Opioids to Prevent Fentanyl Deaths Act of 2018:							
Authorization Level	30	30	30	30	30	0	120
Estimated Outlays	0	11	25	29	29	19	113
H.R. 5587, Peer Support Communities of Recovery Act:							
Authorization Level	0	15	15	15	15	15	75
Estimated Outlays	0	5	13	14	15	15	62

Annual amounts may not sum to totals because of rounding. * = between zero and $500,000.

Specified Authorizations. Table 2 lists the ten bills that would authorize specified amounts to be appropriated over the 2019–2023 period. Spending from those authorized amounts would be subject to appropriation.

H.R. 4684, the Ensuring Access to Quality Sober Living Act, would direct the Secretary of HHS to develop and disseminate best practices for organizations that operate housing designed for people recovering from substance use disorders. The bill would authorize a total of $3 million over the 2019–2021 period for that purpose. Based on historical spending patterns for similar activities, CBO estimates that implementing H.R. 4684 would cost $3 million over the 2019–2023 period.

H.R. 5102, the Substance Use Disorder Workforce Loan Repayment Act of 2018, would establish a loan repayment program for mental health professionals who practice in areas with few mental health providers or with high rates of death from overdose and would authorize $25 million per year over the 2019–2028 period for that purpose. Based on historical spending patterns for similar activities, CBO estimates that implementing H.R. 5102 would cost $100 million over the 2019–2023 period; the remaining amounts would be spent in years after 2023.

H.R. 5176, the Preventing Overdoses While in Emergency Rooms Act of 2018, would require the Secretary of HHS to develop protocols and a grant program for health care providers to address the needs of people who survive a drug overdose, and it would authorize $50 million in 2019 for that purpose. Based on historical spending patterns for similar activities, CBO estimates that implementing H.R. 5176 would cost $50 million over the 2019–2023 period.

H.R. 5197, the Alternatives to Opioids (ALTO) in the Emergency Department Act, would direct the Secretary of HHS to carry out a demonstration program for hospitals and emergency departments to develop alternative protocols for pain management that limit the use of opioids and would authorize $10 million annually in grants for fiscal years 2019 through 2021. Based on historical spending patterns for similar programs, CBO estimates that implementing H.R. 5197 would cost $30 million over the 2019–2023 period.

H.R. 5261, the Treatment, Education, and Community Help to Combat Addiction Act of 2018, would direct the Secretary of HHS to designate regional centers of excellence to improve the training of health professionals who treat substance use disorders. The bill would authorize $4 million annually for grants to those programs over the 2019–2023 period. Based on historical spending patterns for similar activities, CBO estimates that implementing H.R. 5261 would cost $16 million over the 2019–2023 period; the remaining amounts would be spent in years after 2023.

H.R. 5327, the Comprehensive Opioid Recovery Centers Act of 2018, would direct the Secretary of HHS to award grants to at least 10 providers that offer treatment services for people with opioid use disorder, and it would authorize $10 million per year over the 2019–2023 period for that purpose. Based on historical spending patterns for similar activities, CBO estimates that implementing H.R. 5327 would cost $41 million over the 2019–2023 period; the remaining amounts would be spent in years after 2023.

H.R. 5329, the Poison Center Network Enhancement Act of 2018, would reauthorize the poison control center toll-free number, national media campaign, and grant program under the Public Health Service Act. Among other actions, H.R. 5329 would increase the share of poison control center funding that could be provided by federal grants. The bill would authorize a total of about $30 million per year over the 2019–2023 period. Based on historical spending patterns for similar activities, CBO estimates that implementing H.R. 5329 would cost $125 million over the 2019–2023 period; the remaining amounts would be spent in years after 2023.

H.R 5353, the Eliminating Opioid Related Infectious Diseases Act of 2018, would amend Public Health Service Act by broadening the focus of surveillance and education programs from preventing and treating hepatitis C virus to preventing and treating infections associated with injection drug use. It would authorize $40 million per year over 2019–2023 period for that purpose. Based on historical spending patterns for similar activities, CBO estimates that implementing H.R. 5353 would cost $166 million over the 2019–2023 period; the remaining amounts would be spent in years after 2023.

H.R. 5580, the Surveillance and Testing of Opioids to Prevent Fentanyl Deaths Act of 2018, would establish a grant program for public health laboratories that conduct testing for fentanyl and other synthetic opioids. It also would direct the Centers for Disease Control and Prevention to expand its drug surveillance program, with a particular focus on collecting data on fentanyl. The bill would authorize a total of $30 million per year over the 2018–2022 period for those activities. Based on historical spending patterns for similar activities, CBO estimates that implementing H.R. 5580 would cost $113 million over the 2019–2023 period; the remaining amounts would be spent in years after 2023.

H.R. 5587, Peer Support Communities of Recovery Act, would direct the Secretary of HHS to award grants to nonprofit organizations that support community-based, peer-delivered support, including technical support for the establishment of recovery community organizations, independent, nonprofit groups led by people in recovery and their families. The bill would authorize $15 million per year for the 2019–2023 period. Based on historical spending patterns for similar activities, CBO estimates that implementing H.R. 5587 would cost $62 million over the 2019–2023 period; the remaining amounts would be spent in years after 2023.

Estimated Authorizations. Table 3 shows CBO's estimates of the appropriations that would be necessary to implement 19 of the bills. Spending would be subject to appropriation of those amounts.

H.R. 449, the Synthetic Drug Awareness Act of 2018, would require the Surgeon General to report to the Congress on the health effects of synthetic psychoactive drugs on children between the ages of 12 and 18. Based on spending patterns for similar activities, CBO estimates that implementing H.R. 449 would cost approximately $1 million over the 2019–2023 period.

H.R. 4005, the Medicaid Reentry Act, would direct the Secretary of HHS to convene a group of stakeholders to develop and report to the Congress on best practices for addressing issues related to health care faced by those returning from incarceration to their communities. The bill also would require the Secretary to issue a letter to state Medicaid directors about relevant demonstration projects. Based on an analysis of anticipated workload, CBO estimates that implementing H.R. 4005 would cost less than $500,000 over the 2018–2023 period.

Table 3. Estimated spending subject to appropriation for bills with estimated authorizations

	By fiscal year, in millions of dollars—						
	2018	2019	2020	2021	2022	2023	2019–2023
INCREASES IN SPENDING SUBJECT TO APPROPRIATION							
H.R. 449, Synthetic Drug Awareness Act of 2018:							
Estimated Authorization Level	0	*	*	*	0	0	1
Estimated Outlays	0	*	*	*	0	0	1
H.R. 4005, Medicaid Reentry Act:							
Estimated Authorization Level	*	*	0	0	0	0	*
Estimated Outlays	*	*	0	0	0	0	*
H.R. 4275, Empowering Pharmacists in the Fight Against Opioid Abuse Act:							
Estimated Authorization Level	0	*	*	*	*	*	*
Estimated Outlays	0	*	*	*	*	*	*
H.R. 5009, Jessie's Law:							
Estimated Authorization Level	0	*	*	*	*	*	*
Estimated Outlays	0	*	*	*	*	*	*
H.R. 5041, Safe Disposal of Unused Medication Act:							
Estimated Authorization Level	0	*	*	*	*	*	*
Estimated Outlays	0	*	*	*	*	*	*
H.R. 5272, Reinforcing Evidence-Based Standards Under Law in Treating Substance Abuse Act of 2018:							
Estimated Authorization Level	0	1	1	1	1	1	4
Estimated Outlays	0	1	1	1	1	1	4
H.R. 5333, Over-the-Counter Monograph Safety, Innovation, and Reform Act of 2018: a							
Food and Drug Administration:							
Collections from fees:							
Estimated Authortration Level	0	−22	−22	−26	−35	−42	−147
Estimated Outlays	0	−22	−22	−26	−35	−42	−147
Spending of fees:							
Estimated Authortration Level	0	22	22	26	35	42	147
Estimated Outlays	0	6	17	30	44	41	137
Net effect on FDA:							
Estimated Authortration Level	0	0	0	0	0	0	0
Estimated Outlays	0	−17	−6	4	9	*	−10
Government Accountability Office:							
Estimated Authorization Level	0	0	0	0	0	*	*
Estimated Outlays	0	0	0	0	0	*	*
Total, H.R. 5333:							
Estimated Authorization Level	0	0	0	0	0	*	*
Estimated Outlays	0	−17	−6	4	9	*	−10
H.R. 5473, Better Pain Management Through Better Data Act of 2018:							
Estimated Authorization Level	0	*	*	*	*	0	1
Estimated Outlays	0	*	*	*	*	*	1
H.R. 5483, Special Registration for Telemedicine Clarification Act of 2018:							
Estimated Authorization Level	0	*	*	*	*	*	*
Estimated Outlays	0	*	*	*	*	*	*
H.R. 5554, Animal Drug and Animal Generic Drug User Fee Amendments of 2018:							
Collections from fees:							
Animal drug fees	0	−30	−31	−32	−33	−34	−159
Generic animal drug fees	0	−18	−19	−19	−20	−21	−97
Total, Estimated Authortration Level	0	−49	−50	−51	−53	−55	−257
Total, Estimated Outlays	0	−49	−50	−51	−53	−55	−257
Spending of fees:							
Animal drug fees	0	30	31	32	33	34	159
Generic animal drug fees	0	18	19	19	20	21	97
Total, Estimated Authortration Level	0	49	50	51	53	55	257
Total, Estimated Outlays	0	39	47	51	52	54	243

	By fiscal year, in millions of dollars—						
	2018	2019	2020	2021	2022	2023	2019–2023
Net changes in fees:							
Estimated Authorization Level	0	0	0	0	0	0	0
Estimated Outlays	0	−10	−3	*	*	*	−14
Other effects:							
Estimated Authorization Level	0	3	1	1	1	1	6
Estimated Outlays	0	2	1	1	1	1	6
Total, H.R. 5554:							
Estimated Authorization Level	0	3	1	1	1	1	6
Estimated Outlays	0	−8	−2	1	*	*	−8
H.R. 5582, Abuse Deterrent Access Act of 2018:							
Estimated Authorization Level	0	0	*	0	0	0	*
Estimated Outlays	0	0	*	0	0	0	*
H.R. 5590, Opioid Addiction Action Plan Act:							
Estimated Authorization Level	*	*	*	*	*	*	2
Estimated Outlays	*	*	*	*	*	*	2
H.R. 5687, Securing Opioids and Unused Narcotics with Deliberate Disposal and Packaging Act of 2018:							
Estimated Authorization Level	0	*	*	*	*	*	*
Estimated Outlays	0	*	*	*	*	*	*
H.R. 5715, Strengthening Partnerships to Prevent Opioid Abuse Act:							
Estimated Authorization Level	0	2	2	2	2	2	9
Estimated Outlays	0	2	2	2	2	2	9
H.R. 5789, a bill to require the Secretary of Health and Human Services to issue guidance to improve care for infants with neonatal abstinence syndrome and their mothers, and to require the Comptroller General of the United States to conduct a study on gaps in Medicaid coverage for pregnant and postpartum women with substance use disorder:							
Estimated Authorization Level	0	2	0	0	0	0	2
Estimated Outlays	0	2	0	0	0	0	2
H.R. 5795, Overdose Prevention and Patient Safety Act:							
Estimated Authorization Level	0	1	0	0	0	0	1
Estimated Outlays	0	1	0	0	0	0	1
H.R. 5800, Medicaid IMD ADDITIONAL INFO Act:							
Estimated Authorization Level	0	1	0	0	0	0	1
Estimated Outlays	0	*	*	0	0	0	1
H.R. 5804, Post-Surgical Injections as an Opioid Alternative Act: a							
Estimated Authorization Level	0	0	0	0	1	1	1
Estimated Outlays	0	0	0	0	1	1	1
H.R. 5811, a bill to amend the Federal Food, Drug, and Cosmetic Act with respect to postapproval study requirements for certain controlled substances, and for other purposes:							
Estimated Authorization Level	0	*	*	*	*	*	*
Estimated Outlays	0	*	*	*	*	*	*

Annual amounts may not sum to totals because of rounding. * = between ¥$500,000 and $500,000. a This bill also would affect mandatory spending (see Table 1).

H.R. 4275, the Empowering Pharmacists in the Fight against Opioid Abuse Act, would require the Secretary of HHS to develop and disseminate materials for training pharmacists, health care practitioners, and the public about the circumstances under which a pharmacist may decline to fill a prescription. Based on historical spending patterns for similar activities, CBO estimates that costs to the federal government for the development and distribution of those materials would not be significant.

H.R. 5009, Jessie's Law, would require HHS, in collaboration with outside experts, to develop best practices for displaying information about opioid use disorder in a patient's medical record. HHS also would be required to develop and disseminate written materials annually to health care providers about what disclosures could be made while still complying with federal laws that govern health care privacy. Based on spending patterns for similar activities, CBO estimates that implementing H.R. 5009 would have an insignificant effect on spending over the 2019–2023 period.

H.R. 5041, the Safe Disposal of Unused Medication Act, would require hospice programs to have written policies and procedures for the disposal of controlled substances after a patient's death. Certain licensed employees of hospice programs would be permitted to assist in the disposal of controlled substances that were lawfully dispensed. Using information from the Department of Justice (DOJ), CBO estimates that implementing the bill would cost less than $500,000 over the 2019–2023 period.

H.R. 5272, the Reinforcing Evidence-Based Standards Under Law in Treating Substance Abuse Act of 2018, would require the newly established National Mental Health and Substance Use Policy Laboratory to issue guidance to applicants for SAMHSA grants that support evidence-based practices. Using information from HHS about the historical cost of similar activities, CBO estimates that enacting this bill would cost approximately $4 million over the 2019–2023 period.

H.R. 5333, the Over-the-Counter Monograph Safety, Innovation, and Reform Act of 2018, would change the FDA's oversight of the commercial marketing of OTC medicines and authorize the collection and spending of fees through 2023 to cover the costs of expediting the FDA's administrative procedures for certain regulatory activities relating to OTC products. Under H.R. 5333, CBO estimates, the FDA would assess about $147 million in fees over the 2019–2023 period that could be collected and made available for obligation only to the extent and in the amounts provided in advance in appropriation acts. Because the FDA could spend those fees, CBO estimates that the estimated budget authority for collections and spending would offset each other exactly in each year, although CBO expects that spending initially would lag behind collections. Assuming appropriation action consistent with the bill, CBO estimates that implementing H.R. 5333 would reduce net discretionary outlays by $10 million over the 2019–2023 period, primarily because of that lag. The bill also would require the Government Accountability Office to study exclusive market protections for certain qualifying OTC drugs authorized by the bill—a provision that CBO estimates would cost less than $500,000. (If enacted, H.R. 5333 also would affect mandatory spending; see Table 1.)

H.R. 5473, the Better Pain Management Through Better Data Act of 2018, would require that the FDA conduct a public meeting and issue guidance to industry addressing data collection and labeling for medical products that reduce pain while enabling the reduction, replacement, or avoidance of oral opioids. Using information from the agency, CBO estimates that implementing H.R. 5473 would cost about $1 million over the 2019–2023 period.

H.R. 5483, the Special Registration for Telemedicine Clarification Act of 2018, would direct DOJ, within one year of the bill's enactment, to issue regulations concerning the practice of telemedicine (for remote diagnosis and treatment of patients). Using information from DOJ, CBO estimates that implementing the bill would cost less than $500,000 over the 2019–2023 period.

H.R. 5554, the Animal Drug and Animal Generic Drug User Fee Amendments of 2018, would authorize the FDA to collect and spend fees to cover the cost of expedited approval for the development and marketing of certain drugs for use in animals. The legislation would extend through fiscal year 2023, and make several changes to, the FDA's existing approval processes and fee programs for brand-name and generic veterinary drugs, which expire at the end of fiscal year 2018. CBO estimates that implementing H.R. 5554 would reduce net discretionary outlays by $8 million over the 2019–2023 period, primarily because the spending of fees lags somewhat behind their collection.

Fees authorized under the bill would supplement funds appropriated to cover the FDA's cost of reviewing certain applications and investigational submissions for brand-name and generic drugs for use in animals. Those fees could be collected and made available for obligation only to the extent and in the amounts provided in advance in appropriation acts. Under H.R. 5554, CBO estimates, the FDA would assess about $257 million in fees over the 2019– 2023 period. Because the FDA could spend those funds, CBO estimates that budget authority for collections and spending would offset each other exactly in each year. CBO estimates that the delay between collecting and spending fees under the reauthorized programs would reduce net discretionary outlays by $14 million over the 2019–2023 period, assuming appropriation actions consistent with the bill.

Enacting H.R. 5554 would increase the FDA's workload because the legislation would expand eligibility for conditional approval for certain drugs. The agency's administrative costs also would increase because of regulatory activities required by a provision concerning petitions for additives intended for use in animal food. H.R. 5554 also would require the FDA to publish guidance or produce regulations on a range of topics, transmit a report to the Congress, and hold public meetings. CBO expects that the costs associated with those activities would not be covered by fees, and it estimates that implementing such provisions would cost $6 million over the 2019–2023 period.

H.R. 5582, the Abuse Deterrent Access Act of 2018, would require the Secretary of HHS to report to the Congress on existing barriers to access to "abuse-deterrent opioid formulations" by Medicare Part C and D beneficiaries. Such formulations make the drugs more difficult to dissolve for injection, for example, and thus can impede their abuse. Assuming the availability of appropriated funds and based on historical spending patterns for similar activities, CBO estimates that implementing the legislation would cost less than $500,000 over the 2019–2023 period.

H.R. 5590, the Opioid Addiction Action Plan Act, would require the Secretary of HHS to develop an action plan by January 1, 2019, for increasing access to medication-assisted treatment among Medicare and Medicaid enrollees. The bill also would require HHS to convene a stakeholder meeting and issue a request for information within three months of enactment, and to submit a report to the Congress by June 1, 2019. Based on historical spending patterns for similar activities, CBO estimates that implementing H.R. 5590 would cost approximately $2 million over the 2019–2023 period.

H.R. 5687, the Securing Opioids and Unused Narcotics with Deliberate Disposal and Packaging Act of 2018, would permit the FDA to require certain packaging and disposal technologies, controls, or measures to mitigate the risk of abuse and misuse of drugs. Based on information from the FDA, CBO estimates that implementing H.R. 5687 would not significantly affect spending over the 2019–2023 period. This bill would also require that the GAO study the effectiveness and use of packaging technologies for controlled substances—a provision that CBO estimates would cost less than $500,000.

H.R. 5715, the Strengthening Partnerships to Prevent Opioid Abuse Act, would require the Secretary of HHS to establish a secure Internet portal to allow HHS, Medicare Advantage plans, and Medicare Part D plans to exchange information about fraud, waste, and abuse among providers and suppliers no later than two years after enactment. H.R. 5715 also would require organizations with Medicare Advantage contracts to submit information on investigations related to providers suspected of prescribing large volumes of opioids through a process established by the Secretary no later than January 2021. Based on historical spending patterns for similar activities, CBO estimates that implementing H.R. 5715 would cost approximately $9 million over the 2019–2023 period.

H.R. 5789, a bill to require the Secretary of Health and Human Services to issue guidance to improve care for infants with neonatal abstinence syndrome and their mothers, and to require the Comptroller General of the United States to conduct a study on gaps in Medicaid coverage for pregnant and postpartum women with substance use disorder, would direct the Secretary of HHS to issue guidance to states on best practices under Medicaid and CHIP for treating infants with neonatal abstinence syndrome. H.R. 5789 also would direct the Government Accountability Office to study Medicaid coverage for pregnant and postpartum women with substance use disorders. Based on inforation from HHS and historical spending patterns for similar activities, CBO estimates that enacting H.R. 5789 would cost approximately $2 million over the 2019–2023 period.

H.R. 5795, the Overdose Prevention and Patient Safety Act, would amend the Public Health Service Act so that requirements pertaining to the confidentiality and disclosure of medical records relating to substance use disorders align with the provisions of the Health Insurance Portability and Accountability Act of 1996. The bill would require the Office of the Secretary of HHS to issue regulations prohibiting discrimination based on data disclosed from such medical records, to issue regulations requiring covered entities to provide written notice of privacy practices, and to develop model training programs and materials for health care providers and patients and their families. Based on spending patterns for similar activities, CBO estimates that implementing H.R. 5795 would cost approximately $1 million over the 2019–2023 period.

H.R. 5800, Medicaid IMD ADDITIONAL INFO Act, would direct the Medicaid and CHIP Payment and Access Commission to study institutions for mental diseases in a representative sample of states. Based on information from the commission about the cost of similar work, CBO estimates that implementing H.R. 5800 would cost about $1 million over the 2019–2023 period.

H.R. 5804, the Post-Surgical Injections as an Opioid Alternative Act, would freeze the Medicare payment rate for certain analgesic injections provided in ambulatory surgical centers. The bill also would mandate two studies of Medicare coding and payments arising from enactment of this legislation. Based on the cost of similar activities, CBO estimates that those reports would cost $1 million over the 2019–2023 period. (If enacted, H.R. 5804 also would affect mandatory spending; see Table 1).

H.R. 5811, a bill to amend the Federal Food, Drug, and Cosmetic Act with respect to postapproval study requirements for certain controlled substances, and for other purposes, would allow the FDA to require that pharmaceutical manufacturers study certain drugs after they are approved to assess any potential reduction in those drugs' effectiveness for the conditions of use prescribed, recommended, or suggested in labeling. CBO anticipates that implementing H.R. 5811 would not significantly affect the FDA's costs over the 2019–2023 period.

Other Authorizations. The following nine bills would increase authorization levels, but CBO has not completed estimates of amounts. All authorizations would be subject to future appropriation action.

- H.R. 4284, Indexing Narcotics, Fentanyl, and Opioids Act of 2017
- H.R. 5002, Advancing Cutting Edge Research Act
- H.R. 5228, Stop Counterfeit Drugs by Regulating and Enhancing Enforcement Now Act (see Table 1 for an estimate of the revenue effects of H.R. 5228)
- H.R. 5752, Stop Illicit Drug Importation Act of 2018 (see Table 1 for an estimate of the revenue effects of H.R. 5752)
- H.R. 5799, Medicaid DRUG Improvement Act (see Table 1 for an estimate of the direct spending effects of H.R. 5799)
- H.R. 5801, Medicaid Providers and Pharmacists Are Required to Note Experiences in Record Systems to Help In-Need Patients (PARTNERSHIP) Act (see Table 1 for an estimate of the direct spending effects of H.R. 5801)
- H.R. 5806, 21st Century Tools for Pain and Addiction Treatments Act
- H.R. 5808, Medicaid Pharmaceutical Home Act of 2018 (see Table 1 for an estimate of the direct spending effects of H.R. 5808)

- H.R. 5812, Creating Opportunities that Necessitate New and Enhanced Connections That Improve Opioid Navigation Strategies Act (CONNECTIONS) Act.

Pay-As-You-Go considerations: The Statutory Pay-As-You-Go Act of 2010 establishes budget-reporting and enforcement procedures for legislation affecting direct spending or revenues. Twenty-two of the bills discussed in this document contain direct spending or revenues and are subject to pay-as-you-go procedures. Details about the amount of direct spending and revenues in those bills can be found in Table 1.

Increase in long-term direct spending and deficits: CBO estimates that enacting H.R. 4998, the Health Insurance for Former Foster Youth Act, would increase net direct spending by more than $2.5 billion and on-budget deficits by more than $5 billion in at least one of the four consecutive 10-year periods beginning in 2029.

CBO estimates that none of the remaining 58 bills included in this estimate would increase net direct spending by more than $2.5 billion or on-budget deficits by more than $5 billion in any of the four consecutive 10-year periods beginning in 2029.

Mandates: One of the 59 bills included in this document, H.R. 5795, would impose both intergovernmental and private-sector mandates as defined in UMRA. CBO estimates that the costs of that bill's mandates on public and private entities would fall below UMRA's thresholds ($80 million and $160 million, respectively, for public- and private-sector entities in 2018, adjusted annually for inflation).

In addition, five bills would impose private-sector mandates as defined in UMRA. CBO estimates that the costs of the mandates in three of those bills (H.R. 5333, H.R. 5554, and H.R. 5811) would fall below the UMRA threshold. Because CBO does not know how federal agencies would implement new authority granted in the other two of those five bills, H.R. 5228 and 5687, CBO cannot determine whether the costs of their mandates would exceed the threshold.

For large entitlement grant programs, including Medicaid and CHIP, UMRA defines an increase in the stringency of conditions on states or localities as an intergovernmental mandate if the affected governments lack authority to offset those costs while continuing to provide required services. Because states possess significant flexibility to alter their responsibilities within Medicaid and CHIP, the requirements imposed by various bills in the markup on state administration of those programs would not constitute mandates as defined in UMRA.

Mandates Affecting Public and Private Entities

H.R. 5795, the Overdose Prevention and Patient Safety Act, would impose intergovernmental and private-sector mandates by requiring entities that provide treatment for substance use disorders to notify patients of their privacy rights and also to notify patients in the event that the confidentiality of their records is breached. In certain circumstances, H.R. 5795 also would prohibit public and private entities from denying entry to treatment on the basis of information in patient health records. Those requirements would either supplant or narrowly expand responsibilities under existing law, and compliance with them would not impose significant additional costs. CBO estimates that the costs of the mandates would fall below the annual thresholds established in UMRA.

Mandates Affecting Private Entities

Five bills included in this document would impose private-sector mandates:

H.R. 5228, the Stop Counterfeit Drugs by Regulating and Enhancing Enforcement Now Act, would require drug distributors to cease distributing any drug that the Secretary of HHS determines might present an imminent or substantial hazard to public health. CBO cannot determine what drugs could be subject to such an order nor can it determine how private entities would respond. Consequently, CBO cannot determine whether the aggregate cost of the mandate would exceed the annual threshold for private-sector mandates.

H.R. 5333, the Over-the-Counter Monograph Safety, Innovation, and Reform Act of 2018, would require developers and manufacturers of OTC drugs to pay certain fees to the FDA. CBO estimates that about $30 million would be collected each year, on average, for a total of $147 million over the 2019–2023 period. Those amounts would not exceed the annual threshold for private-sector mandates in any year during that period.

H.R. 5554, the Animal Drug and Animal Generic Drug User Fee Amendments of 2018, would require developers and manufacturers of brand-name and generic veterinary drugs to pay application, product, establishment, and sponsor fees to the FDA. CBO estimates that about $51 million would be collected annually, on average, for a total of $257 million over the 2019–2023 period. Those amounts would not exceed the annual threshold for private-sector mandates in any year during that period.

H.R. 5687, the Securing Opioids and Unused Narcotics with Deliberate Disposal and Packaging Act of 2018, would permit the Secretary of HHS to require drug developers and manufacturers to implement new packaging and disposal technology for certain drugs. Based on information from the agency, CBO expects that the Secretary would use the new regulatory authority provided in the bill; however, it is uncertain how or when those requirements would be implemented. Consequently, CBO cannot determine whether the aggregate cost of the mandate would exceed the annual threshold for private entities.

H.R. 5811, a bill to amend the Federal Food, Drug, and Cosmetic Act with respect to postapproval study requirements for certain controlled substances, and for other purposes, would expand an existing mandate that requires drug developers to conduct postapproval studies or clinical trials for certain drugs. Under current law, in certain instances, the FDA can require studies or clinical trials after a drug has been approved. H.R. 5811 would permit the FDA to use that authority if the reduction in a drug's effectiveness meant that its benefits no longer outweighed its costs. CBO estimates that the incremental cost of the mandate would fall below the annual threshold established in UMRA because of the small number of drugs affected and the narrow expansion of the authority that exists under current law.

None of the remaining 53 bills included in this document would impose an intergovernmental or private-sector mandate.

Previous CBO estimate: On June 6, 2018, CBO issued an estimate for seven opioid-related bills ordered reported by the House Committee on Ways and Means on May 16, 2018. Two of those bills contain provisions that are identical or similar to the legislation ordered reported by the Committee on Energy and Commerce, and for those provisions, CBO's estimates are the same.

In particular, five bills listed in this estimate contain provisions that are identical or similar to those in several sections of H.R. 5773, the Preventing Addiction for Susceptible Seniors Act of 2018:

- H.R. 5675, which would require prescription drug plans to implement drug management programs, is identical to section 2 of H.R. 5773.
- H.R. 4841, regarding electronic prior authorization for prescriptions under Medicare's Part D, is similar to section 3 of H.R. 5773.
- H.R. 5715, which would mandate the creation of a new Internet portal to allow various stakeholders to exchange information, is identical to section 4 of H.R. 5773.
- H.R. 5684, which would expand medication therapy management, is the same as section 5 of H.R. 5773.
- H.R. 5716, regarding prescriber notification, is identical to section 6 of H.R. 5773.

In addition, in this estimate, a provision related to Medicare beneficiary education in H.R. 5686, the Medicare Clear Health Options in Care for Enrollees Act of 2018, is the same as a provision in section 2 of H.R. 5775, the Providing Reliable Options for Patients and Educational Resources Act of 2018, in CBO's estimate for the Committee on Ways and Means.

Federal Mandates Statement

The Committee adopts as its own the estimate of Federal mandates prepared by the Director of the Congressional Budget Office pursuant to section 423 of the Unfunded Mandates Reform Act.

Statement of General Performance Goals and Objectives

Pursuant to clause 3(c)(4) of rule XIII, the general performance goal or objective of this legislation is to direct the Centers for Medicare and Medicaid Services to require e-prescribing for coverage of prescribed controlled substances under the Medicare Part D program.

Duplication of Federal Programs

Pursuant to clause 3(c)(5) of rule XIII, no provision of H.R. 3528 is known to be duplicative of another Federal program, including any program that was included in a report to Congress pursuant to section 21 of Public Law 111–139 or the most recent Catalog of Federal Domestic Assistance.

Committee Cost Estimate

Pursuant to clause 3(d)(1) of rule XIII, the Committee adopts as its own the cost estimate prepared by the Director of the Congressional Budget Office pursuant to section 402 of the Congressional Budget Act of 1974.

Earmark, Limited Tax Benefits, and Limited Tariff Benefits

Pursuant to clause 9(e), 9(f), and 9(g) of rule XXI, the Committee finds that H.R. 3528 contains no earmarks, limited tax benefits, or limited tariff benefits.

Disclosure of Directed Rule Makings

Pursuant to section 3(i) of H. Res. 5, the following directed rule makings are contained in H.R. 3528:

- *Section 2(a)(B):* The Secretary shall, pursuant to rule-making, specify circumstances with respect to which the Secretary may waive the requirement under subparagraph (A), with respect to a covered part D drug.
- *Section 2(a)(D):* The Secretary shall, pursuant to rule-making, have authority to enforce and specify appropriate penalties for noncompliance with the requirement under subparagraph (A).

Advisory Committee Statement

No advisory committees within the meaning of section 5(b) of the Federal Advisory Committee Act were created by this legislation.

Applicability To Legislative Branch

The Committee finds that the legislation does not relate to the terms and conditions of employment or access to public services or accommodations within the meaning of section 102(b)(3) of the Congressional Accountability Act.

Section-by-Section Analysis of the Legislation

Section 1. Short title. Section 1 provides that the Act may be cited as the "Every Prescription Conveyed Securely Act."

Section 2. Requiring E-prescribing for coverage of covered Part D controlled substances. Section requires prescriptions for a schedule II, III, IV, or V controlled substance covered under a part D prescription drug plan or MA–PD plan to be transmitted in accordance with an electronic prescription drug program by January 1, 2021. The Secretary may waive this requirement in certain defined cases, such as reasonable technological limitations.

CHANGES IN EXISTING LAW MADE BY THE BILL, AS REPORTED

In compliance with clause 3(e) of rule XIII of the Rules of the House of Representatives, changes in existing law made by the bill, as reported, are shown as follows (new matter is printed in italic and existing law in which no change is proposed is shown in roman):

SOCIAL SECURITY ACT: TITLE XVIII— HEALTH INSURANCE FOR THE AGED AND DISABLED

Part D—Voluntary Prescription Drug Benefit Program

Subpart 1—Part D Eligible Individuals And Prescription Drug Benefits: Beneficiary Protections For Qualified Prescription Drug Coverage

SEC. 1860D–4. (a) DISSEMINATION OF INFORMATION.—

(1) GENERAL INFORMATION.—

(A) APPLICATION OF MA INFORMATION.—A PDP sponsor shall disclose, in a clear, accurate, and standardized form to each enrollee with a prescription drug plan offered by the sponsor under this part at the time of enrollment and at least annually thereafter, the information described in section 1852(c)(1) relating to such plan, insofar as the Secretary determines appropriate with respect to benefits provided under this part, and including the information described in subparagraph (B).

(B) DRUG SPECIFIC INFORMATION.—The information described in this subparagraph is information concerning the following:

(i) Access to specific covered part D drugs, including access through pharmacy networks.

(ii) How any formulary (including any tiered formulary structure) used by the sponsor functions, including a description of how a part D eligible individual may obtain information on the formulary consistent with paragraph (3).

(iii) Beneficiary cost-sharing requirements and how a part D eligible individual may obtain information on such requirements, including tiered or other copayment level applicable to each drug (or class of drugs), consistent with paragraph (3).

(iv) The medication therapy management program required under subsection (c).

(v) The drug management program for at-risk beneficiaries under subsection (c)(5).

(2) DISCLOSURE UPON REQUEST OF GENERAL COVERAGE, UTILIZATION, AND GRIEVANCE INFORMATION.—Upon request of a part D eligible individual who is eligible to enroll in a prescription drug plan, the PDP sponsor offering such plan shall provide information similar (as determined by the Secretary) to the information described in subparagraphs (A), (B), and (C) of section 1852(c)(2) to such individual.

(3) PROVISION OF SPECIFIC INFORMATION.—

(A) RESPONSE TO BENEFICIARY QUESTIONS.—Each PDP sponsor offering a prescription drug plan shall have a mechanism for providing specific information on a timely basis to enrollees upon request. Such mechanism shall include access to information through the use of a toll-free telephone number and, upon request, the provision of such information in writing.

(B) AVAILABILITY OF INFORMATION ON CHANGES IN FORMULARY THROUGH THE INTERNET.—A PDP sponsor offering a prescription drug plan shall make available on a timely basis through an Internet website information on specific changes in the formulary under the plan (including changes to tiered or preferred status of covered part D drugs).

(4) CLAIMS INFORMATION.—A PDP sponsor offering a prescription drug plan must furnish to each enrollee in a form easily understandable to such enrollees—

(A) an explanation of benefits (in accordance with section 1806(a) or in a comparable manner); and

(B) when prescription drug benefits are provided under this part, a notice of the benefits in relation to—

(i) the initial coverage limit for the current year; and

(ii) the annual out-of-pocket threshold for the current year.

Notices under subparagraph (B) need not be provided more often than as specified by the Secretary and notices under subparagraph (B)(ii) shall take into account the application of section 1860D–2(b)(4)(C) to the extent practicable, as specified by the Secretary.

(b) ACCESS TO COVERED PART D DRUGS.—

(1) ASSURING PHARMACY ACCESS.—

(A) PARTICIPATION OF ANY WILLING PHARMACY.—A prescription drug plan shall permit the participation of any pharmacy that meets the terms and conditions under the plan.

(B) DISCOUNTS ALLOWED FOR NETWORK PHARMACIES.— For covered part D drugs dispensed through in-network pharmacies, a prescription drug plan may, notwithstanding subparagraph (A), reduce coinsurance or copayments for part D eligible individuals enrolled in the plan below the level otherwise required. In no case shall such a reduction result in an increase in payments made by the Secretary under section 1860D–15 to a plan.

(C) CONVENIENT ACCESS FOR NETWORK PHARMACIES.—

(i) IN GENERAL.—The PDP sponsor of the prescription drug plan shall secure the participation in its network of a sufficient number of pharmacies that dispense (other than by mail order) drugs directly to patients to ensure convenient access (consistent with rules established by the Secretary).

(ii) APPLICATION OF TRICARE STANDARDS.—The Secretary shall establish rules for convenient access to in- network pharmacies under this subparagraph that are no less favorable to enrollees than the rules for convenient access to pharmacies included in the statement of work of solicitation (#MDA906–03–R–0002) of the Department of Defense under the TRICARE Retail Pharmacy (TRRx) as of March 13, 2003.

(iii) ADEQUATE EMERGENCY ACCESS.—Such rules shall include adequate emergency access for enrollees.

(iv) CONVENIENT ACCESS IN LONG-TERM CARE FACILITIES.—Such rules may include standards with respect to access for enrollees who are residing in long-term care facilities and for pharmacies operated by the Indian Health Service, Indian tribes and tribal organizations, and urban Indian organizations (as defined in section 4 of the Indian Health Care Improvement Act).

(D) LEVEL PLAYING FIELD.—Such a sponsor shall permit enrollees to receive benefits (which may include a 90-day supply of drugs or biologicals) through a pharmacy (other than a mail order pharmacy), with any differential in charge paid by such enrollees.

(E) NOT REQUIRED TO ACCEPT INSURANCE RISK.—The terms and conditions under subparagraph (A) may not require participating pharmacies to accept insurance risk as a condition of participation.

(2) USE OF STANDARDIZED TECHNOLOGY.—

(A) IN GENERAL.—The PDP sponsor of a prescription drug plan shall issue (and reissue, as appropriate) such a card (or other technology) that may be used by an enrollee to assure access to negotiated prices under section 1860D– 2(d).

(B) STANDARDS.—

(i) IN GENERAL.—The Secretary shall provide for the development, adoption, or recognition of standards relating to a standardized format for the card or other technology required under subparagraph (A). Such standards shall be compatible with part C of title XI and may be based on standards developed by an appropriate standard setting organization.

(ii) CONSULTATION.—In developing the standards under clause (i), the Secretary shall consult with the National Council for Prescription Drug Programs and other standard setting organizations determined appropriate by the Secretary.

(iii) IMPLEMENTATION.—The Secretary shall develop, adopt, or recognize the standards under clause (i) by such date as the Secretary determines shall be sufficient to ensure that PDP sponsors utilize such standards beginning January 1, 2006.

(3) REQUIREMENTS ON DEVELOPMENT AND APPLICATION OF FORMULARIES.—If a PDP sponsor of a prescription drug plan uses a formulary (including the use of tiered cost-sharing), the following requirements must be met:

(A) DEVELOPMENT AND REVISION BY A PHARMACY AND THERAPEUTIC (P&T) COMMITTEE.—

(i) IN GENERAL.—The formulary must be developed and reviewed by a pharmacy and therapeutic committee. A majority of the members of such committee shall consist of individuals who are practicing physicians or practicing pharmacists (or both).

(ii) INCLUSION OF INDEPENDENT EXPERTS.—Such committee shall include at least one practicing physician and at least one practicing pharmacist, each of whom—

(I) is independent and free of conflict with respect to the sponsor and plan; and

(II) has expertise in the care of elderly or disabled persons.

(B) FORMULARY DEVELOPMENT.—In developing and reviewing the formulary, the committee shall—

(a) base clinical decisions on the strength of scientific evidence and standards of practice, including assessing peer-reviewed medical literature, such as randomized clinical trials, pharmacoeconomic studies, outcomes research data, and on such other information as the committee determines to be appropriate; and

(b) take into account whether including in the formulary (or in a tier in such formulary) particular covered part D drugs has therapeutic advantages in terms of safety and efficacy.

(C) INCLUSION OF DRUGS IN ALL THERAPEUTIC CATEGORIES AND CLASSES.—

(i) IN GENERAL.—Subject to subparagraph (G), the formulary must include drugs within each therapeutic category and class of covered part D drugs, although not necessarily all drugs within such categories and classes.

(ii) MODEL GUIDELINES.—The Secretary shall request the United States Pharmacopeia to develop, in consultation with pharmaceutical benefit managers and other interested parties, a list of categories and classes that may be used by prescription drug plans under this paragraph and to revise such classification from time to time to reflect changes in therapeutic uses of covered part D drugs and the additions of new covered part D drugs.

(iii) LIMITATION ON CHANGES IN THERAPEUTIC CLASSIFICATION.—The PDP sponsor of a prescription drug plan may not change the therapeutic categories and classes in a formulary other than at the beginning of each plan year except as the Secretary may permit to take into account new therapeutic uses and newly approved covered part D drugs.

(D) PROVIDER AND PATIENT EDUCATION.—The PDP sponsor shall establish policies and procedures to educate and inform health care providers and enrollees concerning the formulary.

(E) NOTICE BEFORE REMOVING DRUG FROM FORMULARY OR CHANGING PREFERRED OR TIER STATUS OF DRUG.—Any removal of a covered part D drug from a formulary and any change in the preferred or tiered cost-sharing status of such a drug shall take effect only after appropriate notice is made available (such as under subsection (a)(3)) to the Secretary, affected enrollees, physicians, pharmacies, and pharmacists.

(F) PERIODIC EVALUATION OF PROTOCOLS.—In connection with the formulary, the sponsor of a prescription drug plan shall provide for the periodic evaluation and analysis of treatment protocols and procedures.

(G) REQUIRED INCLUSION OF DRUGS IN CERTAIN CATEGORIES AND CLASSES.—

(i) FORMULARY REQUIREMENTS.—

(I) IN GENERAL.—Subject to subclause (II), a PDP sponsor offering a prescription drug plan shall be required to include all covered part D drugs in the categories and classes identified by the Secretary under clause (ii)(I).

(II) EXCEPTIONS.—The Secretary may establish exceptions that permit a PDP sponsor offering a prescription drug plan to exclude from its formulary a particular covered part D drug in a category or class that is otherwise required to be included in the formulary under subclause (I) (or to otherwise limit access to such a drug, including through prior authorization or utilization management).

(ii) IDENTIFICATION OF DRUGS IN CERTAIN CATEGORIES AND CLASSES.—

(I) IN GENERAL.—Subject to clause (iv), the Secretary shall identify, as appropriate, categories and classes of drugs for which the Secretary determines are of clinical concern.

(II) CRITERIA.—The Secretary shall use criteria established by the Secretary in making any determination under subclause (I).

(iii) IMPLEMENTATION.—The Secretary shall establish the criteria under clause (ii)(II) and any exceptions under clause (i)(II) through the promulgation of a regulation which includes a public notice and comment period.

(iv) REQUIREMENT FOR CERTAIN CATEGORIES AND CLASSES UNTIL CRITERIA ESTABLISHED.—Until such time as the Secretary establishes the criteria under clause (ii)(II) the following categories and classes of drugs shall be identified under clause (ii)(I):

(I) Anticonvulsants.

(II) Antidepressants.

(III) Antineoplastics.

(IV) Antipsychotics.

(V) Antiretrovirals.

(VI) Immunosuppressants for the treatment of transplant rejection.

(H) USE OF SINGLE, UNIFORM EXCEPTIONS AND APPEALS PROCESS.—Notwithstanding any other provision of this part, each PDP sponsor of a prescription drug plan shall— (i) use a single, uniform exceptions and appeals process (including, to the extent the Secretary determines feasible, a single, uniform model form for use under such process) with respect to the determination of prescription drug coverage for an enrollee under the plan; and

(ii) provide instant access to such process by enrollees through a toll-free telephone number and an Internet website.

(c) COST AND UTILIZATION MANAGEMENT; QUALITY ASSURANCE; MEDICATION THERAPY MANAGEMENT PROGRAM.—

(1) IN GENERAL.—The PDP sponsor shall have in place, directly or through appropriate arrangements, with respect to covered part D drugs, the following:

(A) A cost-effective drug utilization management program, including incentives to reduce costs when medically appropriate, such as through the use of multiple source drugs (as defined in section 1927(k)(7)(A)(i)).

(B) Quality assurance measures and systems to reduce medication errors and adverse drug interactions and improve medication use.

(C) A medication therapy management program described in paragraph (2).

(D) A program to control fraud, abuse, and waste.

(E) A utilization management tool to prevent drug abuse (as described in paragraph (6)(A)).

Nothing in this section shall be construed as impairing a PDP sponsor from utilizing cost management tools (including differential payments) under all methods of operation.

(2) MEDICATION THERAPY MANAGEMENT PROGRAM.—

(A) DESCRIPTION.—

(i) IN GENERAL.—A medication therapy management program described in this paragraph is a program of drug therapy management that may be furnished by a pharmacist and that is designed to assure, with respect to targeted beneficiaries described in clause (ii), that covered part D drugs under the prescription drug plan are appropriately used to optimize therapeutic outcomes through improved medication use, and to reduce the risk of adverse events, including adverse drug interactions. Such a program may distinguish between services in ambulatory and institutional settings.

(ii) TARGETED BENEFICIARIES DESCRIBED.—Targeted beneficiaries described in this clause are part D eligible individuals who—

(I) have multiple chronic diseases (such as diabetes, asthma, hypertension, hyperlipidemia, and congestive heart failure);

(II) are taking multiple covered part D drugs; and

(III) are identified as likely to incur annual costs for covered part D drugs that exceed a level specified by the Secretary.

(B) ELEMENTS.—Such program may include elements that promote—

(i) enhanced enrollee understanding to promote the appropriate use of medications by enrollees and to reduce the risk of potential adverse events associated with medications, through beneficiary education, counseling, and other appropriate means;

(ii) increased enrollee adherence with prescription medication regimens through medication refill reminders, special packaging, and other compliance programs and other appropriate means; and

(iii) detection of adverse drug events and patterns of overuse and underuse of prescription drugs.

(C) REQUIRED INTERVENTIONS.—For plan years beginning on or after the date that is 2 years after the date of the enactment of the Patient Protection and Affordable Care Act, prescription drug plan sponsors shall offer medication therapy management services to targeted beneficiaries described in subparagraph (A)(ii) that include, at a minimum, the following to increase adherence to prescription medications or other goals deemed necessary by the Secretary:

(i) An annual comprehensive medication review furnished person-to-person or using telehealth technologies (as defined by the Secretary) by a licensed pharmacist or other qualified provider. The comprehensive medication review—

(I) shall include a review of the individual's medications and may result in the creation of a recommended medication action plan or other actions in consultation with the individual and with input from the prescriber to the extent necessary and practicable; and

(II) shall include providing the individual with a written or printed summary of the results of the review.

The Secretary, in consultation with relevant stakeholders, shall develop a standardized format for the action plan under subclause (I) and the summary under subclause (II).

(ii) Follow-up interventions as warranted based on the findings of the annual medication review or the targeted medication enrollment and which may be provided person-to-person or using telehealth technologies (as defined by the Secretary).

(D) ASSESSMENT.—The prescription drug plan sponsor shall have in place a process to assess, at least on a quarterly basis, the medication use of individuals who are at risk but not enrolled in the medication therapy management program, including individuals who have experienced a transition in care, if the prescription drug plan sponsor has access to that information.

(E) AUTOMATIC ENROLLMENT WITH ABILITY TO OPT-OUT.— The prescription drug plan sponsor shall have in place a process to—

(i) subject to clause (ii), automatically enroll targeted beneficiaries described in subparagraph (A)(ii), including beneficiaries identified under subparagraph (D), in the medication therapy management program required under this subsection; and

(ii) permit such beneficiaries to opt-out of enrollment in such program.

(E) DEVELOPMENT OF PROGRAM IN COOPERATION WITH LICENSED PHARMACISTS.—Such program shall be developed in cooperation with licensed and practicing pharmacists and physicians.

(F) COORDINATION WITH CARE MANAGEMENT PLANS.—The Secretary shall establish guidelines for the coordination of any medication therapy management program under this paragraph with respect to a targeted beneficiary with any care management plan established with respect to such beneficiary under a chronic care improvement program under section 1807.

(G) CONSIDERATIONS IN PHARMACY FEES.—The PDP sponsor of a prescription drug plan shall take into account, in establishing fees for pharmacists and others providing services under such plan, the resources used, and time required to, implement the medication therapy management program under this paragraph. Each such sponsor shall disclose to the Secretary upon request the amount of any such management or dispensing fees. The provisions of section 1927(b)(3)(D) apply to information disclosed under this subparagraph.

(3) REDUCING WASTEFUL DISPENSING OF OUTPATIENT PRESCRIPTION DRUGS IN LONG-TERM CARE FACILITIES.—The Secretary shall require PDP sponsors of prescription drug plans to utilize specific, uniform dispensing techniques, as determined by the Secretary, in consultation with relevant stakeholders (including representatives of nursing facilities, residents of nursing facilities, pharmacists, the pharmacy industry (including retail and long-term care pharmacy), prescription drug plans, MA–PD plans, and any other stakeholders the Secretary determines appropriate), such as weekly, daily, or automated dose dispensing, when dispensing covered part D drugs to enrollees who reside in a long-term care facility in order to reduce waste associated with 30-day fills.

(4) REQUIRING VALID PRESCRIBER NATIONAL PROVIDER IDENTIFIERS ON PHARMACY CLAIMS.—

(A) IN GENERAL.—For plan year 2016 and subsequent plan years, the Secretary shall require a claim for a covered part D drug for a part D eligible individual enrolled in a prescription drug plan under this part or an MA–PD plan under part C to include a prescriber National Provider Identifier that is determined to be valid under the procedures established under subparagraph (B)(i).

(B) PROCEDURES.—

(i) VALIDITY OF PRESCRIBER NATIONAL PROVIDER IDENTIFIERS.—The Secretary, in consultation with appropriate stakeholders, shall establish procedures for determining the validity of prescriber National Provider Identifiers under subparagraph (A).

(ii) INFORMING BENEFICIARIES OF REASON FOR DENIAL.—The Secretary shall establish procedures to ensure that, in the case that a claim for a covered part D drug of an individual described in subparagraph (A) is denied because the claim does not meet the requirements of this paragraph, the individual is properly informed at the point of service of the reason for the denial.

(C) REPORT.—Not later than January 1, 2018, the Inspector General of the Department of Health and Human Services shall submit to Congress a report on the effectiveness of the procedures established under subparagraph (B)(i).

(5) DRUG MANAGEMENT PROGRAM FOR AT-RISK BENEFICIARIES.—

(A) AUTHORITY TO ESTABLISH.—A PDP sponsor may establish a drug management program for at-risk beneficiaries under which, subject to subparagraph (B), the PDP sponsor may, in the case of an at-risk beneficiary for prescription drug abuse who is an enrollee in a prescription drug plan of such PDP sponsor, limit such beneficiary's access to coverage for frequently abused drugs under such plan to frequently abused drugs that are prescribed for such beneficiary by one or more prescribers selected under subparagraph (D), and dispensed for such beneficiary by one or more pharmacies selected under such subparagraph.

(B) REQUIREMENT FOR NOTICES.—

(i) IN GENERAL.—A PDP sponsor may not limit the access of an at-risk beneficiary for prescription drug abuse to coverage for frequently abused drugs under a prescription drug plan until such sponsor—

(I) provides to the beneficiary an initial notice described in clause (ii) and a second notice described in clause (iii); and

(II) verifies with the providers of the beneficiary that the beneficiary is an at-risk beneficiary for prescription drug abuse.

(III) INITIAL NOTICE.—An initial notice described in this clause is a notice that provides to the beneficiary—

(IV) notice that the PDP sponsor has identified the beneficiary as potentially being an at-risk beneficiary for prescription drug abuse;

(V) information describing all State and Federal public health resources that are designed to address prescription drug abuse to which the beneficiary has access, including mental health services and other counseling services;

(VI) notice of, and information about, the right of the beneficiary to appeal such identification under subsection (h) and the option of an automatic escalation to external review;

(VII) a request for the beneficiary to submit to the PDP sponsor preferences for which prescribers and pharmacies the beneficiary would prefer the PDP sponsor to select under subparagraph (D) in the case that the beneficiary is identified as an at-risk beneficiary for prescription drug abuse as described in clause (iii)(I);

(VIII) an explanation of the meaning and consequences of the identification of the beneficiary as potentially being an at-risk beneficiary for prescription drug abuse, including an explanation of the drug management program established by the PDP sponsor pursuant to subparagraph (A);

(IX) clear instructions that explain how the beneficiary can contact the PDP sponsor in order to submit to the PDP sponsor the preferences described in subclause (IV) and any other communications relating to the drug management program for at-risk beneficiaries established by the PDP sponsor; and

(X) contact information for other organizations that can provide the beneficiary with assistance regarding such drug management program (similar to the information provided by the Secretary in other standardized notices provided to part D eligible individuals enrolled in prescription drug plans under this part).

(iii) SECOND NOTICE.—A second notice described in this clause is a notice that provides to the beneficiary notice—

(I) that the PDP sponsor has identified the beneficiary as an at-risk beneficiary for prescription drug abuse;

(II) that such beneficiary is subject to the requirements of the drug management program for at-risk beneficiaries established by such PDP sponsor for such plan;

(III) of the prescriber (or prescribers) and pharmacy (or pharmacies) selected for such individual under subparagraph (D);

(IV) of, and information about, the beneficiary's right to appeal such identification under subsection (h) and the option of an automatic escalation to external review;

(V) that the beneficiary can, in the case that the beneficiary has not previously submitted to the PDP sponsor preferences for which prescribers and pharmacies the beneficiary would prefer the PDP sponsor select under subparagraph (D), submit such preferences to the PDP sponsor; and

(VI) that includes clear instructions that explain how the beneficiary can contact the PDP sponsor.

(iv) TIMING OF NOTICES.—

(I) IN GENERAL.—Subject to subclause (II), a second notice described in clause (iii) shall be provided to the beneficiary on a date that is not less than 30 days after an initial notice described in clause (ii) is provided to the beneficiary.

(II) EXCEPTION.—In the case that the PDP sponsor, in conjunction with the Secretary, determines that concerns identified through rulemaking by the Secretary regarding the health or safety of the beneficiary or regarding significant drug diversion activities require the PDP sponsor to provide a second notice described in clause (iii) to the beneficiary on a date that is earlier than the date described in subclause (I), the PDP sponsor may provide such second notice on such earlier date. (C) AT-RISK BENEFICIARY FOR PRESCRIPTION DRUG ABUSE.—

(i) IN GENERAL.—For purposes of this paragraph, the term "at-risk beneficiary for prescription drug abuse" means a part D eligible individual who is not an exempted individual described in clause (ii) and—

(I) who is identified as such an at-risk beneficiary through the use of clinical guidelines that indicate misuse or abuse of prescription drugs described in subparagraph (G) and that are developed by the Secretary in consultation with PDP sponsors and other stakeholders, including individuals entitled to benefits under part A or enrolled under part B, advocacy groups representing such individuals, physicians, pharmacists, and other clinicians, retail pharmacies, plan sponsors, entities delegated by plan sponsors, and bio-pharmaceutical manufacturers; or

(II) with respect to whom the PDP sponsor of a prescription drug plan, upon enrolling such individual in such plan, received notice from the Secretary that such individual was identified under this paragraph to be an at-risk beneficiary for prescription drug abuse under the prescription drug plan in which such individual was most recently previously enrolled and such identification has not been terminated under subparagraph (F).

(ii) EXEMPTED INDIVIDUAL DESCRIBED.—An exempted individual described in this clause is an individual who—

(I) receives hospice care under this title;

(II) is a resident of a long-term care facility, of a facility described in section 1905(d), or of another facility for which frequently abused drugs are dispensed for residents through a contract with a single pharmacy; or

(III) the Secretary elects to treat as an exempted individual for purposes of clause (i).

(iii) PROGRAM SIZE.—The Secretary shall establish policies, including the guidelines developed under clause (i)(I) and the exemptions under clause (ii)(III), to ensure that the population of enrollees in a drug management program for at-risk beneficiaries operated by a prescription drug plan can be effectively managed by such plans.

(iv) CLINICAL CONTACT.—With respect to each at- risk beneficiary for prescription drug abuse enrolled in a prescription drug plan offered by a PDP sponsor, the PDP sponsor shall contact the beneficiary's providers who have prescribed frequently abused drugs regarding whether prescribed medications are appropriate for such beneficiary's medical conditions.

(D) SELECTION OF PRESCRIBERS AND PHARMACIES.—

(i) IN GENERAL.—With respect to each at-risk beneficiary for prescription drug abuse enrolled in a prescription drug plan offered by such sponsor, a PDP sponsor shall, based on the preferences submitted to the PDP sponsor by the beneficiary pursuant to clauses (ii)(IV) and (iii)(V) of subparagraph (B) (except as otherwise provided in this subparagraph) select—

(I) one, or, if the PDP sponsor reasonably determines it necessary to provide the beneficiary with reasonable access under clause (ii), more than one, individual who is authorized to prescribe frequently abused drugs (referred to in this paragraph as a "prescriber") who may write prescriptions for such drugs for such beneficiary; and

(II) one, or, if the PDP sponsor reasonably determines it necessary to provide the beneficiary with reasonable access under clause (ii), more than one, pharmacy that may dispense such drugs to such beneficiary.

For purposes of subclause (II), in the case of a pharmacy that has multiple locations that share real-time electronic data, all such locations of the pharmacy shall collectively be treated as one pharmacy.

(ii) REASONABLE ACCESS.—In making the selections under this subparagraph—

(I) a PDP sponsor shall ensure that the beneficiary continues to have reasonable access to frequently abused drugs (as defined in subparagraph (G)), taking into account geographic location, beneficiary preference, impact on costsharing, and reasonable travel time; and

(II) a PDP sponsor shall ensure such access (including access to prescribers and pharmacies with respect to frequently abused drugs) in the case of individuals with multiple residences, in the case of natural disasters and similar situations, and in the case of the provision of emergency services.

(iii) BENEFICIARY PREFERENCES.—If an at-risk beneficiary for prescription drug abuse submits preferences for which in-network prescribers and pharmacies the beneficiary would prefer the PDP sponsor select in response to a notice under subparagraph (B), the PDP sponsor shall—

(I) review such preferences;

(II) select or change the selection of prescribers and pharmacies for the beneficiary based on such preferences; and

(III) inform the beneficiary of such selection or change of selection.

(iv) EXCEPTION REGARDING BENEFICIARY PREFERENCES.—In the case that the PDP sponsor determines that a change to the selection of prescriber or pharmacy under clause (iii)(II) by the PDP sponsor is contributing or would contribute to prescription drug abuse or drug diversion by the beneficiary, the PDP sponsor may change the selection of prescriber or pharmacy for the beneficiary without regard to the preferences of the beneficiary described in clause (iii). If the PDP sponsor changes the selection pursuant to the preceding sentence, the PDP sponsor shall provide the beneficiary with—

(I) at least 30 days written notice of the change of selection; and

(II) a rationale for the change.

(v) CONFIRMATION.—Before selecting a prescriber or pharmacy under this subparagraph, a PDP sponsor must notify the prescriber and pharmacy that the beneficiary involved has been identified for inclusion in the drug management program for at-risk beneficiaries and that the prescriber and pharmacy has been selected as the beneficiary's designated prescriber and pharmacy.

(E) TERMINATIONS AND APPEALS.—The identification of an individual as an at-risk beneficiary for prescription drug abuse under this paragraph, a coverage determination made under a drug management program for at-risk beneficiaries, the selection of prescriber or pharmacy under subparagraph (D), and information to be shared under subparagraph (I), with respect to such individual, shall be subject to reconsideration and appeal under subsection (h) and the option of an automatic escalation to external review to the extent provided by the Secretary.

(F) TERMINATION OF IDENTIFICATION.—

(i) IN GENERAL.—The Secretary shall develop standards for the termination of identification of an individual as an at-risk beneficiary for prescription drug abuse under this paragraph. Under such standards such identification shall terminate as of the earlier of—

(I) the date the individual demonstrates that the individual is no longer likely, in the absence of the restrictions under this paragraph, to be an at-risk beneficiary for prescription drug abuse described in subparagraph (C)(i); and

(II) the end of such maximum period of identification as the Secretary may specify.

(ii) RULE OF CONSTRUCTION.—Nothing in clause (i) shall be construed as preventing a plan from identifying an individual as an at-risk beneficiary for prescription drug abuse under subparagraph (C)(i) after such termination on the basis of additional information on drug use occurring after the date of notice of such termination.

(G) FREQUENTLY ABUSED DRUG.—For purposes of this subsection, the term "frequently abused drug" means a drug that is a controlled substance that the Secretary determines to be frequently abused or diverted.

(H) DATA DISCLOSURE.—

(i) DATA ON DECISION TO IMPOSE LIMITATION.—In the case of an at-risk beneficiary for prescription drug abuse (or an individual who is a potentially at-risk beneficiary for prescription drug abuse) whose access to coverage for frequently abused drugs under a prescription drug plan has been limited by a PDP sponsor under this paragraph, the Secretary shall establish rules and procedures to require the PDP sponsor to disclose data, including any necessary individually identifiable health information, in a form and manner specified by the Secretary, about the decision to impose such limitations and the limitations imposed by the sponsor under this part.

(ii) DATA TO REDUCE FRAUD, ABUSE, AND WASTE.— The Secretary shall establish rules and procedures to require PDP sponsors operating a drug management program for at-risk beneficiaries under this paragraph to provide the Secretary with such data as the Secretary determines appropriate for purposes of identifying patterns of prescription drug utilization for plan enrollees that are outside normal patterns and that may indicate fraudulent, medically unnecessary, or unsafe use.

(I) SHARING OF INFORMATION FOR SUBSEQUENT PLAN ENROLLMENTS.—The Secretary shall establish procedures under which PDP sponsors who offer prescription drug plans shall share information with respect to individuals who are at-risk beneficiaries for prescription drug abuse (or individuals who are potentially at-risk beneficiaries for prescription drug abuse) and enrolled in a prescription drug plan and who subsequently disenroll from such plan and enroll in another prescription drug plan offered by another PDP sponsor.

(J) PRIVACY ISSUES.—Prior to the implementation of the rules and procedures under this paragraph, the Secretary shall clarify privacy requirements, including requirements under the regulations promulgated pursuant to section 264(c) of the Health Insurance Portability and Accountability Act of 1996 (42 U.S.C. 1320d–2 note), related to the sharing of data under subparagraphs (H) and (I) by PDP sponsors. Such clarification shall provide that the sharing of such data shall be considered to be protected health information in accordance with the requirements of the regulations promulgated pursuant to such section 264(c).

(K) EDUCATION.—The Secretary shall provide education to enrollees in prescription drug plans of PDP sponsors and providers regarding the drug management program for at-risk beneficiaries described in this paragraph, including education—

(i) provided by Medicare administrative contractors through the improper payment outreach and education program described in section 1874A(h); and

(ii) through current education efforts (such as State health insurance assistance programs described in subsection (a)(1)(A) of section 119 of the Medicare Improvements for Patients and Providers Act of 2008 (42 U.S.C. 1395b–3 note)) and materials directed toward such enrollees.

(L) APPLICATION UNDER MA–PD PLANS.—Pursuant to section 1860D–21(c)(1), the provisions of this paragraph apply under part D to MA organizations offering MA–PD plans to MA eligible individuals in the same manner as such provisions apply under this part to a PDP sponsor offering a prescription drug plan to a part D eligible individual.

(M) CMS COMPLIANCE REVIEW.—The Secretary shall ensure that existing plan sponsor compliance reviews and audit processes include the drug management programs for at-risk beneficiaries under this paragraph, including appeals processes under such programs.

(6) UTILIZATION MANAGEMENT TOOL TO PREVENT DRUG ABUSE.—

(A) IN GENERAL.—A tool described in this paragraph is any of the following:

(i) A utilization tool designed to prevent the abuse of frequently abused drugs by individuals and to prevent the diversion of such drugs at pharmacies.

(ii) Retrospective utilization review to identify—

(I) individuals that receive frequently abused drugs at a frequency or in amounts that are not clinically appropriate; and

(II) providers of services or suppliers that may facilitate the abuse or diversion of frequently abused drugs by beneficiaries.

(iii) Consultation with the contractor described in subparagraph (B) to verify if an individual enrolling in a prescription drug plan offered by a PDP sponsor has been previously identified by another PDP sponsor as an individual described in clause (ii)(I).

(B) REPORTING.—A PDP sponsor offering a prescription drug plan (and an MA organization offering an MA–PD plan) in a State shall submit to the Secretary and the Medicare drug integrity contractor with which the Secretary has entered into a contract under section 1893 with respect to such State a report, on a monthly basis, containing information on—any provider of services or supplier described in subparagraph (A)(ii)(II) that is identified by such plan sponsor (or organization) during the 30-day period before such report is submitted; and the name and prescription records of individuals described in paragraph (5)(C).

(C) CMS COMPLIANCE REVIEW.—The Secretary shall ensure that plan sponsor compliance reviews and program audits biennially include a certification that utilization management tools under this paragraph are in compliance with the requirements for such tools.

(6) PROVIDING PRESCRIPTION DRUG PLANS WITH PARTS A AND B CLAIMS DATA TO PROMOTE THE APPROPRIATE USE OF MEDICATIONS AND IMPROVE HEALTH OUTCOMES.—

(A) PROCESS.—Subject to subparagraph (B), the Secretary shall establish a process under which a PDP sponsor of a prescription drug plan may submit a request for the Secretary to provide the sponsor, on a periodic basis and in an electronic format, beginning in plan year 2020, data described in subparagraph (D) with respect to enrollees in such plan. Such data shall be provided without regard to whether such enrollees are described in clause (ii) of paragraph (2)(A).

(B) PURPOSES.—A PDP sponsor may use the data provided to the sponsor pursuant to subparagraph (A) for any of the following purposes:

(i) To optimize therapeutic outcomes through improved medication use, as such phrase is used in clause (i) of paragraph (2)(A).

(ii) To improving care coordination so as to prevent adverse health outcomes, such as preventable emergency department visits and hospital readmissions.

(iii) For any other purpose determined appropriate by the Secretary.

(C) LIMITATIONS ON DATA USE.—A PDP sponsor shall not use data provided to the sponsor pursuant to subparagraph (A) for any of the following purposes:

(i) To inform coverage determinations under this part.

(ii) To conduct retroactive reviews of medically accepted indications determinations.

(iii) To facilitate enrollment changes to a different prescription drug plan or an MA–PD plan offered by the same parent organization.

(iv) To inform marketing of benefits.

(v) For any other purpose that the Secretary determines is necessary to include in order to protect the identity of individuals entitled to, or enrolled for, benefits under this title and to protect the security of personal health information.

(D) DATA DESCRIBED.—The data described in this clause are standardized extracts (as determined by the Secretary) of claims data under parts A and B for items and services furnished under such parts for time periods specified by the Secretary. Such data shall include data as current as practicable.

(d) CONSUMER SATISFACTION SURVEYS.—In order to provide for comparative information under section 1860D–1(c)(3)(A)(v), the Secretary shall conduct consumer satisfaction surveys with respect to PDP sponsors and prescription drug plans in a manner similar to the manner such surveys are conducted for MA organizations and MA plans under part C.

(e) ELECTRONIC PRESCRIPTION PROGRAM.—

(1) APPLICATION OF STANDARDS.—As of such date as the Secretary may specify, but not later than 1 year after the date of promulgation of final standards under paragraph (4)(D), prescriptions and other information described in paragraph (2)(A) for

covered part D drugs prescribed for part D eligible individuals that are transmitted electronically shall be transmitted only in accordance with such standards under an electronic prescription drug program that meets the requirements of paragraph (2).

(2) PROGRAM REQUIREMENTS.—Consistent with uniform standards established under paragraph (3)—

(A) PROVISION OF INFORMATION TO PRESCRIBING HEALTH CARE PROFESSIONAL AND DISPENSING PHARMACIES AND PHARMACISTS.—An electronic prescription drug program shall provide for the electronic transmittal to the prescribing health care professional and to the dispensing pharmacy and pharmacist of the prescription and information on eligibility and benefits (including the drugs included in the applicable formulary, any tiered formulary structure, and any requirements for prior authorization) and of the following information with respect to the prescribing and dispensing of a covered part D drug:

(i) Information on the drug being prescribed or dispensed and other drugs listed on the medication history, including information on drug-drug interactions, warnings or cautions, and, when indicated, dosage adjustments.

(ii) Information on the availability of lower cost, therapeutically appropriate alternatives (if any) for the drug prescribed.

(B) APPLICATION TO MEDICAL HISTORY INFORMATION.—Effective on and after such date as the Secretary specifies and after the establishment of appropriate standards to carry out this subparagraph, the program shall provide for the electronic transmittal in a manner similar to the manner under subparagraph (A) of information that relates to the medical history concerning the individual and related to a covered part D drug being prescribed or dispensed, upon request of the professional or pharmacist involved.

(C) LIMITATIONS.—Information shall only be disclosed under subparagraph (A) or (B) if the disclosure of such information is permitted under the Federal regulations (concerning the privacy of individually identifiable health information) promulgated under section 264(c) of the Health Insurance Portability and Accountability Act of 1996.

(D) TIMING.—To the extent feasible, the information exchanged under this paragraph shall be on an interactive, real-time basis.

(3) STANDARDS.—

(A) IN GENERAL.—The Secretary shall provide consistent with this subsection for the promulgation of uniform standards relating to the requirements for electronic prescription drug programs under paragraph (2).

(B) OBJECTIVES.—Such standards shall be consistent with the objectives of improving—

(i) patient safety;

(ii) the quality of care provided to patients; and

(iii) efficiencies, including cost savings, in the delivery of care.

(C) DESIGN CRITERIA.—Such standards shall—

(i) be designed so that, to the extent practicable, the standards do not impose an undue administrative burden on prescribing health care professionals and dispensing pharmacies and pharmacists;

(ii) be compatible with standards established under part C of title XI, standards established under subsection (b)(2)(B)(i), and with general health information technology standards; and

(iii) be designed so that they permit electronic exchange of drug labeling and drug listing information maintained by the Food and Drug Administration and the National Library of Medicine.

(D) PERMITTING USE OF APPROPRIATE MESSAGING.—Such standards shall allow for the messaging of information only if it relates to the appropriate prescribing of drugs, including quality assurance measures and systems referred to in subsection (c)(1)(B).

(E) PERMITTING PATIENT DESIGNATION OF DISPENSING PHARMACY.—

(i) IN GENERAL.—Consistent with clause (ii), such standards shall permit a part D eligible individual to designate a particular pharmacy to dispense a prescribed drug.

(ii) NO CHANGE IN BENEFITS.—Clause (i) shall not be construed as affecting—

(I) the access required to be provided to pharmacies by a prescription drug plan; or

(II) the application of any differences in benefits or payments under such a plan based on the pharmacy dispensing a covered part D drug.

(4) DEVELOPMENT, PROMULGATION, AND MODIFICATION OF STANDARDS.—

(A) INITIAL STANDARDS.—Not later than September 1, 2005, the Secretary shall develop, adopt, recognize, or modify initial uniform standards relating to the requirements for electronic prescription drug programs described in paragraph (2) taking into consideration the recommendations (if any) from the National Committee on Vital and Health Statistics (as established under section 306(k) of the Public Health Service Act (42 U.S.C. 242k(k))) under subparagraph (B).

(B) ROLE OF NCVHS.—The National Committee on Vital and Health Statistics shall develop recommendations for uniform standards relating to such requirements in consultation with the following:

(i) Standard setting organizations (as defined in section 1171(8))

(ii) Practicing physicians.

(iii) Hospitals.

(iv) Pharmacies.

(v) Practicing pharmacists.

(vi) Pharmacy benefit managers.

(vii) State boards of pharmacy.

(viii) State boards of medicine.

(ix) Experts on electronic prescribing.

(x) Other appropriate Federal agencies.

(C) PILOT PROJECT TO TEST INITIAL STANDARDS.—

(i) IN GENERAL.—During the 1-year period that begins on January 1, 2006, the Secretary shall conduct a pilot project to test the initial standards developed under subparagraph (A) prior to the promulgation of the final uniform standards under subparagraph (D) in order to provide for the efficient implementation of the requirements described in paragraph (2).

(ii) EXCEPTION.—Pilot testing of standards is not required under clause (i) where there already is adequate industry experience with such standards, as determined by the Secretary after consultation with effected standard setting organizations and industry users.

(iii) VOLUNTARY PARTICIPATION OF PHYSICIANS AND PHARMACIES.—In order to conduct the pilot project under clause (i), the Secretary shall enter into agreements with physicians, physician groups, pharmacies, hospitals, PDP sponsors, MA organizations, and other appropriate entities under which health care professionals electronically transmit prescriptions to dispensing pharmacies and pharmacists in accordance with such standards.

(iv) EVALUATION AND REPORT.—

(I) EVALUATION.—The Secretary shall conduct an evaluation of the pilot project conducted under clause (i).

(II) REPORT TO CONGRESS.—Not later than April 1, 2007, the Secretary shall submit to Congress a report on the evaluation conducted under subclause (I).

(D) FINAL STANDARDS.—Based upon the evaluation of the pilot project under subparagraph (C)(iv)(I) and not later than April 1, 2008, the Secretary shall promulgate uniform standards relating to the requirements described in paragraph (2).

(5) RELATION TO STATE LAWS.—The standards promulgated under this subsection shall supersede any State law or regulation that—

(A) is contrary to the standards or restricts the ability to carry out this part; and

(B) pertains to the electronic transmission of medication history and of information on eligibility, benefits, and prescriptions with respect to covered part D drugs under this part.

(6) ESTABLISHMENT OF SAFE HARBOR.—The Secretary, in consultation with the Attorney General, shall promulgate regulations that provide for a safe harbor from sanctions under paragraphs (1) and (2) of section 1128B(b) and an exception to the prohibition under subsection (a)(1) of section 1877 with respect to the provision of nonmonetary remuneration (in the form of hardware, software, or information technology

and training services) necessary and used solely to receive and transmit electronic prescription information in accordance with the standards promulgated under this subsection—

(A) in the case of a hospital, by the hospital to members of its medical staff;

(B) in the case of a group practice (as defined in section 1877(h)(4)), by the practice to prescribing health care professionals who are members of such practice; and

(C) in the case of a PDP sponsor or MA organization, by the sponsor or organization to pharmacists and pharmacies participating in the network of such sponsor or organization, and to prescribing health care professionals.

(7) REQUIREMENT OF E-PRESCRIBING FOR CONTROLLED SUBSTANCES.—

(A) IN GENERAL.—Subject to subparagraph (B), a prescription for a covered part D drug under a prescription drug plan (or under an MA–PD plan) for a schedule II, III, IV, or V controlled substance shall be transmitted by a health care practitioner electronically in accordance with an electronic prescription drug program that meets the requirements of paragraph (2).

(B) EXCEPTION FOR CERTAIN CIRCUMSTANCES.—The Secretary shall, pursuant to rulemaking, specify circumstances with respect to which the Secretary may waive the requirement under subparagraph (A), with respect to a covered part D drug, including in the case of—

(i) a prescription issued when the practitioner and dispenser are the same entity;

(ii) a prescription issued that cannot be transmitted electronically under the most recently implemented version of the National Council for Prescription Drug Programs SCRIPT Standard;

(iii) a prescription issued by a practitioner who has received a waiver or a renewal thereof for a specified period determined by the Secretary, not to exceed one year, from the requirement to use electronic prescribing, pursuant to a process established by regulation by the Secretary, due to demonstrated economic hardship, technological limitations that are not reasonably within the control of the practitioner, or other exceptional circumstance demonstrated by the practitioner;

(iv) a prescription issued by a practitioner under circumstances in which, notwithstanding the practitioner's ability to submit a prescription electronically as required by this subsection, such practitioner reasonably determines that it would be impractical for the individual involved to obtain substances prescribed by electronic prescription in a timely manner, and such delay would adversely impact the individual's medical condition involved;

(v) a prescription issued by a practitioner allowing for the dispensing of a non-patient specific prescription pursuant to a standing order, approved protocol for drug therapy, collaborative drug management, or comprehensive medication management, in response to a public health emergency, or other circumstances where the practitioner may issue a non-patient specific prescription;

(vi) a prescription issued by a practitioner prescribing a drug under a research protocol;

(vii) a prescription issued by a practitioner for a drug for which the Food and Drug Administration requires a prescription to contain elements that are not able to be included in electronic prescribing, such as a drug with risk evaluation and mitigation strategies that include elements to assure safe use; and

(viii) a prescription issued by a practitioner for an individual who—

(I) receives hospice care under this title; or

(II) is a resident of a skilled nursing facility (as defined in section 1819(a)), or a medical institution or nursing facility for which payment is made for an institutionalized individual under section 1902(q)(1)(B), for which frequently abused drugs are dispensed for residents through a contract with a single pharmacy, as determined by the Secretary in accordance with this paragraph.

(C) DISPENSING.—Nothing in this paragraph shall be construed as requiring a sponsor of a prescription drug plan under this part, MA organization offering an MA–PD plan under part C, or a pharmacist to verify that a practitioner, with respect to a prescription for a covered part D drug, has a waiver (or is otherwise exempt) under subparagraph (B) from the requirement under subparagraph (A). Nothing in this paragraph shall be construed as affecting the ability of the plan to cover or the pharmacists' ability to continue to dispense covered part D drugs from otherwise valid written, oral or fax prescriptions that are consistent with laws and regulations. Nothing in this paragraph shall be construed as affecting the ability of the beneficiary involved to designate a particular pharmacy to dispense a prescribed drug to the extent consistent with the requirements under subsection (b)(1) and under this paragraph.

(D) ENFORCEMENT.—The Secretary shall, pursuant to rulemaking, have authority to enforce and specify appropriate penalties for non-compliance with the requirement under subparagraph (A).

(f) GRIEVANCE MECHANISM.—Each PDP sponsor shall provide meaningful procedures for hearing and resolving grievances between the sponsor (including any entity or individual through which the sponsor provides covered benefits) and enrollees with prescription drug plans of the sponsor under this part in accordance with section 1852(f).

(g) COVERAGE DETERMINATIONS AND RECONSIDERATIONS.—

(1) APPLICATION OF COVERAGE DETERMINATION AND RECONSIDERATION PROVISIONS.—A PDP sponsor shall meet the requirements of paragraphs (1) through (3) of section 1852(g) with respect to covered benefits under the prescription drug plan it offers under this part in the same manner as such requirements apply to an MA organization with respect to benefits it offers under an MA plan under part C.

(2) REQUEST FOR A DETERMINATION FOR THE TREATMENT OF TIERED FORMULARY DRUG.—In the case of a prescription drug plan offered by a PDP sponsor that provides for tiered cost- sharing for drugs included within a formulary and provides lower cost-sharing for preferred drugs included within the formulary, a part D eligible individual who is enrolled in the plan may request an exception to the tiered cost-sharing structure. Under such an exception, a nonpreferred drug could be covered under the terms applicable for preferred drugs if the prescribing physician determines that the preferred drug for treatment of the same condition either would not be as effective for the individual or would have adverse effects for the individual or both. A PDP sponsor shall have an exceptions process under this paragraph consistent with guidelines established by the Secretary for making a determination with respect to such a request. Denial of such an exception shall be treated as a coverage denial for purposes of applying subsection (h).

(h) APPEALS.—

(1) IN GENERAL.—Subject to paragraph (2), a PDP sponsor shall meet the requirements of paragraphs (4) and (5) of section 1852(g) with respect to benefits (including a determination related to the application of tiered cost-sharing described in subsection (g)(2)) in a manner similar (as determined by the Secretary) to the manner such requirements apply to an MA organization with respect to benefits under the original medicare fee-for-service program option it offers under an MA plan under part C. In applying this paragraph only the part D eligible individual shall be entitled to bring such an appeal.

(2) LIMITATION IN CASES ON NONFORMULARY DETERMINATIONS.—A part D eligible individual who is enrolled in a prescription drug plan offered by a PDP sponsor may appeal under paragraph (1) a determination not to provide for coverage of a covered part D drug that is not on the formulary under the plan only if the prescribing physician determines that all covered part D drugs on any tier of the formulary for treatment of the same condition would not be as effective for the individual as the nonformulary drug, would have adverse effects for the individual, or both.

(3) TREATMENT OF NONFORMULARY DETERMINATIONS.—If a PDP sponsor determines that a plan provides coverage for a covered part D drug that

is not on the formulary of the plan, the drug shall be treated as being included on the formulary for purposes of section 1860D–2(b)(4)(C)(i).

(i) PRIVACY, CONFIDENTIALITY, AND ACCURACY OF ENROLLEE RECORDS.—The provisions of section 1852(h) shall apply to a PDP sponsor and prescription drug plan in the same manner as it applies to an MA organization and an MA plan.

(j) TREATMENT OF ACCREDITATION.—Subparagraph (A) of section 1852(e)(4) (relating to treatment of accreditation) shall apply to a PDP sponsor under this part with respect to the following requirements, in the same manner as it applies to an MA organization with respect to the requirements in subparagraph (B) (other than clause (vii) thereof) of such section:

(1) Subsection (b) of this section (relating to access to covered part D drugs).

(2) Subsection (c) of this section (including quality assurance and medication therapy management).

(3) Subsection (i) of this section (relating to confidentiality and accuracy of enrollee records).

(k) PUBLIC DISCLOSURE OF PHARMACEUTICAL PRICES FOR EQUIVALENT DRUGS.—

(1) IN GENERAL.—A PDP sponsor offering a prescription drug plan shall provide that each pharmacy that dispenses a covered part D drug shall inform an enrollee of any differential between the price of the drug to the enrollee and the price of the lowest priced generic covered part D drug under the plan that is therapeutically equivalent and bioequivalent and available at such pharmacy.

(2) TIMING OF NOTICE.—

(A) IN GENERAL.—Subject to subparagraph (B), the information under paragraph (1) shall be provided at the time of purchase of the drug involved, or, in the case of dispensing by mail order, at the time of delivery of such drug.

(B) WAIVER.—The Secretary may waive subparagraph (A) in such circumstances as the Secretary may specify.

(l) REQUIREMENTS WITH RESPECT TO SALES AND MARKETING ACTIVITIES.—The following provisions shall apply to a PDP sponsor (and the agents, brokers, and other third parties representing such sponsor) in the same manner as such provisions apply to a Medicare Advantage organization (and the agents, brokers, and other third parties representing such organization):

(1) The prohibition under section 1851(h)(4)(C) on conducting activities described in section 1851(j)(1).

(2) The requirement under section 1851(h)(4)(D) to conduct activities described in section 1851(j)(2) in accordance with the limitations established under such subsection.

(3) The inclusion of the plan type in the plan name under section 1851(h)(6).
(4) The requirements regarding the appointment of agents and brokers and compliance with State information requests under subparagraphs (A) and (B), respectively, of section 1851(h)(7).

EXCHANGE OF LETTERS WITH ADDITIONAL COMMITTEES OF REFERRAL

Greg Walden, Oregon
Chairman

Frank Pallone, Jr., New Jersey
Ranking Member

One Hundred Fifteenth Congress
Congress of the United States
House of Representatives

June 7, 2018

The Honorable Kevin Brady
Chairman
Committee on Ways and Means

Dear Chairman Brady:

On May 9 and 17, 2018, the Committee on Energy and Commerce ordered favorably reported over 50 bills to address the opioid epidemic facing communities across our nation. Several of the bills were also referred to the Committee on Ways and Means.

I ask that the Committee on Ways and Means not insist on its referral of the following bills so that they may be scheduled for consideration by the Majority Leader:

- H.R. 1925, At-Risk Youth Medicaid Protection Act of 2017;
- H.R. 3331, To amend title XI of the Social Security Act to promote testing of incentive payments for behavioral health providers for adoption and use of certified electronic health record technology;
- H.R. 3528, Every Prescription Conveyed Securely Act;
- H.R. 4841, Standardizing Electronic Prior Authorization for Safe Prescribing Act of 2018;

- H.R. 5582, Abuse Deterrent Access Act of 2018;
- H.R. 5590, Opioid Addiction Action Plan Act;
- H.R. 5603, Access to Telehealth Services for Opioid Use Disorder;
- H.R. 5605, Advancing High Quality Treatment for Opioid Use Disorders in Medicare Act;
- H.R. 5675, To amend title XVIII of the Social Security Act to require prescription drug plan sponsors under the Medicare program to establish drug management programs for at-risk beneficiaries;
- H.R. 5684, Protecting Seniors from Opioid Abuse Act;
- H.R. 5685, Medicare Opioid Safety Education Act;
- H.R. 5686, Medicare Clear Health Options in Care for Enrollees (CHOICE) Act;
- H.R. 5715, Strengthening Partnerships to Prevent Opioid Abuse Act;
- H.R. 5716, Commit to Opioid Medical Prescriber Accountability and Safety for Seniors (COMPASS) Act;
- H.R. 5796, Responsible Education Achieves Care and Healthy Outcomes for Users' Treatment (REACH OUT) Act of 2018;
- H.R. 5798, Opioid Screening and Chronic Pain Management Alternatives for Seniors Act;
- H.R. 5804, Post-Surgical Injections as an Opioid Alternative Act; and
- H.R. 5809, Postoperative Opioid Prevention Act of 2018.

This concession in no way affects your jurisdiction over the subject matter of these bills, and it will not serve as precedent for future referrals. In addition, should a conference on the bills be necessary, 1 would support your request to have the Committee on Ways and Means on the conference committee. Finally, I would be pleased to include this letter and your response in the bill reports and the Congressional Record.

Thank you for your consideration of my request and for the extraordinary cooperation shown by you and your staff over matters of shared jurisdiction. I look forward to further opportunities to work with you this Congress.

Sincerely,

Greg Walden
Chairman

June 8, 2018

The Honorable Greg Walden
Chairman
Committee on Energy and Commerce

Dear Chairman Walden,

Thank you for your letter concerning several bills favorably reported out of the Committee on Energy and Commerce to address the opioid epidemic and which the Committee on Ways and Means was granted an additional referral.

As a result of your having consulted with us on provisions within these bills that fall within the Rule X jurisdiction of the Committee on Ways and Means, I agree to waive formal consideration of the following bills so that they may move expeditiously to the floor:

- H.R. 1925, At-Risk Youth Medicaid Protection Act of 2017;
- H.R. 3331, To amend title X.1 of the Social Security Act to promote testing of incentive payments for behavioral health providers for adoption and use of certified electronic health record technology;
- H.R. 3528, Every Prescription Conveyed Securely Act;
- H.R. 4841, Standardizing Electronic Prior Authorization for Safe Prescribing Act of 2018;
- H.R. 5582, Abuse Deterrent Access Act of 2018;
- H.R. 5590, Opioid Addiction Action Plan Act;
- H.R. 5603, Access to Telehealth Services for Opioid Use Disorder;
- H.R. 5605, Advancing High Quality Treatment for Opioid Use Disorders in Medicare Act;
- H.R. 5675, To amend title XVIII of the Social Security Act to require prescription drug plan sponsors under the Medicare program to establish drug management programs for at-risk beneficiaries;
- H.R. 5684, Protecting Seniors from Opioid Abuse Act;
- H.R. 5685, Medicare Opioid Safety Education Act;
- H.R. 5686, Medicare Clear Health Options in Care for Enrollees (CHOICE) Act;
- H.R. 5715, Strengthening Partnerships to Prevent Opioid Abuse Act;
- H.R. 5716, Commit to Opioid Medical Prescriber Accountability and Safety for Seniors (COMPASS) Act;
- H.R. 5796, Responsible Education Achieves Care and Healthy Outcomes for Users' Treatment (REACH OUT) Act of 2018;
- H.R. 5798, Opioid Screening and Chronic Pain Management Alternatives for Seniors Act;
- H.R. 5804, Post-Surgical Injections as an Opioid Alternative Act; and
- H.R. 5809, Postoperative Opioid Prevention Act of 2018.

The Committee on Ways and Means takes this action with the mutual understanding that we do not waive any jurisdiction over the subject matter contained in this or similar legislation, and the Committee will be appropriately consulted and involved as the bill or similar legislation moves forward so that we may address any remaining issues that fall within our jurisdiction. The Committee also reserves the right to seek appointment of an appropriate number of conferees to any House-Senate conference involving this or similar legislation and requests your support for such a request.

Finally, I would appreciate your commitment to include this exchange of letters in the bill reports and the Congressional Record.

Sincerely,

Kevin Brady
Chairman

cc: The Honorable Paul Ryan, Speaker, The Honorable Richard E. Neal, The Honorable Frank Pallone, Thomas J. Wickham, Jr., Parliamentarian.

INDEX

A

B

C

D

E

F

J

L

M

N

O

P

Q

R

S

T

U

V

W